Pd 18/7/08

Dr. AC Presents
Horror 101
The A-List of Horror Films and
Monster Movies Vol. 1

University of
Chester
Warrington Campus

University of Chester Library
Tel: 01925 534284

D1494362

Dr. AC Presents

Horror 101

The A-List of Horror Films and Monster Movies Vol. 1

edited by
Aaron Christensen

Midnight Marquee Press, Inc.
Baltimore, Maryland

ISBN 13: 978-1-887664-79-0
ISBN 10: 1-887664-79-3
Library of Congress Catalog Card Number 2007932980
Manufactured in the United States of America
Printed by Odyssey Press
First Printing by Midnight Marquee Press, Inc., September 2007

Dedication

To my beautiful and loving femalien Michelle,
who has never once told me to
"turn that crap off."

Thank you for being so supportive
during the long nights
of bloodcurdling screams and growls
coming from the TV room.

You're the greatest.

ACKNOWLEDGEMENTS

To those who have gone before and lit the way: Denis Gifford, Phil Hardy, John Stanley, Joe Bob Briggs, Mike Mayo, Ed Naha, Bruce Lanier Wright, John McCarty, Jim Harper, David J. Skal, Carlos Clarens, Michael Weldon, James O'Neill, Kim Newman, Nathaniel Thompson, Danny Peary, Howard Maxford, Gene Wright and on and on and on...

My mother, who allowed me to watch Godzilla, Dracula and the gang on late night *Creature Features*, and my Aunt Cathie, who encouraged my interest in monster movies and took me to see quite a few in the theaters (with or without my mom's knowledge).

My "horror mentors": David White, Doug Lamoreux, and Lawrence P. Raffel, all of whom I'm honored to have on board as contributors. You're sick, sick people. I'm damn glad to know you.

Every video store that has ever kept a rare, hard to find item on the shelves rather than dumping it in favor of some new blockbuster. Courage and good taste in the face of commerce! Bless you all, especially Chicago's Nationwide Video.

All of the Horror Boarders at IMDb, who inspire and astound me daily.

All the wonderful people who came on board with this project. Thank you for putting up with my rah-rah email notices and endless hounding about deadlines. Thank you for your incredibly informative, engaging and often hilarious insights. I'm honored to have been able to work alongside each and every one of you. Special thanks to Brett Harrison for his amazing cover design.

No words of gratitude can possibly do justice to the efforts and enthusiasm of Jon Kitley of Kitley's Krypt, who time and time again opened up his treasure chest of personal knowledge, reference books, rare films, publicity stills, and movie paraphernalia to a fellow fan. We are forever indebted to his painstaking quest to find just the right illustrations to enliven the pages of this volume. Plus, he throws one heck of a Halloween party. Thank you, my friend.

And last, but not least, Gary J. and Susan Svehla at Midnight Marquee for taking a chance on a bunch of no-name nut-jobs. Your assistance in guiding this project from a collection of rambling ruminations to its current, slightly less rambling state has been invaluable. We truly wouldn't be here without you. Also, thanks to Tom Savini for his thoughtful foreword.

TABLE OF CONTENTS

FOREWORD

Hi folks. Savini here.

I have to admit, when Aaron first contacted me about writing a Foreword for *Horror 101*, it sounded like an easy task. After all, I've been involved in the art of making people scream and/or gag (preferably both) since the early 1970s, and I've been a fan of the genre myself for even longer than that.

But when I sat down before the keyboard, I found myself at a bit of a loss as to what to say. After all, in my line of work, I prefer to show people my ideas and passions rather than just talk about them. So, I called up a few of my old friends to talk shop, noodle a few ideas, get the, ahem, juices flowing as it were. And in the course of our conversation, it occurred to me—not for the first time—just how much horror movies have meant to me and what an influence they've been on my life. In fact, horror movies are my life, my livelihood, and I wouldn't have it any other way.

My earliest genre memories date back to when I was a six-year-old lad being taken to the cinema on Saturday mornings. Starting around 9 a.m., my older sister Rose and I would plunk down our quarters, grab our popcorn, then settle into the lumpy theater seats to watch 17 cartoons, a couple of serials, tons of previews, and finally, a double feature of horror classics like *Frankenstein, Dracula, The Wolf Man* or *Abbott and Costello Meet*...well, all of them. Around 4 or 5 in the afternoon, we would stumble from the darkened theater, our blinking eyes surprised by the fact that such a thing as sunlight still existed. (Today, just try to get someone to sit through a double feature. Sigh. Those were the days...)

Growing up, there was a part of me—a big part of me—that honestly believed the monsters I was encountering on a weekly basis really, truly existed. Then, one Saturday when I was 11 years old, I saw Jimmy Cagney playing the immortal Lon Chaney in the movie that changed my life forever: *The Man of a Thousand Faces*. I suddenly realized that for every monster, there was someone behind the scenes who created them, and from that moment on, I knew that I wanted to be that someone. I hurried to the library, found books on makeup, and began experimenting at home on family and friends. Nothing has been the same ever since.

Well, that's not entirely true. Even though I'm now one of the monster makers, I'm still hypnotized and enthralled by horror movies. To be blunt about it, horror films and monster movies have come to mean everything to me. Since childhood, they've transfixed me, motivated me, and even saved me from a complete emotional breakdown when I was a combat photographer in the Vietnam War. As I looked through the lens of my camera at horrible physical atrocities, I tried to just think of them as special effects, and wondered how I could later create what I was looking at. It would prove to be an invaluable lesson in anatomy, death, and real horror.

Obviously, I prefer pretend horror, which leads me to the book you hold in your hands. The cinematic art of creating monsters and suspense and scares, followed by the relief of getting up from the theater, stepping back into the sunlight...then finding someone else to talk to about it. This is exactly what Dr. AC and his enthusiastic band of blood brothers (and sisters—horror chicks rule!) have brought to the table with *Horror 101*. Flipping through these pages has been a pleasant walk down memory lane—a lane that is cold and dark, mysterious and terrifying, good and gory.

Sounds like fun, right?

Hopefully, *Horror 101* reminds you, as it did me, of the special thrill that horror films and monster movies can provide—the sense of wonder that hypnotizes and enthralls audiences of all ages. Whether you're a horror veteran or just learning how wonderful getting good and scared can be, you're in for a real treat. And that's quite a trick.

Tom Savini
Pittsburgh, PA,
U.S.A.
June 2007

INTRODUCTION

Greetings. My name is Aaron Christensen, aka Dr. AC.

"I Like Horror Movies."

If you've ever uttered the above four words (which you undoubtedly have, otherwise you wouldn't be reading this) to another person, then you are well acquainted with "the look" that follows. The look comes in three varieties:

Look #1: Shock, dismay, confusion, usually accompanied by the word, "Why?"

Look #2: Mild interest. "Really? What's your favorite one?"

Look #3: Euphoria, followed by "Gooble gobble, gooble gobble, one of us, one of us..."

Herein, you will find nothing but #3's, right down the line. Welcome home, fellow fiend.

The bug bit me at an early age, in the form of a big, green stomping machine known as Godzilla. Thanks to late night TV and the public library, I soon expanded my horizons to include the Universal monsters, Hammer vixens, and big bugs of all varieties, eventually becoming immersed in this wonderful world of thrills and chills. With the advent of cable, home video, and now the Internet, my disease has grown exponentially over the years and I suspect that I may never return to normalcy. At least, that is my hope.

To my mind, this is the greatest time in history to be a horror fan, or a film fan of any ilk. DVD and the Internet have opened up a world of possibilities never before available. Nowadays, pretty much any flick we ever wanted to see, no matter how obscure or bizarre, is available with the click of a mouse and/or the swipe of a credit card. Even better, there is now a worldwide community available, just waiting to rap about our personal reactions to it.

One day, however, it struck me that the most challenging thing about being a fledgling horror aficionado in this age of instant access was simply knowing where to *start*. Which horror flicks and monster movies were the "essentials?" Every October, a multitude of divergent "scariest movies" lists are circulated, usually offering more grief than comfort to fans. Occasionally, we are lucky enough to find a "horror mentor," but knowledgeable as they might be, they are probably going to steer us toward their own personal passions. What was needed was a good jumping off place to discover each new subgenre (after all, not all Italian cannibal films are created equal), as well as an overall look at the genre as a whole.

While my original impulse was to compile a list and write about the essential films myself, a thought suddenly struck me: What if I were to invite individual horror fans to write on each of the films that I had designated as "must-see?" After all, I had encountered a wealth of informed and articulate folks in my travels (both on and off-line), and wouldn't it be far more interesting to read myriad opinions on 100+ different films than to listen to just one person (i.e., me) drone on and on? This way, we would also have a terrific cross-section of viewpoints; young and old, male and female, as well as an international contingent.

The more I thought about it, the more I liked the idea, and things quickly went from concept to action. I invited numerous friends and fans from my various walks of life to participate in the undertaking. The guidelines, in order to preserve the multifaceted dynamic, were simple: *Within a prescribed word limit, celebrate and illuminate the films in question, utilizing personal reactions as well as any background information one finds worth including. Anything goes.* Serving as a producer-editor, I recruited and assembled the talent roster, assigned the essays, proofread, and suggested revisions, etc. While there were a few bumps in the road and more than a few deadlines missed, I'm happy to report that the experience itself was overwhelmingly a positive one.

You now hold the fruits of our labors in your hands. And such sweet, forbidden fruits they are…

Herein, you will find 101 essays on 110 vital cinematic offerings within our beloved genre. In several cases, where it seemed impossible to talk about one film without mentioning another (as in the case of the 1958 and 1986 versions of *The Fly*, or *The Evil Dead* and *Evil Dead II*), we have simply created a longer essay that examines, compares, and contrasts them. Not only did this make good sense thematically, it also allowed us to squeeze in a few more titles. Pretty sneaky, eh?

With this book, we hope to accomplish a number of things: First, to get a list of essentials out there in the world, hopefully inspiring today's younger horror fans to partake of the pleasures to be found within some older films. Second, to create an opportunity for the voice of the everyday horror enthusiast to be heard, allowing them to celebrate his/her favorite fright flick. After all, it has never been the "serious" critics who have helped these films stand the test of time, it has been the tireless masses who have slavishly devoted themselves to the cause. This is for the fans, by the fans.

Also, it seemed like someone needed to step up and put a word in for the monsters out there, particularly of the "giant" variety. Too often these days, the creature features that thrilled and delighted many of us old-timers as children are being pushed out of the room and sent down the hall to the "sci-fi" or "fantasy" departments. (I can't tell you the grief I took from my horror buddies for including *The 7th Voyage of Sinbad*, but darn it, the monstrous Cyclops will always have a champion in me.) So, if that means we needed to add the words "and Monster Movies" onto the title, then so be it. If monsters don't have a place in the horror realm, then there's something wrong with this picture.

But the main reason behind putting this project together was that we hoped to create a tool that will help breed a more well-rounded horrorphile, creating a common ground for all of us to stand upon. Horror fans take enough crap from the "outside" world; we could do with a more united front. For instance, if a slasher fan and a classic Universal fan meet on the street, and the one has seen a couple moldy oldies and the other has seen a few gorefests, then voila! A conversation is possible, a bond is formed, a fellow "outcast from society" has been recognized. It is my firm belief that horror films and monster movies have the ability to bring more divergent people together than perhaps any other force on Earth. And no, I'm not kidding.

To wit, what sets this volume apart from others of its type is its many-voiced format. The participants range in age from 16 to 74. They are male and female. They hail from all over the U.S., England, Belgium, Scotland, Australia, Spain, Finland, Sweden, Denmark, Mexico, and elsewhere. They are actors, clerks, students, librarians, office temps, retired grandparents, graphic designers, warehouse managers... Between these pages is proof positive that horror fans come in all shapes and sizes; we're not all the pierced Goth kids in black t-shirts that the civilians seem to envision (although we do have a few of those as well).

Finally, we offer this as a sampler platter from the massive buffet that is the genre; an introductory class, if you will, at "Horror U." It's for the casual fan who is looking to get into the pool but isn't sure where to start, and it's for the experienced viewer who has seen all the films listed and just wants to hang out with some like-minded folks. Basically, it's for everyone who has ever trolled the horror aisles at the video store or furtively scanned the TV listings for the words, "melodrama," "thriller," or "horror," depending on your age group.

As far as defending the films included, we simply request that before all the experts get up in arms about "How come you didn't include _____? Or ___? OR _____?" please take that chill pill and realize that all the films chosen truly are worthy of attention. The selections within cover a period of 80 years, hail from a wide array of countries, and represent some high water marks in the glorious history of horror cinema. Any collection of this nature is going to be incomplete, but I think we've done a pretty good job here and any nit-picking is just that. However, in regards to more current films, we elected to set the cut-off point at 1999. Time is the true test and, only a few years into the new millennium, it seems unwise to declare any of them "must-see" films at this point. Not to say that there haven't been some bright spots on the horizon. Perhaps in Vol. 2...

Thank you for buying this book. My illustrious crew and I are thrilled that you too have come down with the same wonderful, horrible condition that we all find ourselves afflicted with. (Hear that, gang? We've got another one! Pass the popcorn and shout Hallelujah!)

Now, sit back, relax, and let the screams begin...

Warning to the Reader

Please be advised that the essays to follow often contain *in-depth* discussion of the films in question, including *specific plot points* and *twist endings*, which may "spoil" the movie for the viewer. If you have not yet seen the film, we advise skipping the corresponding essay in order to preserve the viewing experience.

Or just go watch the flippin' movie. Go ahead.

We'll be here when you get back.

ALIEN (1979)
ALIENS (1986)
by Wendy K. Bodine

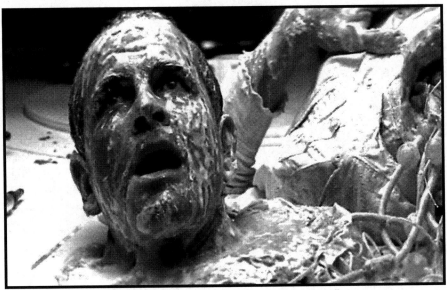

Science Officer Ash (Ian Holm) melts down in *Alien*.

Blessed and happy is the movie lover fortunate enough to experience the great movies of our time in their purity, during the opening weeks, on the big screen as God intended, surrounded by like-minded individuals who have put down their hard-earned cash for a few hours of distraction. While this author was unable to enjoy the *Alien* series' first installment at its genesis, I was present at the advent of its sophomore offering. Fresh out of high school, on the brink of college and a whole new avenue of life, I witnessed *Aliens* in all its flat-out, mind-blowing glory on the big screen.

After reading all that I could about the first film, I was determined to hunt it down and find out what all the fuss was about. Turned out the original *Alien* was the brainchild of several parents: Science fiction veteran Dan O'Bannon and writer Ronald Shusett came up with the original concept and received story credits. Walter Hill, Larry Ferguson, and David Giler wrote the script for the film, as well as the sequels. The plot deals with the crew of the interstellar freighter *Nostromo* being awakened from hyper-sleep by a distress signal coming from a barren planet light-years from Earth. When they investigate the planet, they inadvertently bring back to the freighter a most unwelcome guest (designed by surrealist artist H.R. Giger) and the crew realizes too late that the distress signal is actually a warning to stay away.

It was the second cinematic effort for director Ridley Scott (after *The Duellists* in 1977). Still getting his feet wet in the movie world, the 40-year-old Englishman chose to borrow heavily from another cult sci-fi hit, Stanley Kubrick's *2001: A Space Odyssey* (1968). Scott used a great deal of film showing off the intensely detailed designs of the different spaceships and the alien landscapes created by art director Roger Christian. The long, drawn-out pans along the hull of the *Nostromo* and the lingering wide-views of the crashed alien ship that the crew explores (Scott used children dressed in space suits to emphasize its hugeness) enhanced the futuristic feel. The movie overall has a gloomy and metallic feel, from the sunless planet to the dark recesses of the *Nostromo,* where one by one the hapless crew members meet the alien.

Taking the lead again from Kubrick, Scott and composer Jerry Goldsmith utilized a gentler film score than one would expect in a horror movie, which added to the suspense. Music is sparingly used and is at times conspicuous by its absence, especially during the more intense scenes such as the infamous "chest-bursting" in the dining hall. As this would turn out to be the centerpiece of the picture, Scott perhaps felt the absence of music would help intensify the shock factor. Countless numbers of hopelessly scarred audience members might agree, as this scene was ranked the second most horrifying scene of all time on Bravo TV's *100 Scariest Movie Moments.*

Another theme Scott borrowed from *2001* was the idea of technology overriding human good sense. The *Nostromo* is run by a super-computer called "Mother," which carries on conversations with the crew, much like the astronauts in *2001* did with HAL. Later, it's revealed that Science Officer Ash (played by Ian Holm), who was instrumental in getting the alien aboard the freighter (despite Ripley's orders), is actually an android programmed to further the interests of the almighty Weyland-Yutani Corporation (hereafter referred to as "the Company"). The Company funded the initial *Nostromo* mining mission and is more concerned with financial benefits than the lives of the crew. Classic post-modern ideas are a main focus here, where the ruthless corporate/governmental entity seeks its own existence, its own survival, at all costs, and humans are ultimately devalued and "expendable."

As Lt. Ellen Ripley, Sigourney Weaver embodies a strong survivor-type—not your typical role for a lady of horror. The role established the 30-year-old Weaver as an up-and-coming star. She goes from being a "person in charge" to being the only one clear-headed enough to escape the ever-growing danger. The basic human element of survival, in spite of seemingly insurmountable odds and the harshest workings of nature and the powers that be, brings *Alien* to a satisfying close.

But alas, for our heroine, there can be no happily ever after.

The first sequel was entitled *Aliens*, which turned out to be truth in advertising as the follow-up had more than one. In fact, it had dozens. Opening 57 years after the end of the first movie, Ripley (Weaver again) has been in hyper-sleep the whole time (along with Jones the Cat, who also survived the *Nostromo*). Her escape pod is found by a salvage ship, and she is returned to a world that knows nothing of what happened on the *Nostromo,* save what was recorded in the ship's log, which was salvaged in the pod. No matter how hard she pleads, her story of the alien that massacred her crew and caused her to destroy the ship falls on deaf Company ears. She also learns—to her horror—that the Company has since colonized the same planet where her crew encountered the first alien. Hundreds of people are now living on that rock, doing mining and research, until one of the families (yes, there are kids involved) stumbled upon the same derelict ship found by Ripley's crew. Apparently, the ship is discovered shortly after her return to Earth because soon after that, all the colonists disappear, and the Company turns to Ripley to advise a rescue team of ultra-tough Marines.

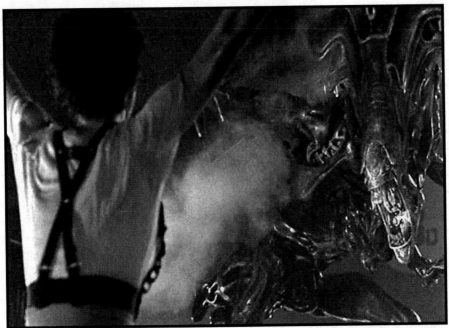

Ripley (Sigourney Weaver) confronts the Alien Queen in *Aliens*.

James Cameron is, well, James Cameron. His love of extreme action and shoot-'em-up resolutions is well-documented in his long, illustrious history of directing, which began with the pseudo-memorable *Piranha II: The Spawning* (1981).

Aliens is probably the most popular and lucrative of the series because of Cameron's vision. The scenery is more colorful, yet somehow still retains an aura of darkness about it. Ripley's character is also more fully developed—an uncut version of the film reveals her past as a mother, which helps explain her deep maternal attachment to the sole survivor of the colony, a little girl called Newt (Carrie Henn). She is also given the chance to evolve into the kick-butt warrior-woman most modern moviegoers associate with her character. Whereas in *Alien* she was in a position of some authority, it wasn't until the end that she finally emerged as a leader. Almost from the outset of *Aliens*, she takes charge of the mission when rescue team's military leaders are eliminated under various, mostly unpleasant circumstances. It was the strength and satisfying growth of Ripley's character that earned Weaver a nomination for the Best Actress Oscar that year—a rarity for an actress in a horror/action film.

There is less emphasis on artistic visuals here, save for the sole purpose of showing off an assortment of Academy-Award winning special effects. Gone are the long, smooth, technical and creative shots of ships, planets, and space; now the audience jumps through rapid scene changes, people running through dimly lit halls, screaming into monitors, and eventually being torn apart by numerous Aliens. Explosions, flame-throwers, machine guns, and grenades dominate most of the action scenes. The Marines are relatively stereotyped, but that seems to work artistically in this movie—the viewer wants these soldiers to be tough-talking and hard-walking, even the women. Cameron doesn't allow anyone to be weak in this film—at least, not for any prolonged period of time. As with Scott, women get their fair share of action time: Each lady Marine goes down fighting, and even Newt (who is about 9 or 10) has the smarts and clear-headedness to be the only survivor out of hundreds of colonists; several times, she helps save the Marines who came to save her.

The post-modern line of thinking takes a turn here, as the old, early 1980s idea that "technology is evil" is challenged with the presence of a new android, Science Officer Bishop (Lance Henriksen) who is instantly distrusted by Ripley because of what happened with Ash on the *Nostromo*. His early fascination with the first alien specimens they encounter (all dead) in the colony's science lab only further Ripley's suspicions. He attempts to earn her trust, citing that he has been programmed not to "harm or allow to be harmed any human being," borrowing from Isaac Asimov's Three Laws of Robotics (it seemed that as the world grew more tech-friendly, so did the movies).

But she later finds out that it's not the machines that she needs to keep her eye on, but rather another human: Company representative Burke (Paul Reiser). It was he who encouraged Ripley to join the mission, with the promise that they were going there "not to study, not to bring back, but to wipe them out." Instead, he has been sent by the Company not to rescue the colonists, but to retrieve the live alien specimens and bring them back for study—once again, at the expense of human life. So another post-modern concept comes into play here: not technology, but big business (science perhaps?) is out to get us. The android ends up saving lives, while the human plots to destroy them. Ripley says it best: "You know, Burke, I don't know which species is worse. You don't see them f**king each other over for a goddamn percentage."

Cameron picks up Scott's mantle admirably. While not denying himself and his fans the hard-hitting action they love, he holds on to the original ideas from the first movie. He remembers what Ripley went through, and brings it into play seamlessly in the beginning of the film. *Aliens* opens a bit slowly, like Scott's movie, as Ripley is rescued and recuperates at the Company hospital, stating her case about the fate of her original crew. But once the action picks up, it almost never lets go. Cameron even continues his tradition of being able to slip a few quotable lines into the script (à la "I'll be back"–*Terminator*; "Hasta la vista, baby"–*Terminator 2*). *Aliens* gives us "Game over, man, game over!" and "Get away from her, you *bitch*!" Cameron's films have a way of becoming cultural landmarks and *Aliens* was no exception. In fact, alongside both of his *Terminator* films, it helped define a decade of movie excess for a whole generation. And once again, after a heart-racing sequence of action, just when audiences thought it was safe to go back into the hypersleep chamber, he winds the action back up with a classic horror second climax that takes us into another episode of suspense. But in the end, all's well that ends well, another airlock is put to good use, and our heroine peacefully lies down for another long sleep.

Sad to say, some people just can't leave well enough alone. The resounding success of the second *Alien* movie gave those deep-behind-the-scenes executives the bright idea of cranking out yet another sequel ASAP. But like a premature baby, it was weaker than its older siblings, without the years of development and careful planning that went into the first two films. The third installment, *Alien³* (1992), felt rushed, lacking the character or plot development of the ones before. It floundered at the box office and scurried off to the video rental shelves without incident. The final piece of the "quadrilogy," *Alien: Resurrection* (1997), fared even worse and is considered by most fans of the genre as the least appealing of the four. Some say it was due to the over-involvement of Weaver in the production and storyline; others felt that despite the added star power (which included Winona Ryder), it just wasn't the *right* power. But although these final two sequels may be the ugly ducklings, they are still part of the family.

It would be unfair to tell a movie lover that if they prefer one movie of a series over another, then they cannot fully appreciate either. *Alien* and *Aliens* were born of two different eras, yet both have the same lineage. *Alien* emerged at a time of theatrical intellectualism where audiences, just coming out of the hippie/disco eras and at the dawn of the computer age, were expected to be more cerebral, more introspective. By the time *Aliens* made the scene, however, audiences were deep into the excess of the '80s—heavy metal hair bands, loud clothes, big hair and America was going to kick everyone's butt, on this planet and every other. Entertainment was all about the *experience*, the *feeling*, and the more intense, the better. To appreciate either movie is to understand the times they were born in. And to be a movie lover born in either time is a blessed and happy thing, indeed.

AN AMERICAN WEREWOLF IN LONDON (1981)
THE HOWLING (1981)
by Sean Robinson

1981 was the year of the wolf, or to be more precise, the year of the werewolf.

With two of the best lycanthrope movies ever made released just months apart, Joe Dante's *The Howling* and John Landis' *An American Werewolf in London* have been inextricably linked in horror fans' minds and hearts. Both movies feature terrific performances, sharp screenplays that wickedly blend horror and comedy, and exceptional transformation scenes featuring groundbreaking special effects.

Let's first take a look at *An American Werewolf in London*, whose taglines teased, "The director of *Animal House* brings you a different kind of animal." *American Werewolf* was perhaps Landis' most personal project, a film that he had been planning to make since 1969. Released on August 21, 1981, the movie opens with two young Americans, David Kessler (David Naughton) and Jack Goodman (Griffin Dunne), on a backpacking holiday in northern England. They head towards East Proctor and the comfort of The Slaughtered Lamb public house. The welcome they receive there is less than warm. After the locals (a fine collection of British character actors: Brian Glover, Rik Mayall, David Schofield, Lila Kaye) caution them to "stick to the road" and "beware the moon," they are on their way again. Despite the warnings, they leave the road and are promptly attacked by some sort of wild animal, which leaves Jack dead and David seriously injured. The locals kill the beast, and the last thing David sees before losing consciousness is the werewolf, now transformed back to a man, lying dead next to him.

When David regains consciousness, he is in a London hospital (there are obviously no hospitals in the north of England), under the care of the lovely nurse Alex Price (Jenny Agutter). He starts to have some very strange dreams and begins to doubt his own sanity when he is visited by his recently deceased friend. Jack has returned from beyond the grave to warn David that he is now the last surviving werewolf and must die in order to release Jack from his tormented limbo. David's nightmares continue to

Jack Goodman (Griffin Dunne) from *An American Werewolf in London*

worsen, becoming more graphic and discomforting. After being released from the hospital, David takes up an invitation from Alex to stay with her. After a romantic interlude in the shower and bedroom with his new flatmate, David is the recipient of another unwelcome visit from the increasingly decomposed Jack, who repeats his warning that David will become a werewolf at the next full moon.

An American Werewolf in London is often called a horror-comedy and it succeeds on both counts, as Landis skillfully mingles genres. Some very funny scenes exist, such as David sitting with Jack's decomposing corpse. When asked about silver bullets, Dunne's delivery of the line "Oh, be serious, David!" is priceless. However, I would describe the movie primarily as a horror film, albeit one with many humorous moments. Landis keeps his tongue firmly in his cheek throughout, incorporating many in-jokes. These include a softcore *See You Next Wednesday* reference, the closing credits congratulating Prince Charles and Diana Spencer on their wedding (presumably because David calls the Royal family various names in a bid to get arrested), and the disclaimer stating "Any resemblance to any persons living, dead, or undead is coincidental." The very final credits urge viewers to "Ask for Babs," a reference to Landis' 1978 film *Animal House*, whose credits listed the future occupations of its characters. (Babs, played by Martha Smith, had become a tour guide at Universal Studios.) References to *American Werewolf* have since appeared in some of Landis' other films, most recently in his *Masters of Horror* episode, *Deer Woman* (2005).

Lots of cameo performances appear throughout the film. Frank Oz makes two appearances: First as Mr. Collins from the American embassy at the hospital and later as the voice of Miss Piggy in the Nazi werewolf dream sequence. We are also treated

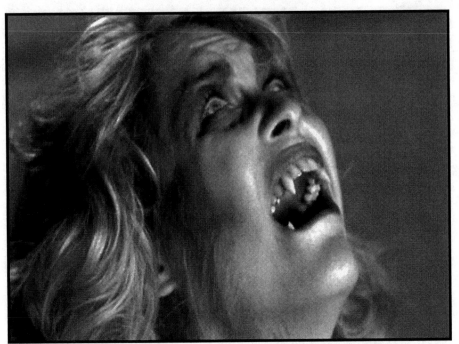

Karen's (Dee Wallace) on-air transformation from *The Howling*

to U.K. glamour girl Nina Carter ("The Naked Truth About Naughty Nina") and porn star Linzi Drew, who stars in *See You Next Wednesday*. The performances throughout the film are excellent and it remains a mystery why stars David Naughton and Griffin Dunne's careers never took off after the potential they display here. *American Werewolf* went on to gross $30,565,000 and later spawned a vastly inferior sequel, *An American Werewolf in Paris* (1997), which failed to recapture the spirit of Landis' classic.

Meanwhile, released just five months earlier, Joe Dante's *The Howling* is perhaps less tongue-in-cheek than *American Werewolf* but also features moments of dark humor and is similarly packed with homages and genre cameos. The film begins with television reporter Karen White (Dee Wallace) participating in a police operation to trap dangerous psychopath and serial killer Eddie Quist (Robert Picardo). She confronts Eddie in the backroom of a seedy porn store, but before the police can burst in and shoot Eddie, Karen witnesses something terrifying, so horrifying that it triggers amnesia of the encounter. In addition to the memory loss, Karen begins having a series of increasingly violent nightmares. With encouragement from her husband Bill (Christopher Stone, whom Wallace would later marry in real life), she admits herself to an isolated recovery resort called The Colony, run by her therapist Dr. Waggner (the always excellent Patrick MacNee).

Back in the city, Karen's friends and co-workers Terry (Belinda Balaski) and Chris (Dennis Dugan) are investigating Eddie Quist's background after his corpse mysteriously vanishes from the morgue. At Eddie's apartment, they discover a collection of strange artwork depicting weird wolf-like creatures and landscapes. They decide to visit an occult bookshop owned by Walter Paisley (Dante regular Dick Miller) and question him on werewolf folklore.

Terry visits Karen at The Colony and, while investigating an isolated cabin is attacked by a werewolf, but she manages to escape by chopping its hand off. She tries to phone Chris to tell him what is going on, but she is interrupted when another werewolf calmly picks a patient's file folder out of her hand. As Chris listens helplessly on the telephone, Terry is brutally murdered.

Meanwhile, Karen has decided to leave The Colony, but before she can, she bumps into her old friend Eddie Quist, who reveals the truth that all The Colony's residents are werewolves, including Dr. Waggner. Dispatching Eddie Quist with a silver bullet, Chris arrives just in time to rescue Karen and, after trapping the werewolves in a blazing barn, the two make their escape. But not before Karen has been bitten by her lycanthropic husband. Returning to her broadcast TV job, Karen's on-air transformation (into the cutest werewolf ever) leads to an exciting conclusion.

Dante fills his film with numerous homages to various other classic horror movies. We are even treated to a few TV clips of 1941's *The Wolf Man*, including the classic "Even a man who is pure in heart" quote. He also manages to cram in cameos aplenty, including Roger Corman (the notoriously penny-pinching producer/director is seen checking for change in a phone booth), Forrest J Ackerman (reading a copy of *Famous Monsters*), the legendary John Carradine, Kevin McCarthy, Kenneth Tobey, and Slim Pickens to name but a few. In further tribute, several of the characters' names are taken from directors of previous notable werewolf films (George Waggner, Terry Fisher, and Fred Francis, the directors of *The Wolf Man*, *The Curse of the Werewolf*, 1961, and *Legend of the Werewolf*, 1975, respectively).

By contrast, the novel by Gary Brandner, on which the film is based, is much more straightforward horror. After initial drafts by original director Jack Conrad (who left the project following problems with the studio) and Terence H. Winkless proved unsatisfactory, Dante hired his *Pirahna* (1978) scribe, John Sayles, to completely rewrite the script. Sayles' final product, it should be noted, bears little resemblance to Brandner's original story.

Despite all the puns and in-jokes, Dante's film has moments of genuine horror, especially whenever Rob Bottin's terrifying werewolves are onscreen. Aided by Pino Donaggio's superb musical score, the transformation scenes are excellent and perhaps second only to Rick Baker's work in *American Werewolf*. In these days of CGI and advanced special effects, Baker and Bottin's efforts still represent the lycanthropic highwater marks. Baker would go on to deservedly win the Best Makeup Oscar for *American Werewolf*. (Although, in yet another grievous Academy oversight, his protégé Bottin's equally impressive accomplishments for *The Howling* were not even nominated.)

At the time, *The Howling* was the first werewolf film to show an onscreen transformation without the use of camera dissolves. Although I would say the main metamorphosis scene in *American Werewolf* has the edge, the two-legged, upright werewolves themselves are, in my opinion, much better in *The Howling* (apart from one terrible animated sequence and some stop-motion werewolves at the end). *The Howling* achieved a theatrical gross of $17,986,000 and managed to spawn six Dante-free sequels of varying but ultimately inferior quality.

Joe Dante has said, "People are always trying to compare those two movies because the transformation techniques are somewhat similar. But it's [*American Werewolf*] lit completely differently and has lots more comedy than our picture. We both wanted to bring it up to the modern day so that people could enjoy the picture the way people enjoyed them in the '30s and '40s."

Both films have stood the test of time, and while arguments still rage over which was the better film, one thing is for certain: Horror fans were the real winners.

ASYLUM (1972)
by Timothy Young

Byron (Herbert Lom) and his manufactured dolls that contain human souls

Asylum is the fifth of seven anthology horror films from Amicus Productions. The firm's founders were the American film producers Milton Subotsky and Max Rosenberg, who had originally suggested the notion of a *Frankenstein* film to Hammer Studios. As the script (which would emerge as *The Curse of Frankenstein*,1957) was extensively rewritten, Subotsky and Rosenberg ended up without a screen credit and had to fight for compensation. But what they did learn was that there was money in horror, and that Britain was the place to make it. For their first horror effort, they poached Hammer's rising star, Christopher Lee, for added insurance and the resulting film, *Horror Hotel* (aka *City of the Dead*, 1960), made enough money to encourage Subotsky and Rosenberg to move to Britain and create their own production company, Amicus Films.

Dr. Terror's House of Horrors (1965) was the first official Amicus production, and its success paved the way for several more offerings. With Hammer stars Lee and Peter Cushing headlining the affair, the movie's format was inspired by the British *Dead of Night* (1945)—instead of a single narrative, the film was divided into five individual tales, linked by a "wrap-around" story. In this case it was that of a fortune teller looking into the future of five passengers in a train carriage (including a youthful Donald Sutherland). *Dr. Terror* fared better than Amicus' follow-up, *The Skull* (1965), a more conventional horror outing (also starring Cushing and Lee), and thus set the stage for a decade of Amicus omnibus horror.

Asylum is a shining example of the Amicus anthology-horror oeuvre: The story opens with Dr. Martin (Robert Powell) arriving at the asylum for a new appointment, accompanied by the over-the-top strains of Mussorgsky on the soundtrack. The asylum's director, Dr. Rutherford (played by the always game Patrick Magee) offers him a challenge: If Martin can identify Dr. Starr—the previous head psychiatrist—from the four incurable lunatics he will be shown, then he can have the job.

Martin first interviews a woman called Bonnie (Barbara Perkins), who tells the tale of her lover Walter (Richard Todd), who had planned to run away with her. But after killing and dismembering his wife, he soon finds that the axed ex's body parts are stalking him around the house. The second story is told by former tailor Bruno (Barry Morse), who is engaged by a mysterious individual (Peter Cushing) to construct a mystical coat. The young doctor then hears the tale of Barbara (Charlotte Rampling), a woman plagued by the murderous Lucy (Britt Ekland), who might just be in Barbara's mind—or might well be real. The final patient is Byron (Herbert Lom), who has manufactured small dolls which contain human souls. With these stories complete, Dr. Martin returns to the asylum director to give his assessment as to the true identity of Dr. Starr. But as one would expect, the horror is not yet over.

Like many of the Amicus horror films, *Asylum* is a mixed bag. The wrap-around story is one of the strongest in the series, giving a solid background to the stories instead of the usual "fortune telling" theme, and the film supplies one of the most satisfying endings. However, while the first story does build a fair amount of tension, the sight of moving body parts wrapped in brown paper is simply laughable and more reminiscent of a comic horror film. (Although Amicus used the roaming body part storyline quite often, including *Dr. Terror's House of Horrors* and *And Now the Screaming Starts* [1973], it never seems to succeed in raising anything but a giggle.) The second and third segments are much more effective, successfully developing *frisson* in very different ways. The story of the astrological coat has a very strange, almost unearthly, ambiance to much of it, that keeps audiences wondering how it will resolve, although the ending itself is a bit absurd. Barbara's story is similarly enigmatic, and while viewers might well guess what is going on, the story keeps twisting and bluffing, so we can never be quite sure what happened. Unfortunately, as with many of the Amicus anthology segments, these two stories have a lot of potential but are not given enough time to develop properly, both running only 20 minutes while they could have easily filled the 50-minute time slot of the *Hammer House of Horror* television series. The final episode ("Mannikins of Horror"), with its miniature robots, is truly bizarre. Though too short to be completely effective, it again displays potential, perhaps even enough to support a feature-length film.

British director Roy Ward Baker takes the helm. Best known for his work on the acclaimed *Titanic* film *A Night to Remember* (1958), Baker shot a variety of later period Hammer films, including the highly regarded *Quatermass and the Pit* (1967) and the less-than-impressive *Scars of Dracula* (1970). His straightforward style brings to mind Hammer's best known director, Terence Fisher. Baker's work on *Asylum* is solid if unspectacular, and the film's pacing and editing are necessarily brisk in accordance with the short stories. Snatches of Mussorgsky's "Night on a Bald Mountain" are also effectively used in several scenes, in addition to the film's wonderfully dramatic opening sequence.

One of the advantages Amicus found with the anthology format was that actors were required for relatively short shooting schedules, allowing Subotsky and Rosenberg to acquire the services of a variety of big-name stars while keeping the budgets low. In *Asylum*, Peter Cushing and Herbert Lom receive top billing despite their minimal screen time, with soon-to-be Bond girl Britt Ekland giving an impressive performance as the mysterious Lucy, alongside a suitably haunted turn from Charlotte Rampling. Robert Powell, who would appear in the little-known, after-death thriller *The Asphyx* (1973) and later star in the TV miniseries *Jesus of Nazareth* (1977), also does a fine job as our nonplussed psychiatrist.

One of the last of the Amicus horrors, *Asylum* performed reasonably well at the box office both in the U.K., where it formed a double bill with *Duel* (1971), and in the U.S.A. It was also re-released in the '80s under the title *House of Crazies*. However, despite continuing to shoot horror in the same vein, the studio never again matched *Asylum*'s success. By the 1970s, the mild-mannered British horror film was on the way out, being quickly replaced by the gritty, realistic, and violent American horror films and the over-the-top bloody and sex-filled Italian *giallo* (murder mystery) films. The Hammer horrors went out on a sour note with *To the Devil a Daughter* (1976) while Amicus bowed out slightly earlier with their last proper horror film, the highly engaging werewolf whodunit, *The Beast Must Die* (1974). The studio stayed in business for a few more years (despite Max Rosenberg returning to America), shooting a series of Edgar Rice Burroughs-inspired fantasy/adventure films, beginning with *The Land That Time Forgot* (1975). The last credited film produced under the Amicus banner was the poorly received anthology horror parody *The Monster Club* (1980), starring Vincent Price, Donald Pleasence, and John Carradine.

For horror aficionados looking to explore the Amicus legacy, *Asylum* is a perfectly good place to start, being a prime example of the studio's anthology films. Fans of the format are also recommended to seek out some of Amicus' other similarly entertaining (if equally flawed) entries: *Dr. Terror's House of Horrors*, *Torture Garden* (1967), *The House that Dripped Blood* (1970), and *Tales from the Crypt* (1972). Happily, many of the studio's works are finally becoming available on DVD in the U.S.A. and U.K., although several of their lesser-known productions still languish in obscurity.

THE BEAST FROM 20,000 FATHOMS (1953)
by Michael Vario

I was fascinated by dinosaurs as a child. I was also in love with horror movies from the time I could first turn on a television. Growing up in the early '60s, my favorite movies were all about giant monsters, especially the 1953 film *The Beast from 20,000 Fathoms*. I liked it more than *Godzilla* (1954) because to me the stop-motion animation was magical. And I liked it more than *King Kong* (1933) because, well, it was a dinosaur. Before home video and cable, we were confined to watching whatever was on the broadcast TV schedule. Fortunately, *The Beast from 20,000 Fathoms* was shown often, and I watched it whenever it was shown.

A nuclear bomb test in the Arctic is presided over by scientist Tom Nesbitt (Paul Hubschmid, billed as Paul Christian) and Army Colonel Jack Evans (Kenneth Tobey). Nesbitt and another scientist, George Elliot, head out to take readings from the sensors.

Ray Harryhausen's masterful stop-motion animated Beast

As a blizzard moves in, Elliot briefly sees what appears to be a huge dinosaur. Nesbitt comes to his aid, but the beast reappears, causing a small avalanche that leaves Elliot dead and Nesbitt unconscious. When rescued, Nesbitt is barely conscious, mumbling something about a "monster." Diagnosed as delusional, he is flown to a New York City hospital.

Later, Nesbitt reads a newspaper story of a fishing boat being sunk in the North Atlantic. Believing it to be the same monster, he leaves the hospital and tracks down a leading paleontologist, Professor Thurgood Elson (Cecil Kellaway), and his assistant Lee Hunter (Paula Raymond). He tries to convince them that the bomb test has released a frozen dinosaur. Though the professor is skeptical, Hunter is more receptive to the possibility.

Meanwhile, on the Maine coast, the beast comes out of the sea and destroys a lighthouse. When Colonel Evans visits the Coast Guard office and discovers the report of the lighthouse, Elson postulates that the beast is heading toward New York and suggests looking for the beast in the underwater canyons. From a diving bell, Elson observes the undersea wildlife when the beast appears and moves to attack. Communication is abruptly cut off and the diving bell is lost, along with Professor Elson. Their worst fears confirmed, the National Guard and Coast Guard are put on alert while Nesbitt and Hunter mourn the death of their friend.

The beast comes ashore near the Brooklyn Bridge and begins wreaking havoc in lower Manhattan. The military attack the beast with bazooka fire, wounding it before it retreats to the river. But the doctors soon realize that the blood from the monster's wound is causing the soldiers to fall ill, suggesting that the beast may be carrying a deadly disease. Evans, Nesbitt, and Hunter come to the conclusion that the only way to stop the monster (without spreading a deadly plague throughout the city) is by shooting it with a radioactive isotope. Just then, the report comes in that the beast has come ashore at Manhattan Beach and is heading toward the Coney Island amusement park. There Nesbitt and a top marksman (played by a young Lee Van Cleef, who would soon put those shooting skills to use in numerous Spaghetti Westerns) confront the beast in a fiery climax.

Watching the film again after many years, I find it holds up exceptionally well. The well-constructed plot and the steady pacing build toward the thrilling climax without ever bogging down. The acting is quite good without being overly melodramatic. For budgetary reasons *Beast* was shot in black and white, but this works to the film's advantage, adding a stark feeling of dread to the beast's scenes which, aside from the initial rampage in Manhattan, usually take place at night.

The Rhedosaurus itself was a stop-motion model created by Ray Harryhausen in his first solo effort after working with *King Kong* maestro Willis O'Brien on *Mighty Joe Young*. To save time and money, Harryhausen developed a technique soon to be labeled Dynamation, which allowed him to combine live action with the model in the same scenes without having to meticulously construct miniature sets. He would use this process on all his future films.

Of course, movies about giant monsters were not new in 1953. O'Brien had been doing stop-motion films since the silent film days, popularizing the genre with *The Lost World* in 1925 and setting the standard with *King Kong* in 1933. In 1949, *Mighty Joe Young* was released, whetting the appetite of filmgoers, with *Kong* enjoying a profitable re-release in 1952. Audiences wanted more.

But by the '50s, the world had changed and audiences had new fears. In 1949 Russia had exploded an atomic bomb and the cold war was on in earnest. The hydrogen bomb was created in 1952 and the U.S. tested 11 bombs the following year. The effects of science and fear of nuclear weapons were very real concerns among people, and *The Beast from 20,000 Fathoms* tapped into those feelings and gave them a shape. *Beast* was the first atom-age monster.

The original idea for the film is an area of some debate. It may have come from a Ray Bradbury story called "The Fog Horn," which features two lighthouse keepers who encounter a strange prehistoric creature. Bradbury and Harryhausen were longtime friends, drawn together by their mutual love of dinosaurs. Both have recounted various tales on the story's origins on different occasions. Bradbury at one time has said his story inspired the writers and that he was given a credit after speaking with the producers; Harryhausen is quoted as saying that the script already existed, but when they became aware of the story, they wished to include the lighthouse scene as part of the action. Whatever the truth, the credits read "Suggested by *The Saturday Evening Post* story by Ray Bradbury."

Another source of genial contention is the film's cost. Harryhausen has estimated the production budget at $150,000 while IMDb.com lists it at $210,000. A Harryhausen fan site credits producers Jack Dietz and Hal E. Chester as saying it cost a mere $65,000. Also, depending on who you believe, the producers of the film, Mutual Pictures of

California, sold it to Warner Bros. for somewhere between $400,000 and $650,000. However, all this became rather a moot point when the film grossed $5 million at the box office and became Warner Bros.' top-grossing film of 1953.

Beast was the first monster to come about because of nuclear weapons, spawning a genre that continues to this day. Warner Bros. would follow up their success with *Them!* (1954), about giant ants created by nuclear bomb tests. The same year, also influenced by *Beast*, Tomoyuki Tanaka created *Godzilla*. In the years to come, cinemagoers would behold a flood of movies about giant monsters resulting from nuclear bombs or radiation. Harryhausen would soon begin work on *It Came from Beneath the Sea* (1955), the first of many successful collaborations with producer Charles H. Schneer. The director of *Beast*, Eugène Lourié, would helm the near-remake, *The Giant Behemoth* (1959), and returned yet again to giant dinosaurs with *Gorgo* (1961). Roland Emmerich's 1998 *Godzilla* remake bears a much closer resemblance in both story and location to *Beast* than to its Japanese namesake.

An interesting bit of trivia is that the dinosaur skeleton that appears in the scene with professor Elson was borrowed from RKO, having originally appeared in the 1938 comedy *Bringing Up Baby*.

The Beast from 20,000 Fathoms is not just an excellent yarn about a giant dinosaur. It remains an important film in the history of horror, inspiring countless imitators and continuing to influence monster movies to this day.

THE BEYOND (1981)
by Jon Kitley

Back in the early '80s, my first job was at a movie theater. Since our manager had no problem in booking horror movies, unrated or otherwise, we played some great stuff, titles like *Evil Dead* (1981), *Re-Animator* (1985), and *Day of the Dead* (1985). As ushers, we would spend most of our time "checking the theater," meaning we'd be standing in the back watching the movies. Sometimes we'd come in on our own time to see the movie from beginning to end, but that was only for the good ones.

One of these good ones was called *Seven Doors of Death*. At that time, I had never heard of the film, the director, or anybody in it for that matter. But from the couple of segments I'd glimpsed, the movie looked pretty gory, so I had to see it all. Sitting in the theater as the lights went down, little did I know that this would be a very important landmark in my life as a horror fan.

The action starts out in 1927, with a group of people arriving at a hotel, seeking out one of its residents whom they believe is a warlock. They bust into his room and take him to the basement. Ignoring his pleas for them to stop, they graphically whip him with chains, blood pouring from the fresh wounds. Then they crucify him by nailing his arms to the basement wall (once again with blood spurting) before throwing some sort of lime and/or acid on him. And, as this character slowly melts into a gooey mess, we get the opening credits.

Now, how's *that* for a start?

We then jump to present time, where a young woman, Liza, has inherited the same old hotel which she intends to renovate and reopen. But, as fate would have it, this particular lodging house just happens to sit atop one of the seven gateways to Hell.

Italian director Lucio Fulci created Hellish imagery.

Tough luck, huh? And even worse, the doorway gets opened somehow, and all hell breaks loose—literally.

As I sat in the theater watching these gruesome escapades, I kept trying to figure out just what the hell was going on. Why would a lady just lay on the ground while acid pours over her face? Why didn't the hero figure out how to shoot a zombie? (After a head shot, they'd drop. But then he'd go and shoot the next one in the body, which had no effect.) The flick may not have made much sense, but it sure was gory. There were eyes being poked out, spiders chewing a guy's face to ribbons, and even a young girl getting most of her head blown off. For a young gorehound, this was sheer bliss.

I would later learn that the object of my adoration was actually called *L'aldilà* aka *The Beyond*, but that it had been drastically cut and re-titled for the American release. Even the director's name had been changed: Instead of "Louis Fuller," the perpetrator of the outlandish events I had witnessed was better known as Lucio Fulci. As I discovered who this Fulci character was, and the other great films that he had contributed to the horror genre, my appreciation quickly grew.

Many uninitiated horror fans are often at a loss when they encounter the Italian style of filmmaking. The phrase "style over substance" perfectly suits this kind of non-plot-driven cinema, and *The Beyond* serves as a prime example. Fulci isn't interested in a coherent storyline, with all the loose ends tidied up at the end of 90 minutes. He is more concerned with creating a series of sequences meant to scare you. Horrify you. And hopefully, even gross you out.

According to Fulci himself, "My idea was to make an absolute film, with all the horrors of our world. It's a plotless film: a house, people, and dead men coming from the beyond. There's no logic to it, just a succession of images. In Italy, we tried to make films based on pure themes, without a plot, and *The Beyond*, like Dario Argento's *Inferno*, refuses conventional and traditional structures."

But because it might not have a strong or coherent plot, does that mean *The Beyond* is a poorly made film? Not at all. The simple fact is that these "successions of images" are some of the most memorable elements of Italian horror. Unfortunately, traditional American audiences are accustomed to having their movies easy to follow, with a neat and clean ending. So for Westerners, Italian horror can take some getting use to. But, once audiences give up the notion of a straightforward plot, it's easy to just sit back and enjoy the full-blooded experience.

Fulci has assembled a terrific cast here, and they give the film their all. Catriona MacColl had worked with Fulci before in *City of the Living Dead* (aka *The Gates of Hell* [1980]), and would work with him again in *House by the Cemetery* (1981). Her co-star, David Warbeck, is also no stranger to fans of Italian cinema of the '80s and '90s. Another notable name here is Al Cliver (real name Pier Luigi Conti), who worked for Fulci many times, most famously in *Zombie* (aka *Zombi 2* [1979]). While Cliver has little more than a bit part in *The Beyond*, he is memorably killed by a bunch of flying broken glass, so I guess that's something. And let's not forget Cinzia Monreale, who has a much bigger and more challenging role than she did in Joe D'Amato's *Beyond The Darkness* (aka *Buio Omega* [1979]), where she was a corpse pretty much the whole movie.

But the picture's ultimate reason for being is the gore, and the splatter-happy Fulci doesn't hold back. One of the most famous scenes in Italian horror history occurs in *Zombie* where Olga Karlatos has her head pulled through a broken door, only to have a sharp wooden splinter slowly puncture her eye. Fulci has always enjoyed including some sort of ocular gore, with his characters' eyeballs constantly being poked in, pulled out, punctured, etc. in an effort to make the audience cringe. For Fulci, that is the idea: To show something simple yet visceral that will generate a great reaction from the crowd.

In *The Beyond*, Fulci displays his considerable talents as a horror director, delivering the gory goods. In one scene in particular, a woman is attacked by one of the living dead. The zombie grabs its victim by the face and starts to push her back toward a wall. As we see a huge nail sticking out of the wall, we *know* what's going to happen. But the real payoff here is not when the head is smashed up against the nail, but when the nail pushes through the *front* of the face, popping the eyeball out on the end of it. What a bonus! That is Italian horror! That is Lucio Fulci!

The living dead here are not the normal Romero-type zombies (i.e. the flesh-eating kind). They are the living dead, but instead of eating you, they are more interested in killing you in some gory and gruesome way. As in *Zombie*, Giannetto De Rossi handled the incredible effects. The makeup and gore are outstanding: When the nails are driven through the forearms of the suspected warlock in the beginning, the carnage sure looks real, and the visual look of the living dead is amazing, from the rotted-away corpses to the more freshly dead ones. (Although, I do feel obliged to point out one effects scene that falls short: the infamous spider attack. Aside from two or three real tarantulas, the other [fake] spiders look silly as hell. Especially when audiences can see them being pulled on a string or wire. But, ahem, let's not dwell on that, okay?)

The music, composed by Fabio Frizzi, fits perfectly into the film. Between the piano and the chanting/singing, Frizzi created one of the best Italian horror scores. It's not one of your conventional creepy/atmospheric scores, filled with musical stingers for the jump scares, but it does add greatly to the feel and mood. Two final assets are screenwriter Dardano Sacchetti and cinematographer Sergio Salvati, both of whom worked on Fulci's most famous films of the '80s: *Zombie, The Beyond, City of the Living Dead,* and *House by the Cemetery.* In my opinion, all four are essential viewing for any hardcore horror fan.

Italian horror may indeed be an acquired taste. But once you've got it, the hunger never goes away.

THE BIRDS (1963)
by Andrew Black

The mystery posed by the intentions of birds has long provided fertile ground for literary horror artists from Poe to Lovecraft. However, cinematically speaking, there is one name that instantly leaps to mind when speaking of our malevolent feathered friends: Alfred Hitchcock.

The Birds was arguably the last of Hitchcock's great works. He directed only five more features, none of which achieved the lasting acclaim of *Rear Window, Vertigo, North by Northwest,* or *Psycho.* The film's themes, attention to detail, and innovative special effects helped make it a hit in its day. However, it is Hitchcock's ability to build suspense and instill fear that has allowed it to stand the test of time.

Based upon the short story by Daphne Du Maurier and scripted by Evan Hunter, *The Birds* starts innocuously outside a pet store in downtown San Francisco where in his cameo Alfred Hitchcock, walking his two dogs, strolls past Melanie Daniels (Tippi Hedren). The story then follows Melanie as she pursues a burgeoning love interest with San Francisco attorney, Mitch Brenner (Rod Taylor). The two have a brief antagonistic flirtation during a chance meeting in the pet store. Melanie then decides to pursue Mitch under the guise of delivering a pair of love birds to his sister, Cathy Brenner (Veronica Cartwright), for her birthday. After discovering that Mitch returns home every weekend to visit Lydia Brenner (Jessica Tandy), his mother, who lives in a small Northern California harbor town, Melanie decides to chase after him. They will soon discover, however, that the avian population is increasing in number as well as dislike for their human co-habitants.

In returning to the film for the first time since childhood, I found that its strength remains the masterful direction. Hitchcock's manipulation of tension never falters, straining the audience's nerves in one scene after another, allowing us to relax, then winding us up even tighter moments later. The attacks begin on isolated individuals, including a haunting scene in which Lydia Brenner walks in on the ravaged corpse of another local resident. Gradually, the birds move to menace smaller groups and ultimately lay siege to the town as a whole, leading to the movie's two most recognizable scenes. First, the attack on a group of school children as they flee the school down the hill to safety; and then the exalted diner/gas station scene, where Melanie is trapped in a phone booth, the assaulting birds cracking the glass pane by pane.

The finale takes place with all the central characters trapped in the Brenner homestead, with the aeronautic assailants attempting to flap, fly, peck, or squeeze their way through every part of the dwelling. The birds begin to overtake the house, room by room, driving Melanie to madness. Her claustrophobia and desire to escape lead to a dramatic showdown (with Melanie trapped in an upstairs bedroom) and an attempted getaway.

Nature goes wild and the birds attack Lydia Brenner (Jessica Tandy).

Hitchcock concludes his final masterpiece with no explanation for the attack and no reprieve for the town. As the curtain closes, the image of a bird-cloaked landscape is left to haunt the audience.

Illustrating how Hitchcock's innovative genius has lasted generations, pop-culture references still turn up on a regular basis in homage's truest form, parody. (The phone booth assault was recently lampooned on an episode of TV's *That '70s Show*.) *The Birds* also features a personal favorite horror "first": The crazy town drunk preaching the end of the world, an idea mimicked in the *Friday the 13th* series with the old man warning camp counselors "not to go into them woods."

Praised for its innovative special effects, the movie employs 370 effects shots and was nominated for the Academy Award for Best Special Visual Effects. Hitchcock did not want to use a blue screen (the standard at the time) for the visual effects shots as it caused a blue aura around the birds and actors, making them appear unnatural. It was determined that the sodium vapor process (yellow screen), under which the actor is filmed against a yellow screen lit by sodium vapor lights, would be utilized. In this process, a camera with a special prism is used to expose two separate elements: regular color film and a special film sensitive to the color of sodium vapor lights. This second element creates a matte, so that the regular color footage can later be combined with another shot without the two images showing through each other. The process creates a less super-imposed look, though it does still reveal a slight white-light halo around the actor—or bird.

It is said that Hitchcock was drawn to the project based on his own fear of birds. Leading to an analysis of the true underpinnings of the production: Is it Man vs. Nature or a visualization of someone's worst fear? In fact, perhaps the most compelling question is, how can that green outfit that Melanie has worn for days on end not smell a little gamey? Maybe the townspeople are right to blame her; sea gulls do seem to circle trash dumps.

In the grisly era of modern horror films, some of the attack scenes may now seem slightly mundane. But *The Birds* remains an enduring classic because of Hitchcock's ability to create paranoia with more than images. Perhaps the feature of the movie that endures better than any other is the sound. The film's climax, with its human characters trapped in the Brenner family home as the birds swarm outside, is highlighted by the constant auditory build of pecking and scratching. The madness and despair it seeks to invoke in the characters is brilliantly illustrated by Hitchcock, who chose to abandon a musical score in favor of highlighting the other sounds.

Alfred Hitchcock elected not to give the film a "THE END" title because he wanted to give the illusion of unrelenting horror. Perhaps the enigmatic director held in mind the terror provoked in Poe's protagonist when first there came a tapping at his chamber door...

This I say...and nothing more.

THE BLACK CAT (1934)
by Charley Sherman

When looking for one adjective to accurately describe *The Black Cat*, the word "delirious" springs to mind. Who could believe that such a rampantly morbid, death-obsessed film, so steeped in perversities such as necrophilia, sadism, incest, human sacrifice, and a bit of mass murder, would be the number one film at the box office for Universal Pictures that year? Directed in full Expressionistic-style, with the nightmarish memories of World War I weighing heavily in the air, it starred Bela Lugosi and Boris Karloff for the first time together, and still remains one of the strangest films to have come out of Hollywood. I also happen to think it is quite wonderful: The work of a great visual artist with a splendidly dark imagination—Edgar G. Ulmer—and one of the purest examples of Expressionism in American cinema.

World War I was a huge influence upon art, as people sought ways to articulate the experience and its effects. German Expressionism was one of the movements inspired by that catastrophe, and filmmaking reflected this. *The Cabinet of Dr. Caligari* (1920) and *The Golem* (1920) are two of the most famous examples. A young Edgar Ulmer assisted the great Expressionist architect and designer Hans Poelzig on the art direction for the latter film (Karloff's character, Hungarian architect Hjalmar Poelzig, is named after him). Ulmer then worked on the art direction and/or set design for several of the most famous and groundbreaking films of the day, like *Die Nibelungen* (1924), *Metropolis* (1926), *Sunrise* (1927), and *M* (1931), with esteemed Expressionist directors F.W. Murnau and Fritz Lang. Although *The Black Cat* was only the fourth film he had worked on as a director—and his first horror effort—if anyone were qualified to bring out the qualities that Expressionism inspired, it was Ulmer.

The idea for the story came from Ulmer, with mystery writer Peter Ruric coming onboard to write the screenplay, which has *nothing* to do with Edgar Allan Poe's story. No doubt the title was used as commercial bait, a "triple horror whammy" if you like:

Werdegast (Bela Lugosi) prepares to skin his rival Poelzig (Boris Karloff) alive.

Bela Lugosi, famous for playing Dracula; Boris Karloff, equally esteemed for his roles as Frankenstein's Monster and The Mummy; and Edgar Allan Poe, probably the world's best known writer of horror fiction at the time. What the film does have in common with Poe is the theme of obsessive love taken beyond death, and when mixed with the other main subject matter—the horrors of the First World War—the resulting combination is a story drenched in death and morbidity. Thus, for a horror film addict, it is filled with potential. And via the visual imagination of Ulmer, we are not disappointed. Indeed, from my own personal perspective, as one who works in theater, the visual elements are the biggest reasons why I can keep coming back to the movie time and again. (Nor have I been afraid to steal an idea or two from its imagery.) What is also fascinating is how Ulmer has taken such morbid elements and fused them into his unique vision.

As *The Black Cat* begins, Dr. Vitus Werdegast (Lugosi) tells the honeymooning couple Peter and June Alison (appealingly played by David Manners and Julie Bishop [billed as Jacqueline Wells]) that he has been in a Russian prison camp for the last 15 years, and spent the three years prior to that fighting in the war. Before their arrival at Poelzig's mansion in the Hungarian countryside, he gives them some background: "All of this country was one of the greatest battlefields of the war. Tens of thousands of men died here. The ravine down there was piled 12-deep with dead and wounded men. The little river below was swollen red, a raging torrent of blood. And that high hill yonder where Engineer Poelzig now lives was the site of Fort Marmorus. He built his home on its very foundations: Marmorus, the greatest graveyard in the world." Thus the scene is set, and we are no doubt expecting to find Poelzig's home to be a creepy, shadowy, Gothic, old haunted house.

Not so. Once we are inside the mansion, we are introduced to a futuristic, art deco, highly cultured, luxurious, brightly lit world—seated atop a landscape of death. This bizarre set (marvelously realized by Charles D. Hall) is a character unto itself, with

Poelzig (Karloff) conducts the black mass in front of the inverted cross.

geometrically pure patterns, sliding doors, jagged-shaped scenic elements, and various weird objects. We never really see outside again, but the characters continually remind us of what happened there years ago. Indeed, the past is the reason that Werdegast is here, as we learn when he tells Poelzig, his comrade during the war: "You sold Marmorus to the Russians. You scurried away in the night and left us to die. Is it to be wondered that you should choose this place to build your house? A masterpiece of construction built upon the ruins of the masterpiece of destruction—a masterpiece of murder. The murderer of 10,000 men returns to the place of his crime."

Not only that, but we also learn that once Werdegast was captured, Poelzig claimed Werdegast's wife and young daughter, never telling them the truth. Werdegast has traveled to learn what happened to them, and to get his revenge. Poelzig, in a brilliantly unsettling sequence, takes Werdegast to the underground part of the mansion, what used to be the old fort. It is here that he reveals several vertical glass cases, which contain perfectly preserved, beautiful, and very dead women, all suspended and facing outward (though one of the actresses can be seen moving, an unfortunate gaffe in an otherwise extraordinary scene). Poelzig reveals Werdegast's wife to be one of them, having died of pneumonia two years after the war. He tells Werdegast, "Is she not beautiful? I wanted to have her beauty—always. I loved her too, Vitus." Werdegast tries to shoot him, but when a black cat appears, he has a seizure due to his fear of them (he has, in fact, already killed one earlier in the film, by throwing a knife at it). This scene is the closest we come to Poe—the obsession with beautiful dead women, and, of course, the black cat itself.

We soon learn that Poelzig has taken Werdegast's daughter for his lover, presumably from a young age, a plot element with undertones of incest and pedophilia, following upon recent hints of necrophilia! Then we find out that Poelzig is a Satanist, and is planning a black mass that night and aims to use June, our newlywed bride, as a sacrifice to Lucifer. Now, correct me if I'm wrong, but it's hard to imagine a character more perversely evil than the character of Poelzig. Therefore it is only suitable that his appearance be striking; his hairstyle best described as a mix of a GI Joe action figure and an '80s punk rocker, atop a bleached-white face etched with deep lines, and clad in sumptuous futuristic robes. Throw in Karloff's genteel British accent and his understated, graceful playing of such a monster, and *voilà*—one of the most unique characterizations in cinema history.

Karloff is perfectly complemented by Lugosi in an atypical tragic-hero role, hell-bent on vengeance, yet weakened by his "intense and all-consuming horror of cats." Lugosi, never one known for holding back, has a blast playing Werdegast right from the first scene as he emphasizes every syllable when describing his life and purpose to the newlywed husband. One might be tempted to accuse Lugosi of being hammy, but this is no ordinary plot or film. It *requires* a heightened approach, and reaches the perfect pitch in the final scene: Werdegast, with the help of his dying manservant, strings up Poelzig on a torture rack, strips him of his robes, and holding a scalpel, exclaims, "Do you know what I am going to do to you now? No? Did you ever see an animal skinned, Hjalmar? That's what I'm going to do to you now—tear the skin from your body. Slowly. Bit by bit!" (It is hard to imagine audiences in 1934 didn't leave the cinema shaking their heads in disbelief at what they had just witnessed.) This is what I mean when describing the film as "delirious."

Unfortunately, Ulmer was virtually blacklisted from Hollywood after completing the film, having had an affair with the wife of a Universal studio mogul. From then on, he would only make low-budget films, though his future credits would include the cult film noir favorite, *Detour* (1945). But his place in film history, already guaranteed with his art design contributions to German cinema, is very much assured with his unique blend of death and perversity in a futuristic world haunted by the ghosts of a terrible past—the dominion of *The Black Cat*.

BLACK CHRISTMAS (1974)
by Andrew Haubert

The sisters of *Pi Kappa Sigma* have been receiving obscene phone calls for quite some time now. Everyone assumes the calls are coming from a fellow student with an overactive imagination (and a total lack of class). What they do not realize is the caller is actually a deranged madman that has recently taken up residence in their attic.

By Christmas Eve, most of the sorority girls have gone home for the holidays, but a handful of the sisters are still in the house. The strong and caring Jesse (Olivia Hussey) is dealing with major personal problems with her unstable boyfriend Peter (Keir Dullea). Meanwhile, her best friends Phyllis (Andrea Martin) and Barbie (Margot Kidder) try to help find out what has happened to their sorority sister Clare (Lynne Griffin). The all-star cast is rounded out by John Saxon as the local police lieutenant, who is trying to catch the killer.

Black Christmas cannot only be argued to be the first slasher film, but it is undoubtedly one of the most effective horror thrillers ever made. I first viewed *Black Christ-*

Olivia Hussey (Jesse) carries the film by giving multiple layers to her character.

mas when I was a sophomore in college. Several acquaintances had mentioned how it was not only a great horror movie, but also one of the most influential of the slasher subgenre. After searching the major video chains, I was able to locate an antique VHS tape at one of the locally owned stores. While my first viewing experience of *Black Christmas* was not through the most state-of-the-art medium, a great work will translate regardless of technical specifications. Director Bob Clark combines a superb mixture of well-developed characters and the utilization of subtle imagery and diegetic sound to amplify the killer's presence.

The most successful horror features are ones where we become emotionally invested in the characters before they are placed in harm's way. Any filmmaker can effectively execute a "jump scare" that might get the audience on a first-time viewing, but in order to create a film that deserves multiple viewings, we should genuinely *want* the characters to survive. Olivia Hussey carries the film, giving Jesse multiple layers; a strong modern woman (indicative of the type emerging in the early 1970s), yet also vulnerable at the climax. Best yet, Clark and screenwriter Roy Moore infuse a suitable level of dark humor, allowing us to laugh without going overboard or losing an ounce of suspense.

Clark also proves himself to be a master of timing, building up the tension over time, then paying off with the scares. The opening shots establish that the killer is living in the attic of the sorority house, so we know the girls are in danger *from the start*. This knowledge provides a solid layer of tension every time we see a shadow lurking in the background. Further, the obscene calls made by the killer, which are extremely profane and flat-out disturbing, add immeasurably. Much of the film's effectiveness can be attributed to its use of ambient sound, with assistance from Carl Zittrer's eerie score. And it is impossible to talk about *Black Christmas* without mentioning the shot of the killer's eye just before he finally makes his move to attack Jesse.

Canadian filmmaker Clark is probably best remembered for his string of successful comedies such as *Porky's* (1982) and the iconic *A Christmas Story* (1983), but his roots are firmly planted in the horror genre. His feature debut was the cult zombie favorite, *Children Shouldn't Play With Dead Things* (1972), that Clark cast with friends and family to stay within his shoestring budget. Clark's next project was the political satire *Dead of Night* (aka *Deathdream* [1974]). A twist on the classic tale "The Monkey's Paw," it featured the return of a recently deceased Vietnam veteran, who mysteriously awakens from the dead and returns home to his family, with dire consequences. For his first two efforts Clark had to rely on independent financiers and primarily used friends as cast and crew. Clark's two-for-two track record gave him the resume to get funding from the Canadian Film Development Corporation, and the chance to finally work with a crew entirely composed of professionals. The result was the critically praised *Black Christmas*. After cementing his status as a legitimate filmmaker, Clark moved away from horror, making a successful string of dramas and becoming famous with the aforementioned comedies.

While there is certainly room for debate in declaring a definitive "original" slasher film, *Black Christmas* has as much, if not more, right to the title as any. The shower scene from Alfred Hitchcock's *Psycho* (1960) is commonly acknowledged as the turning point for onscreen violence in the horror genre and became the blueprint for kill scenes in slashers. Almost every horror filmmaker working today owes a two-fold debt to Hitchcock for his inspired direction and, perhaps more importantly, his legitimizing of the horror genre for adults. Mario Bava's *Bay of Blood* (aka *Twitch of the Death Nerve* [1971]) also holds a rightful claim as the prototypal slasher, being the first to employ many conventions that would become staples of the genre, such as using first-person camera perspective for the killer, incompetent authority figures, "creative" slayings, etc. However, while Bava certainly deserves credit for creating the first "body count" movies, the teen slashers that define the genre are much more than just a series of brutal murders—although cynics may dispute that claim.

The slasher genre is defined by numerous commonalities in both the narrative structure and stylistic techniques, and many of these now-common clichés can be traced to *Black Christmas*. First and foremost is the setting. While small towns have never been safe within the horror genre, slashers almost exclusively tend to be set in rural or small town settings where mass murder is non-existent. Another key component is the progressive representation of strong females. In horror films (and elsewhere), women had traditionally been portrayed as weak and dependent upon men for protection in times of danger. The slasher genre was one of the first to play against this stereotype, presenting female characters that could take care of themselves. Slashers are also well known for employing camera shots from the killer's point of view, a technique often criticized by detractors of the genre, maintaining that the approach promotes viewer identification with the killer. These techniques—utilized so effectively in *Black Christmas*—have since become commonplace.

While *Black Christmas* has since gone on to fanfare and critical praise, it was by no means a blockbuster, as it grossed just over $4 million in theaters in its initial release. John Carpenter's genre classic *Halloween* (1978), which ended up grossing over $47 million, is inarguably responsible for *popularizing* the slasher genre. Regardless of which is ultimately considered the first true teen slasher, Clark definitely deserves credit for his hand in creating the subgenre. According to Clark's commentary track on the *Black Christmas* DVD, Carpenter was a huge fan of *Black Christmas* and asked if there were any plans for a sequel. Clark informed the young director that *Black Christmas* would be his last horror film, but he envisioned the sequel would occur the following autumn when the killer escaped from the asylum where he had been held. The maniac would then ruthlessly stalk the residents of sorority houses, much as he did the previous Christmas. While Clark gives Carpenter full credit for the masterful execution of *Halloween*, it is clear that Clark feels that it was based upon his core idea.

Black Christmas is truly a classic that should be seen by all fans of the horror genre. The influence *Black Christmas* had on *Halloween* is undeniable, and the two together have had a tremendous effect on a multitude of horror films, completely altering the face of popular American horror. *Black Christmas* deserves to be seen simply because it is a very effective fright film. Clark's ability to combine *mise en scène* with genuinely haunting sound effects is enough to scare the most thick-skinned horror enthusiast.

BLACK SUNDAY (1960)
by Anthony Revelas

Black Sunday (aka *The Mask of Satan*) takes a quantum leap in terms of artistic achievement and visceral intensity within the horror genre. But more on that later. First, a little background on its director, the great Italian maestro Mario Bava, and also a bit about the infancy of Italian horror.

Bava directed in every genre, but at the time of his death he was regarded as merely an efficient director for hire. Had he worked in the United States or England, experts agree that he would today be regarded as the equal of Hitchcock. Traditionally, horror films had been frowned upon in Italy since the time of Mussolini, but when director Riccardo Freda accompanied friend and camera operator Mario to his father Eugenio Bava's home and workshop, he was astounded by the sight of numerous tormented-looking wax figurine sculptures. (Eugenio was a sculptor who worked his way into the Italian film industry as a creator of special effects, and later as a cinematographer, a talent that would be passed down through generations of the Bava family.) These wax figurines were produced about the time of the Vincent Price vehicle *House of Wax* (1953) and would ignite the dreams of Freda and Bava to rekindle the horror genre in Italy, which had not been in existence since the silent era.

Freda would take long siestas on *I Vampiri* (1956) and *Caltiki the Immortal Monster* (1959) in an effort to nudge his shy and unassuming friend behind the camera into taking charge of the set, thus priming the unknown Bava for a directorial position. Rewarded

Barbara Steele plays the wild-eyed witch Asa.

for his resourcefulness, Galetea-Jolly Films gave Bava free reign in choosing a property for his directorial debut. Fascinated by Russian folklore, Bava selected a short story entitled "The Vij" written by Ukrainian author Nikolai Gogol. However, *Black Sunday* bears little in common with its source material.

Exquisitely shot in black and white by Bava himself, *Black Sunday* evokes a dreamlike quality difficult to define. It exists somewhere between the Expressionistic corridors of Murnau's *Nosferatu* (1922) and the haunted forests of Disney's classic animated tale of witchery, *Snow White and the Seven Dwarfs* (1937) (the latter not surprising as it would have been one of the few films accessible to Italy at the time). Bava adheres to the Gothic tradition of earlier Universal horrors with superstitious torch-bearing villagers wielding fiery justice, but also takes inspiration from Hammer Film Production's sensational "full blooded" entrees *The Curse of Frankenstein* (1957) and *Horror of Dracula* (1958). However, it is not enough to simply break *Black Sunday* down to its inspirational components to appreciate its creative ingenuity. Bava brings a perspective that is uniquely Italian, rooted in Roman Catholicism, a painterly illumination on themes of resurrection and Martyrdom. (This might bring comparisons to James Whale's *Bride of Frankenstein* to mind, whose monster befalls a Christ-like persecution.) *Black Sunday*'s vampires suffer an even worse fate, their incestuous allure literally hammered away with iron spikes through the face and eyes.

Equal credit for *Black Sunday*'s enduring cult status must be shared with Barbara Steele, who plays the dual roles of the vampire-witch Asa and her virginal descendant Princess Katia. Still in her early 20s, the young Steele had just walked off the set of her first American film, *Flaming Star* (1960), in which she was to play opposite Elvis Presley. Thus severing her ties with 20th Century Fox, her photo had already been sent to Italy for an upcoming biblical co-production, and Bava instantly recognized "the perfect face" for his upcoming horror film. Much is said of Steele's exotic looks and

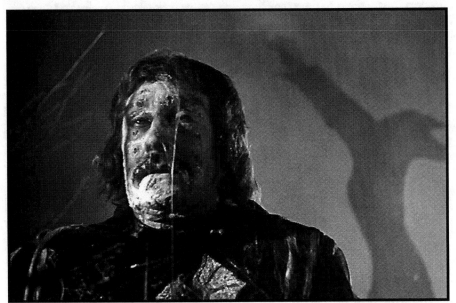

Arturo Dominici plays Igor Javutich (aka Javuto), the witch's companion.

screen presence; she is one of the genre's select female monsters, at once repulsive, alluring, and evil to the core. Steele is regarded as "The Queen of Horror," and in the nearly 50 years since, no actress has ever risen to challenge that title.

The story takes place in 17th-century Muldavia, where fear of Satan holds sway over the land, where practitioners of the black arts are hunted down and burned at the stake. Bound and branded with the Mark of Satan, Asa Vajda issues a curse upon her tormentors: that the blood of their descendants will bring the ruination of their families and bring to her life eternal. The curse is issued moments before Satan's bronze mask is hammered to her face, symbolically damning the witch to hell. (Incidentally, the demonic spiked bronze torture masks were crafted by Eugenio Bava's hands.) Two centuries later, a doctor of medicine and his apprentice journey to a conference in St. Petersburg, but along the way they stumble into Asa's tomb and accidentally revive the witch with drops of blood. While leaving the tomb, the doctors meet a beautiful girl, Princess Katia Vajda. It is love at first sight for the younger man, but the witch in the crypt is intent on taking the maiden's body and life for her own. Soon, a ghoul is risen from the grave to attack the Vajda patriarch and his kin, while Asa regains her strength and takes control of the senior doctor. The old ways of dealing with vampires must win the day, or Katia will be lost.

Black Sunday became AIP's top moneymaker to date, outgrossing Roger Corman's color adaptation of Poe's *House of Usher*, released the same year. Its success catapulted the career of Barbara Steele as the world's premier scream queen, and she would play opposite Vincent Price in Corman's next Poe revision, 1961's *The Pit and the Pendulum*. It is not surprising that *Pit* answers *Black Sunday* with its own erotic allure and heightened sexuality, addressing similar themes of incestuous depravity. Bava's mastery of dreamlike surrealism in *Black Sunday* would anticipate an entire decade of macabre styling from around the globe. Mexico's *Curse of the Crying Woman* (1963) and Spain's *Tombs of the Blind Dead* (1971)—as well as Tim Burton's recent *Sleepy Hollow* (1999)—owe a huge debt to *Black Sunday*.

It wasn't until the end of the '90s that I first watched *Black Sunday* on DVD, alone at night in my house. But soon after, I found myself frantically sharing the experience with like-minded individuals on Internet message boards. The Internet provides strange and wonderful companions from across the land and even across the seas, all sharing our enthusiasm over newfound ancient treasures. *Black Sunday* is a clarion call to all aficionados of the macabre and all things dark and Gothic. This is horror with imagery that sinks right through the skull, more powerful on a subconscious level than most films rendered with realism. In short, it is the first and best of its kind.

THE BLAIR WITCH PROJECT (1999)
by Cory Colock

In October 1994, three student filmmakers disappeared in the woods near Burkittsville, Maryland while shooting a documentary. A year later…their footage was found. This footage provides as many questions as it does answers, as we follow our trio on their unfortunate journey, seeing what they see, hearing what they hear, and experiencing firsthand the terrifying ordeal they found themselves in. They set out to make a simple documentary about a local legend and instead, became a part of it.

The Blair Witch Project opened wide on July 30, 1999 to much critical acclaim, after previous showings at the Sundance and Cannes Film Festivals and a limited release earlier in the month. I was there opening night, the midnight showing to be exact, with two of my college friends. We were anxious to see it, as were many others, judging by the long lines outside. Being in a particularly jovial mood, I recall asking a dozen or so people as they exited the theater if it was scary—if they would spend a night in those woods for $100. Though I received several scoffs from the macho guys in the crowd, most of them declined my offer in a solemn manner. They were genuinely *frightened*. My anticipation grew as we were finally allowed to move into the theater. Once the film started, aside from a few chuckles here and there at the lighter moments during the first half, the audience was dead silent. And they remained silent, and seated, for several minutes after it had ended! In the hundreds of movies I've watched on the silver screen, this has remained a one-of-a-kind experience. For good or bad, *The Blair Witch Project* clearly made an impression on its viewers. And this viewer had trouble falling asleep that night.

According to woodsmovie.com (a truly comprehensive site detailing the making of *The Blair Witch Project*), directors Daniel Myrick and Eduardo Sanchez first came up with their concept, simply called "The Woods Movie," in 1992 while they were still film students themselves. They raised the budget (roughly $35,000) in part by selling two short video episodes of their idea to *Split Screen* (a show that ran on the Bravo network), the first of which aired in 1997. Pre-production began in 1995 with continued development of the plotline and in 1996, under their company, Haxan Films (inspired by Benjamin Christensen's 1922 movie about witchcraft), the audition process commenced. A year later, after over one thousand tryouts, they had found their lead actors, Heather Donahue, Mike Williams, and Joshua Leonard. Shooting began in October 1997, mainly in the Seneca Creek and Patapsco State Parks in Maryland, and lasted for

Heather Donahue as one of the student filmmakers

less than two weeks. Myrick and Sanchez used most of 1998 to edit the footage and, in January 1999, their film finally had its first major audience at the Sundance Film Festival. It was then that Artisan Entertainment bought the picture for $1,000,000-plus, reportedly the first sale of the festival. And here is where the fun really started.

Though the first Internet site for the film appeared in June 1998, the official website (blairwitch.com), which supplied a variety of background information on the Blair Witch legend and the three missing filmmakers, was launched in April 1999. It received 110,000 hits over the first weekend.

The marketing campaign of *The Blair Witch Project* was, in a word, brilliant, and not only for its unprecedented use of the Internet or provocative trailers. A promotional "documentary" appeared entitled *Curse of the Blair Witch*, which aired on the Sci-Fi Channel just weeks before the film's wide release. This short movie, comprised of realistic interviews and news reports, provided a lot of valuable insight into the origin of the Blair Witch (and continues to serve as a fantastic companion piece). With all this phenomenal buzz, *The Blair Witch Project* raked in over $29 million in its opening weekend. It would remain in theaters until early November, ending up with a total of $140,539,000, plus another $108,100,000 in foreign earnings, making it one of the most successful films of all time! Additionally, it spawned books, comics, video games, movie spoofs, and a mediocre sequel in 2000.

1999 was a good year for horror in general. With *The Sixth Sense, Stir of Echoes, Sleepy Hollow, The Ninth Gate,* and *Audition,* the genre had started to break free from the *Scream*-like clones that had bombarded theaters in recent years. *The Blair Witch Project* continued this trend, bringing something fresh to the horror fan's table with its captivating narrative, unconventional presentation, and genuine suspense and scares. The storyline, not counting the promotional media, is a masterful example of minimalist horror. The basic plot of the three lost filmmakers is simple and straightforward, but it is the Blair Witch mythos that really haunts the viewer. Myrick and Sanchez supply just enough of the legend to keep you on the edge of your seat psychologically, while whetting your appetite for more.

Following their purchase, Artisan voiced concern over the picture's ending. Myrick and Sanchez were asked to shoot several new options, one of which had Heather finding Mike crucified on a large "stickman" in the basement. None of these worked any better, so they finally shot another short interview, where a man describes how Rustin Parr made one child stand in the corner as he killed the other. This proved to be a stroke of genius, as it not only tied up the ending nicely but also added another layer to the mystery.

In addition to the compelling mythos, the realistic presentation played an enormous part in the film's success and actually convinced many people that it was real (as well as giving some folks motion sickness from the shaky camerawork). From the beginning of this "authentic" documentary gone frightfully awry, the aim was for complete realism. The actors were separated from the crew during the shoot and had to improvise most of their dialogue and film everything themselves. They were not without directorial guidance though. There were character profiles, a general shooting script, and Myrick and Sanchez came up with a clever method they called "Remote Control Directing" to achieve the natural performances. Everyday, when the actors (using GPS) made their way to the predestined campsites set up by the crew, they would find notes for their characters left amongst their meager supplies. These notes supplied each actor with individual motivation and guidance for their upcoming scenes and were to be kept private from the others. Because of this, in essence, the actors were not acting but reacting with conviction to each other and what was going on around them, and they did an admirable job of it. The group tension and emotional breakdown they display over the course of eight days (cramped into 86 minutes of screen time) is quite believable, a credit to both the inventive directors and their talented cast. The outdoor settings are rough and desolate, providing the perfect atmosphere. The film, understandably, has no music; but its makers added an interesting aural touch in postproduction: As the film progresses, the sounds of birds and crickets become muted little by little, increasing the feeling of isolation and dread.

Though Myrick and Sanchez cite *Chariots of the Gods* (1970), *The Legend of Boggy Creek* (1972), and the television show *In Search of...* as inspirations, because of the film's documentary presentation, it has been accused of stealing from similar films, namely *Cannibal Holocaust* (1980) and *The Last Broadcast* (1998). In the case of *Cannibal Holocaust*, the directors have claimed that they weren't aware of the movie before making their own and in truth, aside from the surface similarities, they are intrinsically different pictures. As for *The Last Broadcast*, Myrick and Sanchez did see it in the early fall of 1998, but by that time, they were nearly done with their film and getting ready for Sundance. And while comparisons can be made between the aforementioned titles, *The Blair Witch Project* is the only one of them that never once breaks from its "found footage" format. Regardless, it's worth noting that the faux documentary approach is still a rarely used concept, unlike the repetitive slasher genre setups, for example.

H.P. Lovecraft once wrote, "The oldest and strongest emotion of mankind is fear, and the oldest and strongest kind of fear is fear of the unknown." If that statement could ever be applied to a film, it would be this one. In *The Blair Witch Project*, so many things are left unanswered—the distinctly unnatural noises at night, the unseen force that shakes their tent, the inescapable woods, the sudden disappearance of Josh, the chillingly somber climax (one of horror's greatest endings, in fact!)—yet somehow, deep within the viewer's imagination, it all conglomerates into primal, nightmarish explanations that are far more powerful than anything that could have been shown on the screen.

Rare is the horror movie that can produce actual horror, and *The Blair Witch Project* is one of them.

THE BLOB (1958)
by Doug Lamoreux

When considering the lasting effect of any horror film, audiences must give weight to the time and place in which it premiered. That done, any true fan must award "classic" status to *The Blob*. Released in 1958 by producer Jack H. Harris' Tonylyn Productions during the drive-in movie craze, *The Blob* was the ultimate drive-in flick. It had a hit theme song and was in garish color. It featured good-looking teens and fast cars. It had one of filmdom's most memorable monsters. More than all that, *The Blob* was about young people and made for young people. The adults in the film don't "get it," and the town is saved only when the adults admit the kids were right all along.

A young couple, Steve (Steven McQueen) and Jane (Aneta Corsaut) are necking on a rural Pennsylvania road when a meteor crashes nearby. Meanwhile, an old man (Olin Howlin) living in a nearby shack finds the space rock first. As anyone would, he jabs the meteor with a stick until it bursts open—revealing a clear gelatinous mass inside. The mass quickly, and painfully, engulfs the old man's hand. En route to investigate the meteor themselves, Steve and Jane nearly run over the old fellow as he stumbles across the road. He begs them to get him to a doctor and they hurry him to Dr. Hallen (Steven Chase). To their alarm, the "blister" now covers the old man's entire forearm. Hallen phones his nurse, Kate (Lee Payton), asking her to return to the office as it may be necessary to amputate the patient's arm to get ahead of the parasite.

With a fast-paced opening, *The Blob* is off to the races. The monster soon consumes the old man, Kate, and Dr. Hallen. Hallen's murder is witnessed by Steve; this sets up the "teens versus adults" theme of the film. The monster serves merely as catalyst.

Steve, Jane, and their friends Tony, Mooch, and Al (Robert Fields, James Bonnet and Anthony Franke, respectively) represent the clear-thinking teens desperate to save the townspeople from the gelatinous monster and their own ignorance. The adult (i.e. wrong) point of view is represented by Police Sgt. Bert (John Benson) and Jane's father (Elbert Smith), men who know kids are no good. Only the good-hearted police chief Lt. Dave (Earl Rowe), and to a lesser extent Steve's father (Hugh Graham), make any attempt to understand the kids. *Believing* them, however, is another matter.

The Blob proves impervious to acid and shotgun blasts as it gobbles its way through town. Though a number of these attacks take place off screen, the film has plenty of tense set pieces to keep the genre fan glued; the attack on the nurse and doctor, a mechanic's demise, stalking victims through a market (where the Blob's aversion to cold is first hinted at), etc. Still, the teens are unable to convince the thickheaded adults anything is amiss.

The old man (Olin Howlin) unfortunately picks up the Blob with a stick.

Eventually, the adults have no choice but to believe. The Blob invades a local movie theater, gobbles the hapless projectionist and oozes its way into the crowd. Minutes later, grown to gigantic proportions, it follows the panicked survivors into the street. One of the best-remembered moments in horror history, this panic sequence was shot at the Colonial Theater in Phoenixville, PA. The stampede from the building required a second take; during the first, an extra fell, taking down a slew of performers in a huge pile. (Gaffe spotters will note the same young couple run from doors on both sides of the ticket booth; first left, then right.) The monster slides and glides across the street and engulfs a diner, trapping Steve, Jane, Jane's brother Danny, and the surprised café staff inside.

Here, to show how fair-minded the film's youthful message is, the wrong-headed Sgt. Bert is given an opportunity to redeem himself. A decision is made to electrocute the Blob and Bert is the only sharpshooter good enough to drop a power line on it. Unfortunately, the attempt fails and the diner catches fire. While keeping the fire at bay, Steve accidentally confirms the Blob can't stand cold—and the hunt is on to find enough carbon dioxide fire extinguishers to freeze the monster into helpless hibernation. Jane's father, the school principal, now has his opportunity at forgiveness and breaks a school window to give the kids access to the needed extinguishers. Once subdued, the inert Blob is flown to the Arctic and dropped by parachute. THE END flashes on the screen, followed by what would become producer Harris' trademark ending: a question mark.

For an inexpensive independent venture, the cast of *The Blob* shines. McQueen, in only his third feature, his first lead, and the last time he would be billed as Steven, displays the charisma and vulnerability soon to make him an international star. Corsaut found fame on the long-running *Andy Griffith Show*. Howlin was a veteran of over 250 features; mostly Westerns. Genre enthusiasts will remember his singing alcoholic in *Them!* (1954). Chase was a successful supporting player who put John Hoyt in his place in George Pal's *When Worlds Collide* (1951). Rowe had one of the strangest careers on record. While *The Blob* was his only feature, his television career spanned four decades. In 40 years, Rowe totaled up six appearances; just over one role every 10 years.

Director Irvin S. Yeaworth, Jr. had a stock company of players for the smaller character roles in his films. Following the success of *The Blob*, producer Harris commissioned another special effects extravaganza from Yeaworth. The result was *The 4D Man* (1959), a nifty thriller starring Robert Lansing and featuring *Blob* alumnus Benson, Smith, George Karas, and Jasper Deeter.

The one lamentable performer was Keith Almoney, who rivals Donnie Dunagan (*Son of Frankenstein* [1939]) and Lee H. Montgomery (*Ben* [1972]; *Burnt Offerings* [1973]) as the most obnoxious child performer in horror history. When Danny takes aim at the Blob with his cap pistol, it is impossible not to root for the monster.

The picture was shot at Yeaworth's studios in Valley Forge and on location in Phoenixville, Royersford, and Downingtown, PA. (The theater and diner are actually 18 miles apart). Locals were used as background performers. The gathering of alarmed townsfolk outside the market, presumably in the wee hours, was actually filmed just after nightfall. Uniformed Little League players dot the crowd as extras.

The creation of the Blob was simplicity itself. Special effects artist Bart Sloane used roughly two gallons of Union Carbide silicone, clear at first, dyed red after it began devouring its victims. A camera was locked down on one end of a table, the silicone monster plopped down on the other, and a miniature locked down in the middle between them. When the table was tipped, the Blob oozed through the miniature and towards the camera. (The silicone was actually quite firm and had to be warmed beneath the movie lights to become pliable enough to creep convincingly.)

The meteor crash and dropping of the power line were both accomplished via cel animation. The screen's first and only "backwards drag race" was shot with the cars going forward and spliced into the movie in reverse. (Note the exhaust flowing *into* the cars tailpipes.) The old man's cabin, seen in the distance, is a six-foot miniature shot in forced perspective.

The memorable theme song was written by Burt Bacharach, who received no screen credit; meanwhile, the credit given to the singers (The Four Blobs) is a hoax. The song was recorded by Bernie Nee, whose voice was laid over itself on separate tracks. The theme became a Top 40 hit and remains the greatest ballad to a gelatinous alien mass ever written; miles ahead of the rock nonsense heralding *The Green Slime* (1968). Ralph Carmichael provided the remainder of the film's music.

As Harris succinctly puts it, "*The Blob* was a landmark movie. It was a runaway hit." Made for $120,000, *The Blob* earned four and a half million at the box office (much to the chagrin of star McQueen, who turned down 10 percent participation in the film for a flat acting fee of $2,000). A black comedy sequel (*Beware! The Blob;* aka *Son of Blob*) followed in 1972, as well as a worthy remake in 1988. A second remake is currently in the works.

Yet, the original Blob lives. It is still shown frequently on television, appears on the big screen at the Colonial Theater's annual Blobfest, and makes personal appearances.

Wes Shank, a collector of horror film memorabilia, owns the original Blob—all two gallons of it—and regularly brings it to Blobfest in the same five gallon can in which it rested when he bought it from Yeaworth in 1965.

Is *The Blob* great cinema? Not at all. But it's great fun, and is *the* drive-in movie you need to see if you're going to claim any knowledge of horror history.

BLOOD AND BLACK LACE (1964)
by Nile Arena

Mario Bava's 1964 film *Blood and Black Lace* jumpstarted the Italian *giallo* subgenre into existence (Italian for "yellow," referring to the popular post-war series of pulp novels distinguished by their yellow covers). Bava and fellow auteur Dario Argento's *giallo* films grew increasingly stylized and were responsible for the advent of the American slasher film. In fact, Bava's own *Twitch of the Death Nerve* (1971) directly inspired much of John Carpenter's haunting opening sequence in *Halloween*.

Also originated in *Blood and Black Lace* (under its original European title *Six Women for the Murderer*) was the idea of an established cinematic "body count." When a prestigious model agency is terrorized by a series of brutal slayings, everyone becomes a suspect. Never before had murder been so eroticized. Starting with the first victim Isabella (Francesca Ungaro), Bava administers an erotic beauty to the murdered women throughout. Often the brutality of the murder scenes is contrasted and therefore elevated by the sensual treatment of the victims after their death. Even Peggy's (Mary Arden) sadistic torture with a hot iron in an infamously Grand Guignol scene ultimately leads to her body's eroticization when it is discovered later.

The brutal and varied nature of each victim's death has gone on to inspire endless films in European and American cinema. The masked killer's utter silence and methodical movements served as the template for many American slasher franchises, most notably *Halloween*'s Michael Myers and *Friday the 13th*'s Jason Voorhees. This silence is brought to a darkly humorous level when the killer takes the time to write out—rather than voice—questions regarding an incriminating diary. While the scene's tension is not diminished by this small touch, it does allow for an almost absurd pause in the killer's brutality.

Blood and Black Lace marked the continuation of Bava's bold lighting effects previously employed with great success in *Black Sabbath* (1963). The second murder's setting within the arcane antique store is made all the more threatening when bathed in pale blues and sickening greens, occasionally punctuated by orange from a flashing neon sign. The silence of the masked killer is particularly chilling in this scene, leaving the audience with only the sound of Ariana Gorini's futile screams.

Carlo Rustichelli's music, while traditional in its moody, almost *noir* sound, is important for its close relationship to building and occasionally misleading tension in a scene. It can be viewed as an omen of music's growing importance to not only the *giallo* films of Mario Bava and Dario Argento (Argento collaborated closely with the band Goblin and individual members of the band to create classic musical scores), but horror movies in general.

By contrast, no suspense is built at all for the fifth victim's horrific end; the audience is violently thrust into the equally shocked and drowning face of Tao-Li (Claude

Claude Dantes meets a watery end as director Mario Bava demonstrates the theme of "beautiful woman as victim" in the Italian *giallo.*

Dantes). Bava then pulls back to reveal her body undressed and drowned in the bathtub, after which the killer cuts Tao-Li's wrists in a Hitchcockian manner—no blood is visibly drawn as the razor passes her wrist. Instead, the camera jumps to a closeup of her face as the blood slowly rises in the water around her, panning out to reveal her exposed body. The murder's savagery, without the "comfort" of a warning, combined with the eroticization of the beautiful and exposed Dantes in the tub, create what may be the most vivid and chilling sequence in *Blood and Black Lace.*

Tragically, Bava's genius is relatively unknown by the average horror aficionado. However, the director and his impressive filmography have garnered a likewise impressive array of fans: Tim Burton, Joe Dante, John Carpenter, and George Lucas to name a few. Without Bava's low budget 1965 cult classic *Terrore nello spazio* (aka *Planet of the Vampires*), there may never have been the 1979 box office hit *Alien.* (For years it has been speculated that screenwriters Dan O'Bannon and Ronald Shusett were heavily influenced by many of *POTV*'s plot elements.) *Sleepy Hollow* (1999), another admittedly Bava-inspired film, liberally borrows elements from *Black Sunday*, as well as the "I Wurdulak" segment of *Black Sabbath*. The opening sequence of the former, with its infamous grisly death mask, is paid homage in several flashback sequences of Tim Burton's film. In fact, *Sleepy Hollow*'s entire design seems an extension of the eerie wilderness from Bava's films of three decades prior, the twisted Expressionist trees and cabins lit in unnatural colors all signature elements of "Il Maestro."

Most recently, Lionsgate Films' lucrative *Saw* franchise has adopted many classic *giallo* elements for a new generation of horror fans. Both *Saw* (2004) and *Saw II* (2005) feature a death mask similar in appearance and brutality to the one hammered onto Barbara Steele's face nearly a half-century earlier. The suspicious characters, murder-mystery intrigue, severe color palettes, and tortuous, often elaborate deaths all have the stamp of *giallo* and its underappreciated patriarch. Additionally, the first *Saw* film boasts the *giallo*-esque use of red herrings and dubious lead characters in an attempt to hide the killer's true identity until the final reveal.

I first saw *Blood and Black Lace* in October of my high school senior year, while taking a college writing class on horror films and their impact on American culture. To get to the screenings, there was a small graveyard and chapel I would have to pass on my way to the building, an eerie detail which became more apparent as the autumn evenings grew darker. The programs usually consisted of two films, either from the same era or sharing a common theme; one week found John Landis' *Thriller* video coupled with Jacques Tourneur's *I Walked With a Zombie*; another paired *Night of the Living Dead* with the musical *Meet Me in St. Louis*. This particular week, *Horror of Dracula* was shown with *Blood and Black Lace*.

Arriving late, I sat down just in time to watch a panicked woman stalked through what looked like an undersea museum, then murdered with a piece of medieval armor. From that point on, I was captivated—it didn't matter how uncomfortable the seats in the classroom were or how many of the students were laughing at the melodramatic dubbed dialogue—there was a terrifying brilliance to all the murder sequences. In spite of the dated audio and the stiff character interaction, I became entranced with how brutal portions of the movie were, especially for a film made during the same era as Roger Corman's entertaining but often kitschy Poe epics. As the practically unsolvable whodunit mystery came to a close with Cameron Mitchell and Eve Bartok murdering each other, their greed outweighing their love, I was sold. I borrowed the movie from my professor, watched it in its entirety, then moved on to Bava classics like *Twitch of the Death Nerve*, *Planet of the Vampires*, *Black Sunday*, *Danger: Diabolik* (1968) and my personal favorite, *Lisa and the Devil* (1973), starring the superb Telly Savalas in a diabolical pre-*Kojak* role.

Re-watching *Blood and Black Lace*, I was struck by how influential it was for both horror and thriller subgenres. Apart from carving out the *giallo* niche for decades to come, the "double-murder in a lover's embrace" would also continue to surface in a vast array of films (from Andrzej Zulawski's *Possession* [1981], to Robert Rodriguez's *Sin City* [2005], to name just a few) within an equally wide range of styles. The appearance of the "Italian Peter Lorre" had also gone unnoticed in previous viewings. Luciano Pigozzi, who plays the suspicious Cesar Losarre (no subtleties spared when naming *his* role), was a character actor in Italian cinema who enjoyed a fair amount of success, building a career around his resemblance to the Hungarian actor.

One final observation: The red mannequins of the fashion house, first seen in the opening credits sequence, provide an unnerving recurring motif. Apart from their striking color, the fact that these mannequins are left nude within the backgrounds of scenes (and never used for their ostensible purpose of modeling clothes) is equally disquieting. Their kewpie-doll faces and unusual hue seem to serve as harbingers of the doomed victims: Gothic dolls—beautiful and lifeless—bathed in garish red.

BLOOD FEAST (1963)
TWO THOUSAND MANIACS! (1964)
by Erika Shoemaker

Mal Arnold as crazed Fuad Ramses in *Blood Feast*

Welcome to Gore 101. We're going to begin today's lesson with a word association exercise:

I say, "Godfather of Gore," and you say…?

That's right, class. For those of you that answered, "Herschell Gordon Lewis," you get a bloody star and a decapitated smiley face sticker. That was fun. Now let's try another.

I say, "First explicit gore film."

If your response wasn't Lewis' 1963 exploitation flick, *Blood Feast*, then you'll need to stay after class for a tutoring session. For now, I ask that you sit up straight, get out your pen and paper, and pay attention. Let's see if we can catch you up to speed with a little history lesson.

Blood Feast, the first in what would later come to be known as the "Blood Trilogy," was the lovechild of the aforementioned Godfather of Gore and one Mr. David F. Friedman. Upon the realization that the market for the "nudie-cutie" films they were currently producing was quickly becoming passé, these two marketing geniuses began to formulate their next shock-and-startle concept.

These self-declared innovators wanted to produce the type of movies that large corporations felt were far too taboo to achieve any type of commercial success and therefore not worth the time nor the effort. As the duo had already begun to amp up the level of violence in their nudist films (branching off into "roughies" with *Scum of the Earth* [1963]), it seemed only natural that the next step in their cinematic evolution would lead them to give birth to the gore genre in all its crimson glory. Their idea was simple: To bring graphic carnage in screaming *blood color* to the screen.

Filmed in only nine days and for less than $25,000, *Blood Feast* is many things. It's a cheezy cult "class-sick." It's groundbreaking trash cinema…a pioneering slasher flick…a splatter fest… a camp comedy. No matter how you describe it, it remains a hallmark in the history of horror.

Blood Feast wastes not a single moment before plunging the audience headlong into, what was at the time of its release, the unexplored territory of explicit celluloid bloodshed. The very first scene depicts a woman arriving home. We hear the ominous sound of a kettle drum, eerily resembling a heartbeat, and are informed by a radio announcer of a recent vicious mutilation murder of a young woman. We hear the police advisory that all women should stay inside after dark. The audience knows full well that this advisory is futile, at least for the woman on the screen. Here she is, seemingly safe within the confines of her home, settling in for an engrossing read and a relaxing soak in the tub, when a shadow falls across her unsuspecting face. She looks up and shrieks, as our killer is revealed in all his maniacal glory, from his insanely bug-eyed stare to his wildly unkempt eyebrows. As he grimaces while plunging the knife into his victim, the audience is given its first delicious taste of the bloodbath to ensue. Much to our horror and delight, the victim's now eyeless socket is exposed. Our killer then grins, thoroughly enjoying the impending gruesome task of removing this bathing beauty's leg. Hack! Hack! Hack!

So begins the tale of Fuad Ramses (Mal Arnold) and his unhealthy relationship with a gold painted mannequin. He is completely consumed with his desire to appease and restore his adored Ishtar, whose resurrection can only be achieved through a grisly ancient rite known as the "blood feast." A rite that will culminate once Ishtar's faithfully fixated follower has collected various body parts from unfortunate young ladies and prepared them as entrees.

The story unfolds through a series of rather amazing occurrences. Mrs. Fremont (Lyn Bolton), who adorns herself in furs, large crazy hats, and speaks as though she hobnobs regularly with the Queen herself, is organizing a banquet for her daughter. She is seeking something "unusual" and "totally different." (To impress all those high society folks milling about suburban Florida, I assume.) And where else would you go for an exotic feast, but to an exotic caterer?

Now let me take a moment to further illuminate Fuad's entrepreneurial enterprise. It appears as though an elderly man, one with a prominent limp no less, can single-handedly run an exotic catering business equipped with nothing more than a couple of crusty old pots, a butcher's block, and a pizza oven. What about a refrigerator you ask? Fuad don't need no stinkin' refrigerator! Speaking of stinking, Ishtar apparently also doubles as an air freshener since the smell of the two week-old meat strewn about the place doesn't seem to raise any concerns from neighbors or customers. In fact, Fuad's business is such a success, he even gets customers to refer their friends to him. Where are the County Health Inspectors throughout all this?

It turns out Mrs. Fremont's daughter, Suzette (Connie Mason), has a fondness for ancient Egyptian culture. She is so fond of it, truth be told, that she and her boyfriend are enrolled in a class on the very subject and attend a lecture on none other than the mighty Ishtar herself! Coincidentally, Suzette's boyfriend just so happens to be Detective Pete Thornton (William Kerwin aka Thomas Wood), the cop heading up the investigation of the rash of recent murders. Given Suzette's historical interests, Mrs. Fremont is ecstatic to discover Fuad has been searching for the perfect opportunity to prepare something "unusual,"…an authentic Egyptian feast!

Will Fuad succeed in releasing the violent deity Ishtar upon the world? Will Suzette become the main course in a heinous feast of flesh? Will the only two cops in town continue to do nothing but hang out in the only office their police station appears to have?

Having broken the skin, let's now carve deeper into the meat of things. Lewis himself readily admits that *Blood Feast* was experimental. Not having any idea how audiences would receive this type of film, every possible corner was cut during production to minimize prospective losses. This resulted in a film simultaneously shocking and amusing.

Blood Feast is by no means the type of movie that audiences can go into maintaining a serious frame of mind. It needs to be approached open-mindedly and with a love for the beautiful schlock that it is. Joe Bob Briggs, notorious drive-in critic, noted that, "It's one of those films that gets better the more you know about it. In some ways, it's a little more fun to talk about than to sit through."

There is no denying that it contains a copious supply of enjoyable absurdities. The script is ridiculously crude. In order to achieve its 70-minute runtime, it was padded with a gratuitous poolside scene featuring several bikini-clad ladies. The acting is abundantly hammy. Connie Mason, a former *Playboy* playmate, was hired solely for her "decorative" charms, so we're not talking about skilled artisans here. Several actors and actresses couldn't remember their lines and can be plainly seen reading them from a variety of places such as their palms or nearby furniture. Ahh, but these are all things that only add to *Blood Feast*'s charm.

When we combine these unintentional hilarities with Lewis' passion for shamelessly drenching the set red with sticky blood and visually assaulting the audience with grand scenes of violence (such as the notorious tongue dismemberment), it's hard *not* to have fun.

Blood Feast was first screened at a drive-in in Peoria, Illinois, intentionally chosen for its distance from larger cities. The theory being that if the movie bombed, the negative reviews would not proliferate as fast in a less populated area. Taglines teased, "Nothing so appalling in the annals of horror!" Moviegoers were issued vomit bags and an ambulance was parked out front in plain view. Yet, even with all the gimmicky build up, people were still so shocked by what flickered before their eyes, they fled the premises. By the second screening word of mouth had gotten out, drawing floods of curious folks. A legend was born and *Blood Feast* immediately secured its place in horror history.

Encouraged by their success, Lewis and Friedman were quick to collaborate on another project of the same ilk, which would become the second film in the "Blood Trilogy." Raise your hand if you can name it.

That's right! *Two Thousand Maniacs!* I'll make an Honor Roll student of you yet!

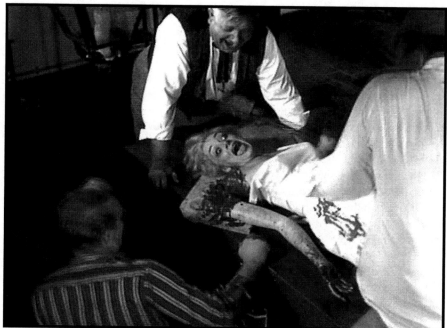

Bea Miller (Shelby Livingston) is a victim of crazed rednecks in *Two Thousand Maniacs!*

By now, Lewis and Friedman were well aware of their audience's blood-soaked expectations and were anxious to keep the crowds captivated. With nearly triple the budget of *Blood Feast*, they produced a film even more outrageous and over-the-top than its predecessor.

Two Thousand Maniacs! is a *Brigadoon*-inspired tale that takes place in the Deep South, in the quaint little town of Pleasant Valley, GA, where its citizens are preparing a Centennial Celebration. The only thing they need to get their shindig flying is six guests of honor. Did I mention they have to be Yankees? Those cunning Pleasantvillians devise a not-so-intricate plan (a road sign switcheroo) to waylay unsuspecting Northerners. Some hapless Yanks are about to discover that Pleasant Valley has a secret…one that's not so pleasant.

Okay, so with taglines like "An entire town bathed in pulsing human blood! Madmen crazed for carnage!" it's really not much of a secret. However, despite what we might think, being clued into the secret doesn't detract from the fun in the least. If anything, it enhances it, allowing the audience to snicker right alongside the bloodthirsty yokels.

Right from its opening sequence, the down-home flavor of this film is firmly established as we are greeted with lively, banjo-heavy music that proclaims (in the enthusiastic voice of Lewis himself), "Yeehaw! Oh, the South's gonna rise again!"

The movie begins with an overall atmosphere of good-humored hijinx. We observe Rufus (Gary Bakeman), a fine specimen of Pleasant Valley living, garbed in a crusty Tom Sawyer hat and dirt-laden dungarees, chewin' tobacky as he scans the intermittent traffic from his perch amongst the tree branches. When he spies a car with Illinois plates containing four passengers, he eagerly signals to his buddy, Lester (Ben Moore), to erect the *faux* detour sign. (How a suspicious man leaping into the road and erecting a detour sign before disappearing into a ditch goes unnoticed remains a mystery to me. But then again, these Northern folks will later prove oblivious to quite a few happenings.)

The next vehicle to be detoured contains two occupants. We discover straight away that Tom (Kerwin/Wood, again) is intelligent. He must be: He's a schoolteacher. He reminds us of this fact several times throughout the movie lest we forget which character has the brains to uncover Pleasant Valley's terrible secret. Terry (Connie Mason…again), on the other hand, picks up strange hitchhikers on desolate backroads. Need I say more? Thanks to Ms. Mason's inability to emote, there are several moments in which it is impossible to determine if Terry is deep in thought or if perhaps she just has a toothache. Terry also manages to ask some of the film's most inane questions. For example, after stopping at a detour sign, she asks Tom, "Now, what do you think this means?" Tom, though a mere stranger, has already come to the realization that you really need to spell things out with this broad, so he replies with, "Well, it means detour, lady."

When the town of Pleasant Valley is introduced, there is quite a hullabaloo taking place on the main street. The townsfolk proudly wave Confederate flags, street musicians wander about, and children frolic joyously. There is an almost Norman Rockwell appeal as this community unites in this time of celebration… at least until we discover that the joyous frolicking of the town's children includes a noose and a "Damn Yankee" effigy in the form of a cat. It doesn't take long for the initial impression of harmless gaiety to shift to one of ominous foreboding.

The six Northerners are greeted by an overzealous crowd and the rather boisterous Mayor Buckman (Jeffrey Allen). Turns out, they're the lucky guests of honor for the town's ambiguous Centennial Celebration, and although reluctant, it seems they just can't refuse Pleasant Valley's Southern-fried hospitality.

Two Thousand Maniacs! resembles a deranged episode of *Hee Haw* as it lays on the hayseed humor with a slew of stereotypical hicks; from the big lug, Harper Alexander (Mark Douglas), who sports a versatile rope belt that is not only fashionable but functional, to Betsy Gunther (Linda Cochran), the flirtatious Daisy Mae of the town. The townsfolk frequently make wisecracks and snide comments that cause them to giggle hysterically like mischievous school children.

There's plenty of dark humor to be found as the celebration quickly becomes a psychotic state fair. Maintaining a lively carnival spirit, the creative kills include a deadly "horserace" and a fatal barrel roll. Especially endearing is the barbeque scene in which the denizens gather around singing "Rollin' in My Sweet Baby's Arms" as one hapless victim's severed arm rotates on the spit.

Although *Two Thousand Maniacs!* was not as successful as its precursor, it remains a favorite among schlock connoisseurs today. Even Lewis and Friedman dub it the favorite of their joint efforts.

Blood Feast and *Two Thousand Maniacs!* (along with *Color Me Blood Red* [1965], the third "Blood" movie) established the classic Lewis formula that audiences would see in future flicks as he and Friedman continued to push limits and cross lines. As the proud purveyors of violence that they are, the pair made undeniably significant contributions to the advancement and broadening of the horror genre. Their vivid portrayals of onscreen gore and violence began a trend that filmmakers the world over would build upon.

Nearly 40 years after drive-in audiences first bore witness to the deadly obsession of Fuad Ramses, the legendary team of Lewis and Friedman reunited in 2002 to respectively direct and executive-produce *Blood Feast 2: All U Can Eat*. This intentionally over-the-top horror/comedy follows the story of Fuad's grandson who, although ignorant of his grandfather's heinous legacy, soon discovers that bloodlust is hereditary.

Okay, class, that concludes today's lesson concerning the origin of those lovely splatter flicks we've all come to know and love. Your homework assignment for this evening…go spread the gospel of gore! Class dismissed!

THE BODY SNATCHER (1945)
by Peter Christensen

Each of Val Lewton's films has its fine qualities, but these often exist within stories that can be jerky, confusing, and almost incoherent. *The Body Snatcher*, with its compelling narrative thrust, is a significant exception to this rule. Philip MacDonald and Lewton (credited as Carlos Keith) transform Stevenson's confused tale into a magnificent example of cinematic storytelling. Discarding the source material's unsuccessful use of flashback, the script stays in the present, unfolding as a continuous, uninterrupted narrative. Since the film depends on our knowledge of events from the past, a certain amount of exposition in the dialogue is required, but MacDonald and Lewton are gifted enough to provide the necessary information without disrupting the narrative's flow (ably assisted by Robert Wise's sharp direction and much fine acting). This seems a simple change, but without it we would have a different and probably lesser result.

The story is complex enough to require close attention, although the screenplay is never unclear. From the opening, the main plot seems to be about the robbing of graves in order to provide cadavers for Dr. MacFarlane's medical students. But the idea of "knowing where the bodies are buried" will soon extend itself into the themes of dark secrets and blackmail. John Gray (a superbly subtle Boris Karloff) is the "resurrectionist" who provides corpses for the highly respectable doctor (Henry Daniell, in one of the best performances of his long career). As it turns out, however, Gray has a history with MacFarlane, a history with which he can blackmail his "colleague." Years ago, as another doctor's assistant, MacFarlane had worked *with* Gray in the robbing of graves and in the receiving of "resurrected" bodies. When the most important culprits were tried for their crimes, Gray served his time without impeaching the young doctor. ("Toddy," Gray's memorably chummy nickname for MacFarlane, carries equal measures of mockery and menace.)

Gray is also aware of MacFarlane's other secret—the fact that, in his youth, he had married a woman who belonged to a lower social class than his family (and their circle) would find acceptable. She lives with him now in the guise of his housekeeper, and the deep love between the two is immediately apparent. What makes Daniell's performance so remarkable is that he manages to be two things at once. The actor utilizes the chilly, aloof persona, which gave him so many suave villain roles during his career, but also his actions inform us that this is not MacFarlane's true nature. His scenes with his wife and, on occasion, with his assistant Fettes, suggest that there's a loving and generous nature inside him, which he fears to show to the world. He doesn't ask for our pity, but he gets it. It's a very moving performance.

MacFarlane isn't the only complex figure in the film, since Gray is far from being a simple stereotype. We see plenty of cold-blooded savagery from him, and no

MacFarlane [left] (Henry Daniell) confronts Cabman Gray (Boris Karloff).

one will forget the killing of a small dog that refuses to leave its master's grave. The killing of the dog isn't presented graphically, nor is the murder of a blind street singer (a shadow-cloaked demise signaled by her song's abrupt end), but both episodes are shocking reminders of John Gray's dark side. He's a thug, to be sure, but we see and believe that there are also better qualities in him. The resurrectionist's kindly treatment of the crippled young girl under MacFarlane's care seems sincere. Indeed, it ultimately leads the girl to take her first steps (after an operation which seems to have failed). It's also no accident that Gray berates the doctor, not for a lack of medical skill but for a lack of essential humanity—a trait in MacFarlane which Gray, ironically enough, is largely responsible for. We are not meant to take Gray's comments lightly, however, and Donald Fettes, MacFarlane's assistant, will later echo his words.

An ugly but understandable element in Gray's character is that, like MacFarlane, he feels himself the victim of the social stratification that exists in his world. His most powerful speech comes after MacFarlane, in an effort to free himself, has offered to make his blackmailer rich. Gray refuses the offer simply because, as a member of a lower order, he enjoys the idea of being able to taunt and torture the doctor. He and MacFarlane both frequent a pub which advertises itself as serving both the gentry and the commonality, although the accommodations for the two groups are clearly separate and unequal. Gray delights in forcing "Toddy" to sit and hobnob at his lower-class table. This is clearly a man who won't go away for a few extra coins in his pocket, preferring to exact a higher price.

The breaking point comes when Joseph, one of MacFarlane's servants (Bela Lugosi, playing a Portuguese), has learned enough about his master's business to attempt blackmailing Gray himself. *The Body Snatcher* was the final film in which Karloff and Lugosi would appear together. Lugosi's role is a small one, and he spends most of his time lurking around the doctor's house trying to pick up information about what's going on there. His one substantial moment comes after he knows enough to blackmail Gray. The scene between the two veterans is a good one, but Karloff dominates it—very appropriately, since the hapless Joseph has wandered into something which he's incapable of handling. In this version of "the biter bit," Gray murders Joseph and places him in a vat in the doctor's basement—a deed which will lead to the doctor's subsequent murder of Gray.

Here, however, we can be virtually certain that every body will rise to the surface, and Gray, even as a dead man, will have his revenge. His spectral apparition will manifest itself to MacFarlane—and *only* to him, despite Fettes' presence in the scene. We realize that Gray's body stands not just for itself but for all of the dirty deeds and secrets that haunt the doctor—things which he now understands will never go away. The doctor's climactic "accidental" death will leave Fettes alive, presumably a sadder and wiser man than he was before the story began.

Fettes is a significant figure in the story, not least because he is the only survivor among the major characters. (Russell Wade sounds the right notes of sincerity and idealism in his performance, but his unabashedly American accent is deplorably out of place, even within a film where few of the accents are really appropriate.) His experience has been, to say the least, an interesting one. His love of medicine includes a human interest in his and others' patients, and his interest in the crippled girl's windowed mother may lead viewers to believe that a conventional happy ending lies just beyond the credits.

On the other hand, he has participated in actions which he wouldn't want the girl and her mother to know anything about. He has done so because he knows that the stolen or murdered bodies will lead to good, yet he's sensitive enough to be aware that his actions taint him in dangerous ways. As Fettes walks away from the wrecked carriage and his dead mentor, we have no idea what his destination might be. The path he walks leads into a great darkness, and we wonder if the little girl and her mother now belong only to his past. All we can be sure of is that he, too, will be a man with secrets.

The Body Snatcher, with its complex characters and dense thematic structure, is a brilliantly subtle and ironic work. It works a splendid series of variations on the theme of resurrection (i.e. digging things up) and on the ironic discrepancies between appearance and reality. Its horrors are those of the soul, of how easily and quickly such an entity can be corrupted and of what the consequences of such corruption might be. It's a bleak film, and even the "happy" ending, in which its young hero walks away, is ambiguous in the extreme. It creates a dangerous, claustrophobic world in which only those who can't see find it possible to sing, and it shows that they do so at their peril.

THE CABINET OF DR. CALIGARI (1920)
by Aaron Christensen

For the casual or uninitiated horror fan, approaching *The Cabinet of Dr. Caligari* might be something akin to encountering the Mona Lisa for the first time: Instantly recognizable, yet somehow more famous for being famous than for anything inherently unique. One might, out of ignorance, easily dismiss it as "just another silent movie"

Conrad Veidt, as the sonambulist Cesare, menaces Lil Dagover.

in the way that the latter is "just another painting of a woman." Yet like Da Vinci's masterpiece, once encountered firsthand, *Caligari* exudes an undeniable raw power that has nothing to do with its reputation or historical context. While its genesis is every bit as fascinating as the onscreen fantasy, and its innovative, groundbreaking role in the legacy of the horror film (and cinema in general) undeniable, the picture itself remains far from being just a museum piece.

Confession time: Prior to researching for the purposes of this essay, I didn't know a damn thing about the modern art movement. In fact, the only reason I was already aware that *The Cabinet of Dr. Caligari* is an "Expressionist" film was that every horror reference book I had ever read as a youth had told me so. From these, I had divined that it had something to do with the bizarre shapes of the sets, the unusually stark art direction, and the broad gestures and makeup, but really, that's about all. As a genre fan, I was much more interested to learn of its significance as the first true horror feature, making it, from a historical standpoint, a must-see for aficionados.

Ah, there's that nasty word again. *Historical.* These days, most newcomers to the horror genre have grown up with geysers of blood, are on a first-name basis with Michael, Jason, and Freddy, and think of Tom Savini's once-vanguard f/x as "old-school." For them, horror means flesh-eating zombies and axe-toting maniacs. Assuming they've even heard of this historic chestnut, their interest is not likely piqued by its being a black and white (strike one…) silent picture (…two…) that doesn't feature Boris Karloff,

Bela Lugosi, or either of the Chaneys (...that's three, and down the Blockbuster aisle we go!) The idea of a murderous sleepwalker might appeal on some level, but the oddball quality of the film's design and the flamboyant acting is more likely to induce yawns and giggles from today's audiences than the *frisson* it inspired decades ago.

However, as any viewer of Shakespeare, Kabuki, or opera will tell you, once you give over, surrendering oneself to the world presented, things once alien soon become familiar. Eager to follow *Caligari*'s murder-mystery narrative, the viewer quickly accepts the fantastic settings, allowing the film to work its spell. The picture was considered wildly radical upon its original release in 1920, and the passage of time has only served to heighten its peculiar qualities. The dreamlike atmosphere, even more pronounced for the modern viewer, is unlike any world we have ever encountered. The landscape is off-kilter and skewed, lending the viewer the feeling of being ungrounded, out of one's element. Yet, and this is the film's genius, it possesses enough familiar elements that we can relate to it. People laugh, love, walk, talk (albeit through dialogue panels), and giggle at the antics of an organ grinder's monkey. As Mike Budd points out in his excellent DVD audio essay, it is this combination of familiarity and innovation that spurs audiences to return again and again.

The year was 1919 when Hans Janowitz and Carl Mayer met with the director of Berlin's Decla Film Co., Erich Pommer, to discuss an original script. Colored by recent years of war and tyranny, their screenplay focused on a traveling sideshow barker and his somnambulist assassin. Pommer purchased it and handed the directorial reins to Fritz Lang, who in turn brought aboard Lil Dagover for the female lead. But, due to previous obligations on his serial *The Spiders* (1919-1920), Lang revealed that he would not be available to direct *Caligari*. He instead suggested Robert Wiene, a journeyman director known within Berlin's artistic circles. Painters Hermann Warm and Walter Rohrig and costumer Walter Reimann rounded out the cutting-edge creative unit.

Cinema at the time (with the exception of Georges Melies' fantasy offerings) had focused on realistically recreating everyday events. Following WWI, Germany's struggling film industry realized that it couldn't compete with Hollywood's technical expertise and budgetary advantages. As has often been the case, less money in the coffers inspired more imagination. While U.S. production companies built lifelike sets of entire Western towns, Germany's growing legion of filmmakers sought to create something different (beginning with *Caligari*) by creating dreamlike scenarios and landscapes for such horror classics as *The Golem* (1920), *Nosferatu* (1922), *Waxworks* (1924), and *Faust* (1926). (There's a reason why these titles are still viewed today, while the silent oaters have long since been put out to pasture.)

Perhaps regrettably, the design team was so focused on artistic innovation that they ignored the implications of adding (accounts differ on whether this was Lang's or Wiene's suggestion) a framing device around the central story that showed its narrator to be an asylum inmate, his addled brain thus justifying the film's insane world. While this change ultimately provided audiences with one of the genre's first twist endings, Phil Hardy points out in *The Overlook Encyclopedia of Horror* that "instead of suggesting that 'the authorities' were insane criminals who ordered wholesale murder to be committed by blindly obedient soldiers, the film now created the impression that only strongly authoritarian institutions ruled by benign dictators can contain the insane fantasies of intellectuals." With this, the picture's political spine was snapped. In the

Cesare (Conrad Veidt) awakens.

words of historian Siegfried Kracauer, "A revolutionary film was thus turned into a conformist one."

In spite of this, it is impossible to overstate the impact *Caligari* had on filmgoers, who felt they were bearing witness to a landmark event, one comparable to the later coming of sound. With cinematic storytelling techniques a recent phenomenon, *Caligari*'s modern art sensibilities served as an assault on established conventions, the distorted sets (as well as the subtitles) utilizing sharp and angular shapes, with shadows and light beams painted onto the walls and floors. *The Monster Show*'s David J. Skal puts it succinctly: "Because of its indelible imagery, a photograph from *Caligari* simply cannot be mistaken for one from any other picture." The shock was softened by the recognizable melodramatic characters, which included a mad scientist, a sleepwalking murderer, a heroine whose beauty arrests the monster, and an amateur detective as our hero.

The film's artistic nature appealed to intellectuals, while the horror elements captivated the worldwide masses. Upon its premiere, a *New York Times* review stated, "The uninitiated are not asked to understand cubism, for the settings are the background, or rather an inseparable part, of a fantastic story of murder and madness such as Edgar Allan Poe might have written." In France, because of *Caligari*, theaters lifted their ban on German films. In the weeks following its opening, Parisian readers would encounter a new term to express anything irregular or bizarre: "Caligarism."

Precursors to countless monsters and psychos to come, Caligari and Cesare are the most dynamic and memorable characters. One seminal horror moment is the first sequence of Cesare (Conrad Veidt) awakening; in closeup, we see his eyelids fluttering, nostrils flaring, eyes bulging, blackened lips parting. None of this is violent, gory, or even deliberately menacing; it's just good and creepy. Veidt would go on to become horror's first genre star, seen in such classics as *Waxworks*, *The Student of Prague* (1926), and *The Man Who Laughs* (1928), although he is probably better recognized by mainstream audiences for his Nazi roles in such films as *Casablanca* (1942). Another highlight features Werner Krauss' obsessed doctor descending into madness, the words "*Du Musst Caligari Werde*" ("You Must Become Caligari") appearing in the air around him, pushing the already heightened nightmarish atmosphere to its limits.

I recently had the distinct pleasure to view *The Cabinet of Dr. Caligari* on the big screen at the Music Box Theatre in Chicago, with live organ accompaniment. As the picture unspooled before me, I was struck again and again by the haunting imagery, the starkness of the jagged forms, the eccentric performances (which only add to the film's otherworldliness). And when the twist ending eventually arrived, it was a slow methodical dawning, like a sleeper awakening from a dream, as opposed to the slam-bang, complete-with-flashback-inserts that seem to mark the modern era (Get it? Get it? Did you get it? What you thought was happening, *wasn't happening at all*! Get it?? Ha ha, fooled you!!) After wildly applauding our organist maestro, I walked out of the theater feeling elevated, inspired, wondering why I had only seen this master-piece one time before, and realizing that I too had bought into the "historical chestnut" myth. Now, as though by revelation, I had finally "gotten" the film after years of just "knowing that it was important." Elated and enlightened, I went into the restroom, where I heard another occupant's voice echo off the tiles: "Well, *that* was the longest 72 minutes of my life."

Hey, you can't please everyone.

CANNIBAL HOLOCAUST (1980)
by Lawrence P. Raffel

Often cited as inspiration for *The Blair Witch Project* (1999), the story of Ruggero Deodato's *Cannibal Holocaust* centers around four American documentary filmmak-ers, presumed dead after they go missing somewhere in the Amazon. A rescue team heads deep into the jungle in an attempt to track down the unaccounted-for filmmakers, eventually stumbling upon a primitive tribe. Not only does the rescue team manage to make peace, but also reacquires the film canisters that belonged to the missing docu-mentarians.

What follows is an unofficial screening back in the U.S. for a group of unemotional, money-hungry TV executives/investors. This "found footage" consists mostly of the four filmmakers traipsing around the jungle, taking time out only to taunt and abuse the local tribe members. Their utter disregard for regional customs leads us to our grand finale in which we see (in up-close and morbid detail) their eventual fate.

While many filmmakers dipped their fingers into this popular pot of gut-munching stew known as "the Italian Cannibal film," none were more infamous than Umberto Lenzi and Ruggero Deodato. Through the years these two tried to outdo one another (and out-gross the general public) by raising the bar of onscreen nastiness with each successive film. With nearly 10 films between them, they celebrated this most outra-geous horror subgenre like no other.

"I wonder who the real cannibals are?"Jack Anders (Perry Pirkanen) captures more un-savory footage.

A widely known fact among the inner horror circle (a circle that you are now a proud member of, mind you) is that Lenzi and Deodato were in constant cannibal conflict with one another over the years. This isn't to say that there weren't other directors chiming in with their quick cash-in cannibal films (of which there were many), but the battlefield was simply dominated by Deodato and Lenzi, both of whom are responsible for some of the sickest, most vile moments of cinematic/cannibalistic history ever. During their ongoing fight for the almighty grindhouse dollar, each upped the ante every time they got behind the camera.

Lenzi was first with his film *Man from Deep River* (1972) and Deodato followed with *Jungle Holocaust* (1977). Both efforts contained an odd, yet sentimental love story angle and were far less graphic than those to come. Lenzi then struck back with *Eaten Alive* (1980) and Deodato took the largest chunk out of the industry with *Cannibal Holocaust* the same year. Lenzi's answer to *Cannibal Holocaust* was the only *slightly* inferior and campier *Cannibal Ferox* (aka *Make Them Die Slowly* [1981]), which is now just as famous a title. Deodato would return yet again only a few short years later with an even campier film called *Cut And Run* ([1985] starring an unlikely Willie Aames), a forgettable outing that pretty much signified the end of the battle.

While each of these offerings had its moments, none of them ever reached the sheer level of audacity as the two films that changed the subgenre forever. After Deodato released *Cannibal Holocaust* in '80 and Lenzi released *Cannibal Ferox* in '81, things would never be the same.

Extreme violence was at the core of these flicks, including but not limited to real animal violence. For some unknown reason, these filmmakers relished having real animal torture and violence thrown into the mix. My least favorite aspect of subgenre—and the hardest to watch (for obvious reasons)—I find it's not appropriate to celebrate these films for this footage, but it is valuable to place them in their historical context. In turn we should adhere a "what's done is done" attitude towards the movie in support of our examinations. Also of note is the fact that Deodato was allegedly dragged to court over *Cannibal Holocaust* and had to prove that the cast hadn't actually been killed. It's told that eventually he was only slapped with a fine for animal cruelty.

So why does *Cannibal Holocaust* remain today the most infamous of all cannibal films? It's not a tough a question to answer. Very few of these over-the-top, graphic films took themselves as seriously as *Cannibal Holocaust*. *Cannibal Ferox* runs a close second, mind you, but still exudes more of a campy vibe with its silly dialogue and score. There is not one frame of *Cannibal Holocaust* that plays for laughs or comes off as camp. It's serious business through and through, and the *cinéma vérité*/documentary-style footage only adds to its uncomfortable feeling. Nearly all of these efforts play off of the same social commentary angle: White man steps into the jungle, disrespects local customs and is eventually given his/her just desserts. *Cannibal Holocaust* is applauded less for its inclusion of this overused morality tale and more for its unique approach and execution of the subject matter. *Cannibal Holocaust* rightfully holds its place in horror film history. Unofficial sequels, soundtrack remixes, shirts, posters, and even rumors of the theme song being played at weddings highlight its effect on underground pop culture over the years.

The first time I saw *Cannibal Holocaust* was during my tape-trading days back in the early '90s. Unavailable in the U.S. at that time, the only way to see uncut foreign horror was to trade import tapes and/or laser discs. During this time, I had acquired a copy of *Cannibal Holocaust* from what I believe was a boot of a Venezuelan tape from one of my tape-trading buddies. Having not even heard of the film at the time, the promised shock money-shot that drew me in was a rumored "fetus eating scene." I only wish I could remember what I traded for it.

In 1997, *Cannibal Holocaust* was released (as a limited run edition) in the U.S. on laser disc and, while the video quality was still far from perfect, the film had never looked better. While I no longer own a laser disc player, I still own this disc, with the jacket autographed by Deodato himself. Also of note is that this release was one of the first to address the legendary missing "piranha scene" by featuring a couple of still photographs that were supposedly taken during filming. Speculation still abounds about a scene in which human flesh was allegedly fed to hungry piranhas. No footage has turned up, just a few stills and Deodato has vacillated over the years by both confirming and denying that the footage was ever shot.

On Friday, June 29, 2001, at the Hoyts Theatre in New Jersey, Exhumed Films showed (for the first time anywhere) a completely remastered and uncut print of *Cannibal Holocaust* on a double bill with the "Nazi zombie-out-of-water" tale *Shock Waves* (1977). I was a member of the audience for this monumental screening, accompanied by a friend who had never seen the film before. How I envied him for experiencing *Holocaust* like this for his first time.

In October 2005, Grindhouse Releasing put out a 2-Disc Special Edition DVD of *Cannibal Holocaust* and, while the print used had a few seconds of footage trimmed from the "Last Road To Hell" sequence (a short documentary film within the film), the entire sequence was available as a DVD extra. In addition, over the years, numerous import VHS tapes and DVDs have been released of varying quality despite the film being banned in over 60 countries.

Distributors have tried to cash in on the cannibal craze by renaming their films accordingly. A handful of films have been renamed *Cannibal Holocaust 2* by unscrupulous distributors worldwide. Note: As of the time of this writing, there has *not* been an official sequel to *Cannibal Holocaust* released. However, Deodato may or may not currently be in production on an "official" sequel himself.

CARRIE (1976)
by Mark Allan Gunnells

A teenager is ostracized and tormented by her peers at school. Her home life provides her with no support system. Feeling different and alone, she becomes angry and unstable. When she can no longer take the humiliations of cruel classmates or the indifference of adults around her, she exacts vengeance by massacring students and teachers indiscriminately, then returns home to murder her mother, and finally takes her own life.

In this post-Columbine age, the above could be heard on any newscast around the country. School shootings have become almost an epidemic in the United States, occurring with disturbing frequency. Yet what I've just described is not the latest headlines; it is the plot of Brian De Palma's *Carrie*.

Based on Stephen King's 1974 novel and scripted by Lawrence D. Cohen, *Carrie* seems even more relevant today than when it was first released. The telekinesis angle aside, the picture offers a startlingly accurate glimpse into the pecking order of high school life. It depicts the sort of daily humiliation and scorn heaped upon those at the bottom of that hierarchy. One of the film's greatest strengths is that it portrays the character of Carrie White not as a heartless monster, but as a girl with whom we sympathize. While her ultimate actions cannot be condoned, they can at least be understood.

In the title role, Sissy Spacek is an example of perfect casting. Unlike modern movies that slap a pair of glasses on a model and call her a geek, people in the movies of the 1970s look real. Spacek, though beautiful in her own way (as evidenced in the prom sequence), is very believable as an awkward, uncoordinated girl, who is the victim of unrelenting harassment from her peers. The success of the film hinges on her look and performance, and Spacek delivers like a seasoned pro. We identify with her pain in a very real way, eventually becoming willing accomplices to her climactic fiery vengeance, looking on with a mixture of horror and glee.

Right from the start, De Palma and Cohen establish the misery of Carrie's life. The opening volleyball scenes (where Carrie stands out like the proverbial sore thumb against a court full of beautiful, athletic girls) capture perfectly the life of a high school outsider. The other team's strategy is to hit the ball to Carrie, knowing she won't be able to hit it back, while her own teammates consider her nothing but a liability. The following locker room sequence is brutal in its intensity and cruelty. The other girls, led by Chris (Nancy Allen) and Norma (P.J. Soles), turn a female rite of passage (Carrie's first menstrual cycle) into an utterly degrading and traumatic event. Indicative of the type of group mentality that pervades high school, even nice girl Sue (Amy Irving, in

Carrie White (Sissy Spacek) is humiliated by her peers and her own body.

a wonderfully understated performance) takes part. After being sent home for the day, Carrie finds neither support nor comfort. Instead, her puritanical mother Margaret (Piper Laurie, in a tour-de-force of over-the-top excess) only heaps on more abuse. For Carrie, there is no safe haven.

Then something special surfaces in our young protagonist's life. In a wonderful symbolic representation of puberty, where young people feel their own bodies are strangers to them, Carrie realizes that she is acquiring an unusual ability: With just the power of her mind, she can make objects move. An ashtray flies off a desk, a mirror shatters, a kid topples off his bicycle—all Carrie has to do is think it, and it is so.

Chris, angered by the administration's reprisal for the locker room stunt, plans an elaborate public prank to play on Carrie, eliciting the help of her slacker boyfriend Billy (John Travolta, obviously enjoying himself every second onscreen). Sue, on the other hand, has a very different reaction. Feeling guilty, she accepts her punishment with grace, even going so far as to entreat her boyfriend Tommy (William Katt) to invite Carrie to the prom as recompense. Fearing this is just another setup to humiliate her, Carrie initially refuses, but she eventually gives in to Tommy's charms and agrees to go to the dance.

As Carrie's telekinetic abilities continue to grow, so does the realization that she now has the power to change her life. When Mrs. White forbids her to attend the prom, Carrie employs a dramatic display to cow her mother, making it clear that she will not be controlled nor intimidated anymore. When Carrie says, "Things are going to change around here," she finally has the power to back it up.

The night of the prom starts out like a Cinderella story. Carrie makes her own dress and walks into the school gym on Tommy's arm. While some snicker behind her back, others are warm and welcoming to her. Tommy, initially doing this as a favor to Sue, seems to develop a genuine attraction to shy, sweet Carrie, even giving her a first kiss. Life almost seems like a fairytale, and De Palma and cinematographer Mario Tosi photograph it accordingly. It is Chris and Billy—banned from the prom, but secretly in attendance—who bring Carrie's dream crashing down in one of the genre's most memorable sequences.

Chris, with the aid of Norma, has fixed the voting, ensuring that Tommy and Carrie are elected Prom King and Queen. When the couple takes the stage, a strategically placed bucket of pig's blood is dumped onto the couple from the rafters, dousing them in gore. Standing before the entire class and faculty, drenched in blood, listening to others laugh at her, Carrie simply…snaps. The breathtaking scenes that follow (utilizing De Palma's trademark split screens) are nothing less than a systematic massacre of everyone in the gym. Not just those that participated in the prank, but anyone in her sights, including the only teacher who ever tried to help her, Miss Collins (a warm, winning performance from Betty Buckley). After trapping everyone inside and setting the gym ablaze, Carrie walks home in her ruined prom gown. Mrs. White is waiting and attempts to kill her daughter, whom she now views as a witch. But Carrie crucifies her mother with flying kitchen implements, then brings the house down on both of them.

A surreal dream serves as the heart-stopping coda. The final shot (Carrie's hand reaching from her grave to grab Sue) has become an iconic image in horror, and while many films since have tried to recreate its shock ending, not one has surpassed it.

Carrie enjoyed great success upon its release, bringing fame to its young cast as well as a certain little-known author of the source material. Both Spacek and Laurie were nominated for Academy Awards, a rarity for genre efforts. The film was so successful that it even inspired a Broadway musical (which has subsequently gone down in history as one of the most infamous blunders ever to stumble upon the Great White Way). An unfortunate, unlikely film sequel, *The Rage: Carrie 2,* also followed 23 years later in 1999, with Amy Irving reprising her role as Sue.

While I cannot speak for every horror fan out there, I for one was a Carrie White in my own way. I knew what it was like to be picked last for any sport in gym; I knew what it was like to be made fun of just because I didn't have the right clothes; I knew what it was like to feel powerless to change my circumstances. If I had discovered I had Carrie's talent, I would not necessarily have killed everyone at the prom, but I would have known the temptation.

Carrie has endured over the years, becoming a certified horror classic. There is rarely a prom sequence, even to this day, that does not contain some reference to De Palma's effort. Considered one of the best adaptations of a Stephen King work, why does it hold up so well after 30 years? Because the problems it deals with still exist. Fashions may change, fads may come and go, but the microcosm that is high school is very much the same as it was in the 1970s. With all the violence in schools today—violence perpetrated by and upon the students themselves—the tale still feels fresh and vital.

CAT PEOPLE (1942)
by Aaron Christensen

Irena's dream sequence demonstrating good vs. evil

From 1942 to 1946, when rust was appearing on the Frankenstein Monster's neck bolts, Dracula was growing longer in the tooth, and swaddled, swollen Mummies were limping along (both figuratively and literally), a savior appeared on the horror horizon, who would provide counter-programming to the usual parade of fur, fangs and putty. That man was Val Lewton, and his debut production would herald a new style of horror where less was infinitely more, where shadows grew ripe with menace lurking just beyond the edge of the screen.

Like Universal's *The Wolf Man* (1941), *Cat People* began as a "concept" title, suggested by RKO. Lewton, a 37-year-old former story editor for David O. Selznick, was given the producing assignment. (Ironically, Lewton was an ailurophobe, suffering from the irrational fear of felines.) According to David J. Skal, Lewton's first treatment was envisioned as a war story: A Nazi division is summarily destroyed when it invades a Serbian village inhabited by giant were-cats. Later, from this hamlet, a girl would flee to Manhattan. The Nazi subplot eventually fell by the wayside, but the cat-cursed female would remain the focal point of Lewton's vision.

A twist of the lycanthropy tale (or tail), DeWitt Bodeen's wonderfully understated script teems with disturbing psychological and sexual undertones, implying everything while stating nothing. The enigmatic and beautiful Irena, a recent Serbian emigree, is befriended near the panther cage at the zoo by a charming naval architect named Oliver.

Ollie (Kent Smith) tells Irena (Simone Simon) that he is giving her a divorce.

The two soon grow closer, eventually marrying, but Irena is reluctant to be physically intimate with her new husband, believing she is descended from "the Marmalukes," a strange race that transform into killer panthers when their emotions are aroused. As time passes, the understandably frustrated Oliver begins to show interest in his female co-worker, Alice. Did he forget that jealousy is a strong emotion as well?

Lewton eschewed the obvious, his assertion being it was the monster *unseen* that truly frightened. Director Jacques Tourneur, who had seemingly inherited much of his filmmaker father Maurice's aesthetic talent and was fresh from his success with the popular *Nick Carter* detective series, shared Lewton's vision. Together, aided by a solid production team, the two created a minor masterpiece hailed by audiences and critics alike. Produced for a mere $135,000 and shot in a frenzied 22 days (five days over schedule!) on the scavenged sets of Orson Welles' *The Magnificent Ambersons* (1942), RKO's gamble paid off to the tune of over four million dollars in box-office receipts.

Much more than the sum of its parts, there are myriad highlights in *Cat People*. First, there is the "bus stop walk" where Irena follows after Alice, their matched pairs of clicking heels providing a terrific counterpoint until suddenly…there is only one set of footsteps. We imagine the stealthy, silent step of a panther trailing along, and our tension grows as Alice's pace increases, rushing away from her unseen predator. Tourneur then provides one of horror's first aural jump scares with the startling hiss of the bus brakes as it pulls up. Later, the equally famous swimming pool scene appears, a masterpiece of suspense, showing the audience just enough to keep us terrified. With the echoes of Alice's panicked breathing, the reflected light from the pool's surface shimmers off the walls and ceiling, and ultimately, the reverberated growls and Alice's subsequent ear-shattering screams erupt. This is a flawlessly constructed sequence, a model for today's would-be horrormeisters to emulate.

The next jewel in the crown occurs in the layout department where Oliver and Alice are cornered. As the panther (inserted at the insistence of Lewton's superiors) closes in on them, a now convinced Oliver cries out, "Irena, leave us!" On the verge of committing Irena to the booby hatch just moments before, the former skeptics now plaintively appeal to a giant cat for mercy. This dramatic shift registers strongly with viewers. Despite having never seen her actually transform (à la Chaney, Jr.'s celebrated metamorphosis, one year earlier), we are convinced that this is Irena, jealously defending her territory against a potential romantic interloper. The use of a T-square as a makeshift cross that drives the menace away might raise a few eyebrows (is this a Transylvanian panther?), but the firmly committed players sell the hokum admirably.

The final showstopper occurs when Dr. Louis Judd seduces Irena, attempting to prove that her sexual feelings are harmless (and it seems he would like nothing better than to pinch-hit for Oliver's desire for matrimonial consummation... all in the name of psychiatry, of course). With a simple shift in lighting, we absolutely buy Irena's transformation. A fierce battle ensues, much of it played out through the combatants' struggling shadows on the wall (an effect that would show up again three years later in Lewton's *The Body Snatcher*). Shadows play an important role throughout *Cat People*, as Irena is often seen fading in and out of them, in the same manner that we suspect she fades in and out of her panther guise.

Without a doubt, alongside Lewton and Tourneur, the main attraction of *Cat People* is the stunning Simone Simon as Irena; with her exotic French accent she laps up dialogue like a bowl of milk. (All right, she's supposed to be Serbian, but who's keeping score?) With a striking combination of tender childlike features and dark, predatory poses, she captures perfectly the essence of the cursed character. Sexy without being slutty, strong yet fragile, Simon is hypnotically watchable, lodging in our minds even when she is not onscreen. She also provides the voice for Elizabeth Russell's cat-lady, lending her words of "*Moja sestra* (my sister)" a creepy subliminal resonance.

Jane Randolph is superb as Alice, an obviously attractive lass whose playful forthright banter makes her an ideal gal pal. Like Oliver, we are drawn to her, yet remain just as intrigued by Irena. It's a marvelous tactic by Lewton and Co., dividing our alliances such that there are no villains, only victims. As Oliver, Kent Smith is a little stiff at times but still comes off as a solid character, the vanilla to set off Simon's spice. The only nefarious one in the group is Tom Conway's deliciously arrogant and smarmy Dr. Judd (Conway would return to Lewton's stable in two other films, *I Walked With a Zombie* and *The Seventh Victim* [both 1943]). When Irena turns on him, we watch with glee as he struggles, cringing only when he fatally wounds *her* with his sword-cane.

If not for the clues that Tourneur leaves behind, such as the animal tracks that turn into those of a woman's high heels (a neat trick, as Irena doesn't have to worry about where to stash her wardrobe; it apparently just comes along for the ride), we might be inclined to wonder whether it is in fact all in Irena's mind. The shots of the panther among the drafting tables and in the battle with Dr. Judd are the only unequivocal giveaways. I have often wondered, as Lewton must have, whether it was necessary to specify whether Irena physically changes into a beast. With a few edits, the explicitness would be gone and yet the film would remain just as effective, without ever letting the cat out of the proverbial bag.

CHILD'S PLAY (1988)
by Lucas Matheson

Child's Play introduces one of the most iconic villains of the horror universe. Let's recount those striking features: Two-foot tall, red hair, freckles, sky blue eyes, cute little outfit, and a devilishly, smart-mouthed manner. Oh yeah, it's the "Good Guy" doll known as Chucky, who like many '80s horror icons went on to spawn a rather successful (and still growing) franchise. His humble roots began in 1988 when the collaboration between director Tom Holland, producer/designer David Kirschner and writer Don Mancini resulted in United Artists' *Child's Play*. For some fans, the late '80s were a time when quality horror flicks were at a real low point. But upon reflection, it was simply a different breed of horror, where the flavor had changed to cheesy and gruesome fun. Let's examine this minor modern horror classic/box office hit (roughly over $44 million worldwide) that changed the way we looked at childhood toys.

Just thinking about the lifeless expressions on dolls, with their beady eyes following us around the room, can make anyone shiver. This is one factor that drew producer Kirschner to the project, who remembered "being frightened by my sister's dolls when I was very little." Meanwhile, Mancini came up with his basic story idea while in college in the mid-'80s: "Cabbage Patch dolls were very popular at the time; being a lifelong horror fan, I realized that the venerable 'killer doll' concept was ripe for updating, especially since that in the wake of movies like *Gremlins*, animatronic puppet effects had advanced to the point where you could now treat the doll as a full-fledged character, with a vivid personality and lengthy dialogue scenes."

My introduction to the series happened to be Ronny Yu's darkly comic *Bride of Chucky* (1998), so when I finally got my hands on the original flick, I was expecting a comedy as well. Whoops, how wrong was I? Holland crafted an extremely chilling little picture that benefits highly from its tongue-in-cheek approach, avoiding broad humor and in-jokes. However, the franchise moved with the times, evolving from its simple, serious-minded slasher origins to the "slay and joke about it, wink, wink" attitude of the later *Chucky* films. The original *Child's Play* is by far still the best of the lot, and a trendsetter for lesser imitators (the *Puppet Master* and *Demonic Toys* flicks).

The story centers on Andy Barlow (Alex Vincent), a six-year-old boy who joyously receives a Good Guy doll named Chucky as a birthday gift from his overworked single mother (Catherine Hicks). However, when people soon start meeting horrible bloody ends, guess who just happens to be there when this occurs? Well, Andy and Chucky, of course. Detective Mick Norris (Chris Sarandon) believes Andy has something to do with the deaths, but Andy maintains that his doll is committing the murders, possessed by the soul of serial killer Charles Lee Ray (Brad Dourif). Of course, while Andy's story is dismissed as lies, we the audience know his unlikely tale to be the truth. To add to the horror, Chucky has plans to use Andy as a way to return to human form.

Andy (Alex Vincent) and Good Guy doll Chucky

How about that for a premise? Incredibly silly and rehashed (*Dead of Night* [1945], *Trilogy of Terror* [1975], and *Twilight Zone* episodes) B-grade material, but it's so well made and slickly directed, audiences can't help but go along with the flow and enjoy the clever thrills. Director Holland knows how to pull out a bluff, only to catch us off guard with the real scare. The film grips you tight, really tight, with its controlled suspense, precise timing, and confident, fine-tuned performances.

Audiences might think credibility would be thrown right out the window, but the horror within is so atmospherically eerie, the viewer forgets how ludicrous and cliché some plot devices are. While the idea seems ridiculous, Holland and Mancini voted against treating it as such. The script (also contributed to by John Lafia, who would direct the first sequel) doesn't limit itself entirely to playing it straight, as there are numerous witty stabs of dark humor streaming through it. But according to Mancini, this morbidly comic streak is thanks mainly to Holland, who had written and/or co-written such films as *The Beast Within* (1982), *Class of 1984* (1982), *Psycho II* (1983), and *Fright Night* (1985). The humorous element doesn't detract from the film's unnerving factor drummed out by Mancini's enterprising storyline, involving diverse facets of commercialism, voodoo, possession, family bonds, and loneliness. Quite a handful, but Mancini managed to distill a suspenseful and taut script, ably assisted by Holland's energetic verve.

As the viewer, we sit there knowing that it's the doll causing the havoc, with poor little Andy being blamed, and we want to tell the long list of non-believers so. Originally though, this wasn't the case. In his original draft, Mancini had the idea that he would mess around with the audience, making them think Andy might be the killer. In the finished film, however, things are pretty clear from the get-go.

While Holland's sharp direction is impressive, another key player in the film's success is that of designer/controller Kevin Yagher's inspired special effects, bringing the Chucky doll to screaming life. As many as nine separate figures were made with a range of different actions to perform. Nine puppeteers (including Yagher) operated the doll (although in some scenes we can clearly tell that it is a tiny person in costume). According to the DVD liner notes, "Chucky's wide range of frightening expressions were made possible by 17 small motors operated by three puppeteers using remote control units. Two puppeteers operated the arms, one the hands, another the head and the lead puppeteer controlled the body and directed the others." Yagher and his team's grueling efforts to get Chucky's complicated figure working ultimately pay off time and again. In one of many cracking scenes, Andy's mother irrefutably learns the doll has a life of its own (after discovering the batteries still in the box). Chilling stuff!

While the f/x team gave it life, it was Chucky's personality that a lot people took a shine to, with much of the credit going to Brad Dourif's vocal performance as the demonic doll. "Brad is indispensable—a great actor who has made the role his own," recalls Mancini. "I think he built on some of the stuff I had in my original script, which Tom Holland amplified a little in his version of the film. He [Brad] amplified the dark, sarcastic sense of humor that Chucky has." In the opening scenes, Dourif is seen fleeing the authorities as mass murderer Charles Lee Ray, (derived from the names of ill-famed murderers Charles Manson, Lee Harvey Oswald, and James Earl Ray). But from the moment his onscreen character transferred his soul into the Good Guy doll, Chucky instantly became the versatile actor's benchmark role. With that wickedly dry voice and venomous tinge, Dourif succeeds in making Chucky a (somewhat) endearing cult character despite his sadistic turns.

Alex Vincent, while very raw and cutesy at times as Andy, portrays his character genuinely and quickly gains our sympathy. Catherine Hicks plays Karen Barlow superbly as a fragile and emotionally charged character struggling with the possibility of losing her son. The supporting roles of Chris Sarandon, Jack Santos, Maggie Peterson, and Jack Colvin are all well grounded, with the charming Sarandon great as the skeptical detective.

Among the other facets contributing to the gripping and haunting experience are Joe Renzetti's understated score, stringing along a somber tone with uncanny sounds and music cues. The dreary urban environment is also part of the film's character and is laid on thick, as we feel the cold wintry air of Chicago take hold. Bill Butler's polished and rather fluid photography adds to the atmosphere with plenty of inventive POV shots. The way some sequences were framed (the shots of Chucky's legs as he's sneaking about, for example) reminds one very much of the British 1964 cult horror flick *Devil Doll*. If there is a weak point, it is in the film's final 10 minutes where one climax is piled onto another, until reaching the outrageous finale. However, the rollercoaster-like, pressure-packed experience manages to remain fun and quite spooky. And how to end it? Well, the door is *literally* left open for a sequel.

CREATURE FROM THE BLACK LAGOON (1954)
by M. Binning

The captured Creature (Ben Chapman/Ricou Browning) gasps for breath.

Creature from the Black Lagoon tells the story of a scientific expedition into the Amazon, which soon turns into a desperate struggle for survival when the hunters become the hunted. David Reed (Richard Carlson) and his beautiful fiancée Kay (Julia Adams) are conducting underwater research when they are approached by a fellow scientist. The colleague reveals that he has unearthed an ancient fossilized hand which appears to have belonged to a prehistoric amphibian and a research team is swiftly put together to find the rest of the fossilized remains. Among the team's members are the head of the department, Mark Williams (Richard Denning), and Lucas (Nestor Paiva), the captain of the ship who speaks of a "black lagoon," a paradise from which no man has ever returned. Upon following a remote Amazonian river into the lagoon, they discover far more than they bargained for: The prehistoric creature is still alive... and looking for companionship. Setting its sights on Kay (after observing her in a beautifully photographed swimming sequence), the lovesick creature blocks the exit to the lagoon. What ensues is a frantic battle for survival, combined with conflicts of personal interest, and a bizarre tale of unrequited love, in one of the most chilling, yet endearing, stories ever told.

This Universal film was directed by Jack Arnold, a highly acclaimed director in the era of '50s monster movies with a filmography that includes *It Came from Outer Space* (1953), *Tarantula* (1955), and *The Incredible Shrinking Man* (1957), all pictures that deal with exploration of the unknown. However, *Creature from the Black Lagoon* is probably the most renowned of his films due to its breathtaking cinematography, one of the most recognizable music scores in horror movie history, and for the monster itself.

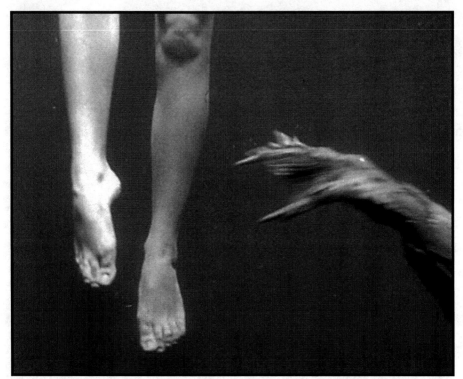

The Creature is just inches away from grabbing Kay's (Julia Adams) legs.

While quintessentially just a man in a rubber suit, the titular creature has achieved iconic status and is recognized as one of the classic Universal monsters alongside the ilk of Dracula, Frankenstein's Monster, The Mummy, and The Wolf Man.

The movie was originally photographed in 3-D, and is also unique for being the first underwater 3-D film. Ricou Browning, a professional swimmer and diver, plays the creature in the underwater sequences, while Ben Chapman dons the fish face and flippers on land. The success of the film spawned two sequels: *Revenge of the Creature* (1955) and *The Creature Walks Among Us* (1956). The former tells the story of the creature being captured, brought to an aquarium, and being attracted to a female researcher, while the latter entails the unfortunate Gill Man being surgically altered so as to no longer be able to breathe underwater, while simultaneously being caught up in a love triangle. As is often the case, the sequels, although entertaining, are not nearly as innovative or involving as the original film.

The differing perceptions people hold are the key to *Creature*'s magic and continued success. In my case, as it was made 32 years before I was born, I first saw it almost half a century after the initial release. The one thing that I regrettably missed out on was viewing this extraordinary effort in its original 3-D format. However, seeing it in simple black and white is hardly anything to complain about; in fact it becomes even more breathtaking, with the excellent use of light and shadow amid the backdrop of the unexplored Amazon. The black and white medium also helps us forget that we are watching a '50s monster movie, evoking instead the folkloric essence of the 1930s classics.

William E. Snyder's cinematography is simply awe-inspiring: from the imagery of the ferocious waves accompanying the opening narration, to the breathtaking depiction of the mysterious Amazon, to the poetic yet thrilling underwater sequences. These scenes are complemented perfectly by the menacing and powerful score, created by some of the studio's greatest composers including the legendary Henry Mancini and Herman Stein. We hear it at intervals alongside abrupt glimpses of the creature, gradually becoming louder and more sinister toward the finale, mirroring our growing sense of dread and fear.

Ultimately, the film works for me as a result of its simple-yet-complex storyline. On the surface, it seems like a typical B-movie plot (i.e. "a group of scientists battle with a monster"), but much more is to be found within its 79-minute running time. There is the exploration of the unknown, the notion of man's curiosity knowing no bounds, and an analysis of themes that include evolution, science, greed, and love. Above all, however, the question arises as to why is it that the "monstrous" creature evokes sympathy from the viewers? Why is it that, although the lives of the human team are in danger, it is the creature's welfare that we are most nervous for?

I personally find the creature endearing because he unwillingly becomes the victim of a tragic "beauty and the beast" tale, akin to that of *King Kong* (1933). When David and Mark initially go diving in the lagoon, the creature observes them from a distance. However, when Kay takes a swim, we bear witness to one of the most breathtaking (yet in hindsight, heartbreaking) scenes in cinematic history, as the creature swims beneath her, admiring her beauty and grace. It is this moment that leads to the creature's downfall, just as Kong's first vision of Ann Darrow led to his. The Gill Man makes his existence known, leading to his uncertain yet ominous fate. (I say uncertain because although he appears to die, he is resurrected for the sequels in the time-honored Universal tradition.)

Framing this doomed love story is the conflict between David and Mark, which ultimately conveys the battle between righteousness and self-righteousness. David's motivations are made clear when he says that the team is "out for photographs, for study, not trophies. This thing, alive and in its natural habitat, is valuable to us," contrasted with Mark's response of, "Why settle for a photo when we can get the real thing?" Later, as the stakes rise, Mark's self-serving "We must have the proof!" is met with David's retort, "We are trapped and fighting for our lives and you are worried about whether people will believe us?" Mark's greedy attitude and desire for fame and glory are illustrated as immoral, and when he gets his inevitable comeuppance, no genre fan is surprised. The film does not solely entertain, but also echoes truths about the nature of man, truths which are clearly emphasized in its powerful, heart-wrenching ending.

Creature from the Black Lagoon is one of the most popular and influential Universal movies, an absolute must-see for any fan of the genre. A most notable homage appears in Steven Spielberg's *Jaws* (1975), which incorporates elements of its forbearer's underwater swimming scenes in its equally famous opening sequence.

Even after half a century, *Creature from the Black Lagoon* has lost none of its magic and is still as admired and appreciated today as it was back in the '50s. There is currently a remake in the works and, regardless of how it turns out, it will undoubtedly raise awareness of this cult classic for modern audiences. Although the creature was the last of Universal's classic monsters, he is by no means least. He embodies elements of all his predecessors. Like Frankenstein's Monster, he is a savage killer yet displays great appreciation for beauty and longs for female companionship. Like Dracula, he abducts his female victims, bringing them to his otherworldly lair. Like The Mummy, he lived ages before and has witnessed the rest of the world evolving while his has stood still, and like The Wolf Man, he is only half a man, a rare and lost species that does not seem to belong. However, despite these similarities, he is wholly unique; a missing link between man and fish, an anomaly of evolution, a mystery from the deep.

THE CURSE OF FRANKENSTEIN (1957)
by Sven Soetemans

Although perhaps not Hammer's finest production, *The Curse of Frankenstein* is the one film (along with their 1958 follow-up, *Horror of Dracula*) that single-handedly regenerated the European horror-boom in the second half of the 1950s. Approximately two decades after the heyday of the immensely popular Universal monster movies, Hammer Films gained their first success in the sci-fi/horror arena with 1955's *The Quatermass Experiment*, a big-screen adaptation of Nigel Kneale's TV sensation. The popular and critical success of *Quatermass*, and its follow-up, *Quatermass 2 (*aka *Enemy from Space)* the following year, indicated to Hammer Film Productions heads that there was clearly an insatiable audience hungering for morbid tales and horrific effects. In an effort to capitalize on this demand, they eventually hit upon the notion of updating Universal's famous franchises, only this time *in color.* They began with *Frankenstein* in 1957, with *Dracula* and *The Mummy* immediately following in the next few years.

Working from a script by Jimmy Sangster and directed by Terence Fisher (both of whom would produce numerous memorable horror/thriller offerings for Hammer), *The Curse of Frankenstein* revives the basic premise of Mary Shelley's classic story while adding numerous horrific aspects that would become trademarks of Hammer. For example, the scenes in Frankenstein's lab featured blood and gore the likes of which had not been seen before, all in full Eastmancolor glory. In addition, the creature's makeup (designed by Phil Leakey) is for the first time on film truly monstrous. (Admittedly, this is also due to the fact that Jack Pierce's original monster design, worn by the legendary Boris Karloff, was copyright protected and not allowed to be imitated.)

Hammer's implementation of these and other minor modifications clearly indicated that their interpretation of the genre was to be much more brutal and spectacular. Pushing the boundaries of onscreen flesh and blood, they appealed to a new generation of fans. Sufficed to say, the success was immense and sequels to both the *Frankenstein* and *Dracula* franchise were quickly released as well as other new, original horror tales. For nearly 20 years, Hammer set the tone of pretty much everything that concerned horror in Europe.

The Curse of Frankenstein stars Peter Cushing as the obsessive and dangerously devoted Baron/scientist, a role he would reprise several times (five, to be exact). Today, more than a decade after his death, Cushing is still revered as a legendary icon of the horror genre, and much of it is due to his indelible stamp as the obsessed Victor Frankenstein.

Here, the morality-lesson that "nobody is entitled to play God and create life himself" is not excessively emphasized as in the majority of other *Frankenstein* adaptations.

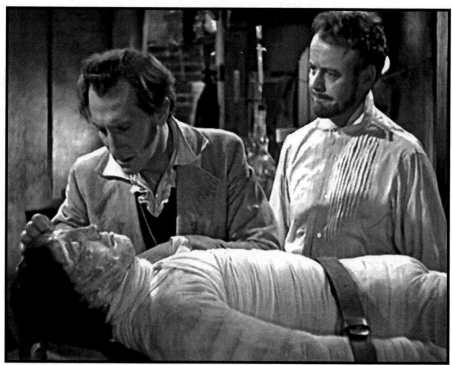
Peter Cushing as Baron Frankenstein, Robert Urquhart as Dr. Krempe, and Christopher Lee as the Creature

The film opens with images of the degraded Baron sitting in a filthy prison cell, clarifying his life-story to a priest. Orphaned at a young age, the wealthy and intellectually gifted Victor Frankenstein works together with his mentor Dr. Paul Krempe (Robert Urquhart) in the field of re-animating dead tissue and brain activity. After the two reach a medical breakthrough, Frankenstein wants to take his experiments to a higher level and create entirely new life by assembling various body parts of deceased persons. Since not every part of his ideal creation is easily available (like, for example, an intelligent brain), Frankenstein turns to murder.

When Victor commits his first murder, exclusively to procure the brain of his former professor, everything changes. Without realizing it, he descends into madness, no longer able to see the difference between science and moral corruption. Driven by blind obsession, Victor alienates Paul and neglects his loving fiancée Elizabeth (Hazel Court). Victor continues his experiments undeterred, and the creature he eventually brings to life is an aggressive, hideous-looking monster that doesn't hesitate to attack its creator. Eventually, the monster escapes, is killed, and resurrected a second time. Frankenstein ends up battling it out with the monster on the rooftop, eventually setting it ablaze with an oil lamp. The creature then falls into a vat of acid, destroyed without a trace. Of course, with the monster gone, Frankenstein is left to explain the murders, a task made impossible when Paul and Elizabeth refuse to corroborate his story. Back in the prison, the priest cannot offer Victor any salvation, and the movie ends with the once-prominent heir of the Frankenstein fortune walking towards the guillotine.

I initially stated that *Curse* isn't Hammer's finest film. Some of their later horrors, notably *Quatermass and the Pit* (1967), *The Devil Rides Out* (1968), and even some of the *Frankenstein* sequels look more appealing, more properly orchestrated. The reasons for this, however, are primarily monetary. The budget for *Curse of Frankenstein* was quite low (a mere £65,000), resulting in occasionally tacky special effects by today's standards, with a notable lack of diversity in scenery. The movie's action takes place largely in one location—the Baron's laboratory—simply because no money existed for other sets! The limited budget is also noticeable in the absence of a vast Gothic atmosphere (despite production designer wunderkind Bernard Robinson's best efforts) and the modest use of color-shades.

However, *The Curse of Frankenstein* remains a milestone in the genre, with some great suspense and a truly powerful acting performance by Peter Cushing. Additionally, the film is significant for an entirely different reason, as it represents the first of many onscreen collaborations between Cushing and Christopher Lee. (Both appeared in Laurence Olivier's *Hamlet* [1948], and John Huston's *Moulin Rouge* [1952], although not in the same scenes.) The duo would eventually turn out 19 features together. As the monster, Lee's participation in this production is very brief but oh-so-memorable, and Leakey's makeup effects still look nightmarish nearly half a century later. Real fans of the genre freely acknowledge that *The Curse of Frankenstein* is a genuine classic that set the Hammer standard for many years and wonders to come.

DAWN OF THE DEAD (1978)
DAY OF THE DEAD (1985)
by Laurent Kleinblatt

One of Tom Savini's zombies emerges from a mall elevator in *Dawn of the Dead.*

The dead are rising, killing, and eating everyone in their way, destroying mankind itself. *Dawn of the Dead* and *Day of the Dead* both tell the story of surviving groups of humans in different situations (*Dawn* is mainly situated in an abandoned shopping mall, while *Day* features scientists and soldiers in an underground military base).

While it's obvious that *Day of the Dead* was made as a direct result of the success of *Dawn of the Dead*, what is less known is how George A. Romero came to create a sequel to his enormously influential and groundbreaking zombie film, *Night of the Living Dead* (1968).

The official story goes that Romero was visiting the shopping mall in Monroeville, PA with a friend (whose company was running the mall in question) in 1974. During this visit, he saw lesser known parts of the mall, parts that weren't accessible to the general public, which he thought would prove very useful in the event of a catastrophe. Romero's mind went to his zombies…imagining them as materialistic consumers…all of which eventually led to the script of *Dawn* with its social commentaries and a very fitting survival theme. The rest is history…

Dawn of the Dead was immediately met with resounding critical acclaim. It was so successful at the box office (grossing $900,000 in the first week despite its limited release, and eventually earning $55 million worldwide, on a budget of $500,000) that many other filmmakers tried to cash in on its success, the most famous example being Lucio Fulci's movie *Zombie* (also known as *Zombi 2* [1979]). *Dawn of the Dead* is widely regarded as being one of the best horror movies of all time, even finding a spot on Roger Ebert's "Great Films" list.

Day of the Dead, on the other hand, was deemed a failure when released, its only redeeming factor the brilliant makeup effects by Tom Savini, also responsible for the gore in *Dawn*. Often cited is the fact that the original budget of $7,000,000 (by no means a princely sum) was cut *in half* during shooting due to Romero's refusal to trim the more gruesome scenes in order to receive an R rating from the MPAA. (Romero's original, more ambitious script for *Day* can still be found on various sites on the Internet, with many horror fans opining that if that script could have been used, the movie probably would have been much better.) However, the film's reputation, like its undead masses, has been revived in recent years. Many fans reject the movie's initial status as a "failure," now regarding it as a worthy companion to the two previous *Dead* movies. Indeed, I personally consider *Day of the Dead* the best of the series.

Dawn of the Dead was the first movie of Romero's series that I saw. I was 18 and, to be honest, didn't like it very much. I found it boring, not frightening, and not very well made. In retrospect, I suppose my discontent stemmed from it not being what I expected. Like most teenage horror fans, I thought that being a "good" horror movie meant that you'd get scared, and in the case of *Dawn*, I was more preoccupied with *not* being terrified than in realizing just how interesting the movie was. Since everyone kept saying how good it was, I viewed it again a few months later to see what I'd missed, and was quite simply blown away. I realized that zombie movies (and horror films in general) could be more about psychology and sociology than about cheap scares. While I still believe that *Dawn* is far from scary in a straightforward way, what is unnerving are the ideas behind it, that danger often comes from ourselves more than from the monsters. *Dawn* makes the comment that in many cases the monsters are (to quote one of *Dawn*'s characters), in fact, us. Besides, Romero's vision of a society wherein people no longer respect the law, nor each other, is a chilling one, one where people can't rely on anything anymore. Scary stuff, indeed.

I'm not an unconditional convert to the movie, as some parts are still a bit over-the-top (the pie throwing, for example) for my tastes, but *Dawn* will always be the movie that made me realize that I could seek out more than cheap thrills from a horror film.

The first time I saw *Day of the Dead*, it was on a Belgian TV program where they show bad horror flicks. The movie was still considered a complete failure at that time, and I admit I hated it too. Then, two years ago, I bought a box set containing the complete *Dead* trilogy, and my girlfriend and I decided to watch all three movies in a row. To my dismay, she admitted that she had been a bit disappointed by the first two. Then came the incredible opening sequence in *Day*, and we both got scared as hell. (My girlfriend even suffered a muscle injury from the shock!) From then on, we were so captivated that I still don't understand my previous disenchantment. Yes, it's mostly a dialogue-driven film, with the zombies featured primarily at the beginning and the end. But the script is intelligent, and the zombie scenes and effects are some of the best ever. After multiple viewings, to this day we still both get jump-scares from that well-timed opening scene, making it the only jump-scare in history that keeps working (for us).

While *Dawn of the Dead* and *Day of the Dead* are parts of the same series, and even made by the same team, these are very different movies, especially in tone. *Dawn* is set at the moment of the breakdown of society; people are panicked, but exalted too, which is why the tone is quite upbeat and sometimes even comical. *Day* focuses on a small group of grim and depressed survivors, who have been isolated for a long time, gradually causing them to break down mentally, emotionally, and spiritually. The fact that almost all the action occurs in an underground bunker only emphasizes the feeling of confinement and isolation…

In the case of *Dawn of the Dead*, the movie was made in the consumerist '70s, and this became a key theme of the movie. It certainly isn't a coincidence that the main action happens in a shopping mall, and various attempts are made to show that, in life, the primary focus of the now walking dead was shopping. ("They come here because this place was very important in their life," says one of the surviving humans.) Another recurring Romero theme included in *Dawn* is the fact that the threat doesn't come from the zombies as much as from the humans themselves. It is often only when humans make mistakes (such as when the blond soldier Roger [Scott H. Reiniger] becomes reckless in the truck sequence and gets bitten) or fail to cooperate (the conflict between the quartet of survivors and the mall-raiding bikers) that their undead antagonists are able to catch up with them.

Day of the Dead was made during Reagan's presidency, a time where militarism was very lively, so Romero focuses on this. Most people consider *Day* as being purely a criticism of the military, which is a logical conclusion, since the military characters are depicted as aggressive, stupid, and short-tempered. But what many people fail to realize is that as vivid as the anti-militaristic approach is, the film also functions as a comment on Western society's blind belief in science. Due to the fact that we are led to sympathize with our main character Sarah (Lori Cardille), who happens to be a scientist, this aspect is often overlooked.

To my mind, the military is completely justified in getting angry at the scientists, as their experiments to this point have yielded nothing, while the soldiers continue to

Sarah (Lori Cardille) flees the zombie arms from *Day of the Dead*.

risk their lives. True, the scientists are searching for a cure for zombieism, but with the equipment they have, it's highly improbable they will ever find anything, and even if they do, what good would it do in a world that has completely been wiped out? Also, the work of Dr. Logan (Richard Liberty), aka "Dr. Frankenstein," is seemingly pointless. We see how much effort it takes to train one zombie, and with billions of others out there, how could a few living people ever be able to perform such a task? Still, the scientists continue their research, because they don't know what else to do, risking their lives—and the lives of the military—for nothing. The voice of reason here is the common man, the pilot John (Terry Alexander), who suggests the only logical way out: Simply start again on a deserted island, and never come back to the old civilization.

Another element of *Day of the Dead* (later expanded in 2005's *Land of the Dead*) is the concept of the evolving undead. Indeed, one of the most engaging characters in *Day* is Logan's star zombie pupil, "Bub," a zombie to whom Logan has taught tricks. Wonderfully played by Howard Sherman, Bub is in fact the only flesh-eater in Romero's universe to have an actual line of dialogue. ("Hello… Aunt… Alicia.")

However, nobody's perfect. Both films, while great achievements, contain flaws for almost the same reasons:

Bad acting: I can't find one good actor in either movie, the best being Howard Sherman's inspired portrayal of Bub in *Day of the Dead*.

The Ending: *Dawn* always disappointed me with its lack of a satisfying conclusion (I'd probably prefer them all to die). The ending leaves uncertainty, which can be good at times, but in this case just doesn't work for me. This is still considerably better than the ending of *Day*, which is just plain awful. (And this is my favorite of the series!) While escaping the bunker, they flee to a helicopter, where a zombie grabs Sarah. But then we find out this didn't really happen (or did it?), as Sarah wakes up from a dream on a deserted island where the survivors have flown. Now, especially when we factor in that Romero's budget was cut because he didn't want to compromise his artistic vision for the sake of an MPAA rating, this is truly disappointing. Why, having made that gutsy choice, *why* would you ruin your film by putting in a final scene that sours everything? I'm still trying to figure that one out.

However, the rest is irreproachable.

I'd like to make a special mention of the highly lauded music used in *Dawn of the Dead*, provided by Italian filmmaker Dario Argento's band The Goblins. Argento (who served as producer for the movie) also made a special European cut of the movie, in which he trimmed 20 minutes off the film's running time, making it gorier and bloodier. I personally consider this the more successful cut, as it removes scenes that I find unnecessary (such as the *awful* refueling scene).

John Harrison's score for *Day of the Dead*, by contrast, is usually considered by horror fans as below par, an assessment with which I disagree. Granted, the music is minimalistic and definitely of the '80s, but I actually like it very much. Harrison's darker tones add considerably to the nihilistic, oppressive feel of the movie.

Of course, a zombie movie often rises or falls on its special effects, and *Day of the Dead* boasts some of the best gore and makeup designs ever. Tom Savini's work here is absolutely stunning! *Dawn of the Dead*'s effects are also good, but not *quite* as impressive. Most of the zombies in *Dawn* are just people with blue paint over their faces and arms, some with occasional flesh wounds, with only the featured zombies getting extensive makeup (though Savini's work on these select few is quite admirable). The practical (no CGI here) effects are great. One of the best examples is the zombie that gets its head mangled by a helicopter rotor, a gag that is brilliantly (pardon the expression) executed.

In conclusion, these are two great films, but then again, they wouldn't be in this book if they weren't.

DEAD OF NIGHT (1945)
by Chris Benedict

Between 1939 and 1945, no horror movies were shown on the island of Great Britain. Horror movies had always had a tough slog in England—some of the horror movies that weren't banned outright were often edited beyond recognition. Horror movies that were banned in England outright included *Freaks* (1932), *Murders in the Rue Morgue* (1932), and *Island of Lost Souls* (1933). In fact, *Freaks* remained unseen in England until 40 years after its release. So it's no surprise that the British Board of Film Censors would ban horror movies en masse during the war years. Britain produced relatively few horror movies during the Golden Age of 1930s horror to begin with. That began to change when the war ended.

Dead of Night was the first British horror movie to be produced following the war, and as such, it is a landmark of sorts. It is also the prototype for the anthology film, in which a number of short films are gathered together under a single heading. *Dead of Night* ties its various stories together with a framing sequence. The anthology movie would later become a specialty of British horror filmmaking under the aegis of Amicus Productions, among other fly-by-night operations. *Dead of Night*'s studio pedigree is

During the surreal montage finale, ghastly images bombard poor Walter Craig (Mervyn Johns).

a bit more rarified. It was produced by Ealing Studios and directed by several of the studio's top hands—Alberto Cavalcanti, Robert Hamer, Charles Crichton, and Basil Dearden. Ealing is best known for the comedies it produced in the following decade and the directors of *Dead of Night* went on to make such droll films as *Kind Hearts and Coronets* (1949), *The Lavender Hill Mob* (1951), and *The Titfield Thunderbolt* (1953). At least one segment of *Dead of Night*—the golfing story—prefigures the great Ealing comedies, but otherwise, the film couldn't be more different. The uniformity of the film's various segments and their integration into an organic whole suggests that the guiding hand behind the picture was producer Michael Balcon, who, of course, signed his name to all of those great Ealing films.

As with all anthology movies, the quality of the stories varies. Two of the stories—the first two—are barely more than anecdotes. They are the sort of brushes with the uncanny that people can relate to second hand, though the culmination of the "hearse story," with its cheerful driver declaring that there's "room for one more inside," sticks in the memory, and the weeping child in the "Christmas" story provides a certain amount of creepiness. The third segment is a full-on horror story about a haunted mirror that reflects a dark reality in the minds of the couple who gaze into it. This segment, directed by Robert Hamer, is a model of filmmaking control as the stately photography that opens the story gives way to wild invention as it climaxes. The oblique approach to horror-on-display in this segment plays with the audience's perceptions and demonstrates the ever-widening influence of the Val Lewton movies from earlier in the decade.

The golfing story, contributed by H.G. Wells of all people, acts as comedy relief and as set-up for the film's final blaze of glory. This story is the one that most fans of the film dislike, in part because it breaks the spell of the previous segment, but also because it seems a bit too genteel. The plot finds a pair of golfers breaking their friendship over a woman, but it's the fact that one golfer cheats on the links that causes the other to haunt him from beyond the grave. While this story is generally disliked, it performs a function within the overall movie of tempering the horror of the preceding story while providing a stark contrast with the next. More than that, though, it's emblematic of the kind of ghost stories to which audiences of the day were accustomed. It's only a short step from this story to Cary Grant and Constance Bennett in *Topper* (1937) or Bud Abbott and Lou Costello in *The Time of Their Lives* (1946). Serious ghost stories were relatively rare in the 1940s.

The final story, in which Michael Redgrave plays a tormented ventriloquist whose dummy wants to move on to greener pastures, is the segment that everyone seems to remember. Unlike the other stories, there is only a small breath of other worlds in this segment. It is more a psychological tale than a ghost story—its narrator is a psychologist, no less—and is more dependent on its central performance than the other stories. In this, the movie is fortunate, because Redgrave is superb. As a portrait of psychological disintegration, his performance is wonderfully nuanced. That all said, the story suggests a supernatural world at a couple of points, and here, the segment's reticence pays dividends. Those hints manage to tickle the hindbrain. What is most striking about this segment is the way that it prefigures *Psycho* (1960). The elements are all in place: the split personality, the psychological exegesis at the end, and—most importantly—the final shot of our imprisoned lunatic, grinning a hideous grin at the camera. Hitchcock wasn't above swiping things—he appropriated the pet store sequence from Lewton's *Cat People* for *The Birds*, for example—so it's not a stretch to suggest that Hitch swiped this, too.

Unlike most anthology movies, where the framing sequences are often the weak link regardless of the relative excellence of the stories, *Dead of Night*'s framing sequence is integral to the success of the film. The various stories are told by the assembled guests to one Walter Craig (Mervyn Johns), an architect who has been summoned to a country house. Craig has a sense of *déjà vu* about the whole thing, as if he has dreamed the events of his visit. Ominously, he knows that horror lurks at the end of his visit. The climax of Craig's experience finds him moving through a nightmare world composed of bits and pieces of the stories he has heard. And then he wakes up.

"And then he wakes up," is usually a cop out in horror movies. It is the crutch of timid filmmakers who refuse to stare for long into the abyss, or of screenwriters who have written themselves into a corner. *Dead of Night* certainly teeters on the brink of both possibilities, but virtually alone among films that use this device, it makes something of it beyond the dissipation of its unease. At the very least, the ending of *Dead of Night* is a case study in film theory. The *very* end of the movie is composed of the same shots that open the film. The filmmakers have changed but a single element—the score—but the context framed by the rest of the film dramatically changes the meaning of these shots.

This is cinematic sleight of hand of the first order, the sort of thing that the Russians pioneered in the 1920s when they placed an identical shot of an actor in juxtaposition with a bowl of food, a casket, and a baby, and saw the audience's perception of the actor's expression change with each new juxtaposition. At the end of *Dead of Night*, the music has changed from the airy tones that opened the film to ominous strains that underline the notion that we are now privy to Craig's *déjà vu*, having dreamed his dream with him. Thus, the film becomes a kind of cinematic möbius strip, in which time turns back on itself and we are presented with a world without end. Horror movies rarely suggest cosmologies, but the framers of the "Steady State" model of the universe (a rival to the "Big Bang" theory) cite *Dead of Night* as their inspiration. Is *Dead of Night* the world's first topological horror movie? It might be.

LES DIABOLIQUES (1955)
by Don Bapst

Nicole (Simone Signoret) dunks Michel (Paul Meurisse) in the tub.

Take two glamorous leading ladies and a wife-beater. Put them near a murky swimming pool and give them a bathtub with a leaky faucet. Throw in a bronze mantelpiece and a bottle of Johnnie Red laced with knockout drops, and we've got the recipe for terror that laid the groundwork for thousands of films to follow. No cleavers, no color. Just a couple of excellent performances and a lot of long, lingering attention to a couple of creepy details.

Les Diaboliques, promoted to U.S. and U.K. audiences in the '50s simply as *Diabolique*, has barely aged in the more than half-century since it first shocked audiences right out of their seats. Based loosely on the novel *She Who Was No More* by Pierre Boileau and Thomas Narcejac (who later penned the screenplay for *Eyes Without a Face* [1959]), the taut film has often been compared to Hitchcock's thrillers. Actually,

Hitchcock attempted to buy the rights to the novel, but director Henri-Georges Clouzot beat him to it by a couple of hours…or so the story goes.

Hitchcock would film another Boileau and Narcejac novel, *D'Entre Les Morts*, in 1958 as *Vertigo*, and many horror aficionados agree he took more than a little inspiration from *Les Diaboliques* for 1960's *Psycho*. But what the "master of suspense" accomplished with razor-sharp edits and violins, Clouzot did with no fancy cutting and hardly any music—save for that creepy title score by Georges Van Parys. The music plays for less than two minutes over the opening credits and only 24 seconds at the very end, but it stands as one of the earliest examples of just how creepy a kids' chorus can sound in harmony, particularly while staring at the seething surface of a pool filled with frothy, black funk, an image that foreshadows a body getting dumped in there…

First, though, bring on the babes. Not those scantily clad scream queens of American or Italian horror, just a bashful Brazilian and a frosty *femme française*. Véra Clouzot, the director's real life wife, plays Christina, the rich Spanish wife of Michel (played selflessly by Paul Meurisse), a womanizing headmaster, who only has his job at the all-boys boarding school with the stagnant swimming pool because his wife happens to own the place. A case of life imitating art perhaps? More on that later. In any case, Michel is pretty mean. At one point he tells his wife—in front of all the students—that it would be better for all of them if she were dead. No Hollywood sugarcoating here.

Meanwhile, enter Simone Signoret as Nicole, wearing a pair of seriously fabulous sunglasses. She's a teacher at the school, as well as Michel's mistress. We know it. Christina knows it. Even the boys at the school know it. The sunglasses, turns out, are covering a bruise, though Nicole, unlike Christina, isn't going to take Michel's slaps lying down. She's got a pack of Gitanes (or are they Gauloises?) and a pair of power pumps. And isn't that a Chanel she's wearing? And, hey, didn't Christina just look at her like she'd rather she wasn't wearing anything?

This is the stuff the French used to lure Americans to art houses in 1955, the same year Disneyland opened in California. That the film's director had worked for a Nazi propaganda production company during the occupation was all but forgotten now, though his reputation as a real tough cookie on the set got a bit of media attention. More on that later too.

So, anyway, mistress Nicole runs off with mean Michel's wife. Did I mention Christina has a heart condition? She's only a breath away from cardiac arrest when Michel threatens her over the phone. And we're only a third through the flick. From then on, Véra Clouzot's big, black, saucer eyes just keep getting bigger.

Nicole says they need to kill him. She pours out some of the Johnnie Walker into a glass—just enough to make room for the sleep serum—and drinks it straight from the glass without wincing. "No sense in wasting it," she shrugs. Women weren't supposed to drink whiskey in the 1950s, much less kill men in suits, and they certainly weren't supposed to look so stunning doing it. But Simone Signoret personified that icy *sang-froid* chic from across the pond, making her Stateside splash a full decade before Deneuve.

And speaking of splashes, let's get back to the ladies and the doped dope. They've dumped him in the bathtub. "Get the bronze," Nicole orders Christina, a seemingly filterless cigarette poised in one corner of her mouth. Christina gets the heavy statue off the mantel. Nicole drops it on top of him. It weighs him down as the water sloshes about. They cover him with a crinkly plastic tablecloth. Later they haul him into a squeaky Citroën in a rickety basket. There's no music, mind you, just these highly textural sound effects.

The tension between the two ladies by now is palpable, with Christina's whimpering getting on Nicole's last nerve. Seems the two actresses playing these characters despised each other in real life. But that's yet another story, and one that no one can confirm with any certainty since both actresses have long ago passed away.

Next follow the painfully long scenes of this pair struggling to get the dead body dumped into the seething swimming pool. Painful in that you're biting your nails down to bloody stumps. They encounter a nosy neighbor, a drunken soldier, a concerned guardian... Suddenly an impossibly bright bathroom light flashes from overhead just as they open the creaky basket to reveal a watery Michel, his eyes rolled back in his head to expose the whites...

It's these simple little details, dwelled on with clinically sterile precision, that make it all so real. Absent is any of the playfulness or morality that Hitchcock would later stir into the mix. *Les Diaboliques* is a high-definition closeup of the step-by-step details of one murder: From the misogynistic behavior that inspired it, to the planning and execution of the crime, right down to the dumping of the body in that black, frothy water. We even get to watch until the gurgling stops and the body settles, temporarily, at the bottom.

Then, like the ladies, we wait. And while we're waiting, this would be a nice time to point out that along with the leads in this picture, a few other famous French actors got their first big break in *Les Diaboliques*, including Michel Serrault, best known to American audiences as the lead in the original *La Cage aux Folles*, and French rocker Johnny Halliday, who plays one of the bourgeois kids running around the dark and slimy pool. On another interesting side note, when the film was first released, it was promoted with a massive campaign that included a warning: No spectators would be permitted to enter the theater after the film started in order to preserve the shocking ending (six years before Hitchcock's *Psycho*, thank you very much). Oh, and one other bit of trivia: The film was produced by Henri-Georges Clouzot's own company, Véra Films, which was named after his wife and lead actress. Hmm, a bit like the boarding school funded by Christina in the film. As Clouzot himself once said, "I believe the truth always makes a scandal." The plot, like the water, thickens.

Okay, so I'm stalling. Just where is that body, anyway? Actually, it never surfaces. Well, it does, sort of, but to explain how would be to ignore the anti-spoiler warning at the end of the film and give away what is simply one of the greatest moments in cinema. The fact that the notorious scene has been so often interpreted, imitated, and flat out ripped off does little to distill the surprise of seeing it for the first time or even the tenth time. Still, it's best if you clear your mind and let it hit you full on.

If it doesn't, consider a couple of other interesting trivia points surrounding this flick: The director, who shot on a set closed to all outsiders, was supposedly so sadistic that if any actors had to swallow poison in his films, he insisted they take a non-lethal dose of the real thing. Meurisse, as Michel, had to spend an entire day submerged in a full, cold bathtub in a full suit, which was a sharp career move in retrospect, given the longevity of the project. He also had to keep ice cubes in his mouth while filming outdoor sequences in the dead of winter to avoid forming steam with his breath.

There's no telling what the director's own wife had to put up with, but Véra Clouzot, like the character she played in *Les Diaboliques*, died of a heart attack only a few years after the release of the film. A fact that only added to the lore and hype surrounding the movie.

As one of the inspectors in the movie observes, "Plenty of people who know how to swim end up drowning. They're the ones who can't stay away from the edge."

DR. JEKYLL AND MR. HYDE (1932)
by Danny Fuller

A loose adaptation of Robert Louis Stevenson's 1886 novella, *The Strange Case of Dr. Jekyll and Mr. Hyde*, Dr. Henry Jekyll (Fredric March) is a scientist who believes that every man has two sides—one good, one evil. He theorizes that these opposites are in constant struggle with each other, but that by separating the two, the evil in Man can be isolated, and, in fact, eliminated. Attempting to prove his hypothesis, Jekyll experiments on himself, creating a chemical potion that succeeds in releasing his own inner evil in the hirsute, snaggletoothed persona of Mr. Edward Hyde. Once liberated from the "good" Jekyll's control, Hyde commits vicious crimes and forces prostitute Ivy Pearson (Miriam Hopkins) to become his mistress.

The movie shows a huge contrast between the two characters. Dr. Jekyll is a loving fiancé who does volunteer work for the poor, as well as being a respected member of upper class society who often attends grand parties. On the other end of the spectrum, Hyde is portrayed as a brutal Neanderthal who starts fights in bars and sadistically whips Ivy in order to dominate her. Interestingly, while the first appearance of Hyde is quite unexpected and accidental, Jekyll continues to use the potion even after he understands its consequences.

Hyde is shown to be an aberration of Jekyll's sexual frustration and addiction, the outlet of a young man who *desperately* wants to expedite the marriage (and its consummation) with his fiancée Muriel (Rose Hobart). When her father, Danvers Carew (Halliwell Hobbes) refuses to give his blessing to an earlier wedding date, Jekyll uses Hyde as an excuse to relieve his sexual frustrations with the sassy Ivy. Hyde also provides the doctor with a disguise to infiltrate the lower class of society, where he can engage in immoral acts without reprisal. Jekyll believes he can control Hyde, despite the fact that his alter ego seems to be growing stronger all the time...

When Muriel's father finally agrees to an imminent wedding date, Jekyll decides to give up the potion. However, on the night of their engagement party, spurred by the sight of a cat attacking a bird in the park, he unexpectedly turns into Hyde. Once again at liberty and smoldering with animalistic rage, he goes to Ivy (who has confessed to Jekyll how much she hates Hyde) and murders her. Hyde is finally cornered back at the laboratory, and is shot down by the police. As he dies he changes back into the benevolent Dr. Jekyll.

For its time, the movie was nothing less than cutting edge. Paramount felt like it needed a movie even more controversial and exciting than Universal's two box office hits of 1931, *Dracula* and *Frankenstein*. A young and energetic director, Rouben Mamoulian, was well chosen to direct and produce this masterpiece. While his stage experience gives the movie its grand theatrical feel, Mamoulian also embraced the

Fredric March as Dr. Jekyll and Mr. Hyde

cinematic medium, willing to explore new filming techniques, such as point-of-view (POV) shots.

It is easy to see why cinematographer Karl Struss received an Oscar nomination for this film. The groundbreaking transformation scenes may seem commonplace for today's f/x savvy audiences, but filmgoers of the early 1930s were stunned and amazed. (Also worthy of note are Wally Westmore's unheralded makeup efforts, completely obscuring March's matinee-idol good looks beneath Hyde's bestial, simian-like features.) Struss was given a lot of freedom to experiment in unusual filming methods, employing the aforementioned POV (a relatively unexplored convention at the time), as well as swipes and double screens.

The biggest difference between the novella and the film lies in the addition of the love interests. These relationships really help add spice and are now common aspects of the Jekyll and Hyde legacy. The acting in the movie is first rate. Fredric March would bring home his first of two Academy Awards for Best Actor (the second being for 1946's *The Best Years of Our Lives*) for his fine portrayal(s) of the sophisticated doctor and socialite, Dr. Jekyll, and the brute known as Hyde. As Ivy, the ill-fated prostitute, Miriam Hopkins is similarly outstanding. Watching the character's sizzling enticements during her first meeting with Dr. Jekyll, compared with her palpable dread and terror in the later Hyde scenes, one cannot help but be impressed. Sadly overlooked by the Oscars, one suspects that the unsavory nature of Hopkins' character probably hurt her chances.

Dr. Jekyll and Mr. Hyde was well received by critics and audiences alike in 1932. Released soon after Universal's twin smashes, audiences were in the mood to be terrified. In addition to March and Struss' Oscar nods, the script by Percy Heath and Samuel Hoffenstein was recognized with a nomination. The film also garnered two awards at

Mr. Hyde (Fredric March) strangles Ivy (Miriam Hopkins).

the inaugural Venice International Film Festival in 1932, for Most Original Fantasy Film and for Best Actor (March). Unfortunately, the censors in the 1930s were not as easily swayed, and several of the more risqué scenes fell victim to the shears. (Luckily, MGM has done a wonderful job on their DVD, restoring the 17 minutes that were cut from the film, so that it can now be seen in its full glory.)

In 1941, MGM purchased the rights to the 1932 movie and promptly sealed it in a vault for the next 36 years. They then remade the picture almost scene-for-scene as a lavish production with all the trimmings. Victor Fleming, who had just completed *Gone with the Wind*, was chosen to direct and produce the film. Hollywood heavyweight Spencer Tracy was chosen for the title role, with Lana Turner playing his fiancée, and Ingrid Bergman as Ivy (now a barmaid instead of a prostitute.)

However, audiences, expecting a more physical Hyde, did not embrace Tracy in the dual role, as the actor opted for a more subtle and psychological approach. Additionally, the film lacked the raw energy and sexual power of the Mamoulian production, hindered by the increased scrutiny of the Hays Code. (The Code, which went into effect in 1934, provided a "moral" guideline for films made between 1934 and 1967, and was eventually replaced in 1968 by the MPAA rating system.) Ingrid Bergman does an admirable job as Ivy, but her performance pales next to that of Hopkins.

Both versions are available on a double-feature MGM DVD, and I strongly recommend watching them in chronological order. Although Fleming's film is the inferior of the two, it offers the viewer a striking contrast of pre- and post-Hays Code horror movies in Hollywood. It is technically well made, with great atmosphere and lavish sets, and deservedly received Academy Award nominations for Cinematography, Score, and Editing.

Unfortunately, though finally unearthed from MGM's vaults, Mamoulian's *Dr. Jekyll and Mr. Hyde* remains almost a lost gem, overshadowed by the great Universal horror films made during the same time period. I first came across the DVD in my public library. Intrigued, I decided to give it a viewing, and it instantly became one of my favorite classic horrors. The raw sexual power of this film makes it unique among genre offerings of the same era. I enjoyed the performances of March and Hopkins, as well as the great internal battle of Jekyll vs. Hyde. The only part of the movie that I disliked was the excessive use of the experimental camerawork. (The POV shots were interesting in small doses but eventually got on my nerves.)

Fans of silent films should also watch the 1920 offering of *Dr. Jekyll and Mr. Hyde*, the closest adaptation to the Stevenson source material. I personally prefer the Mamoulian film, due to the addition of the love interests. But the silent version, with stage and film legend John Barrymore quite captivating in the title roles, is well worth seeking out.

DRACULA (1931)
by Brett Neveu

As a kid, I was hypnotized by horror. Horror comic books were the biggest source of my horror fix and I pored over titles such as *Witching Hour* and *The Unexplained,* looking for the most frightening and gore-related imagery I could handle. I firmly believe that if my mom or my dad had taken the time to look at a few pages of these comics, they would have tossed them out with the Thursday trash pickup (which my mom did with several of my copies of *MAD Magazine*, for which I'm still upset).

There are a few stories and panels from that stash of comics that have stayed with me well into my adulthood. There was the skull-faced flight attendant; a hunchbacked, drippy gravedigger-guy; a large-mouthed giant-squid carnival-sideshow-killer-animal-thing. But of all those comic book panels I remember, one stands out above the rest. It was of a vampire—Dracula, actually—emerging from the darkness, near the side of a horse-drawn carriage that had crashed in a rainstorm. Dining on the victims of the crash, Dracula appeared in the previous panels of the story as a man-sized, wild-eyed wolf, tearing apart his victims as they lay bleeding near the side of the muddy road.

This ravaging continued until a panel featured a beautiful young woman who had been nearly crushed by one of the wheels of the carriage. Suddenly Dracula, having spied her dying in the muck, became oddly compassionate. His face transformed into that of a solemn savior as he knelt down to save her life the only way he knew how—by turning her into an undead creature of the night. Spooky, weird, and complex, I suddenly wanted to understand more about what sort of guy Dracula was. He was a man, but he was also a beast, and he never died. How does a person deal with that sort of internal conflict? I immediately went to the local drugstore (thankfully it was October) and found a life-sized paper cutout of Dracula and hung it on my bedroom door, where it proceeded to give me the ultimate creeps for weeks.

It took me a number of years to finally see the "real" Dracula, after having seen various incarnations on television (supplied by local Iowa TV horror host, M.T. Graves).

Bela Lugosi as Count Dracula

Fortunately, I had become a Halloween addict by that time and come October I watched all things Halloween on television that I could find (including every television Halloween episode ever shown, such as the shriek-inducing Halloween episode of *Little House on the Prairie*). On one of these occasions I was able to check out a dim, grainy copy of a copy of the "original" *Dracula*, featuring Bela Lugosi as The Count. I found that I recognized that guy—the medallion, the cape, the strange clawed hands—Bela was that vampire from my comic book and my bedroom door! I realized that he was the one that defined all the others. He taught them how to speak, how to move, where to live, how to dress. The imagery in Tod Browning's *Dracula* created the living, breathing world of the vampire. All other creations would be only ghostly, pale imitations.

I hadn't seen the movie in a number of years, so I watched it again recently. Focusing on the film's storytelling, I tried to decipher what it was that made everything stick in our mythological consciousness of vampire-dom. Was it the terrible ruins of the castle? Was it the calm demeanor of Count Dracula as he attended the symphony? Was it Bela's wild and pointed accent, his words dripping from his lips as he spun slow circles around two young British beauties? Yes. All that. And more.

Because of Tod Browning's strong connection to his previous work in silent film, *Dracula* is filled with eerie silence. Not often do films of any era (since the advent of sound in cinema) exist with as much "nothing" as this film gives the audience. Long stretches of image alone show us Dracula staring at the screen, his lips curling, his fingers bent. Browning allows Lugosi to walk casually among a crowd, the deep tones of the street giving way to soundlessness. As an audience, we can hear our own breath and feel our own heartbeat. We connect to the action of the movie because the silence is our way in. Browning trusts his audience, knowing we will notice the body language and imagine the horrors within the minds of the characters ourselves.

German Expressionism also has a strong foothold in the film, which tugs the script away from its roots in the popular Hamilton Deane-John Balderston stage play of the time. The screenplay was meant to capture more of the lavish destinations and the grandness of Bram Stoker's novel, but due to the American Depression, the budget was scaled back to a minimum. The result being that the filmmakers were forced to rely more on the stage version, with location shooting becoming a much more modest affair. This problem was uniquely solved by the presence of cinematographer Karl Freund, a gifted Expressionist who brought his love for the tracking and dolly shot to the set of *Dracula*. His ability to enhance the storytelling is shown early on in the film as the camera slides along the floor of Castle Dracula, coming to rest beside the decaying coffin of the Count himself. Being so close to something so terrible forces audiences to confront its fears and challenges us to watch while the twisted and pale hand of the creature emerges from the darkness within the coffin.

This creature was uniquely personified by a Hungarian actor who gave fully of himself in the creation of such an intricate character. Bela Lugosi's performance captures an actor at the top of his game (literally, in a way, as he was sadly typecast as the Count for the rest of his life). The rhythms of the movie follow Lugosi's own rhythms, echoing his elongated speech patterns, his mood-affected facial expressions, his spikey-thin fingers, and his stiffened gait. There is a depth to his Count Dracula, unequaled in all other portrayals. Lugosi is that creature that I remember from my comic book, that frightening cutout on my bedroom door. His portrayal is that of one who is beast and aristocrat, monster and man. Lugosi's Dracula speaks eloquently, holds a person in his sway, and then sucks them dry. (Clean, quick, and intelligent, Count Dracula will never die because he's got the world figured out.)

The other actors, including Edward Van Sloan as Van Helsing and Helen Chandler as Mina Harker, bring honesty and careful thought to their portrayals. The roles feel lived in (Edward Van Sloan certainly had a leg up, having played Van Helsing on Broadway opposite Lugosi) and the intimacy of relationships surpasses nearly all films of the period. The movie is creepy due to its story and setting, but the creep-factor is raised tenfold as we watch the actors relating to each other with such careful ease. Dwight Frye, playing the businessman-turned-psychotic Renfield, seemingly and solely births the horror movie tradition of the wide-eyed thrall. His screeching speech, his arched back, and the constant baring of his teeth (after he succumbs to Dracula's wiles) is a portrait of semi-restrained wild-man bravura that nearly surpasses Bela Lugosi's own wonderfully odd character choices. Renfield eats bugs and becomes a bug—ultra-fantastic and ultra-creepy.

A classic in most people's minds (meaning that somebody once called it "classic" or perhaps the same somebody called it "old"), *Dracula* is what the essence of horror should be—unsuspecting, weird without explanation (armadillos?), and fully invested in the world that it creates. This is the reason the images within this movie have staying power, and this is the reason Tod Browning's *Dracula* still frightens and fascinates.

DRACULA (1958)
(aka HORROR OF DRACULA)
by Charley Sherman

It's 10:30 on a Friday night, the early 1970s, in a cottage in England. I'm seven years old sitting on a couch waiting for the *Appointment with Fear* weekly slot to begin on the television. This week, the film is *Dracula* (re-titled *Horror of Dracula* for the U.S.). The opening frames come on—the statue of an eagle in front of a castle, the thunderous, foreboding music, and the blood-red credits roll. Scared witless, I dive behind the couch—and this is before anything has actually happened onscreen. My other memory of that night is seeing a voluptuous woman bearing fangs at Jonathan Harker, followed by a terrifying appearance by the Count himself. Once again, I dove behind the couch to protect myself from seeing more. But I could hear the action, and I pictured all manner of terrible things happening—all of which, as I discovered years later, were probably worse in my imagination than what actually appeared onscreen. Such was the terror the film induced in me.

The reason I mention these memories is because I believe that being exposed to this film, at this particular juncture in my life, conspired to make me the horror film fanatic I became. Countless repeated viewings have not diminished my love for what also happens to be one of the most groundbreaking films in the genre. For the first time onscreen, blood and sex and vampirism oozed from the screen together in stunning Technicolor. For the first time, Dracula was portrayed as a dashing, sensual, erotically charged Count, and Van Helsing was seen as a dashing, heroic, athletic opponent.

The film opens with Jonathan Harker journeying to Castle Dracula in order to serve as the Count's librarian. However, we soon learn he is really there to put an end to this vampire's reign of terror, by putting a stake through his undead heart. Unfortunately, although he manages to get rid of one of Dracula's concubines, he fails to complete his job, and he is turned into a vampire himself by Dracula. Dr. Van Helsing comes looking for him at the castle, and after finding Harker laying in a coffin, drives a stake through his friend's heart. Van Helsing must then track Count Dracula down, a trail which leads him right to Harker's own family and friends…

With a running time of 82 minutes, and produced by Hammer Film Productions on a budget of £82,000, Jimmy Sangster's adaptation locates all the action seemingly within the same country, allowing for a flowing and fast-paced narrative drive. He has also removed major characters like Renfield and significantly altered others, like Harker. So, though it may lack the overblown grandeur and attempted "faithfulness" of later filmed versions of Bram Stoker's novel, it makes up for this by bringing out the story's sexuality and violence—something which was rather shocking for its time. And it looks bloody gorgeous, with rich and luscious art direction, cinematography, sets, and costumes. This is complemented by a classical, atmospheric, and terrifying musical soundtrack by James Bernard, one of the best ever scored for a horror film. All of these elements are stylishly put together by director Terence Fisher, with a keen sense of period, which would influence much of the later Hammer films. Then there is the cast…

One of the biggest problems with the direct sequels to this film is that the adversaries to Christopher Lee's Dracula are so uninteresting. Not so in this case. Peter

In Hammer's *Dracula*, Christopher Lee played the most enraged vampire ever.

Cushing, who had previously played Frankenstein with a consummate air of incarnate evil, takes the part of Van Helsing by the scruff of the neck and makes him a powerful opponent for the Count. Highly proficient with a tourniquet and needle in his professional capacity as a doctor, he is just as formidable when leaping into hand-to-hand combat with Dracula. Cushing dominates the film with his charismatic performance: coolly intelligent, fearless, yet with genuine warmth for the people he ends up trying to protect (note the lovely moments with the little girl in the graveyard, when he puts the crucifix around her neck to protect her). Cushing would play the part again, equally fine, in the marvelous *Brides of Dracula* (1960), battling different vampires this time, but with similar gusto. He also made a splendid Sherlock Holmes in *The Hound of the Baskervilles* (1959). It is a shame we didn't see more of the younger Cushing in such heroic roles.

As for Christopher Lee, he only has a few lines, all delivered with charm and aristocratic grace to Jonathan Harker (and significantly, none spoken with any menace). It's not really the voice that made the impact, silky and melodious though it is, but rather Lee's screen presence and striking physical prowess that was shocking. He can be seductive and charming, vicious and terrifying—all the time being aware of the rapturous pleasure this Dracula derives from inflicting pain and ecstasy in his victims. There is no hint of the novel's sadness, no sense of romance or longing. After all, unlike the novel, he doesn't travel across a sea to get to his female victims. His journey is just a coach ride away from Castle Dracula, in the same country. But he is there, insidiously infecting them, and clearly taking pleasure in doing so.

His first appearance in vampire mode would have been incredibly shocking to 1958 audiences—a startling closeup of his face, his eyeballs swimming in blood and rage, his blood-soaked fangs bared in an animalistic snarl. It's still powerful, his menace has not diminished with time, and I'm sure there are plenty of seven year olds these days who might find themselves hiding behind a couch to avoid the sight of him. It would be eight years before Lee next played the part again, appearing in the direct sequel *Dracula—Prince of Darkness* (1966), and then in the dark and sensual *Dracula Has Risen from the Grave* (1968). Though Lee himself is given little to do or say in these films, they are both well worth watching. The same cannot be said of the four sequels to follow.

The other male cast members in *Horror of Dracula* are not quite as memorable, but the females give striking performances: Valerie Gaunt makes an alluring vampire, Carol Marsh is a very sensual Lucy, and Melissa Stribling is an intelligent, mature Mina. There is also a sweet performance from Janina Faye as the young Tania.

Then there is the ending. I think it is fair to say that the chase and fight at Castle Dracula is the most exciting and memorable climax to any vampire film ever made. Van Helsing pursues Dracula, the pair leaping over stairs and tables, flinging themselves at each other like two young swashbucklers. Their tussle results in a spectacular piece of invention by Van Helsing, and with the help of some old-fashioned special effects, we get the terrific ending the film deserves.

Made after the stunning success of Hammer's *The Curse of Frankenstein* (1957), also starring Lee and Cushing, and directed by Terence Fisher—*Horror of Dracula* immediately became a global box-office hit. It was so successful that distributors Universal-International smiled all the way to the bank as Hammer remade their classic horror movies. The floodgates opened, and soon Hammer saturated the market with sequels, remakes, originals, variations on old stories, and forays into different genres. The production company would dominate British horror filmmaking until the mid-1970s, using the same sets, actors, directors, etc. for different films. It was like a repertory company in a way, churning out film after film, often for the purposes of a double bill.

Horror of Dracula, with its fresh injection of sex, blood, and vampirism into the genre and its phenomenal worldwide success, certainly secured itself as a landmark in the history of the horror film. On a personal level, no other movie has scared me as much as this one, and no matter the tender age I was when I first saw it, one can't praise a horror film any more highly than that.

ERASERHEAD (1977)
by Alexander Gold

While *Eraserhead* is certainly not a picture that appeals to a wide audience, the images contained within are the type which stay in a viewer's mind forever. In 1977, through the use of Alan Splet's brilliant sound design and Frederick Elmes' stark black-and-white cinematography, director David Lynch (*Mulholland Dr.*, *Blue Velvet*) fashioned a debut feature that actually lives up to the cliché: It is a film to be "experienced" rather than simply seen.

Not yet born when the film was making its "midnight movie sensation" rounds in New York and elsewhere, my firsthand experience came much later. By then, I was already a big fan of Lynch, and after months of hearing how disturbing and shocking *Eraserhead* was, I decided I should watch the film myself. However, despite having seen the majority of his filmography, I was hesitant. I'd just bought a bootleg of *The Short*

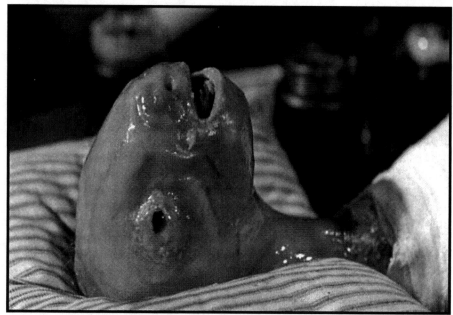
The mutant "premature" child

Films of David Lynch at a horror film convention and, after witnessing Lynch's early work, most significantly *The Alphabet* (1968) and the very creepy *The Grandmother* (1970), I was unsure whether I truly *wanted* to see Lynch's infamous feature debut. But as time progressed, my curiosity continued to increase, and one fateful day I gave in.

On its decidedly unconventional surface, the film follows the story of a young man residing in an industrial wasteland, a mutant child and a tiny woman who lives in the heating system. However, while full of bizarre imagery and characters, *Eraserhead* lies completely within each viewer's individual interpretation (I have friends who have conjured up reasons for every offbeat aspect). I prefer not take any of it as literal, electing to see it instead as a nightmare set to celluloid.

While the onscreen events are never really specified as to whether they occur in reality or in a dream state, they have a decidedly surreal quality. The film begins with an ominous Man in a Planet (Jack Fisk) pulling a lever that releases an odd worm-type creature out of Henry Spencer (excellently played by Jack Nance). The worm then emerges from a puddle in what appears to be our world. (It is not clear as to whether these two places are different dimensions, but there is definitely some expansion of space and time in the Man in the Planet's domain.) In Henry's world, the planet has become covered in industrialized factories, one of which has recently put Henry "on vacation." As he goes home to his Cocteau-inspired apartment, his beautiful neighbor from across the hall tells him to go to his girlfriend Mary X's (Charlotte Stewart) house for dinner.

After a disturbing dinner with the X family, Henry learns he is the father of a mutant "premature" child, who looks very similar to the creature released by the Man in the Planet in the opening sequence. Henry is forced to care for the "baby" with Mary, but she soon leaves due to the baby's incessant crying. Forced to care for the child alone, Henry is slowly driven mad and begins to have visions of sex, murder, and heads being turned into pencils... not to mention a creepy thumb-sized girl who lives in his radiator and sings eerie songs all night. Eventually, he cuts the child open with a pair of scissors, then takes his own life. When he appears in Heaven, he is welcomed by the strange Lady from the Radiator.

Eraserhead was developed from an earlier script about adultery called *Gardenback*, which landed Lynch a $2,200 grant from the American Film Institute. (Most of the sets were based in the basement of the AFI conservatory.) Due to the lack of funds, the project took a whopping five years to complete, finally premiering in March 1977. Under the guiding hand of distributor Ben Barenholtz, *Eraserhead* made its way to many "midnight movie" theaters across the country, its word-of-mouth reputation developing rapidly. Upon seeing Lynch's work, filmmaker Mel Brooks, best known for his raucous comedic epics *Young Frankenstein* and *Blazing Saddles*, handpicked the young director to helm Brooksfilms' award-winning *The Elephant Man* (1980).

While many horror films work with an established method of jump scares (creating audience tension and then finally releasing it with some loud noise, causing the viewer to jump—also known as a "bus" from the bus scene in Val Lewton's 1942 *The Cat People*), *Eraserhead* does exactly the opposite. Employing Splet's harrowing sound design, Lynch creates a great deal of tension, but he never provides the release the audience is expecting. By doing so, something much more frightening is created: a profound sense of lingering dread.

But *Eraserhead* is a defiant film that is not exclusively horror. While many aspects are horrific, something deeply personal and almost beautiful can be felt within. I see it as Lynch's autobiography of his early life in Philadelphia. Like many American cities, the "City of Brotherly Love" was morally bankrupt and, plainly speaking, not a nice place to live. Lynch was a student at the time, with his life bearing many similarities to that of his lead character. Like Henry Spencer, Lynch was a young man thrust into "maturity" with the birth of a deformed child. While Lynch's daughter only suffered from webbed toes, the idea of being a first-time father and having one's child coming out not perfect is universally haunting. While others have played upon this idea—mostly notably Larry Cohen's *It's Alive!* (1974)—I doubt that Lynch was influenced by that film or, to be honest, any film at all. While many have drawn comparisons to Expressionist efforts like *The Cabinet of Dr. Caligari*, it is my belief that Lynch had no filmic influences, only ideas that stemmed straight from the subconscious.

However, another director was profoundly affected by the young filmmaker's work, even going so far as to screen Lynch's debut to his cast and crew for the picture he was making. That director was Stanley Kubrick, and the picture was 1980's *The Shining*. Kubrick claimed that *Eraserhead* was one of his favorite films, and a distinct kinship can be felt in his adaptation of Stephen King's novel. Perhaps the strongest link between the two is the usage of dark, ambient music. Similar to Splet's work on *Eraserhead*, Wendy Carlos' music for *The Shining* maintains a constant background presence throughout. For both films, this adds an eerie sense of atmosphere and sets a great mood. When watched back to back, viewers can easily identify the cinematic connections between the two.

Despite launching its director's well-regarded career, *Eraserhead* has never really enjoyed huge popularity within the mainstream, though the image of a backlit, bug-eyed Spencer/Nance with his hair standing on end is a pop culture touchstone. Additionally, for the majority of people that see the film, the image of the mutant child is something they never forget. It has been referenced in countless forms of pop culture, be it the Dead Kennedy's song "Too Drunk To F**k" (which features the lyric "But in my room/ Wish you were dead/ You bawl just like the baby in *Eraserhead*") or the 1988 remake of *The Blob*, in which Jack Nance cameos as a doctor who, when faced with the Blob's first victim, offers up a facial expression almost identical to his reaction to the mutant, spore-covered child. Another aspect of *Eraserhead* appropriated by the masses is the song "In Heaven," eerily sung in the film by The Lady in the Radiator. It has been covered by many artists, most notably the Pixies, who perform it on their *Purple Tape* demo.

    Eraserhead is truly a film like no other, one that deserves to be seen by anyone who calls themselves a fan of horror films or film in general. A disturbing masterpiece, and one of the best of the 1970s independent American cinema movement.

THE EVIL DEAD (1981)
EVIL DEAD II (1987)
by Kevin Matthews

Betsy Baker as Linda, in her possessed (smiling and singing) demon state from *The Evil Dead*.

Three words for you: Demons... Kill... Youngsters.

That is the brilliantly simple premise behind both *Evil Dead* movies. Based on Sam Raimi's (infamous amongst horror fans) template-setting short *Within the Woods*, the first film sees a group of young adults venturing to a cabin in the woods and unleashing a force that attacks and possesses them, one at a time. The second movie continues the storyline. Despite what many people like to say, it is *not* a remake. Legal wranglings forced the filmmakers to shoot an abridged recap for the uninitiated, before pushing the demonic madness further and further.

Of course, if the movies were *only* about demons killing people, they would have still been pretty enjoyable for similar-minded fans like myself, but probably not half as successful. No, these movies are also about writer/director Raimi and his dedicated troupe. From his formative years spent making 8mm movies in his backyard with friends, many of whom would still be working with him over 20 years later, it's no surprise that these movies are infused with adolescent glee and energy, walking a fine line between clear-eyed narrative vision and cramming as many crazy ideas as possible into every scene. Raimi knew, certainly on the first movie anyway, that a horror flick was his best shot at finding an audience. He succeeded beyond his wildest dreams.

Like many 30-something U.K. residents, I actually saw the second *Evil Dead* movie before the first. This was all thanks to the BBFC, who (I can only hazard a guess here) seemed to think that any viewers seeing a woman raped by a tree would be so mentally disturbed that the British populace would form a lynch mob to clear the surrounding areas of particularly virile-looking flora.

So if one doesn't mind, I will, in a rather unorthodox manner, start with some comments on the second movie (still the best of the lot, in my opinion). The main characters are slightly older here but none the wiser and just as susceptible to demonic bullying. The primary difference this time around is that Bruce Campbell is, let's face it, *mas macho* (ripped, buff, call it what you will) and ready to kick ass. His anti-hero, Ash, is one of the finest and most enduring human characters in modern horror. This is in no small way thanks to the brilliant hamminess/knowingness of Campbell's performance, and it's no surprise that Raimi has consistently rewarded his good friend over the years whenever possible.

The second film takes all of the madness and horror of the first movie, amplifies it, and then adds humor. Furthermore (unlike the often labored comic stylings of Raimi's third installment, *Army of Darkness* [1992]), it does so with great success. Anyone can see this, unless you happen to have been me at 12 years old. Yes, I have to admit that my first encounter with Mr. Raimi's creative output left me, as I'm sure he would be happy to hear, a whimpering, traumatized mess who had taken everything at face value and found no solace at all in the humor I would eventually be able to see. Now, of course, I can barely get through a minute of the thing without laughing out loud.

From the re-imagined recap of the first film through every blood-soaked moment and right up to the final punchline, we have a perfect mix of gore, scares, and belly laughs. Although still *very* bloody, there was less trouble with the censors upon *Evil Dead II*'s release as Raimi used every trick in the book, whether it was using green blood instead of red (something that can help you sneak past archaic censorship rulings), or simply pushing the envelope to embrace the absurdity of it all. Necessity is indeed the mother of invention.

Any horror fan will tell you that a good horror-comedy is one of the hardest things to get right, but Raimi easily earns himself a place alongside the likes of John Landis (*An American Werewolf in London*), Dan O'Bannon (*The Return of the Living Dead*), Mel Brooks (*Young Frankenstein*), and Edgar Wright (*Shaun of the Dead* may be a recent release, but it already deserves a place among the elite). The sparse script provides a surprisingly high amount of quotable material while the visual gags go flying by, sometimes literally, every few minutes. It doesn't matter that everything is still a little bit rough around the edges. It's unimportant that we can see the top of the set during an impressive display of "Raimi-cam" or that we can see the wire holding the flying eyeball or even the rip in the back of Henrietta's (played by Sam's brother Ted, who is tortured almost as regularly as Bruce Campbell) body suit. It's the unbridled enthusiasm that matters.

For viewers, the fun to be had is not only in the mayhem happening onscreen, but also snickering at just how far Raimi pushes his leading man, Bruce Campbell (he of the mighty chin and master of "reverse motion acting"), through the insane paces. It really is a balls-out, white-knuckle ride that audiences should enjoy on the first encounter and then truly savor on repeat viewings. Here, the tone of the comedic violence is pitched perfectly, unlike other occasions when Raimi appears to want to do nothing more than recreate Three Stooges moments (hello, *Army of Darkness* and *Crimewave* [1985]).

Great moments abound, and people already well-acquainted with the film will instantly smile whenever someone says "groovy" or "work shed" in their best Bruce Campbell voice. The chainsaw has its finest moments onscreen since Leatherface met his McCullough, and a dismembered hand hasn't been this much fun since "Thing" from *The Addams Family*. Throw in the "But baby, I ain't holdin' your hand" moment and (one of my favorite scenes of all time) the image of Campbell trapped in a fruit cellar while he hears a tape recording above him revealing that a man has killed and buried his possessed wife…in the self-same cellar. I hope readers are either already smiling in recognition or rushing out to see the movie right now.

To dismiss this fine sequel as either too dumb or for gorehounds only is to dismiss, arguably, the most important film in this A-list director's canon. Sound as if I'm overrating the film? Maybe, but not by much. The first film undeniably launched Sam Raimi's career, but *Evil Dead II*, more importantly for "the suits," showed that Raimi knew his target audience and that he could make his wacky sensibilities a bit more palatable for the masses. This ability to adapt and harness his talents has doubtlessly helped Raimi to go from Horror Bad Boy to Superhero King without losing his loyal fanbase. His style is stamped all over efforts as diverse as *The Quick and the Dead* (1995) (an enjoyable Western that alternates between twisting clichés and exaggerating the very essence of the genre) and the *Spiderman* films (I'm sure every horror fan was as pleased as I was to see "Raimi-cam" giving us a POV shot from the end of Doc Ock's tentacles). *Darkman* (1990), *A Simple Plan* (1998), *For Love of the Game* (1999), and *The Gift* (2000) provide us with a much more diverse selection, and yet his fingerprints are clear, especially for fans of *Evil Dead II*, the movie that *really* made him.

And now, a bit belatedly perhaps, we rewind.

As mentioned a while ago, the first film was a simplistic affair (albeit a film shot over a four-year period), content to give us a bunch of characters and then putting them through the wringer as they succumbed to the evil forces battering down their paltry

Ash (Bruce Campbell) confronts a demon in *Evil Dead II*.

defenses. The cast is enjoyably fresh-faced, yet not completely beautiful and glamorous—that would detract from the main event.

From the inauspicious start of a fly buzzing around (the same sound would be placed at the end of *Army of Darkness* to herald the end of the trilogy), it really doesn't take long for *The Evil Dead* to start racking up the atmosphere and ballsy, bloody entertainment. It only takes the first playing of a tape featuring a translation of *The Necronomicon* and audiences start seeing Raimi's hyperactive talent shine through. The impressive sound design, especially considering the budget, complements the dazzling, appropriately crazy camerawork, especially the demonic POV shot that drags us hurtling through the woods.

Like some other things I could mention, we never forget our first time.

My first encounter with this fine, dare I say seminal, horror actually happened on Christmas Day. At the age of 16, I had finally managed to unearth an uncut VHS copy of the movie but, living in foster care as I was at that time (ahem, no violins please, I am merely providing detail to set the scene), I wasn't allowed to watch an 18-certificated film, even though it was mine.

Except on Christmas Day! As a special treat, because my foster parents were basically fed up with me whining about not being able to watch my own property, they relented.

Of course, by this time I had seen the second movie repeatedly and enjoyed the comedic slant, so there was some apprehension in my mind when I finally settled down to watch this infamous alleged classic. How bad could the first film be? How powerful could it remain after so long in the metaphorical wilderness while the likes of Freddy, Jason, and Pinhead had already taken their deserved spaces in my deep, dark fears?

I was soon to find out that some movies could remain *very* powerful.

At the end of this wild onslaught, I felt as if I had been grabbed by the scruff of the neck and dragged alongside our hapless hero through the demonic travails centering on that rather "unimportant" cabin in the woods.

Despite the fact that it couldn't gloss over its budgetary limitations, despite the many moments during the first half when the actors clearly showed how amateurish they were (hey, I love them, but there were no Oscar-winning performances here, even from Bruce), and despite its Claymation finale, *The Evil Dead* still managed to thrill, shock, and disturb me. It was an all-too-rare case, especially in the post "video-nasty" era, where a hyped-up horror movie actually delivered the goods.

Alongside the possessions in the movie, Raimi's humor was already seeping into the celluloid. Sometimes it takes the form of a subtle in-joke: the ripped poster of *The Hills Have Eyes* (starting off a fun series of jabs between himself and Wes Craven), the voice on the tape being that of American Movie Classics' host Bob Dorian, etc. Other times it can be a skewed, childish giggle in the middle of a particularly horrific moment, emphasizing the playfulness of the demonic entity and the hopelessness for the protagonists.

The movie also works so well for fans because it realizes all of our dreams; one of us making good, a quality product on a tiny budget and, hell, even a poster quote from Stephen King when the guy was still in his prime.

Incorporating the corruption of innocence, the violation of the body, paranoia, helplessness, and more, *The Evil Dead* checks off all of those boxes and then goes even further than many of us could have envisaged. More evident in *Evil Dead II* than in any other installment, there isn't any clear "good" and "evil" as characters are prone to be controlled like puppets. Nobody has any real control over their destiny and many of the characters manage to last as long as they do by simply weathering the storm until the evil grows weary of toying with them. Like most great movies of the genre, nobody is indispensable.

The Evil Dead is a film full of familiarity, while the second movie is content to drag us into the realm of the sublimely ridiculous. Who hasn't played a game with friends where they tried to guess the next playing card? Who hasn't heard those childish taunts when we were all younger? Who hasn't been stuck in a cabin in the woods, attacked by demons and raped by trees? Okay, maybe not quite that last bit, but the movie certainly plays on those easy fears of isolation, ineffectuality, and more. The sequel seems to carefully avoid any familiarity, with the exception of the inherent, primal fears. We are treated instead to limbs being chain-sawed off, a hero who becomes cockier by the minute instead of more afraid, and a series of situations that grow increasingly perilous and amusing at the same time.

Another thing that fans of the genre will surely appreciate, as I do, is Raimi's love for the old Harryhausen–style of animation and effects. From the finale of *The Evil Dead* through the "dance of the dead" toward the beginning of the sequel, Raimi creates many wonderful little touches completed in this older style. Everything culminates in the wonderful, affectionate display taking up much of *Army of Darkness*, allowing us all to enjoy a modern take on those classic skeleton armies that used to impress and entertain us so much.

The trilogy, particularly the first two movies, remains essential viewing for any true horror fan. Candarian demons have never been so much fun!

THE EXORCIST (1973)
by Sean Robinson

Over the years, the Devil has been depicted in many different cinematic forms, usually as a horned, cloven-hoofed beast. However, for horror fans, the most terrifying depiction of Satan would come in the form of an innocent 12-year-old girl in one of the most chilling and controversial films ever made: *The Exorcist*.

Even in these seen-it-all-before times, *The Exorcist* still retains its status as the scariest film ever made. It might be hard for today's younger fans to imagine just how much controversy surrounded this film in the '70s. I clearly remember all the stories from my youth; of ambulances being called out to screenings, of people fainting in the aisles, even stories of people committing suicide or being committed to lunatic asylums after viewing the film. It was the stuff of urban legend in school playgrounds across the country. One might become a hero overnight if he/she managed to sneak into a screening. I had an older friend who had seen it and was always telling me not to bother watching it, as it was "nothing special." I later found out he had found it so terrifying he could not bear to watch it again. For some people, seeing *The Exorcist* represented their first tentative steps into adulthood.

Adapted by William Peter Blatty from his own bestselling 1971 novel, the film graphically depicts an epic battle between the forces of good and evil. Blatty supposedly based his story upon a real event that took place in Washington, D.C. in 1949. In *On The Exorcist: From Novel To Film*, Blatty writes that as an English major at Georgetown University, he saw an article in *The Washington Post* that told of a 14-year-old Maryland boy who had been freed from demonic possession by a Catholic Priest using the ancient Exorcism Ritual. The story obviously planted a seed in Blatty's mind.

Produced by Blatty and directed by William Friedkin (who had recently won the Best Director Oscar for *The French Connection* [1971]), *The Exorcist* plays brilliantly upon the darkest of parental fears: Cherubic 12-year-old Regan, the daughter of divorced Hollywood actress Chris MacNeil, begins to exhibit increasingly disturbing personality changes. As the episodes escalate past medical comprehension, the distraught mother seeks aid from a Jesuit priest, Father Karras (who is confronting his own crisis of faith), and later, from the elderly but experienced Father Merrin.

The fact that the majority of the action is set in an ordinary house somehow makes it all the more harrowing. In the basement of Chris' house, Regan amuses herself with arts and crafts. Her mother comes across a Ouija board that her daughter has found in the closet. Obviously lonely and without friends, Regan demonstrates to her mother how she plays with one of her imaginary friends, "Captain Howdy." (A wonderful touch by Friedkin: when the planchette abruptly jerks from Chris' hand—the first evidence of telekinesis or supernatural activity in the film—it is handled almost as an afterthought.) Later however, during a dinner party at Chris' house, things grow more sinister. Regan walks downstairs seemingly in a daze and, in front of the horrified guests, announces to a visiting astronaut, "You're gonna die up there," then proceeds to urinate on the carpet.

In the film's most iconic moment, Merrin arrives by taxi and stands, briefcase in hand, illuminated by a lone streetlight, staring up at the house. What follows are some

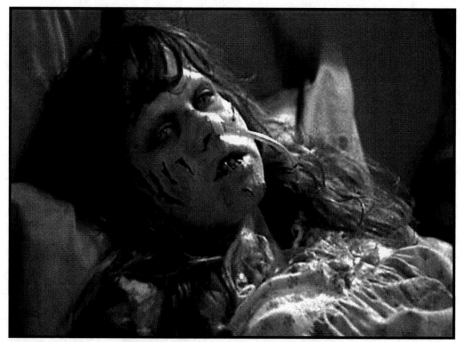

Linda Blair as the demon-possessed Regan

of the most disturbing and terrifying scenes ever committed to celluloid, with Dick Smith's excellent makeup becoming the stuff of legend. During the exorcism, the possessed Regan proceeds to vomit a green bile-like substance (Campbell's split-pea soup, according to popular legend), spin her head completely around 360 degrees, speak in Karras' dead mother's voice (*"Why, Dimmy, why? Why you do this to me?"*), levitate off the bed, and unleash an unrivaled spree of profanity and blasphemy in a rasping, distinctly un-childlike voice. (Mercedes McCambridge would later sue Warner Bros. when she was given no screen credit for Regan's demonic vocal stylings.)

At the film's climax, after the elderly Father Merrin suffers a fatal heart attack, Karras hurls himself at the giggling, possessed Regan, demanding: *"Take me. Come into me. God damn you. Take me. Take me!"* Just as the demon takes possession of him, he screams in defiance and throws himself from the window in Regan' room, hurtling down the cement steps outside. Karras gives his own life to save Regan's life and soul.

The Exorcist was released on December 26, 1973, playing to packed cinemas, and went on to cause widespread controversy. The inevitable media outcry focused on the scenes depicting a child possessed by the devil and the fact that author Blatty claimed it was based on a true story. Reviews were mixed, equally divided between those who loved it and those who hated it. And although the Catholic Church was involved in the making of the film, they instantly condemned it. Odd, when those who have actually watched the film realize it is one of the most affirming religious films ever made, confirming the existence of good and evil, and celebrating the ultimate triumph of God over the Devil (or in this case the demon Pazuzu).

The Exorcist was nominated for 10 Academy Awards (including Best Picture), eventually winning two: Blatty for Best Adapted Screenplay, and Robert Knudson and

Chris Newman for Best Sound. The movie has retained a faithful and devoted following and was for many years one of the highest-grossing films of all time. The film's recognizable instrumental tune—Mike Oldfield's "Tubular Bells—eventually became a #1 single on the Billboard charts and will forever be known as "the *Exorcist* music." Due to the film's popularity, the steep stairway at the end of M Street in Georgetown has since become a minor tourist attraction.

It all came at a price though. Friction often developed between Friedkin and cast/crew members. To make the room authentically cold, Friedkin had the "Regan room" set refrigerated to extreme temperatures. There were also post-production conflicts between Friedkin and Blatty (such as the infamous spider walk, later restored in "The Version You've Never Seen," and a protracted ending). Numerous other disturbing events (including injury and death) also plagued the production.

The Exorcist deserves its place as a true classic of the genre, a truly remarkable, disturbing 121-minute film that leaves its audience drained (both emotionally and physically) but ultimately satisfied and entertained. A cultural phenomenon, it still stands as one of the most horrifying films ever made and a legendary cinematic achievement.

"What an excellent day for an exorcism."

EYES WITHOUT A FACE (1959)
by David White

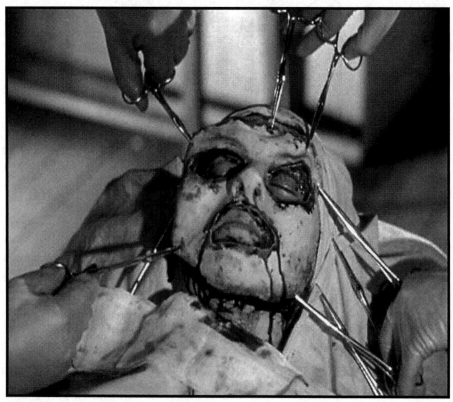

The gruesome face transplant sequence

In the mid-'80s, horror fans began getting their information from fanzines. Spelling errors aside, the unbridled enthusiasm for forgotten cinema informed an entire generation of artsy slackers, like me, of celluloid atrocities lurking in the back shelves of the mom & pop video stores. It was in one of these hastily scribbled, xeroxed "zines" that I read an article about the birth of the gore film and the two movies that opened the floodgates for bloody cinematic mayhem. The first was H.G. Lewis' *Blood Feast* (1963). The second was *The Horror Chamber of Dr. Faustus*.

I located both videotapes at a Kansas City outlet called Tivoli Video. It was a classy joint, stuffed with Sonia Braga videos. *Blood Feast* was there because Michael Weldon's *Psychotronic Encyclopedia of Film* and RE:Search Publication's *Incredibly Strange Films* had wrenched it away from purveyors of tasteless juvenilia and pimped it as hip and ironic.

Sitting on the same shelf was *The Horror Chamber of Dr. Faustus*, now under the name *Eyes Without a Face*. The clerk knowingly assured me that this was the film's *real* title. "*Les Yeux Sans Visage*," he said over and over, chewing the French in his mouth like so much candy.

That night, I treated myself to a double-feature. I loved *Blood Feast*. I adored the amateurishness of it and reveled in its accidental art. It was genius.

Then I watched *Eyes Without a Face*. Eh... it was okay.

I could tell it was an important film. It was artful, in black and white and, most importantly, it was in French. But it was… slow. I dug the infamous "face surgery" scene, but it was nothing compared to Fuad Ramses' Egyptian feast. I wanted to love it, knew I should love it, and eventually professed to love it. I recommended it to friends. I began referring to it by its French title only, refusing to utter the parochial English translation.

But I didn't *get* it.

My loss. Because when I finally watched the film again, I was overwhelmed by it. I had been telling people for years that it was one of the greatest horror films of all time, but it took me more than a decade to really understand why.

Pierre Brasseur plays Dr. Génessier, a sad sack genius who's one-part compassion to two-parts arrogance. In addition to his experimental work on dozens of dogs that he keeps locked up in a cellar, he's been working on perfecting a skin grafting process ever since his daughter Christiane (the extraordinary Edith Scob) lost her face in a car accident. Since then, the mad doc's secretary, Louise (Alida Valli), has been kidnapping young women so Génessier can surgically remove their faces and transplant them onto Christiane. Sadly, all of the experiments thus far have ended in failure.

When Louise coerces a young co-ed into taking a room at the good doctor's mansion, the unwitting girl becomes the latest victim of Génessier's cruel experiments, leading to an excruciatingly long sequence that depicts the face removal process in all its queasy detail. The victim wakes with her face in bandages and attempts an escape, but she falls from a balcony and dies. The resulting transplant appears to be a success, but over the course of several weeks, Christiane's fragile body begins to reject her new face. Christiane, desperate to make contact with the outside world, places a phone call to Jacques (her former lover and colleague of Génessier who believes Christiane to be dead). While Christiane only whispers Jacques' name before hanging up, it's enough to convince Jacques to go to the police.

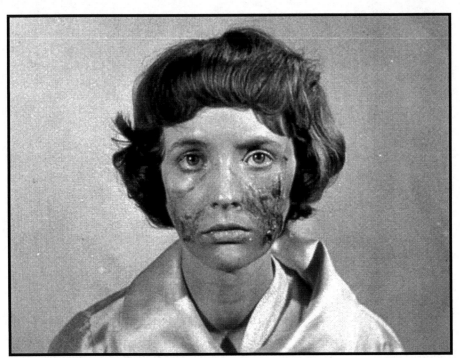
Christiane (Edith Scob) finds her facial transplant does not work.

A police detective sets a trap using a young, female criminal as bait. The trap fails, leaving the detective convinced that Génessier is on the up and up, but it gives Christiane the opportunity to free the young woman, stab Louise, free Génessier's savage dogs and wander off into the night.

Reading the preceding synopsis might unwittingly prepare one for a Poverty-Row potboiler with Bela Lugosi as a scenery-chewing mad doctor. Franju has a wholly different agenda, however. *Eyes Without a Face* is a quiet masterpiece of horror, a film that keeps the characters' desperation simmering beneath the surface and the true horror around the edges of each scene. The violence is clinical and detached. The film doesn't assault the viewer, nor does it creep. Instead, it glides: seducing us with its visual beauty and insinuating its horror bit by bit, piece by piece.

One of director Georges Franju's earliest influences was the series of *Fantomas* thrillers that shocked Parisian audiences in the early 20th century. Franju was fascinated by their juxtaposition of reality with the *fantastique*. The *Fantomas* thrillers weren't novels of the supernatural, but of grotesque criminal acts that may have strained the bounds of credulity, but always stayed bound, however tentatively, to the laws of nature.

After a few years building sets for the Folies Bergère, Franju founded the Cinematheque Francaise in 1937, with his colleague and friend, Henri Langlois. He then embarked on a series of short films that combined the visual poetry of daily, Parisian life with shocking violence. In his first film, *Blood of the Beasts* (1949), he opens with beautiful black-and-white shots of Paris, only to gradually lead us into a real slaughterhouse, where we witness dozens of slaughterhouse workers casually killing cattle, their knives severing the throats so quickly that the heads virtually separate from the necks while pools of blood drain into metal tubs below.

When Franju agreed to make *Eyes*, he was given a clear dictum: Not too much blood, no mad scientists, no animal torture… In short, the producers wanted a horror film that wouldn't upset anyone. Franju, in his devious, gentlemanly way, catered to their demands. Instead of shocking audiences with blood, he shocked them with amoral depravity.

Much has been made of the visual panache Franju brings to *Eyes Without a Face*. Euro-horror fans expecting the Baroque visuals of a Mario Bava or Riccardo Freda film will likely be disappointed. Franju's visual sense is more direct and simple. Each shot focuses on a single image, usually a central character, without the accompanying flora and fauna we often associate with the familiar Euro-horror stylists. In addition, horror fans may be scared off by those often misunderstood adjectives "poetic" and "lyrical." Like the stanzas of a poem, Franju's images defy easy analysis or categorization. Viewers who are willing to breathe in these images, to allow them to speak for themselves without the convenience of language, will find themselves imbued with a sense of longing, despair, and fear. But Franju's is not the fear of bodily harm that permeates most horror cinema, but fear of the loss of identity.

The face removal scene is not horrifying because it is gory, but horrifying because it taps into this collective fear. Whereas things like spirituality or religion are often ill-defined, based on abstract notions like faith, our identities are concrete. We can see them and touch them. Nowhere are our identities more in evidence than in our faces. Despite the studio's mandate, Franju had the last laugh. He created the ultimate blaspheme: the violation of the self.

In an illuminating interview on Criterion's excellent DVD of *Eyes Without a Face*, Franju states that what frightens him are not abnormal people doing abnormal things, but *normal* people doing abnormal things. Génessier embodies this principle perfectly. His devotion and love for his daughter is perfectly understandable, as is his need for success. His passions cause him to veer into murder so easily that the viewer is unsure where Génessier's nobility ends and his corruption begins.

The success of *Eyes Without a Face* isn't entirely due to Franju. The screenplay was authored by the team of Boileau and Narcejac, who also wrote the source novels for *Les Diaboliques* (1955) and *Vertigo* (1958). Boileau and Narcejac had a penchant for tightly wound plots that revolved around psychologically fragile characters. This psychology was further illuminated by the "mad calliope" score by Maurice Jarre. Divorced from the visuals, Jarre's jaunty opening theme would have far less power. Jarre counterpoints the somber proceedings and adds a layer of irony to the film.

But Franju's most valuable collaborator is the amazing Edith Scob. Scob's performance becomes even more impressive when the viewer realizes that her scenes in the mask are no less emotive than the scenes with her face revealed. Her body is so expressive that the viewer begins to see a range of emotion in her unmoving mask. It's an illusion that a lesser actress would never be able to pull off.

Almost 20 years after my initial viewing of Franju's masterpiece, I find myself wishing that more filmmakers would take a chance on meditative, lyrical horror cinema. The artistry of horror has been replaced by some bizarre top banana contest in which the only goal seems to be creating new, violent atrocities that top the previous ones.

The danger of prolonged exposure to cinema violence is not that it may make us immune to real violence. It's that it may make us immune to art.

THE FLY (1958)
THE FLY (1986)
by J. Luis Rivera

Ideally, a remake gives a filmmaker the chance to experiment, attempting something different and original with a previously released story. He/she is granted the opportunity to explore new options, probe different themes and ideas inspired by (or not completely realized within) the original version. Unfortunately, most remakes don't follow this ideal—the differences existing only on a technical level—with the result often being an inferior work beyond the visual flare. However, George Langelaan's short story "The Fly" has a place in history as the rare example of a story that has twice been brought to the screen (first in 1958 by Kurt Neumann, then in 1986 by David Cronenberg) under different conditions by two very different directors exploring two diverse sets of themes. Yet, despite all the differences, both end up with similarly excellent results.

Both films keep faithful to the main plot: A man of science who, while experimenting with an innovative system of teleportation, gets transformed into a mutant monster due to the intervention of a little fly. The consequences of the tragic accident in his life, and specifically in his relationship with his significant other (wife in the original picture, girlfriend in the remake), become the central theme of this modern tragedy of horror and science fiction. The point of departure between the versions lies in the directors' individual takes on Langelaan's story.

With a screenplay written by *Shogun* novelist James Clavell (his first), Kurt Neumann's version of *The Fly* focuses on the scientist's wife, Hélène Delambre (Patricia Owens), who is introduced gruesomely murdering her husband André (Al Hedison) by crushing his head in a giant machine press. The crime confuses the police and disturbs her brother-in-law François (Vincent Price), who cannot believe that his brother's wife is a murderer. Even more confusing is Hélène's obsession with finding a white-headed housefly in her home, leading the police to suspect she is insane, despite evidence pointing to the contrary. The film continues as a flashback as Hélène tries to explain the bizarre circumstances that made her kill her husband.

With an elegance akin to earlier melodramas, Neumann tells the Delambres' tragedy from the family's point of view, and the horrors presented become harsher as we discover that the Delambre family was a happy one before that tragic day. André and Hélène are a happily married couple, and even though François harbors a secret pining love for Hélène, the family functions well. Contrary to the sequels that followed, Neumann doesn't use the monstrous transformation to scare us, preferring to keep its results hidden for the better part of the 94-minute running time. This allows the suspenseful story and our morbid curiosity to become the bearers of the thrills. We keep wondering what could be so horrible that André's family has been affected in such a brutal way?

At the time of filming, Neumann was an experienced director with a career spanning almost 30 years, specializing in melodramas and *Tarzan* films with Johnny Weissmuller during the '40s. Not only that, he was preparing to direct *Bride of Frankenstein* (1935) before the studio convinced James Whale to take up the monster-making reins again. All of Neumann's pains directing below-the-radar B-movies were finally rewarded when he got a nice budget, enabling him to finally make the horror classic he wanted in the

Mrs. Delambre (Patricia Owens) as seen through fragmented human/fly eyes, from the 1958 version

way he wanted. Personally, I find *The Fly* easily comparable with the classic Universal horrors of the '30s, only in color. Sadly, it would be Neumann's swan song, with the director passing away days before the picture's opening. Though its maker wouldn't live to see its success, the film's influence is enormous, and it had a hand in developing the new "Gothic-in-color" style that came to prominence around this time.

Soon, plans for the perhaps inevitable sequel were announced. However, as the follow-up was designed mostly to earn some easy cash, the production values were considerably minimized (being shot, for example, in black and white instead of color). Directed by veteran journeyman Edward Bernds, *Return of the Fly* premiered in 1959 with a drastic change in tone from Neumann's masterpiece. The story had become a mixture of film noir and typical science fiction, with the horror and suspense exchanged for action and special effects. Six years later came *Curse of the Fly*, but by that point the story had been completely reworked, putting more emphasis on the teleportation machine and the disastrous consequences of using it without ethics—becoming a social commentary on the misuse of science rather than in the personal horror of the first movie (and the subsequent remake). What once was a terrifying tragedy of love and horror had become a parody of itself, an example of the low-budget excesses of the times.

Due to the poor sequels, it was no wonder that by the time the production of a remake was announced, most people remembered *The Fly* more for its "cheesy special effects" than for the powerful mix of science fiction and Gothic horror the 1958 original had delivered. Fortunately, when producer Stuart Cornfeld and writer Charles Edward Pogue decided to remake the film, the project went to the hands of an up-and-coming Canadian director—one who just had surprised American audiences in 1983 with a remarkable film version of Stephen King's novel *The Dead Zone*—David Cronenberg.

Seth Brundle (Jeff Goldblum) becomes less human and more fly in David Cronenberg's remake.

Unlike Kurt Neumann, Cronenberg was just starting his career in the U.S., after creating a reputation as the new master of horror in his native Canada. After a time on Canadian television, he surprised horror fans across the globe with a powerful pair of films featuring graphic violence and grotesque special effects, *Shivers* (1975) and *Rabid* (1977). But Cronenberg would soon demonstrate that he was more than just a director with a taste for blood. In the following years, he delivered the deep and emotional *The Brood* (1979), the visceral "mind vs. body" duel of *Scanners* (1981), and finally, the extraordinary *Videodrome* (1983), a horror tale that provides an acidic commentary on modern society and its TV-dependence. His success with *The Dead Zone* only confirmed to U.S. producers something that the fans already knew: Cronenberg was no ordinary horror filmmaker.

The final script for *The Fly* (Pogue and Cronenberg would eventually share screen-writing credit) follows Seth Brundle (Jeff Goldblum), a brilliant and reclusive scientist, who has finally discovered the secrets of teleportation, and a magazine reporter, Veronica (Geena Davis), who is interested in Brundle's discovery, and who later falls in love with him. But their lives are unexpectedly and irrevocably changed after a teleportation experiment goes wrong, causing the young scientist to slowly transform into an hideous hybrid of man and fly. Aside from the alterations in the original film's characters and other plot points, this is the primary difference between the original and the remake:

that the effects of the scientific blunder are gradually revealed. Instead of a sudden and brutal change, the metamorphosis here is slower, akin to a severe disease that begins to change not only Brundle's body, but also his mind.

This metamorphosis element accords perfectly with the frequent themes in Cronenberg's work, but surprisingly, the themes one might recognize as typical of Cronenberg were already in Pogue's original script. According to the director, these ideas are what most attracted him to the project. And while the mental deterioration aspects are in the original, since the film hints (although Neumann doesn't fully explore it) that the scientist is also losing his mind, Cronenberg takes this one step further. By identifying with Brundle (rather than the female character), we explicitly discover how the change affects him not only physically, but mentally as well.

In fact, a case could be made for the film being a metaphor for chronic diseases (AIDS or cancer) and the isolation that surrounds those infected by them. By way of example, Brundle exclaims at one point that his disease has a purpose, and that is to change him. Contrary to the '50s version, where the scientist accepts his change as a punishment for going "too far," Brundle sees his "disease" as something alive, new and dangerous, something that inevitably will lead him to equally new and dangerous discoveries and new experiences. Cronenberg has been quoted as saying, "It's my conceit that perhaps some diseases perceived as diseases which destroy a well-functioning machine, actually turn it into a new but still well-functioning machine with a different purpose." That is the essence of his version of *The Fly*, and despite its horrific nature and tragic story, it is possible that Cronenberg has a positive note to offer, albeit one that can't be noticed at first sight.

Finally, just like in the original, the film profits from the awesome performances of two of the best actors of the time. Goldblum and Davis share a great onscreen chemistry (no surprise that they were also once a couple in real life), effortlessly projecting feelings of love, joy, pain, fear, and finally, loss. This is *The Fly*'s main theme in both versions: The tragic fallout from a single unforeseen moment—lives ruined by a minuscule intervention of fate—and how the characters face the irremediable metamorphosis. Sure, the remake yielded its own inferior sequel, *The Fly II* (1989), but fortunately, its impact was not enough to tarnish the great film Cronenberg had delivered.

The remake of *The Fly* left a powerful impression in my young mind. Watching this brilliant scientist evolve slowly into a monster was a shock that still gives me shivers. It was something beyond Chris Walas' Oscar-winning makeup effects (which are excellent, by the way), something beyond the wonderful heartfelt performances by the actors. It was something rooted in how human the characters were, how real the change. It's not just a switch of heads and hands (which, in the original version and its sequels, appears quite simple), but the brutal rape of what is human in a man and its gradual change into something else, something new, something that the world has never seen. That said, I thought that watching the 1958 version would be a bore by comparison, but I was shocked to find that despite being completely different movies, my feelings of dread and shock from the remake were still there, just delivered in a completely different way.

In the end, what makes the two versions of *The Fly* special is that while each is based on exactly the same story, they don't feel at all like the same movie. Both explore the story's potential in different directions, showing something completely original. No scene from either film is interchangeable with one from its counterpart, and yet both share the essence of Langelaan's tale. To my mind, that's what a remake should be, a completely new experience, rather than an updated retread of the original. In *The Fly*'s case, the feeling is one of three-fold admiration; of how original the tale's source material is, how well it was originally adapted to the screen in 1958, and how Cronenberg and his creative team were to give us a new tale that delivered the same horror and suspense with quite a different style.

FRANKENSTEIN (1931)
BRIDE OF FRANKENSTEIN (1935)
by Jon Kitley

"Mr. Carl Laemmle feels that it would be a little unkind to present this picture without a just a word of friendly warning... I think it will thrill you. It may shock you. It might even horrify you. So if any of you feel that you do not care to subject your nerves to such a strain, now's your chance to uh...well, we've warned you."

With this warning, much like a carnival barker to his crowd, we are enticed into the darkness to witness the unusual, the terrible, the horrifying. Can you handle it?

For any young horror fan, the movie *Frankenstein* is one of the earliest introductions to the horror genre. We might have seen it as a kid as a Saturday matinee on television, or possibly one of the many parodies of the film and/or its monstrous character over the years. Although there have been many sequels and remakes, it's the original *Frankenstein* that set the standard. It truly is one of the founding fathers of monster movies, and has always been one of my personal favorites.

As the film begins, a funeral is in process. As we watch, we see two onlookers hiding from the mourners. Waiting. Once the funeral is over and they are alone, these

Dr. Frankenstein (Colin Clive) brings life to his creation in *Frankenstein*.

two strange characters will step out of the shadows to dig up the freshly buried corpse. This is Henry Frankenstein...scientist. He's on the verge of the greatest discovery known to man. The other is his hunchback assistant, Fritz.

We quickly learn of the exploits of Henry Frankenstein and his fanatical experiments to create life. He is determined to go beyond the boundaries, to explore where man is afraid to go, to discover the secrets of life and of death. All this theorizing occurs without a single thought for the consequences of his actions.

Colin Clive portrays this arrogant genius. Many movie scientists (especially in the horror genre) often become misguided, mad, even evil during their journey toward the unknown. But Clive's Frankenstein is not working for the good of mankind. He's using science to prove to the world that *he* has the power of creating life, that he has discovered the secrets of life and death. His is an example of simple maniacal arrogance.

Witness this exchange between Henry and Fritz (Dwight Frye) during their last minute preparations: "Think of it. The brain of a dead man waiting to live again in a body I made with my own hands. With *my own hands*." Clearly, advancing science is the last thing on his mind. He is doing this for his own ego, with little forethought for what may result. When the experiment is successful, he screams, "Now I know what it feels like to be God!" (The censors thought that line was a bit too much for 1931 filmgoers and had it covered up with the sound of thunder on the original release.)

But shortly after the creation, Henry starts to realize his error, and his mind begins to crack. On the one hand, he still feels the power and drive of crossing that line, uncovering the mysteries of life and death. But on the other, he realizes the grave mistake that he has made, and what he has created.

Frankenstein's Creature is as innocent as a child, only becoming violent when provoked or faced with violence. Fritz torments the Creature with fire, and as a result, meets a grisly end. When Dr. Waldman (Edward Van Sloan) tries to put an end to the Creature's existence, the Creature kills him as an act of self-defense. Does this make the Monster evil?

As the Creature wanders the countryside, he stumbles across a young girl, Maria, who does not see him as a threat, but as a friend with which to play. When their game of throwing flowers into the water goes horribly wrong, audiences can see the torment and sadness in the Creature's face. This was not the act of a monster, but a confused newborn.

I've always found it amusing that the townspeople never seem to hold anything against Henry Frankenstein for creating this Monster. At least not until *Son of Frankenstein* (1939) and the later sequels, where the name of Frankenstein has become a curse. But at this point, they're all willing to help Frankenstein capture and destroy his evil Monster. They knew who created it, so why not hold him responsible?

In the end, the Creature meets a fiery demise after being trapped in a burning windmill by the angry mob. In the original script (perhaps as payment for his sins?), Henry Frankenstein was to be killed at the end of the movie. But Universal later decided it would be better for his character to live. So with Henry recovering under the care of his family and soon-to-be wife, all is well in the House of Frankenstein as the film closes. But has Henry learned his lesson?

Of course, the name of Frankenstein is now synonymous with Boris Karloff, or as he was billed at times, simply Karloff. The story of his landing the role as the Creature

Gothic romance with the Bride (Elsa Lanchester) and Monster (Boris Karloff), from *Bride of Frankenstein*

is the stuff of Hollywood legend. Director James Whale sees Karloff in the Universal commissary eating by himself, goes over and starts to talk to him, telling him that he would be perfect for Whale's new movie. Karloff, who just wants to keep working, jumps at the chance. The rest is movie history.

Who's to say that this movie would still be around, talked and written about for the last 75 years, had it not been for the incredible and passionate performance given by Karloff? The 44-year-old actor was able to bring a deep pathos to the Creature, showing that he wasn't evil, just innocent. Despite the hindrances of heavy makeup and a laborious wardrobe, Karloff managed to make his Creature more human than most of the other characters in the story. Makeup man Jack Pierce is justly credited with giving the Creature his look, but it was Boris Karloff, not Henry Frankenstein, who really brought this character to life. Many actors have played the Monster over the years, but not one has come close to giving the performance that Karloff did.

I've always felt it a tragic oversight that makeup man Jack Pierce, who single-handedly created most of the famous Universal monsters, continues to be recognized only by devoted genre fans and fellow makeup artists. Through the combined efforts of Whale, Karloff, and Pierce, something was created that would truly live forever.

After the huge success of *Frankenstein*, Universal Studios wanted a sequel. Four years later, James Whale finally gave in, making *Bride of Frankenstein*. But what he gave them (and us) was quite a different movie than the first film. *Frankenstein* did have its moments of dark humor, but was still a basic morality play. In *Bride*, considerably more dark comedy exists, as well as standard vaudevillian-style humor.

Now, I know that *Bride* is highly regarded as a classic film, which it is. But I don't feel, as a *horror* movie it's as good as many people think. The gaudy humor not only detracts from the horrific elements of the film, but also waters down any attempt to make a serious moral statement. Silly humor dilutes the somber message. Maybe this was Whale's way to get the darker elements of the film past the censors? That is always a possibility, but it's still unfortunate.

The main offender in *Bride*'s over-the-top-humor department is Una O'Connor. Much like Mantan Moreland in the Charlie Chan movies, she was known for her wide-eyed screams and running about. Right from the beginning, with the first of many of these episodes, I find her very, *very* annoying. Don't know what Whale was thinking on that one.

But besides Una and a few other moments, the rest of the humor is very dark. Ernest Thesiger portrays Dr. Pretorius, out to persuade Henry Frankenstein to continue his experiments. Thesiger's flamboyant performance goes way over the top and is the source of much of the film's dark humor. He doesn't show any signs of fear from the Monster. If anything, it's the normal people with whom he seems to be out of place. But once again, while I do enjoy his performance, it turns the seriousness of the subject into parody.

The sequel starts out on a stormy night, in the presence of Lord Byron, Percy Shelley, and his wife Mary Shelley. Byron is going on and on about how Mary's story of Frankenstein scared him to bits. And now, he wants more. So Mary (Elsa Lanchester) continues her story of the Creature and the man who made him. Picking up right where the first film ended, we see the fiery windmill collapsing to the ground with the Monster inside. But we know the Creature is not dead, and a few minutes later, we see him rise from the ashes.

Whale seems intent on making the character of the Monster a lot more sympathetic in this sequel. The poor Creature is quickly captured by the townspeople and strapped to a long pole, with some stunning near-crucifixion imagery. He is then taken to the jail and chained and imprisoned. However, this doesn't last too long, as he breaks free and is on the loose once again. (Strange that this same mob, that had no problem capturing him moments before, all run in terror as he escapes.)

Pretorius shows up at Frankenstein's door (on the young scientist's wedding night, no less), demanding Henry continue his experiments. Pretorius shows Henry the results of his own efforts to create life. This is yet another segment that takes the wind out of any attempt at serious horror. The little "homunculi" characters that Pretorius has created are just plain silly, and the scene seems to be done purely for laughs.

Meanwhile, as the Creature wanders the countryside, he encounters a blind hermit. Looking for a companion to help pass the time, the blind man happily welcomes this lost soul into his home. Soon, he will teach the Creature to speak his first important words: "Good." "Bad." "Friend."

A multitude of psychobabble has been written about the hermit sequence. One prominent theory is that the hermit represents homosexuality and has been driven to the outskirts of the town by normal society. This is why he lives by himself and is so lonely. When two hunters happen upon the hermit and the Creature enjoying each other's company, they are obliged to stop what they consider an unholy companionship. And to this, I say...bullshit!

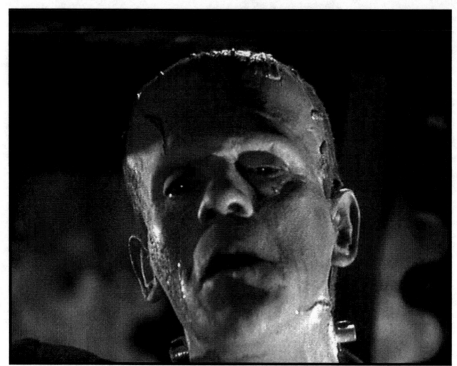

The Monster cries before blowing everyone to atoms, from *Bride of Frankenstein*.

I guess we'll never know what Whale's true underlying intentions were. The sequence can be interpreted in many different ways. However, what this homosexual interpretation does is take a very dramatic and emotional sequence where both the Creature and the hermit have found peace and solace together and view it solely in a sexual context. During the emotional scene where the blind hermit is thanking God for sending him a companion, we lose any sense of horror. The hermit is blind, so he does not see the hulking Monster before him. What he does sense is a fellow tormented soul looking for peace and companionship. At least that's how I interpret the sequence.

As the Creature is being chased by the mob once again, he finds shelter in an underground burial tomb. In this place of death, he finds another moment of peace. He meets up with Pretorius, who convinces the Monster that he is a friend, one who can make a mate for him. When Henry, beaten down by his conscience, refuses to help, Pretorius uses the Creature to threaten Henry into working again.

The experiment seems to be more of a success this time around, as far as the female Creature's looks are concerned. But the Bride (Elsa Lanchester, again) is a little out of touch on her people skills. When the Creature shows up to meet his mate, the joy and love in his eyes are shattered when the Bride screams at him in horror. The Creature realizes that even his own kind see him as a monster. Unable to bear this rejection, he turns again to the most primal emotion there is...anger.

The Creature decides to blow up the whole laboratory (thanks to a convenient lever that does just that), allowing Henry to escape with his bride, Elizabeth. As for the monstrous Bride and Pretorius, the Creature puts it best, "We belong dead." The last shot before the explosion is of the Creature's face, tears running down his cheeks, his heart broken.

Every horror fan, every movie fan, and virtually everyone else in the civilized world now knows the name of Frankenstein. It has become synonymous with "monster," conjuring the image of the Creature. But who is the real monster here? The poor misunderstood newborn, treated harshly from the beginning and looked upon in terror? Or the man who brought the undead Creature to life, only to soon abandon it?

Volumes have been written about the possible meanings behind these films. Could it be man's attempt to replace women? Or maybe to show the consequences of dabbling in things that man shouldn't? Or the mistake of ignoring the consequences of one's actions? Or even that the Creature represents homosexuality (as director James Whale was himself homosexual)? But I prefer to look at the film in the most basic of terms: The Creature is one of the original outcasts from society, born out of carelessness and ignorance.

Sure, its creator is a brilliant scientist. But one who has given no thought to what will happen if and when his experiment is a success. When his creation is not the perfect being that he'd hoped for, he dismisses it as a mistake, wants nothing to do with it, even abandons it and asks his mentor to dissect it.

Taking responsibility for our actions is one of the fundamental morals of the Frankenstein tale. Right or wrong, we must accept our fate and deal with it. And secondly, and most importantly, we learn that we cannot judge people solely on their outward appearances. Some that are considered freaks, weirdos, oddities, and even abominations are really just as normal as anyone else. I'm sure any serious horror fan can relate to that one.

Or maybe it's just about a monster on the loose. What do I know?

FREAKS (1932)
by Gregory Black

As a teenager, Charles Albert Browning fell in love with a circus dancer, leading him to run away from home and join the circus himself. Humble beginnings for a man who would soon become a successful Hollywood film director known by the name of Tod, the German word equivalent of "death." In 1931, Browning directed Bela Lugosi in his most famous role as *Dracula* and soon, many Hollywood studios were feverishly looking to capitalize on the box-office success of horror films. MGM studios, poised to make the most horrific film audiences had ever seen, sought out Browning's collaboration. The result was the 1932 film *Freaks*, which shocked audiences all over the world. It was consequently cut severely by distributors and finally banned outright in England for over 30 years. Today, while still unsettling, Browning's film is viewed differently as our social climate has changed, allowing audiences to see a more compassionate story.

Our movie begins as a freak show barker introduces the assembled masses to the story of how a beautiful trapeze performer has become the source of horrified shrieks among women and children at the sideshow.

At its core, the film is one of camaraderie and unconditional love. What builds *Freaks*' reputation as a horror film is the extent to which this camaraderie is exercised.

Schlitze the Pinhead shows off her new dress.

The first half focuses on the myriad performers at the sideshow. Browning depicts all of these events behind the curtains, where there is no audience for the characters to present themselves to, providing a sense of intimacy and identification. Through everyday moments—ranging from heartache, dating, the birth of a child, engagements, and fights—the talents, relationships, and personalities of those in the circus are unveiled beyond physical abnormality. An understanding is established that while the people performing in the circus are different, the moments that make up their lives are not so far removed from anyone else's.

Freaks is often discussed as being exploitative of the disabilities of the performers it puts on the screen, such as an extraordinary moment in which Prince Randian, a man with no arms or legs, takes a match out of a box and lights a cigarette using only his mouth. These moments could easily be viewed as gratuitous, being placed in the story only to show off the cast's unique abilities. The beauty of *Freaks* lies within the context of such scenes, forcing the audience to refashion their notions as to what is "normal," what is "strange"; it defines how a viewer sees the film. I savored my first viewing of *Freaks* because it was a unique experience, full of beautifully strange moments I had never seen, and will likely never see again. Upon later viewings, I found the fluid, graceful skills of these performers provided a sense of ease and peaceful relaxation; a comfortable state of normalcy amongst the bizarre.

The film's primary relationships are between the midget couple Hans and Frieda (played by real-life brother and sister Harry and Daisy Earles), and the trapeze artist

Cleopatra (Olga Baclanova) and the strong man Hercules (Henry Victor). As Hans' interest gravitates toward Cleopatra, "the most beautiful big person" he's ever seen, Frieda's unwavering devotion begins to drive the film's theme of unconditional love. Cleopatra and Hercules, the "normal" characters, are despicable and manipulative people. When they learn of a fortune that awaits Hans through a family will, they capitalize on Hans' desire for Cleopatra by forming a plan to unite the two in marriage, then kill Hans and run away together with the money. Frieda, ignorant of the plans to kill Hans but well aware of Cleopatra's bogus affections, does not intervene in the marriage. In her love for Hans and concern for his happiness, she allows him to make his own choice, and despite her heartbreak, briefly shows up to the marriage party.

At this celebration, the film's most famous scene, the story takes a dramatic shift into the horrific. The circus gathers for a dinner to celebrate the marriage of Hans and Cleopatra, with all the performers prepared to embrace Cleopatra as one of their own. They fill a goblet with wine, chanting, "Gooble gobble, gooble gobble, we accept her, we accept her, one of us, one of us!" as each takes a drink. A drunken and disgusted Cleopatra lashes out, refusing to drink from the same cup, an act which not only embarrasses her new husband, but also insults and degrades all the freaks. After the dinner, Cleopatra continues to slowly poison Hans who, while aware of her scheme, simply appears resigned to his fate. The film grows quieter, as we see the other freaks watching from the shadows, waiting and plotting. The resulting climax is a defining moment in horror cinema.

As the circus moves to a new town during the night, the carriages bump along a dark, muddy trail. Hans, laying in bed surrounded by his friends, alerts Cleopatra that he knows she's been poisoning him. She looks up to see Half Boy (Johnny Eck) holding a gun, the midget Angeleno (Angelo Rossitto) wielding a knife, and the rest staring her down. It is a chilling moment—one that calls into question everything the audience believes they know about these characters. As Cleopatra tries to escape by running through the woods, the viewer is left to watch the freaks crawl through the mud, weapons in hands, eyes gleaming as though stalking prey. Cleopatra's image fades, leaving only the sounds of her apprehensive screams. However, these are not the last screams heard. The camera fades back to the present where the freak show barker has finished his tale. He unveils the new Cleopatra—a frightening duck-woman monstrosity left squawking amidst the "normal" people. Alone...afraid...a freak.

The restored film closes with a scene that was long missing from many prints. After several years, Frieda finally gains an audience with Hans, who has isolated himself and refuses to see any visitors. Filled with guilt over what has happened, Hans cannot bear to look her in the eye. But when Frieda assures him, "You tried to stop them, it was only the poison you wanted, it wasn't your fault," the film concludes with Hans crying into his devoted Frieda's arms as she repeatedly tells him, "I love you." It is Frieda's unconditional love that has helped drive the story, and now that love gives Hans a crutch to support himself at the end. In spite of the ridicule, distrust, unease and murder of their past, Hans and Frieda will go on, together.

As the social timeline has advanced, so has the word "freak," and how *Freaks* is received by audiences has changed along with perception of the word itself. To be a freak does not mean that you are inferior or irrational; it just means you are different. The timeless factor of the film is apparent in how the reception has changed, but reactions never have. Over 70 years since its original release, *Freaks* does not pass through a viewer's mind; rather it lingers, waiting to be addressed, a testament to its greatness and the power of horror films.

In 1932, however, the film was a giant risk, not only financially, but also as a career move for Browning. After its disastrous reception by audiences and critics, Browning's career never again fully recovered. Though he would sporadically continue to make pictures, including *Mark of the Vampire* (1935) and *The Devil-Doll* (1936), his star had lost considerable luster in the eyes of Hollywood. He quit the business in 1939 and retired to Santa Monica, where he lived until his death on October 6, 1962.

Browning's film has influenced many facets of horror cinema. To pull no punches and tell the story using real people with real deformities and unusual talents, as opposed to makeup or special effects, is unlike anything seen since in mainstream cinema. It is almost impossible to believe that such a daring effort was made in the early 1930s by a major American studio. *Freaks* sticks out like a sore thumb in a period that placed elegant, graceful, and noble Hollywood actors and actresses on the screen. It forces the viewer to reflect on where true horror lies, and who or what are the real freaks; creating a flurry of emotions, but not giving us time to make sense of them, raising questions without easy answers. All of these themes have found a niche in horror cinema and have helped define not only *Freaks*, but the genre's intrigue and popularity among fans.

FRIDAY THE 13TH (1980)
by Don Bapst

My mom took a friend and me to see *Friday the 13th* when I was 13. Like millions of other kids that summer, I'd been lured by the trailer in which a dozen teens were shown in various poses of distress, each one about to get it, each one counted off with a giant white numeral, as if tagged for the slaughter on some twisted parody of *Sesame Street*. If we went to see this movie, the ad seemed to promise, we'd see each of these murders in graphic detail. Could audiences actually take it? Would we see intestines? Brain matter? What else? Like passing by the scene of a horrible accident, it was impossible to look away.

I needed Mom along because of the R rating. I convinced her it wasn't supposed to be so bad. What did I know? I was only 13, after all, so this horror thing was new to me. Only later would I catch up on cult classics like *The Texas Chain Saw Massacre* and *Dawn of the Dead*, which were rarely seen at major cinemas like the one at the strip mall where we went on that hot day in 1980...

We giggle as the lights go black. The movie starts off at some camp in the late 1950s. A couple of counselors are caught making out...by us. We find ourselves looking out of the killer's eyes, stalking our victims. Music that sounds like the killer's breathing sets the mood: "Jee, jee, jee, huh, huh, huh." When the first victim bites the dust, we're holding the knife. The camera slows down and freezes on her helpless scream, which is quickly replaced by the film's logo hurled at us through a smashing pane of glass...

Next, some hip, "present day" teen camp counselors set up camp at Crystal Lake, despite warnings from the country bumpkin locals about what happened back in '58. Both the boys and the girls show off equal amounts of skin along with the objects with

Betsy Palmer as Pamela Voorhees, mother of future slasher icon Jason

which they will eventually be slaughtered. We watch from out in the forest through the killer's eyes.

Suddenly, we are chasing a helpless hitchhiker through the woods. We pin her against a tree. As she pleads for her life, our big gloved hand reaches out with a serrated hunting knife and slowly, deliberately, slashes her throat clean across, about two inches deep. The gaping wound fills with dark arterial blood and she drops to the ground with a gurgling sound.

This isn't fun anymore. Deep inside, I feel that I've crossed some sort of line and there's no going back. I look over at Mom to see if she's okay. She's covering her eyes as she'd advised us to do if it got too scary. So she isn't really seeing just how gory this picture is...

See, not having caught the scathing reviews, my mom didn't know that this movie had crossed a big fat line in mainstream horror. *Friday the 13ᵗʰ* was to *Psycho* what the double-upside-down-corkscrew coaster was to the old wooden dipper. It rattled you so badly in the harness you got a headache. No more tricky edits, just chop, slice, bleed, and then cut to the next shot. A cheap, easy recipe that became so immediately familiar to modern audiences that it lost its shock-value almost as quickly as it became popular. But seeing it for the first time on the big screen in 1980, I was beyond terrified.

I sneak a quick peek at my friend who seems to be having as little fun as I am, and just as reluctant to admit it. We have to get through this rite of passage, even if we end up puking in the process. Enter Mrs. Voorhees. "Oh, it's Betsy Palmer," whispers my mom. "She was on television when I was kid!" Oh good, so everything's going to be okay...

Turns out it wasn't. See, even though Gene Siskel had already published his notorious "zero star" spoiler review (which included Palmer's home address along with an open call to send her hate mail), none of us had read it. So we weren't prepared for that last little, um, scene. You know, the one that shocked the world and put the movie on the map. That scene.

My friend and I are jolted clean out of our seats. We fall back into them. The credits roll. We pry ourselves off the padded theater cushions where we've been cowering for 90 minutes and find they're actually indented with our butt prints. "That movie scared the crap out of you," Mom says as we hobble into the daylight, mere pulpy lumps of flesh. "I should never have taken you."

I don't think I slept a full night for at least a week after that. Sure, no monster was going to come through my window now, but a real life freak with a serrated knife who was way faster than me was *out there*. And all my friends would already be dead with their throats slashed by the time I opened my mouth to scream, just as the cold knife flashed across my throat…

Eventually, I got over all that…only to realize I needed more. But more what? I needed something so scary it would take me back to the innocence of that pre-slasher flick kid watching the original body count trailer and wondering what he'd see if he followed the camp counselors into the dark forest. And I suppose that's part of what has me—and millions of other horror hounds—watching terror movies right up till today.

There are much better horror films than *Friday the 13th*, which in retrospect is about as sophisticated as an amateur porno shot in a barn on Super 8. For one thing it blatantly rips off at least 10 other films, most notably *Halloween* (1978), the success of which soap opera writer Victor Miller and hack director Sean S. Cunningham capitalized on, and *Carrie* (1976), which was the original twist ending to end all twist endings. It nails down the rather rigid, almost puritanical form of the body count/death scene genre that has become so familiar to modern audiences, a form which has its roots in B-monster movies and Italian *gialli* but strips away all humor and glamour from the mix to deliver one moral: Get laid and you're dead. The message is delivered bluntly, with an almost complete absence of style and love, a lack of care surpassed only by the film's numerous sequels, which Victor Miller claims to have never seen since they resurrect one of his dead characters (Jason) to make him into the killer. Judging from numerous commentaries on the web, young audiences watching for the first time at the start of the 21st century find it little more than silly fun or just plain bad.

Hell, if it weren't for the downright militant campaign to get the flick pulled from theaters mounted by newspaper and television film critics Siskel and Ebert, *Friday the 13th* probably wouldn't have gotten a fraction of the attention it did. That it has generated 10 sequels and has made a veritable cultural icon out of the resulting franchise's anti-hero is a testament to just how badly their plan backfired. The original flick, shot on location in Northwestern New Jersey, cost only $700,000 and served up only 10 bodies (including Kevin Bacon and Bing Crosby's son Harry), but it grossed around $40 million in America alone. As of 2005, the collective series has slashed 146 cinematic victims and grossed around a third of a billion dollars in a quarter of a century (according to the-numbers.com).

In those 25 years, Jason has been killed, resurrected, and impersonated. He has terrorized Manhattan, gone to hell, turned into a zombie, soared off into space, fought with Freddy…on and on it goes. There are countless websites (most notably fridaythe13thfilms.com, which hosts multiple forums and discussions and gives detailed background info and even body counts for each film in the series), a complete written history (*Crystal Lake Memories* by Peter M. Bracke), and even actual campsites (such as campblood.com) that plunge guests into a (hopefully) simulated slasher scenario.

Having said all that, the original *Friday the 13th* still has something undeniably terrifying, and I'm not just saying this because of the job it did on me at age 13. Maybe it's the adrenaline-rush performance by method actress Betsy Palmer that steals the third act. Maybe it's the sharp contrast between the almost Brady Bunch naïveté of the first act and the cold, clinical closeups of arrows forced through necks or axes buried in skulls that occur later on. Or maybe it's the flawless set-up of that final horrible shot, which gave birth to one of cinema's most instantly recognizable characters. Then again, maybe it's the breathy introduction to Harry Manfredini's relentless score (which is otherwise almost directly pilfered from Bernard Herrmann). Many would say it's simply the über-realistic effects of makeup artist Tom Savini.

But I would have to argue that *Friday the 13th* continues to work so well precisely because it fails on so many other levels. That it's unapologetically cheap, voyeuristic, and sadistic gives it the quality of a semi-professional snuff film—with that commercial studio input making it all the more sinister. If there's one film that brought mutilation and torture into *mainstream* cinema, this is the one. America, if not the world, lost more than a little innocence on that Friday the 13th Jason Voorhees was born, and there's something undeniably chilling about watching him come onto the screen for that split second that changed the shape of modern horror forever.

GOJIRA (1954)
(aka GODZILLA)
by Gert Verbeeck

Gojira becomes a metaphor for all the ills of the atomic age.

A good friend of mine recently wrote: "Along with the 1933 version of *King Kong*, the original Japanese release of *Gojira* is the most essential giant monster movie ever, and one of the very few horror movies that every film lover has to see at least once." As much as *Gojira* is a full-blooded monster movie, it also transcends the genre. No one, not the film's makers, the critics, or the first audiences could have predicted the worldwide impact *Gojira* would have over the next 50 years. When it was first released in 1954 in Japan, critics were not enthusiastic. But Japanese audiences loved it. *Gojira* became an icon of Japanese pop culture during the '60s and '70s, was revived in 1984 with *Gojira* (aka *Godzilla 1985,* a direct sequel to the original that ignored all previous installments) and became even more profitable during the '90s. At present, there are a stunning 28 official Toho-produced *Gojira* movies in the series.

But exactly what *is* Gojira? Scientist Kyohei Yamane (Takashi Shimura) speculates it to be a huge prehistoric amphibious bipedal dinosaur-like creature, somehow surviving all those centuries by inhabiting caverns under the sea, living off of various sea animals, remaining unseen to mankind. Apparently, some of the older villagers of the local population of Odo Island have already seen glimpses of the monster, referring to it as some sort of sea god. Then, due to hydrogen bomb tests performed in its habitat, Gojira mutates. It grows in strength and size (approximately 164 feet tall), its breath becoming 100% radioactive. Now it will angrily stomp its way through Tokyo, leaving destruction and chaos in its path…

In addition to its obvious ecological message (Mankind tampers with Nature—in this case, nuclear testing—with disastrous results), the deeper meanings are far more profound than one would expect from a monster movie. Firmly grounded in its historical era, *Gojira* is a credible allegory of nuclear warfare, as well as an indictment against it. Coming from the only country ever to have suffered a nuclear attack and its devastating aftermath, this was one way to make sure the world would never forget. Director Ishiro Honda was a prisoner of war during WWII. Returning to Japan after the war, he passed through Hiroshima and saw the devastation with his own eyes. According to his wife Kimi Honda, this experience yielded the horrific images of Tokyo being destroyed.

Another reason behind the film's genesis was of a commercial ilk. In 1952, *King Kong* was re-released worldwide in cinemas, followed by Ray Harryhausen's hugely successful *The Beast from 20,000 Fathoms* (1953). Japan's answer? *Gojira*.

Concerning the origin of our favorite Japanese monster's name, the most plausible one is that Gojira is a compound of the Japanese words for "gorilla" (*gorira*) and "whale" (*kujira*). It supposedly also was a nickname for a rather upstanding crew member of Toho at the time. But the fact is, during production, the film was secretively referred to as *Production G*. Even when actor Haruo Nakajima (who played Gojira) received the script, his character was only named "G."

When the Toho logo first appears onscreen, it is accompanied by three loud pounding noises, like a 20-ton hammer hitting solid earth. As the title appears, we hear a deafening, spine-chilling roar. (A better introduction for the King of the Monsters cannot be imagined.) The opening scene has the ship's crew of the *Eiko* witnessing an intense white light from what appears to be a massive underwater explosion. Moments later, we are treated to the sinking of a charming miniature ship on fire, staged as if it were the dark and desolate waters of the Pacific Ocean. Salvage officer Hideto Ogata (Akira Takarada) and his girlfriend Emiko Yamane (Momoko Kochi) are then presented; later

These haunting images from *Gojira* intentionally resemble nuclear devastation.

we learn that Emiko is also beloved by scientist Dr. Daisuke Serizawa (Akihiko Hirata). To be completely honest, this whole love triangle thing, while blending in nicely with the monster action, is portrayed in a rather clinical fashion. Dr. Seriwaza, however, is a very interesting character. He has the look of a typical movie mad scientist, complete with eye-patch. But instead, he is an intelligent and sad man who carries the burden of having invented a weapon of mass destruction, the Oxygen Destroyer.

Approximately 21 minutes into the movie, Gojira makes its first appearance by stretching its neck over a hill while people are running for cover. Surprisingly, the film-makers made the decision to have this scene take place in broad daylight. (They also apparently decided to use a Gojira *hand puppet* and a photographed composite shot to craft the scene. Rest assured, things do get better.) At the time—and even now—the fully realized monster was a terrifying and truly menacing creation. During pre-production, producer Tomoyuki Tanaka and director Ishiro Honda, both being admirers of Harryhausen's stop-motion work, contemplated using the same technique for their monster. They soon realized that they had neither the time nor the budget for the process, so the decision was made to have Gojira played by an actor in a monster suit. *Kaiju eiga* [Japanese monster movie] history was made.

At exactly 45 minutes running time, Gojira hits Tokyo. Its giant feet crush buildings. It picks up trains and munches on them. Bridges are lifted up and thrown away. We also learn what kind of mutated powers Gojira has gained from all that radiation. As the scales on its back start to glow, out of its mouth comes burning atomic plasma breath, incinerating everything within sight. The demolition of Tokyo takes place at night and it is these scenes, with their scarcely lit miniature sets, that add to the dark and foreboding atmosphere this movie is known for. The combined efforts of special effects director Eiji Tsuburaya and director of photography Teisho Arikawa are simply astonishing. Their images of a burning Tokyo, drenched in a frightening murkiness, are downright infernal, with the black and white photography certainly adding to the gloom. Yet not all effects are as convincing. In particular, the air raid the army launches on Gojira has a pretty high Ed Wood factor; Gojira stands motionless in a pool filled with water, on a very obvious set with a grey backdrop, while miniature planes on visible strings fly around his head. Additionally, the editing is pretty sloppy, and a few irritating jump-cuts can easily be spotted.

In 1956, the movie was released in American theaters and the American producers re-baptized the movie: *Godzilla, King of the Monsters!* But, as everyone knows, that's not all they did. Fearing that an all-Japanese movie would do poorly at the box office, they hired director Terry O. Morse to shoot extra scenes with actor Raymond Burr as an American reporter who happens to be in Tokyo at the same time that Godzilla decides to have some fun. After dubbing the rest of the movie in English, the extra footage blended in quite well with the original material. Unfortunately, the producers also cut the original from 98 minutes to 80 minutes, thereby losing a lot of the original characters' background.

There's just one guy we haven't mentioned yet: Composer Akira Ifukube. His musical score is highly memorable, especially *Gojira*'s main theme, which would be featured repeatedly in the many sequels. (Ifukube was also responsible for creating Gojira's famous roar.) During the final scenes, when the army takes to the ocean to destroy Gojira, Ifukube's score works on many levels. Its tragic theme is two-fold, with Gojira's death linked to an unexpected and perhaps unnecessary human sacrifice.

Now, if someone asks me if all *Gojira* movies are good, I would have to answer with a firm "No!" Some of them are pretty goofy, plain hilarious, or totally inept. There isn't much continuity in Gojira's timeline; at one point our fearsome monster even became a child-friendly hero, and ultimately the uncrowned protector of Japan! The best way to introduce any serious monster movie fans to the *Gojira* phenomenon is to start with the original.

On a production note: A few months after shooting *Gojira 2000* (1999) in Tokai-mura, a serious nuclear accident happened in that very same town, with the environment surrounding the power plant (actually a fuel processing facility) severely polluted with radiation. The news generated worldwide headlines. Toho Company, however, decided to keep the Tokaimura scene in the movie in order to warn the people about the dangers of nuclear energy. A message *Gojira* cried out to the world for the very first time in 1954.

THE GOLEM (1920)
by Lee Price

I first saw *The Golem*, projected from a ping-pong table onto a roll-up screen in my family's basement, when I was a pre-teenager in the early 1970s. After seeing pictures of the Golem makeup in *Famous Monsters of Filmland*, I simply had to see the whole movie. I saved up money from a weekend job, and purchased the entire multi-reel 8mm movie from Blackhawk Films.

The Golem (Paul Wegener) and Famulus (Ernst Deutsch)

Needless to say, these were not ideal conditions to view a classic piece of cinema. There was no sound accompaniment except the monotonous sputter of the projector. No comfortable chairs. And if the film jammed, you had approximately five seconds to rescue it before a melt pattern would spread across the screen.

But the movie worked its magic in our dark unfinished basement, and I've loved it ever since.

To really appreciate *The Golem*, it's best to relegate an enormous amount of historical and sociological baggage to the "hold" compartment. If humanly possible, forget that Hitler and his minions were young adults when the *Golem* movies were made in Germany. Ignore the way the plot punishes a Jewish/Christian love affair with the subtlety of an '80s slasher flick. Overlook the suggestions that black magic is practiced by Jewish elders.

Forget all that, because it's simply not necessary for an appreciation of the movie itself. All these seemingly negative points can be reasonably rebutted by complex arguments that the movie is relatively enlightened in its approach to Jewish culture. But why go that route at all? Approaching *The Golem* in the context of the Holocaust is like looking at *The Thief of Bagdad* for insight into Islamic jihads.

Better to watch *The Golem* because it offers one of the first great depictions of a cinematic dream landscape, with a production design that would influence the future prowling grounds of countless man-made monsters and werewolves. Even better, *The Golem* placed its own fully realized monster right in the center of the dream.

To fully appreciate *The Golem*, keep your mind focused on setting and monster, and lose yourself in timeless fantasy, temporarily relegating the real horrors of our time to the very back row of the theater...

The genius of *The Golem* sprung from a collaboration of some very talented people, namely Paul Wegener, Henrik Galeen, Karl Freund, and Hans Poelzig.

Paul Wegener was a widely respected leader in the early German film industry, known for his skills as an actor, writer, director, and producer. His first major movie, *The Student of Prague* (1913), survives today. Released seven years before *The Cabinet of Dr. Caligari* (generally considered the first Expressionist movie), *The Student of Prague* is Expressionist in everything except its style, where it falls dismally short. In fact, it lacks any style whatsoever, except for a tedious, primitive one reminiscent of Georges Melies' stagebound fantasy shorts of the early 1900s drawn out to feature length. Regardless, *The Student of Prague* was a hit in Germany and internationally, establishing Wegener as a major force in the German film industry.

Obviously fascinated by the Jewish legend of the Golem of Prague, Wegener made three *Golem* movies in all: *The Golem* in 1914, followed by a comic variation in 1917 (*The Golem and the Dancing Girl*), and finally *The Golem: How He Came Into the World* in 1920. Although the 1920 version is usually grouped with the post-*Caligari* German Expressionist movies, it can be viewed as the final installment of a trilogy that began well before *Caligari* was conceived.

For the 1914 *Golem* movie, Wegener recruited Henrik Galeen, who shared writing and directing credits with Wegener and had a co-starring role. Subsequently, Galeen plunged deep into the dark heart of German Expressionism, serving as co-writer on the 1920 *Golem*, screenwriter on F.W. Murnau's *Nosferatu* (1922) and Paul Leni's *Waxworks* (1924), and as writer/director of the 1926 remake of *The Student of Prague* and *Alraune* (1928).

The legendary cinematographer Karl Freund was assigned to *The Golem* team in 1920. Already solidly established at Germany's famous UFA Studios, Freund had been in the movie business since 1907, when he was just 17. His future horror credits would include his cinematography of Fritz Lang's *Metropolis* (1927) and his direction of the Hollywood horror classics *The Mummy* (1932) and *Mad Love* (1935).

Creator of the massive, strange sets that dominate nearly every scene, the influence of Hans Poelzig on *The Golem* is enormous, felt in every frame of the movie. Already firmly established as a leading German architect, *The Golem* was Poelzig's first movie, and he only worked on a handful of others during his brief time in the movie business. Under Poelzig, future director Edgar G. Ulmer served as an uncredited set designer on *The Golem*. As a tribute to his mentor, Ulmer would eventually assign the name "Hjalmar Poelzig" to Boris Karloff's villain in *The Black Cat* (1934).

The Golem is one of those rare movies that seems to exist outside of time, like a folk tale come to life or a living woodcut from a medieval book. If we are attuned to the movie's unique spell, it's a testament to the quality of the production design, costumes, makeup, cinematography, and Paul Wegener's performance. If audiences can't catch the magic, they're probably being distracted by the supporting cast's performances, which too frequently fall back on silent film clichés. This is unfortunate, because the inconsistency of the acting is the only element that holds *The Golem* back from fulfilling its status as a no-holds-barred masterpiece, as opposed to being merely a great movie.

The Poelzig-designed architecture sets the tone. Although *Caligari* often receives the credit for establishing the look of German Expressionism, *The Golem* takes a different approach that turned out to be much more influential. *Caligari*'s designs are flat, daringly two-dimensional. *The Golem*'s production is deeply three-dimensional, with sets conveying an impressive sense of weight and size. They look almost as if they were molded from cookie dough (or, more likely, from the same clay as the Golem himself), with off-kilter rounded shapes predominating and hardly a right angle in sight. The rabbi's home is defined by a winding staircase that sets the model for many of horror's great staircases to follow. The huge gate that separates the ghetto from the rest of the city suggests a model for the great gate of Fritz Lang's *Destiny* (1921) and maybe even the memorable gate of *King Kong* (1933). The ghetto buildings are the prototype for the production design of the Universal horror movies of the 1930s, from *Frankenstein* (1931) through *The Wolf Man* (1941), the direct spiritual offspring of *The Golem*.

The figure of the Golem itself is often presented architecturally. He's a mass of clay in the beginning, serves as a column that supports a collapsing roof in one of the key set pieces, and ends as a bench for Aryan children to sit on. None of this would be believable if it weren't for the seamless integration of the Golem's costume, makeup, and acting into the environment of Poelzig's amazing sets. Wegener's Golem is otherworldly, always a monster, but with intimations of the pathos that Karloff would fully explore a decade later as the Frankenstein Monster.

The images are fairy tale etchings come to life, vividly composed by Karl Freund. Strangely, considering that he would soon astonish the world with his dizzying camera movements in *The Last Laugh* (1924), Freund's camera never moves in this world. Plenty of sophisticated editing abounds within the scenes, but the individual shots are tightly framed to accommodate all the action without a need for tilts, pans, or tracks. Fortunately, there is such depth and imagination displayed within the composition of the images, that the static nature of the camerawork becomes one of the movie's strengths, anchoring its timeless style.

It's no wonder that so many scenes in *The Golem* reverberate down through the years. When the Golem pursues a man up a spiral staircase, corners him on a rooftop, and tosses him to the street below, the low-angle shots and the precision cutting from monster to the monster's point-of-view have been imitated countless times in the decades that followed. Even more famously, the climactic scene with the Golem and the child established an iconic contrast between monster and innocence that has been duplicated often but rarely matched.

With the advent of sound, silents went out of style for many years, thoughtlessly dismissed as primitive art. But in the time of *The Golem*'s initial creation, the art of the silent movie was fully in place, with the best filmmakers finding all the tools needed to create authentic fantasy worlds on the screen. And, when presented respectfully, *The Golem* can still weave its magical spell today.

HALLOWEEN (1978)
by Dan Stearnes

In the autumn of 1978, director John Carpenter introduced cinema fans to the boogeyman.

Carpenter wrote the screenplay for *Halloween* with writing partner and producer Debra Hill. The script, originally titled "The Babysitter Murders," drew inspiration from

The Shape claims another victim, the brazen Lynda (P.J. Soles).

Alfred Hitchcock in its simple but thrilling premise. Talented cinematographer Dean Cundey began a long and successful partnership with Carpenter, collaborating on *The Fog* (1980), *Escape from New York* (1981), *The Thing* (1982), and the underrated cult classic *Big Trouble in Little China* (1986). In addition, Carpenter took on the role of film composer, contributing one of the creepiest and most effective film horror scores ever recorded.

Newcomer Jamie Lee Curtis (daughter of the cinema's most famous shower victim, Janet Leigh) got her big break in this, her film debut. *Halloween* would serve as her first foray into horror, and she proceeded to build a solid "scream queen" reputation (thanks to her 1980 hat-trick of horror—*The Fog, Prom Night,* and *Terror Train*—as well as three *Halloween* sequels). P.J. Soles (*Carrie* [1976]) and Nancy Loomis (*Assault on Precinct 13* [1976]) round out the babysitting trio that becomes the focus of the boogeyman. Headlining the cast of mostly unknown performers was revered international character actor Donald Pleasence. Oddly enough, Pleasence was not the director's first choice; only after Christopher Lee and Peter Cushing turned the part down did the soft-spoken Englishman come into the role of his career.

Halloween began filming in March 1978 on a very thin $300,000 budget. These financial constraints limited shooting locations, with Pasadena, California standing in for the fictitious Illinois suburb of Haddonfield (if you keep a watchful eye out you'll catch the occasional palm tree or California license plate). The low budget forced the filmmakers to come up with creative shoestring solutions such as using (and reusing) a batch of painted leaves to give the obviously springtime landscape a more autumnal flavor. But the most creative, and in the end wisest, decision was to change Michael's mask from the originally planned clown mask (mask-maker Don Post was consulted but was deemed too expensive) to a modified "Captain Kirk" mask. A few imaginative alterations (flaring out the hair, opening up the eye holes and painting the face white) yielded one of the most terrifyingly simple maniac masks in movie history.

In October 1978, *Halloween* hit theaters with a resounding thud. The release covered only a few towns at a time and the initial numbers were very low. The film's woes were further compounded by being either ignored by the press or receiving the typically bad reviews horror films usually get. But after the second or third week, something happened. The audiences came…in droves. Little by little, the favorable word-of-mouth finally kicked in, and some reviewers who initially panned the film later changed their opinions drastically. *Halloween* eventually became the most successful independently released film to date, earning close to $50 million domestically.

Around the age of seven or eight, I started taking in all the horror flicks I could sink my teeth into. From the classic Universal features of the '30s and '40s to the outlandish fare Elvira unreeled every Saturday, from *Sci-Fi Theatre* on the weekends to the deepest darkest rows of the local mom-and-pop video store, I devoured it all with a gleam in my eye. One afternoon, while stalking the video aisle, a cassette box with a pumpkin and knife caught my eye.

From that fateful day forward, *Halloween* became my favorite horror film. I may have not been able to express it back then, but my reasons are now crystal clear. The thing that works is how *simple* the story is: A masked maniac, the epitome of all that is evil and wrong in the world, enters the suburbs. This faceless menace terrorizes the population with no rhyme or reason and murders the teen population. He never utters a single word and his glassy stare sends a chill down audiences' collective spine, just before he severs it.

Carpenter wisely chose to spend a large chunk of the budget on Panavision cameras for the exquisite widescreen imagery, creating some of the film's most brilliant and potent images. Who can forget the Shape's glancing over his handiwork after the killing of Bob, as though it was the Mona Lisa of murder? Or the light raising ever-so-slightly to reveal Michael lurking in the darkness behind Laurie? But the thing that really makes the film is the soundtrack. Carpenter's score is bloody brilliant. The unmistakable theme and the stingers that accompany the scares are, quite simply, the work of genius.

Halloween was a huge influence on the horror genre, especially the slasher subgenre prominent during the '80s. While not wholly original itself, *Halloween* did inspire a slew of imitators and half-baked retreads. In addition to the popular *Friday the 13th* series, everything from *Just Before Dawn* (1981) and *Madman* (1982) to spoofs like *Student Bodies* (1981) can thank *Halloween* for opening doors for them. The shoestring budget and simple structure promised big returns to any filmmaker who could halfway harness the vibe of *Halloween*.

And of course, it also inspired its own string of sequels…

Forever will Halloween night be known as "the night *HE* came home!" The old adage "less is more" catapulted *Halloween* into the forefront of horror cinema with the plucky and resourceful nature of the filmmakers and cast. John Carpenter's breakout film will always hold a special place in this fan's heart. I've seen it over 70 times and it is one of a handful of films I can watch over and over (while preparing to write this piece, I saw it no less than five times, including three consecutive viewings). Thank the maker for DVD.

THE HAUNTING (1963)
by Matt Black

An evil old house, the kind some people call haunted, is like an un-
discovered country waiting to be explored. Hill House had stood for
90 years and might stand for 90 more. Silence lay steadily against the
wood and stone of Hill House, and whatever walked there, walked
alone.

So begins *The Haunting*, director Robert Wise's 1963 adaptation of Shirley
Jackson's classic novel *The Haunting of Hill House*. The story tells of a group of four
researchers investigating paranormal activity at Hill House; an eerie Victorian-era
mansion that was "born bad" and holds a morbid history of murder, misfortune, and
madness for all who've dwelled there.

Anthropologist Dr. John Markway (Richard Johnson) leads the group. Intent
on scientifically proving the existence of supernatural phenomena, he has selected
psychic Theodora (Claire Bloom) and Eleanor Lance (Julie Harris) for their previous
encounters with the "abnormal." Accompanying them in their research is skeptic Luke
Sanderson (Russ Tamblyn), the young nephew of the owner of Hill House, intending
to keep a watchful eye on his future inheritance. What begins as a simple investigation
into the unknown soon becomes a battle against dark unseen forces that threaten their
very lives.

As with the novel, *The Haunting*'s primary focus is the character of Eleanor, the
elder of two sisters who's spent her life thus far in domestic servitude, caring for their
ailing yet demanding mother until her death. While her younger sister is married with
a family, Eleanor is a spinster; she's been nowhere and seen nothing. For Eleanor the
invitation to Hill House is a means of escape from her entrapment of living with her
belittling sister and brother-in-law, her first step towards freedom and a new life. Yet
more than this, she feels Hill House will be a place where she belongs, as if it were
destiny calling her to go there. Even though Eleanor's initial reaction upon first seeing
the house is that it is "vile," "staring at her," and she should run away while she still
has the chance, she is still drawn in as if being beckoned inside.

It is more apparent in the novel, but several parallels can be drawn between Eleanor's
life and those who have lived (and died) at Hill House before her, such as Abigail Crain,
daughter of Hugh Crain who originally built Hill House. Abigail had to fight with her
sister for the inherited house after their father's death, just as Eleanor had to fight her
own sister for ownership of the car so she could leave for Hill House. Abigail spent
her entire life at Hill House as a spinster, until she died a bedridden invalid, her final
bangs for help going ignored by her paid companion. This mirrors Eleanor's guilt for
her own mother's death under somewhat similar circumstances.

These parallels are made even clearer by Eleanor's rather complex interactivity
with, and certain quips made by, the clairvoyant Theodora. When the two first meet,
in response to Eleanor stating, "We're going to be great friends, Theo," Theo replies,
"Like sisters?" This double-sided remark offers both the hand of friendship yet takes
a stab at Eleanor's family life. These characters are complete opposites, with Eleanor

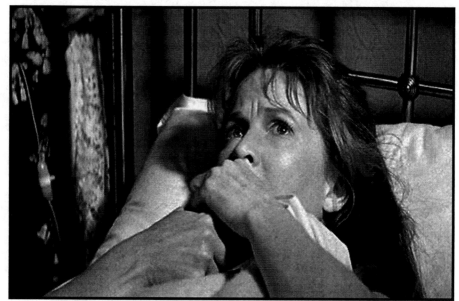
Eleanor Lance's (Julie Harris) ghosts are internal as well as external.

mild, timid, positively mouse-like, and somewhat conservative in her appearance, and Theo far more forthright, abrupt, openly flirtatious (to members of both sexes), and stylishly dressed in a designer wardrobe (supplied by Mary Quant).

What is more apparent is that Eleanor has a longing to belong and feel loved. She develops a crush upon Dr. Markway who, though he seems to have a clear affection for her, is a married man. He becomes instead more of a fatherly figure, concerned for her welfare and, when her erratic behavior puts her in danger, he urges her to leave. This behavior also leads the audience to question if Eleanor's experiences at Hill House are the result of her own imagination and guilt.

It would seem that the combined factors of Eleanor's character; her naiveté, lack of life experience, and needing to belong all make her more susceptible to whatever dark forces lie within the walls of Hill House. Not only is she the central focus of the film, but she is the central focus of the house itself.

Wise, already responsible for several genre classics including *Curse of the Cat People* (1944), *The Body Snatcher* (1945), and *The Day the Earth Stood Still* (1951), did a truly masterful job of bringing the novel to the screen. After seeing a review in *Time* magazine, Wise was prompted to read the novel and, along with screenwriter Nelson Gidding, approached Shirley Jackson about ideas for the film.

Although Wise retained the novel's location of Massachusetts, the film was partly shot on location at Ettington Park in Stratford-Upon-Avon, England. (Ettington Park is now a hotel which claims to have a haunting of its very own!) This Gothic manor setting works to the advantage of the movie, becoming a character itself within the film. Along with the use of wide angles within the crisp black and white cinematography, this setting helps to create a feeling of visual distortion, mirroring the unease and foreboding so beautifully described in the novel. The ghosts are never actually seen, but their presence is vividly *felt* through sound effects, roaming camera work, and "breathing" doors, allowing the viewer's imagination to go to work.

Another major asset is the film's flawless cast. Richard Johnson (who at the time was also appearing in a stage production of John Whiting's *The Devils*) works well as the strong, sensible Dr. Markway, the voice of reason and scientific approach. Johnson, once married to Kim Novak and whose suave good looks made him a one-time consideration to play James Bond, also went on to play the Bond-like role of Bulldog Drummond (1966's *Deadlier Than The Male* and 1969's *Some Girls Do*), but he is better known to horror fans for his appearances in Lucio Fulci's *Zombie* (aka *Zombi 2* [1979]) and Pete Walker's *The Comeback* (1978).

Russ Tamblyn provides the cynical approach to the experiment, echoing some viewers' disbelief of the supernatural. Among his countless screen appearances, including Wise's *West Side Story* (1961), Tamblyn may also be known to B-movie fans for his turns in Al Adamson's Z-grade classics *Satan's Sadists* (1969) and *Dracula vs. Frankenstein* (1971), or as Dr. Lawrence Jacoby in the cult favorite TV series *Twin Peaks*.

It is, however, the casting of Julie Harris and Claire Bloom that are the strongest links here. Harris, who was already well known for starring opposite James Dean in Elia Kazan's 1955 adaptation of *East of Eden*, plays Eleanor with perfect paranoia and insecurity. (An interesting side note, she is the most honored member in Broadway history, with a total of 10 Tony nominations and five victories, a tribute to her abilities.) Bloom is also flawless in her role, carrying off the chic look and almost predatory manner of Theodora. In addition to a very active movie career, Bloom has been even more successful on stage, winning rave reviews in London and on Broadway. One of the well-known on-set stories about *The Haunting* is that Bloom got along with all of the cast—except Harris, who seemed to make a point of avoiding her. She was relieved when Harris visited her home (after filming was completed) to deliver a present and explain that she had been merely trying to remain in character as an outsider!

The Haunting is an important film within the horror genre as it is one of the best examples of how to unsettle an audience through the mere power of suggestion and intelligent filming, rather than with the standard fare of graphic "blood and gore" cinema. By many it's considered *the* landmark haunted house film, a benchmark by which all others are measured, and rightly so. I first saw the film around the age of 11 or 12 and it still remains one of my favorite movies today (fast approaching 20 years and countless viewings later), a testament to its well-crafted filmmaking.

Along with Lewis Allen's *The Uninvited* (1944), Ealing Studios' anthology *Dead of Night* (1945), and Jack Clayton's *The Innocents* (1961), *The Haunting* is a precursor and influence upon numerous ghost/haunted house movies, including *The Changeling* (1980), *The Sixth Sense* (1999), *The Others* (2001), *An American Haunting* (2005) and, in particular, *The Legend of Hell House* (a 1973 adaptation of Richard Matheson's *Hell House*), which bears more than a passing resemblance to the plotline of *The Haunting*.

While the film may have influenced many others, in my personal opinion, it's never been topped. One need only watch Jan de Bont's 1999 big budget remake, which casts aside the subtle plot qualities and eeriness of the original film—replacing them with full blown lesbianism and overused CGI special effects—for clear evidence how good Wise's film really is.

A perfect example of how modern Hollywood fails to live up to its former glory; it's sad but true when fans say, "They just don't make them like that anymore."

HELLRAISER (1987)
by Crystal Porphir

Julia (Clare Higgins) and Frank Cotton (Oliver Smith) are reunited once again.

Hellraiser premiered in U.S. theaters September 18, 1987. Since it was rated R, and I was not yet 17 at the time, I did not get to see the film until a couple of years later on video. While I cannot give you an exact date when I actually first saw the film, I can tell you this: It haunts my dreams still. Thanks to writer/director Clive Barker's twisted, nightmarish imagination and style, *Hellraiser* is one of the few horror movies that still drips originality today, two decades after its initial release.

At a bizarre trinket shop, a man named Frank Cotton (Sean Chapman) visits with the shopkeeper, who asks him, "What's your pleasure, Mr. Cotton?" "The box," Frank responds, and as he pays for it, the shopkeeper says, "Take it, it's yours." The customer leaves the shop with the puzzle box, with the shopkeeper solemnly adding, "It always was." Frank soon meets with a mysterious, horrific end.

Meanwhile, Frank's brother Larry (Andrew Robinson) and his wife, Julia (Clare Higgins) are moving back into the Cotton family house. It has been 10 years since Larry has visited, and though he had wanted to sell the house, Frank wouldn't allow it. Larry also invites his daughter, the young and beautiful Kirsty (Ashley Laurence), to stay with them. However, due to previous friction with Julia, Kirsty declines, deciding to get a room in town instead.

Though he is nowhere to be found, remnants of Frank's presence are apparent all over the house—rotting food, covered with maggots and cockroachs, litters the kitchen and there is a spot in one of the upstairs rooms where he had been sleeping. While the couple looks around the house, Julia finds a box full of snapshots and takes out a picture of Frank and another girl. Julia proceeds to tear the girl out of the picture, sliding the remaining half into her pocket. Courtesy of several steamy flashback scenes, we soon learn that Frank was her lover before she and Larry were married.

The fun really starts when Larry cuts himself badly on a nail in the hallway. Bleeding profusely, he runs up the stairs to get Julia to help him, eventually finding her in the attic. However, before she can look at the wound, some of Larry's blood spills on the floor. As they leave the room, the blood flows through the floorboards, and we see a heart spontaneously form and begin pumping. As the coagulations continue, a horrible looking monster assumes its humanoid shape, step by step, minus any skin and with most of its vital organs still showing. The scene climaxes with the monster coming through the attic floorboards. Frank (now played by Oliver Smith) has been resurrected!

Meanwhile Kirsty finds and solves the puzzle box, thus opening a gateway to another dimension and its inhabitants. The Cenobites, who describe themselves as "Demons to some, Angels to others," all look different. But it is apparent they have all been through some…modifications. The Lead Cenobite has pins shoved into his head; among his compatriots, piercings and mutilations abound. Kirsty is informed that they are "explorers," in charge of inflicting the pain and/or pleasure tortures that coincide with the opening of the puzzle box. As the Cenobites advance on Kirsty, she informs them that Frank has returned to the land of the living, and that she can lead them to him. However, Frank still has a few surprises left, and Kristy's life is in danger since she has also opened the puzzle box...

Hellraiser is based on Barker's novel *The Hellbound Heart*, and its success heralded Barker as one of the foremost horror writer/directors of our time. Stephen King has been quoted as saying, "I have seen the future of horror and his name is Clive Barker," a ringing endorsement, indeed. Barker's writing career started out with some short horror stories found in his collection *Books of Blood*, then a novel, *Damnation Game*, followed by *Hellbound Heart*. Born in Liverpool in 1952, he is also a visual artist and has published several comic books. Barker is currently developing a film based on his "Tortured Souls" toy line and its accompanying 2001 novelette.

In 2000, I was living in Hollywood, California. My roommate had heard that they were having a special showing of *Hellraiser* down the street at the Egyptian Theatre and got us tickets. We arrived an hour early, were second in line, and I was so excited I could barely breathe. Not only had I never seen the film in a theater before, but Clive Barker and star Ashley Laurence were both going to be there. During the Q & A session held before the movie, I learned just how much of the movie had to be shaved down to appease the MPAA ratings. Several scenes had to be re-shot, including most of the sex scenes with Frank and Julia.

One of the more interesting aspects of this film is the fact that actor Doug Bradley's character is listed in the credits as "Lead Cenobite," but was later dubbed "Pinhead" by fans. Bradley has since become the de facto face of *Hellraiser*, his many-punctured visage indelibly linked with the franchise.

As far as influence, *Hellraiser* has also spawned seven sequels (to date), and to this day, Pinhead remains one of America's top modern horror icons. Barker reports that he still gets e-mails from women who want to have Pinhead's children. There have also been fan spin-offs, parodies, and video games, as well as action figures, t-shirts and other memorabilia. There has also been a lot of talk over the past couple of years of making a "versus" movie, along the lines of *Freddy vs. Jason*, but as of yet, nothing has surfaced. Additionally, several music groups have sampled *Hellraiser* quotes into their music. Rosetta Stone, a Goth band from the early '90s used the quote, "What's your pleasure sir?" at the beginning of their song, "Shadow," on the *Adrenaline* album (which I still own to this day).

HENRY: PORTRAIT OF A SERIAL KILLER (1986)
by Fawn Bartosch

Henry likes to kill.

Henry initiates Otis, his roommate and former prison pal, into a world of depravity shortly after Otis' sister Becky comes for an extended stay at their Chicago apartment. Unaware of their murder and mayhem, Becky is clearly infatuated with Henry. As Henry draws Otis ever deeper into his black hole, Becky's affection seems to be pulling Henry out. Can Becky temper Henry's murderous impulses? Will Otis surpass Henry's boundaries?

Henry: Portrait of a Serial Killer opens with the camera slowly pulling back from the dead stare of a murdered young woman, bringing her naked body (save for a pair of orange socks) into full focus for one long minute before fading out. This jolting introduction anchors the foreboding feel of this first film from director John McNaughton, which plays like a twisted "week-in-the-life" documentary of a serial killer.

"Orange Socks" is but the first of many victims on display in the opening sequence, contrasted with shots of Henry (Michael Rooker) drinking coffee, finishing up his meal

Otis (Tom Towles) and Henry (Michael Rooker)

in a diner, driving a car while listening to the radio, etc. This is the give-and-take during the first minutes of the film—scenes showing the aftermath of dead bodies that have been violently shot, stabbed, and violated countered with a cool and collected Henry executing the mundane activities of an everyday citizen. The montage sets the bleak and hopeless tone, while revealing Henry as totally unemotional. He kills without conscience, regret or reason—and is apparently unstoppable.

Richard Fire and McNaughton's bare-bones script was roughly inspired by the real-life serial killer Henry Lee Lucas, after McNaughton viewed a *20/20* TV episode on the murderer. In reality, Lucas was only pegged with killing three people. The writers were unaware of this in 1983 when Lucas' story was just breaking, as McNaughton explains in the documentary *Portrait: The Making of Henry*. Despite his less "impressive" body count, the essence of Lucas—the fact that *anyone* could be capable of random and motiveless murder while traveling across the country—became the heart of the script for *Henry*.

Even though the movie is not a completely accurate account of Lucas' life, certain authentic aspects are interspersed within the story. For example, the opening shot is a recreation of one of Lucas' real-life victims—for which Lucas received a life sentence— who was found wearing only a pair of orange socks. Later, in one of the film's most revealing exchanges, Henry confesses to Becky that he killed his mother (though the method of how he killed his mother eludes him). This reflects the true murder of Lucas' mother, whom he killed after years of physical and emotional abuse. The predominant similarity between Lucas and Henry is the relationship with Becky, which ends up being the most poignant aspect of the film.

Becky (Tracy Arnold) escapes her abusive husband back home, coming to stay with her oafish brother Otis (Tom Towles) in Chicago. She meets Henry, and what follows is a mutant variation of the typical cinematic love story. She thinks she's found someone who listens and understands her troubled past, and she feels that she understands his—it's a match made in white-trash heaven.

The film also provides the dynamic between Henry and Otis, that of teacher and student. At first, Otis is a goofball character, who provides some comic relief to the moody and starkly realistic film. However, as Otis grows into his new role of killer, the pendulum swings. While Henry seems to have some moral gravitas—stopping Otis from kissing his own sister, disapproving when Otis insists on continually re-watching a family's murder on videotape—Otis comes off as increasingly depraved, becoming the film's true villain. (Towles explains in the documentary that the character of Otis was made more reprehensible in order to make Henry look better.) The viewer is lulled into the sense that Henry is the hero of the film, however unusual, and this heroic perception climaxes as he rescues Becky from being raped by Otis.

Love does not conquer all, however, and the writers of *Henry* refuse to tie a nice little Hollywood ending onto the story. Instead, it ends with a feeling of complete hopelessness and devastation, coldly symbolized by a deserted suitcase on the side of the road. Whatever glimmer of hope the viewer had in Henry's repenting and changing his ways are dashed. He still goes on to murder.

The success of *Henry* owes much to Michael Rooker's performance. Rooker confesses that, while preparing for the role, he went through all the available information on Henry Lee Lucas but ultimately did not draw much influence from it for his interpretation, preferring to let his imagination fill in the character's chilling personality. Liberties were similarly taken with Otis and Becky's characters, and the performances are equally impressive. Towles and Arnold were both culled from Chicago's Organic Theatre troupe where they honed their acting skills—though I'm sure none of their stage performances could have prepared them for this gig. Towles' character was based on Lucas' partner and rumored lover Ottis Elwood Toole, and in the film he becomes the over-the-top culmination of every pervy uncle in the world. Arnold's real-life inspiration was actually a pubescent niece of Toole, though the writers rejected the idea of having someone that young play the part. Arnold fit the bill in more ways than one: She was actually raised in Georgetown, Texas—the city where "Orange Socks" was found lying dead in a culvert.

Henry is aging quite well, too. Though the film was released some 20 years ago, it still stands as a unique and harrowing horror movie, owing much to the writers' choice to steer clear from editorializing. They present a snippet of a serial killer's life with such stark realism and immediacy that, according to McNaughton, it was given an "X" rating by the MPAA when it was originally reviewed, due to its "overall moral tone." The rating was in response to the film's heavy, gritty approach, which foregoes any offering of guilt, remorse, or sympathy for the victims. The story is told from the murderer's point of view (not a police detective's or investigator's) and does not offer any easy explanation as to why he murders, leaving the door wide open for uneasy speculation on why a human being would kill with no obvious motive. Many films since *Henry* have walked the same route, most notably Michael Haneke's *Benny's Video* (1992) and *Funny Games* (1997).

More than any other film I've seen, however, McNaughton manages to evoke a sense of "being there"—of witnessing the horrible crimes firsthand, as though we are participating with the killer. This is most evident when Henry and Otis capture on videotape (with no edits) the murder of an entire family, otherwise known as the "home invasion" scene. The viewer is transformed into a fly on the wall, actually watching Henry kick and stab the husband, seeing Otis molest the wife before (and after) breaking her neck.

Shooting with a handheld camera, McNaughton achieves a similar tone in my favorite scene: Henry and Otis drive down onto lower Wacker Drive, on the prowl for blood, while the eerie green-glow of neon light floods the seedy streets as ominous music by Robert McNaughton (no relation to the director) plays on the soundtrack. This scene evokes something in me each time I watch it. It's hard to explain the feeling that comes over me, one that is surely dark and formidable. It's a feeling of connecting, understanding what it's like to be Henry, even if just for a moment.

Due to the low ($100,000) budget, the production is austere and minimalist, and the grainy and homemade-looking footage adds to the realism of the story. Everything in the film is well thought out, including the props. The guitar, which shows up many times throughout the movie, was taken from a hitchhiking musician, one of Henry's earlier victims. The camcorder/video that records the "home invasion" scene (*and* the television set that plays it) was stolen during a previous murder by the pair. These subtle details permeate the film, contributing to its overall foreboding tone.

This is a true horror movie because it's a reflection of the horror that goes on in real life. No monsters in latex suits with the zipper visible appear; no ephemeral spooks, poltergeists or fictionalized demons. The horror is the guy next door—your new neighbor, the grocery bagger, the gas attendant—serving as a reminder that we can never truly be sure about anyone. And we are never really safe.

HOUSE OF USHER (1960)
by J. Luis Rivera

Honestly, a few years ago I would have never considered a Roger Corman movie to be important in the history of the horror genre, as I had always associated Corman's name with cheap sci-fi stories and absurd drive-in pictures with poor production and even poorer acting. Of course, that was due to my inexperience and ignorance about Corman's place in history. When I finally watched the first installment of the so-called "Poe cycle" in Corman's filmography, I was as shocked as critics must have been when the film was originally released. *Usher* heralded a significant departure from his usual output, proving that inside the effective businessman, there existed a director who really knew how to create a horror film. It is safe to say that this movie, along with others like Alfred Hitchcock's *Psycho*, is one that changed the face of the American horror genre forever.

Scripted by Richard Matheson, the film is loosely based on Edgar Allan Poe's famous short story "The Fall of the House of Usher," a tale of madness and horror detailing the "curse" of the ancient Usher family, specifically the last surviving members, Roderick and Madeline. Written in 1839, the story has become one of the most characteristic examples of Poe's work, as it conveys many of his common themes such as fear, death, and resurrection, all framed by the ominous Gothic atmosphere of the Usher mansion. Ideal material for the silver screen, the first two adaptations were produced in 1928, one by the French director Jean Epstein (*La Chute de la Maison Usher*), and the other by American director James Sibley Watson. Another version was filmed in 1949, but Roger Corman, teaming with Matheson and actor Vincent Price, would make the most famous version of the classic tale.

Matheson's screenplay was not a straightforward adaptation, as the skilled writer did much more than simply lift Poe's terrifying, haunted narrative onto the screen. As the short story could hardly sustain a feature-length film, Matheson incorporated elements from other Poe works to create an original narrative that was not only an excellent horror yarn, but also conveyed the emotions Poe expressed in the original tale. Shortening the title to simply *House of Usher*, the revised script follows the basic path of Poe's chiller, using the name Philip Winthrop (played by Mark Damon) for the anonymous narrator, and changing his reasons for visiting the Usher household.

In this version, Philip is looking for his fiancée, Madeline Usher (Myrna Fahey), but as he arrives he is informed that both Madeline and her brother Roderick (Vincent Price) are affected by an unknown malady that Roderick believes is a manifestation of the ancient family curse. Philip refuses to believe Roderick's explanation, and bent on taking Madeline away from her brother's insanity, forcefully gains entry into the house. However, as Philip (and the audience) venture deeper inside, we discover that within every legend there is at least *some* truth.

Matheson's adaptation, which expands while faithfully respecting the tone and the mood of the original, is without a doubt an amazing gem of scriptwriting. But it

Philip (Mark Damon) approaches the dreaded house.

is Corman's direction that really distinguishes the film, allowing it to stand out among the many horror efforts of its time. At this point in his career, Corman was accustomed to directing two low-budget black-and-white films to be released as a double feature. But for *House of Usher*, the erstwhile producer/director decided that the material deserved better than that. So he convinced American International Pictures (AIP) to use the budget of his usual two black-and-white films to make one, in color, and with better production values, including CinemaScope photography. As Corman had proven to be an effective director, AIP agreed. Thus, the burgeoning artist inside the businessman was set free, proving AIP's risky bet to be, literally, right on the money.

Moving away from the sci-fi/horror genre popular in double features through the '50s (a model that he himself had helped develop), Corman looked ahead and crafted his new film in a style that had been forgotten for decades, the slow and elegant Gothic style. After the success of Kurt Neumann's *The Fly* in 1958, and the new *Dracula* and *Frankenstein* movies made in the United Kingdom by Hammer in the late '50s, Corman realized that Gothic horror was not exclusive to black-and-white films, and so determined that his *House of Usher* would be the American answer to Hammer Studios' Gothic offerings.

Finally, to complement Matheson's script and Roger Corman's direction, a decisive element was added: Vincent Price. By 1960, Price was already a recognized actor in horror films, having enjoyed success with Andre de Toth's *House of Wax* (1953), Neumann's *The Fly* (and its inferior sequel), and William Castle's *House on Haunted Hill* (1959). However, his fame would reach legendary status in *House of Usher*, where he imbued the insane Roderick with a magnetic presence that is both haunting and charming. Despite being an apparent madman, intent on doing anything to halt his sister's union with Winthrop, he inspires sympathy and is indeed very likeable. Roderick Usher is a perfect villain, and Price was the perfect choice to portray him, as the emotionally complex character suits the actor's hammy melodrama like a glove. It's no surprise that this would be the role that Price considered one of his finest.

The first time I sat down to watch *House of Usher*, I quickly realized that this was a different kind of monster. Gone were the loud shocks and paranoia of the atomic age, with subtler psychological themes such as madness and schizophrenia in their place, as well as a new touch of elegance that gives the film the melancholy and sorrowful tone of Poe's story. This new style of filmmaking took me by surprise in the same way it affected audiences in 1960. *House of Usher* became Corman's biggest hit to date, and was likewise praised by notable critics of its time (something no other Corman movie had managed to date). In Ed Naha's book, *The Films of Roger Corman: Brilliance on a Budget*, Corman admits that: "We anticipated that the movie would do well, but not half as well as it did."

Certainly nobody expected that AIP's bet would be a hit, but it was only the beginning. Corman would revisit Edgar Allan Poe's works seven more times, joined by Vincent Price in all of them (except for 1963's *The Premature Burial*, where Ray Milland would attempt to fill Price's shoes, without much success). These eight films, which would become known as "the Poe cycle" or "the AIPoes," would peak with 1964's critically acclaimed *The Masque of the Red Death* (often touted as Corman's best film) and conclude with *The Tomb of Ligeia* later that same year.

Corman, of course, went on to become a legend among independent filmmakers and his numerous protégés would go on to become important, award-winning filmmakers both within and outside the horror genre, including Francis Ford Coppola, Martin Scorsese, Jonathan Demme, Monte Helleman, Joe Dante, Paul Bartel, and the list goes on and on. However, none of this might have occurred without *House of Usher*, the picture that turned Vincent Price into a legend and proved "King of the B's" Roger Corman to be much, much more than just a clever exploitation film racketeer.

HOUSE ON HAUNTED HILL (1959)
by Joel R. Warren

Annabelle Loren (Carol Ohmart), a spoiled rich-man's wife, decides that she wants to have a party in a dangerous haunted house (seven people have mysteriously died here), with each of the five invited guests to be paid $10,000 if they stay the night. However, her plans are ruined by her husband Frederick Loren (Vincent Price), who insists on inviting people that Annabelle neither knows nor feels are worthy of her lofty station. The party guests are:

Lance Schroeder (Richard Long): Generic hero-type (a test-pilot, no less!)

Ruth Bridgers (Julie Mitchum, sister of Robert Mitchum): Matronly newswoman, desperate for money because of her gambling problems.

Watson Pritchard (character actor Elisha Cook, Jr.): Owner of the house, who lost a brother here, but is along to provide exposition as well as doom and gloom.

Dr. David Trent (Alan Marshal): Mercenary and vaguely sinister psychologist who focuses on the group's hysteria.

Nora Manning (Carolyn Craig): Mousy lady who works for Frederick Loren's company. Her innocence means she will spend the majority of the time swooning and/or screaming.

The housekeeper Mrs. Slydes (Leona Anderson) surprises Nora (Carolyn Craig).

The house has various unpleasant elements, from the blood that continuously drips from the ceiling to the pool of acid in the basement (acid which dissolves everything except bones). Speaking of the basement, while left alone down there Lance and Nora become separated when Lance is locked in a closet and given a bump on the noggin. In the dark, Nora becomes more and more frightened until she sees a scary-looking figure in a different closet, causing her to flee upstairs.

Despite the bump on his head, Lance remains curious as to what might be going on downstairs. Despite her earlier encounter, Nora accompanies him, and the two proceed to tap the walls in search of secret passages. The scary figure reappears to Nora, and then floats out of the room (as if on roller skates). All this goes unseen by handsome Lance, who treats Nora with all the respect due a deceptive child. Nora resentfully runs upstairs where she encounters a severed head left in her bag. She then wanders out into the hall where she is grabbed by the caretaker and warned that she needs to leave. Unluckily, the guests find they're trapped in the house, but Frederick soothes them by providing everyone with a pistol ("party favors"), each in its own matching coffin. All save Watson retire to their bedrooms for the night, but things shall not be quiet long.

House on Haunted Hill is as cheesy as a film can get. However, it was never meant to be Shakespeare. It is a B-movie, and its intention simply to entertain...like Shakespeare in his day. All of the clichés of the horror genre—from splitting up when in danger to hands reaching around corners to grab the heroine—are here. And while the story itself is something of a bust (the plan to kill Frederick is far too complicated, as well as other plot holes), the dialogue is wonderfully wry, especially when delivered by professionals like Price and Cook, Jr. Far from perfect, the film is a great deal of fun to watch.

William Castle, who has often been derided as more of a marketing huckster than a director, started as an actor trying to find stage work in New York City and, through a series of breaks and examples of pure bravado, managed to work his way up the ladder, eventually directing in (and out of) the studio system of the 1940s. He was a man who could be relied upon to bring a film in on time and have a marketing plan arranged that would maximize profits. Castle became notorious for his gimmickry, bringing the showmanship that had long been a part of the stage world to the somewhat respectable B-cinema (though others in the exploitation road show circuits had been doing the same thing for years). Ultimately Castle's success became a liability and he was, in effect, typecast as a salesman of silly films (with excellent gimmicks) rather than as a skilled director. This image cost him dearly when Paramount Pictures only allowed him to produce, rather than direct, what he knew would be a great film, *Rosemary's Baby* (1968).

The gimmick of *House on Haunted Hill* was called EMERGO. Each theater would have a dark box put on the stage near the screen from which, during the climax when the skeleton rises from the acid, a plastic skeleton on wires would be drawn upwards and flown over the heads of the often less-than-terrified audience. EMERGO became something of a problem when mischievous boys discovered that the skeleton could be knocked down if pelted with a barrage of popcorn boxes and slingshot fire. This caused many theaters to retire the skeleton, but audiences came anyway. While it might be difficult for modern filmgoers to understand the impact of a simple gimmick, Joe Dante's *Matinee* (1993) (about a Castle-like filmmaker) gives us a taste.

Robb White, the writer of *House on Haunted Hill*, was the creative partner in William Castle's stated goal to "scare the pants off America." The dialogue of the film, while not up to the standards of Dashiell Hammett, is quite snappy and arch. The interplay between Frederick and Annabelle Loren is especially notable, as, despite his strong screen presence, Vincent Price does not dominate these scenes. Rather, the dialogue is good enough (and Carol Ohmart has the right mix of beauty and cruelty) that it seems real, though no less bitter.

According to Castle, Price took the parts in *House on Haunted Hill* (and *The Tingler* later that same year) after having been passed over for a role in a major studio film. Price had not been particularly successful in big studio pictures, but had become something of a staple in the horror genre. These two Castle films caught producer/director Roger Corman's attention, leading to the AIP boom in Price's career that made him a beloved horror icon.

No discussion of the cast would be complete without a mention of the house itself. Designed by Frank Lloyd Wright, the Ennis-Brown House is built of concrete blocks meant to give it something of an Aztec appearance. The house has appeared in several films and other media—most notably as the exterior of Deckard's (Harrison Ford) apartment in *Blade Runner* (1982). As of 2007, it is in danger of being destroyed by instability caused by an earthquake and floods.

House on Haunted Hill stands as a testament to what makes films great: sheer entertainment. According to his autobiography, *Step Right Up!: I'm Gonna Scare the Pants Off America*, William Castle loved entertaining people more than anything besides his family (and sometimes even that was close). He made a mark on American horror cinema by showing big studios (and many say Alfred Hitchcock as well) that horror could be profitable. He was also an innovator in marketing which, unfortunately, has been used often by people concerned less with creating a quality film than making a profit (the inferior 1999 remake of *House on Haunted Hill* being a perfect example).

THE HUNCHBACK OF NOTRE DAME (1923)
by Joel R. Warren

Lon Chaney portrays Quasimodo, the bell-ringer of Notre Dame.

The streets of Paris are alive with the celebration of the Festival of Fools. The deformed Quasimodo (Lon Chaney) mocks the rabble from his perch near the bells of Notre Dame Cathedral high above the square. He eventually clambers down the side of the great building, evoking disgust in all those who view him. But on this day the ugliest man in Paris will be crowned the King of Fools.

Quasimodo sees the lovely Gypsy Esmeralda (Patsy Ruth Miller) dancing and is as attracted to her beauty as she is repulsed by his ugliness. Quasimodo is not the only man enchanted by Esmeralda; the captain of the guards, Phoebus de Chateaupers (Norman Kerry), sees her from his noblewoman fiancée's balcony and decides he must meet her. Jehan (Brandon Hurst), brother of the saintly Dom Claud (Nigel de Brulier), also lusts after Esmeralda and wants her for himself, costs be damned. The film ends with Quasimodo sacrificing his life and ringing his bells one final time; wedding chimes for Esmeralda, a funeral knell for himself.

This film is impossible to discuss without discussing the Man of a Thousand Faces, Lon Chaney. The son of two deaf-mutes, Chaney, to better communicate with his parents, learned to be very expressive in body language and facial expression. Equal to the greatest of mimes, he further honed his abilities when his mother was confined to a sickbed for several years. Despite his working-class origins, Chaney drifted toward the theater where his skills and passion were soon rewarded. His natural ability to project emotions without words, combined with his drive to create and astound, earned his status as one of the greatest silent film actors of all time.

In addition to his acting ability, Chaney created his own makeup effects. For the role of Quasimodo, Chaney developed innovative facial prosthetics and a harness that both held his hunchback in place and kept him from standing upright. There have been many myths about his makeup in this film being exceptionally difficult, but the false hump was made of plaster and weighed less than 20 pounds. The harness set did cause him some small back problems, but only insofar as it made existing problems worse. The makeup that Chaney used to cover his eye, however, during the more than six months of filming caused such stress on the other eye that he was forced to wear glasses for the rest of his life.

Chaney was as active behind the scenes of this film as he was in front of the camera. He had to push to get the film produced to his high standards and succeeded in getting Universal to put up approximately $1,250,000 (in an era in which a full-time factory worker made $1,500 a year) to build several sets and hire hundreds of professional crew and thousands of extras. It was only because of an unusual arrangement of power within Universal in which Irving Thalberg had been given almost unlimited authority that this film was possible. Thalberg's decision was a good one, as the film brought Universal prestige and profit, as well as making Lon Chaney a household name. It also opened the way to the Universal classics of the 1930s and '40s.

The Hunchback of Notre Dame, like all movies before 1951, was filmed on unstable nitrocellulose film stock. Nitrocellulose burns very easily (even continuing to burn underwater) and deteriorates over time. As a result, no original prints of *Hunchback* still exist; all current copies come from scratchy 16mm prints from the 1970s. Careful restoration work has gotten the film back to the look it might have had originally, but some 15 minutes of footage have been (presumably permanently) lost. Though the film is often called "black and white," in a properly restored edition it is rarely black and white, with each scene instead tinted an appropriate color (blue for nighttime for example), which is quite visually striking. The age of the film also means it is in the public domain and may be reproduced freely (even legally downloaded from the Internet). Of the DVD editions I examined, the one from Image Entertainment was far and away the best.

Victor Hugo's novel *Notre Dame de Paris* has been adapted for the screen several times (and had already been made at least six times by 1923). Most, including the excellent 1939 version with Charles Laughton and Maureen O'Hara, have followed the lead of the 1923 version and made several departures from Hugo's novel, most probably due to censorship as much as to give the audience a happy ending. Certainly any version is better than Disney's wretched 1996 animated film that replaces tragic horror with an admonition against prejudice toward the ugly. But Chaney's renowned version took an epic approach to a tale of Gothic horror; tickling people's fear through the freakish Quasimodo, thrilling them with quality stunt work and leaving them tearful with a final act of love…performed by a monster.

THE INCREDIBLE SHRINKING MAN (1957)
by Patrick Mathewes

While vacationing, Scott Carey (Grant Williams) is enveloped in a mysterious mist. A few weeks later, Scott notices that all of his clothes are growing larger. His wife Louise (Randy Stuart) and his doctor are skeptical, but X-rays reveal that he is indeed shrinking.

Medical science now steps in and proceeds to examine Scott in every imaginable way until a litmus test finally reveals a radioactive element in his metabolism. Scott will continue to shrink. Adding to Scott's troubles, his brother is unable to continue helping out financially.

Cut to a scene where Scott is actually so tiny that he has moved into a dollhouse in his own home. When Louise accidentally allows the family cat inside, the now-deadly predator chases Scott from his dollhouse. He manages to get away but ends up trapped in the cellar, too small to climb the stairs to freedom. Returning home, Louise finds a torn bloody scrap of Scott's shirt and the paw-licking cat. Scott's brother convinces her to leave the house where so much tragedy has occurred.

Scott awakens in the cellar much like a shipwrecked castaway coming to on a deserted island. He quickly begins to deal with his urgent need for food, water and shelter, and he establishes his new home in a discarded kitchen matchbox. But his trials are not over. He will have to cope with a deadly mousetrap, a sudden flood when the hot water heater bursts, and most frightening of all, a spider that wants to make a meal out of him. Overcoming all those obstacles through his ingenuity, courage and perseverance, Scott ultimately finds a renewed self-respect and the movie ends with him finding comfort in his new status as just a speck in a vast universe.

From the opening strains of the Joseph Gershenson score featuring haunting, melancholy trumpet solos by Ray Anthony, it is clear that *The Incredible Shrinking Man* is more adult-oriented than the usual '50s science fiction fare from Universal-International. Using music, flirtatious dialogue and the physicality of Grant Williams and Randy Stuart, director Jack Arnold quickly establishes in the first few moments that Scott and Louise have a loving physical relationship, without showing anything that would lose the kid audience. This is key to understanding the psychological dilemma that Scott faces as he begins to shrink. Unlike most '50s sci-fi heroes, he is not facing a monster that is an "other" (not yet anyway), but the failure of his own body to maintain a reasonable size—his own diminishing manhood. It is a terror that comes from within, placing the film as a very early predecessor to the so-called "venereal horror" films of David Cronenberg.

By the time Jack Arnold directed *The Incredible Shrinking Man*, he had already established himself as Universal's top choice for their science fiction films, having helmed such groundbreaking works as *Creature from the Black Lagoon* (1954) and *Tarantula!* (1955). He set many of the standards of the genre with his sci-fi film, *It Came from Outer Space* (1953), which was the first movie made from an original screenplay by Ray Bradbury, the first big-budget 3-D film, the first sci-fi picture to make extensive use of the American desert landscape, and one of the first to feature the prototype for scientist/heroes in most subsequent ones. Although he made films in a number of other

Scott Carey (Grant Williams) must face his strange new world alone.

genres from Westerns to teen comedies, it is his intelligent and visually exciting flair for the fantastic that places Arnold among the most important and influential directors of the science fiction/horror genres.

As Scott Carey, Grant Williams is not the usual pipe-smoking, scientific nerd hero often associated with '50s flicks. He is an average guy whose physical prowess serves him well once he has shrunk to a size where cats and spiders are gigantic monsters. It is this later turn of events that connects the film to the more typical sci-fi/horror craze of the '50s—the fear of the other as represented by a monster of gigantic proportions. This era produced countless films like *Godzilla* (1954), *Them!* (1954), and *The Deadly Mantis* (1957), creatures that have grown to an enormous size (usually after being exposed to atomic radiation) and threaten mankind. In all those films though, there was always a group of experts led by the military and scientific elite, who banded together to combat the menace. In *The Incredible Shrinking Man*, Scott must fight his demons alone. Clint Eastwood will not jet in at the last minute and set fire to Scott's giant spider nemesis with napalm—as he did in Arnold's *Tarantula!*.

As much as I love the combination of men in rubber suits and miniatures in *Godzilla*, or the dazzling stop-motion animation of Ray Harryhausen in *20 Million Miles to Earth* (1957), the spider that Scott must battle is all the more terrifying because it is real. In conjunction with special-effects photography wizard Clifford Stine, Arnold and his crew filmed live tarantulas on normal-sized sets and then timed that footage so that Williams' actions and reactions (filmed separately on sets expertly scaled to match his character's current size) would perfectly match when the images were combined. The painstaking use of mathematics and a metronome, along with the use of back projection and mattes, resulted in the nearly flawless realization of an inch-high Scott Carey fighting a six-inch spider. When Scott manages to fatally spear the monstrous spider as it crouches above him and the arachnid's vital juices cover him from head to toe, it is the climax of one of the scariest man vs. monster battles ever filmed.

Richard Matheson based the screenplay on his own novel, *The Shrinking Man* (1956). There are some key scenes in the novel that did not make it into the film, such as those in which a youthful-appearing Scott Carey encounters a child molester and a gang of teen bullies. He also develops a Lolita-like sexual obsession with his daughter's babysitter, who is both taller and younger than he is, and it is clear that he and new-found diminutive friend Clarice have a brief sexual relationship. It's understandable why that material isn't in the film given the era in which it was made, but it does add a much darker edge.

In the most important change, it is his brother on the boat with him in the opening scene of the novel, so we never really see how physical and teasing Scott and Louise are together before his shrinking begins. In the film, this scene adds an important emotional level that makes up for all the omitted scenes.

The success of *The Incredible Shrinking Man* sparked a slew of reverse imitators, where a character grew to astounding proportions, such as *The Amazing Colossal Man* (1957) and *Attack of the 50 Ft. Woman* (1958), but none of them managed to be as convincing, intelligent, or downright scary as this one. In 1981, a remake entitled *The Incredible Shrinking Woman* appeared, which changed the gender of the hero and attempted to turn the story into a comedy. The film is generally regarded as a failure. As I write this, a remake directed by Keenen Ivory Wayans is in development, to be released in 2008, probably also a comedy.

THE INNOCENTS (1961)
by Jorge Didaco

Squeezed between two milestones in the adult horror canon, *Psycho* (1960) and *The Haunting* (1963), Jack Clayton's *The Innocents* remains likewise a remarkably mature work. Here, horror is presented in its most primeval manifestations, ones that, without neglecting its possible supernatural elements, are more akin to what Bergman calls "horrors of the soul." Not dissimilar to Val Lewton's RKO films of the '40s, *The Innocents* is a marvel of sustained sinister atmosphere and artistic invention maintained solely through tactful, restrained direction, evocative performances, brilliant black-and-white camerawork, and sound design. No shock tactics are on display here; instead, the terror slowly insinuates itself into our hearts, inscrutably creeping under our skin. I was in awe the first time I watched *The Innocents* and it is undoubtedly one of the sources for my fascination with horror films.

The first readers of Henry James' novella *The Turn of the Screw* embraced, without questioning, its possible supernatural/evil manifestations, accepting the protagonists' experiences as indeed arising from the otherworld. However, in light of Freud's studies, critic Edmund Wilson introduced another reading in 1934: a psychoanalytical one. For Wilson, the hallucinations experienced by the protagonist are the products of her internal conflicts. He cites the ghosts in Shakespeare, that only appear to characters already emotionally shattered and predisposed for their manifestations. Wilson purports that the governess, Miss Giddens, despite a brave, authoritative facade, is an obviously haunted, obsessive, prim, sexually repressed woman. Of course, James favored ambiguity, obliquity and allusion, so that this dispute between the veracity of the ghosts' apparitions and the governess' sanity remains the source of endless fascination.

This interpretation of events centers itself on the governess and her reactions, but what about the children, Miles and Flora? Were they sexually abused or victimized in any way by the previous governess, Miss Jessel, and the valet Peter Quint? Are the children possessed by their wicked spirits? Were they witnesses of the lustful and disturbing sexual encounters between Miss Jessel and Quint? Or rather, are they now being subjected to the hysterical, obsessive paranoia of the new governess, Miss Giddens? Who are in fact the innocents—the victims, the abusers? These questions are not easily nor comfortably answered. And if there was a director that could dwell in these uncertainties with extreme sensitivity, aesthetic prowess, and great knowledge for the vagaries between reality and fantasy, it was Jack Clayton.

In Victorian England, a wealthy man (Michael Redgrave) hires a young governess, Miss Giddens (Deborah Kerr) to take care of his orphaned niece and nephew, who live in Bly, a sprawling country estate. Miss Giddens is at first quite pleased but finds herself at a loss dealing with the two precocious and secretive children, Flora (Pamela Franklin) and Miles (Martin Stephens). From the housekeeper Mrs. Grose (Megs Jenkins), Giddens learns that Miss Jessel (Clytie Jessop) had a wild and sordid affair with the brutal valet Peter Quint (Peter Wyngarde), both of whom died under bizarre circumstances. Soon Miss Giddens becomes certain that the children are possessed by the evil spirits of Quint and Miss Jessel. Her suspicions intensify when she begins to see the ghostly appearances of the previous servants. She therefore decides that something has to be done, with catastrophic consequences. The ending remains as ambiguous as that of the novel.

The Innocents begins unforgettably: a black screen with the voice of a child singing a song of sorrow and sadness:

> We lay my love and I, beneath the weeping willow,
> But now alone I lie and weep beside the tree,
> Singing "Oh willow waly" by the tree that weeps with me.

We then witness, on the left side of the screen, a tortured figure crying and praying feverishly behind the titles. Critics often compare *The Innocents* with Robert Wise's *The Haunting*, another adaptation of a classic ghost/haunted house novel. However, this affecting opening reminds me of another 1961 horror masterpiece, Jerzy Kawalerowicz's *Mother Joan of the Angels*. Here too, as the credits appear, we hear a litany and see the fragile, lean figure of a priest prostrated on the floor. These two susceptible creatures, the governess and the priest, will soon enter a world of their own (and others') demons; both films' protagonists will, by the conclusion, find themselves forever devastated.

Two things stand out in this opening scene: the atmospheric use of sound, augmented by eloquent silences and eerie music, and the unusual framing and composition by ace cinematographer Freddie Francis (who would embark on a successful career as director himself). He uses startling effects of *chiaroscuro*, where strange, artificial luminosities invade nights and dark areas, producing shadowy effects that permeate the clarity of bright and humid days (the classic Gothic imagery of dark shadows creeping into a ring of candlelight, for instance). He constructs closeups of Miss Giddens positioned

Dead valet Peter (Peter Wyngarde) watches young Miles (Martin Stephens).

along the corner of the frame, while events occur on the opposite side, sometimes "trapping" her alongside windows, stairs, corridors, achieving a sense of inescapability and claustrophobia.

Francis and Clayton (ably assisted by William Archibald and Truman Capote's shrewd screenplay) achieve particularly startling results in dealing with the possible manifestation of the ghosts of Miss Jessel and Quint: In one sequence the highly exaggerated buzzing of a fly does the preparatory work, evoking the daze of a summertime illusion. The governess sees Miss Jessel as a substantial figure inside the house, briefly glimpsed at a desk and then gone again, but leaving behind a teardrop that evaporates on a piece of blotting paper. More daringly, yet with equal persuasion, a game of hide and seek is punctuated by the sudden vision of Quint at the window, his breathing heavy and sensual, his handsome face luminous, yet cruel.

The contrast between sunlit gardens and moody shadows wonderfully reflects the psychological drama, but strongest of all are the individual, baroque images of death and decay, of sexual repression and sensuality: a fat, black beetle crawling between the lips of a fallen statue of Cupid in the garden; the unsettling poem/ballad Miles recites at night (*"What shall I say when his feet enter softly? Leaving the marks of his grave on my floor"*) just before the windows inexplicably fly open; or the goodnight kiss Miles gives Miss Giddens—or is it the contrary?—which somehow becomes indecently sexual (critic Shoshana Felman points out that in this memorable scene it is as if the spectator's innocence, along with those of the characters, is no longer intact; we have been violated).

Another stylistic device Clayton favors is the use of dissolves (a technique also utilized in Val Lewton's productions, like 1946's *Bedlam*). In an interview with Gordon Gow for *Films and Filming* (1974) Clayton stated: "*The Innocents* is completely mood-orientated, and it gave me opportunities to explore this field: to create, in those multiple dissolves, images which hang there, and have a meaning which applies to the end of the last scene and the beginning of the next." One such image that just "hangs there," becoming something akin to Japanese *haikai*, (a poem/metaphor open to multiple meanings), is one of a large white rose, another striking symbol of lost innocence.

Clayton was arguably one of the most celebrated directors of children and the performances he elicits from Pamela Franklin and Martin Stephens are so emotionally devastating and exhausting, filled with such complexity and impeccable middle-class creepiness, that one cannot help but marvel. As Flora, Franklin is delicate, playful, and cheerful in her screen debut, but possessing a palpable menace in her expressive eyes. Even more astonishing is Stephens as Miles, who had played the demonic alien offspring from the previous year's *Village of the Damned*. His angelic looks convey prescience and innocence, his manipulative, obnoxious behavior counter-balanced by sudden affability and a strange, precocious sensuality that belies his tender age.

But it is Deborah Kerr who is the film's center, giving one of her most memorable performances: nervous and genteel, veiling repressed feelings and an escalating hysteria under a controlling facade, working layers of meaning in her well modulated gestures, voice and facial expressions. By the time the film ends as it began, with the credits rolling under the praying hands of Miss Giddens, we, like she, have been irredeemably doomed by the onscreen events, by those inexplicable, incomprehensible acts, words, and gestures.

Though not a huge success on its initial release (Hammer's "blood in color" productions were more in vogue), *The Innocents'* reputation and influence has continued to grow through the years. Such films as Alejandro Amenábar's *The Others* (2001), Guillermo del Toro's *The Devil's Backbone* (*El Espinazo del Diablo* [2001]) and even M. Night Shyamalan's *The Sixth Sense* (1999) are indebted to Clayton's picture in their use of ambiguity and an oblique narrative. By not relying solely on jump frights but rather upon atmosphere and ambiance, these recent works mark a very welcome return to the Gothic, that wondrous mixture of the uncanny and the marvelous.

INVASION OF THE BODY SNATCHERS (1956)
by Darren Callahan

There are some core ideas in horror that always "play," as they say in the business. Threat of physical harm is certainly one of them, which explains the proliferation of serial killers, chainsaw killers, monster killers, and slasher killers. Another would be the threat from supernatural evil—ghosts and devils that take over the world, your house, or your car named Christine. But no horror is higher on the list than having a person we know become someone…different. Very few of us, thankfully, have been chased by madmen with axes or lived in haunted houses, but many of us have become disconnected from friends, or family, or ex-lovers. In their own way, films like *The Shining, The Exorcist, Rosemary's Baby,* and Romero's zombie movies tap into this basic fear, but very few films provide such a pointed example as the original 1956 version of *Invasion of the Body Snatchers*.

Directed by Don Siegel (*Dirty Harry, The Shootist*) and starring Kevin McCarthy, this film tells of strange events in Santa Mira, an idyllic American town, where the residents have been suddenly gripped by a "mass hypnosis." People believe that duplicates have replaced all their friends, lovers, and families. Returning from a trip is resident doctor Miles Bennell (McCarthy), a good man in a budding romance with too-beauti-

Miles Bennell (Kevin McCarthy) realizes when a kiss is not a kiss!

ful-for-this-town Becky Driscoll (Dana Wynter). Investigating the town's perplexing mindset, Bennell begins to uncover the truth—that alien seedpods are hatching exact replicas of each person. The replicas then steal the victim's remaining spiritual and mental attributes when the person falls asleep, resulting in the destruction of the original body. The replica is the same in every way—except they are emotionally hollow. But Bennell and his sweetheart realize this too late, for soon they are the last remaining humans in Santa Mira.

I should be very clear here that this film is *not* the one with the dog. The horrific "dog with man's head" scared the wits out of many audiences and is considered a core image from *Invasion*. That memorable scene is from Philip Kaufman's 1978 remake starring Donald Sutherland, Jeff Goldblum, and Leonard Nimoy. The '78 version also introduced "the voice"—the screeching alarm bell out of the pod people's mouth when ratting out a human—which was carried into Abel Ferrara's 1993 updating, *Body Snatchers*. These are fine touches, to be sure, but they were not in the original.

However, the 1956 film based on Jack Finney's novel *The Body Snatchers* (originally serialized in *Harper's*) is no drive-in throwaway from the atomic age. When Kevin McCarthy takes a pitchfork to his half-formed double, we know this isn't some quaint monster movie. This is the real deal—a film ahead of its time in content and character. The only thing that feels a little stiff over the decades is the rather forgettable thriller score by Carmen Dragon and the over-politeness of Dr. Bennell's courtship of Becky Driscoll. Often thought of as a McCarthy-ism, Communist-scare parable, producer Walter Wanger insists his only goal was to deliver a popcorn alien invasion movie. But the source material, the commitment of the cast, and the realism of director Siegel (displaying his *Riot In Cell Block 11* grittiness) serve to elevate the film and connect it with true human experience.

There is one particular moment where *Invasion* shows its stuff. Dr. Bennell, searching for anyone in the town still human, goes to the house of his loyal assistant. Peeping in the windows, he witnesses a meeting of a dozen pod people. They are discussing, quite casually, who should put a seedpod in the baby's crib upstairs, so the child can be replicated and the original destroyed. We never see the child, the child is never introduced as a character, and we never learn if the child escapes this fate. In one brief scene, the evil of the aliens is fully established.

Children actually suffer quite a bit in the film (though not as much as in Ferrara's remake). Bennell's first strange incident when returning to Santa Mira is calming a child who believes his mother is not his mother. Anyone with a hint of the film's premise watches the scene with shaking head as Bennell injects the boy with "something to help him sleep," unaware that he is making the boy completely defenseless.

Bennell and his friends, the Belicecs, catch on very quickly to the alien mission. The audience is not led around for reel after reel of stupid and dense character behavior. (It's worth mentioning that Bennell abandoning the Belicecs with a half-formed replica of the husband, Jack, to go on a date with Becky is pretty ludicrous. But it's a rare plot contrivance rather than the first in a series of predictable blunders.)

Is it scary? Made on a shoestring budget and containing few special effects, if anything, *Invasion* often resembles a stage play with long exchanges of dialogue between the main characters. The frights don't come from blood or pyrotechnics, but from what we think of ourselves and those we know. What would a world be like if we surrendered all our hopes, fears, desires, and personality over to an alien collective?

In fact, things in this "new world order" of pod people seem pretty ideal. No one fears each other and no one fights. They have a common goal based in logic and have apparently discarded all the emotions that get humans into trouble.

In one famous scene, Bennell and Becky look down on the town square from a hiding place. Santa Mira is as blissfully normal in its midday bustle as any American small town. Then, as if pulled by invisible wires, everyone breaks from their random activities to form a perfect shape in the town square. It must have been a very difficult shot to orchestrate, and it has a lasting, chilling effect. The people they knew are no longer thinking, but instead are joined together like a single-cell organism, whose only goal is to assimilate, Borg-style, everything different from itself.

The film makes us ask *questions*. That's uncommon in a genre mainly known for aural or visual stabs—things that make audiences jump in their seat. Throughout the film, the audience wonders, how would I act in the same situation? What would it be like in a world without individual identity or emotions? How *well* do I know the person next to me in the theater, on the sofa? What might it feel like to be the last person standing, to be different from everyone else around? After all, one of the prime causes of sadness is a feeling of isolation. I'm not talking about being alone, but of loneliness—a very different thing. People are naturally "joiners"—churches, clubs, MySpace, horror conventions, you name it. We all want to belong. But there is an absolute line drawn: We will only belong if we can remain ourselves. Once self is surrendered, it's no longer a community. It's servitude. Community binds common interests, common purposes, but not at the expense of individuality. Miles Bennell runs into the night (famously shouting "You're next!") because he knows, as all humans know, that a life without individualism is a terrible fate.

Of course, in all three versions of the film, there is a beautiful caveat to the transformation. When it's over, we will be happy, and we will understand. We merely feared what was not yet known. Everyone watching the film will also be transformed.

THE INVISIBLE MAN (1933)
by Charles S. Lore

Jack Griffin (Claude Rains), the Invisible One

In the 1979 film *Time After Time*, there are scenes in a museum exhibit trumpeting H.G. Wells as a man ahead of his time—and rightly so. A Reuters news story dated July 31, 2006 carried the headline: "Scientist Thinks Invisibility Possible In Future." It goes on to state that "in research published in the New Journal of Physics, Dr. Ulf Leonhardt described the physics of theoretical devices that could create invisibility. It is a follow-up paper to an earlier study published in the Journal of Science."

We can also consider Universal's 1933 screen version of Wells' *The Invisible Man* to be a film ahead of its time; still able to entertain with all of its powers undiminished.

I watched the film recently for perhaps the 40th time in as many years. This time I did so with my 15-year-old son, who is more receptive to the current state of special effects. Still, even he found this 70-year-old film to be most enjoyable, declaring the effects as "awesome."

What makes such a film retain its freshness? Many offerings of equal vintage creak more than they speak to today's filmgoers. While watching, I pointed out to my son how director James Whale kept his camera moving, while so many other efforts of that period appear stagebound, with the camera stuck in one position and the actors all in frame. Only two years separate Whale's classic from Browning's *Dracula*, but it might

Jack Griffin, in death, turns visible for the first time in the movie.

as well be two generations. Even Browning's *Freaks* (made at the much bigger MGM in 1932) still looks as if it were filmed as a silent, or at the least, as if it were a Mascot release rather than one from the most opulent of the major studios.

A static camera was often blamed on primitive sound recording techniques, yet here again, Whale shows his flair, as the story depends greatly on an unseen character (Jack Griffin, our titular "Invisible One") often moving and speaking at the same time. Some of these lines from R.C. Sherriff's delightful screenplay deserve recall, especially Griffin's scenes with fellow scientist Kemp:

"It came to me suddenly. The drugs I took seem to light up my brain. Suddenly I realized the power I held, the power to rule, to make the world grovel at my feet."

"We'll start with a reign of terror. Murders of little men and murders of big men—just to show that we make no distinction."

"You must always be at hand to wipe off my feet. Even dirt beneath my fingernails can give me away."

This last line comes from a scene where Griffin is describing the ins and outs of invisibility, which include not going out in the rain or areas of heavy soot (such as the mining town in which Whale was raised), nor going out in public until his food is digested. The film also contains what might be the first uttering of that oft-cited mantra of mad-scientist movies: "He meddled in things that Man should leave alone."

That Claude Rains would never have to worry about work for the rest of his life is a testament to his performance here, despite not being seen until the last 30 seconds of the film. Universal would subsequently star a much more visible Rains in the marvelously titled *The Man Who Reclaimed His Head* (1934) and *The Mystery of Edwin Drood* (1935). A decade after *The Invisible Man*, Rains' voice would again be more prominent than his features in Universal's 1943 remake of *The Phantom of the Opera*.

However, Rains' talents might not have been visible, or invisible in this case, were it not for the studio's greed. As noted by Pablo Kjolseth on the Turner Classic Movies web site:

"Boris Karloff had originally been slated for the role of Griffin but walked out after producer Carl Laemmle, Jr. pressed him one too many times for cuts in his contractual pay. This was just fine with Whale who was dead-set against Karloff anyway, feeling Karloff's followers would expect a ghoulish monster film rather than an extraordinary tale of a scientist trying to escape his fate. From the beginning, Whale wanted Claude Rains, whom he knew from earlier years as a respected teacher at the Royal Academy for Dramatic Art (Charles Laughton was one of his students)."

Dr. Kemp, played by William Harrigan, is truly contemptible, less so for his cowardly (but understandable) reactions to Griffin's demands than for his hitting on the Invisible One's lovely fiancée, Flora Cranley (Gloria Stuart), just as she's bemoaning Griffin's disappearance. Stuart, the elderly "Rose" of James Cameron's *Titanic*, has little to do beyond fretting as Flora, but she does so most attractively. Henry Travers is acceptable as Dr. Cranley, though present day audiences probably can't help but identify him as Clarence the angel in *It's a Wonderful Life*. His part does not have much going for it, but does set the standard for the elderly scientist with the hot daughter (or niece) that would appear in so many horror and sci-fi films of the future.

Dwight Frye, of Whale's *Frankenstein* and *Bride of Frankenstein* (as well as Tod Browning's *Dracula*), can be glimpsed briefly as a spectacled reporter, while John Carradine turns up calling the police with suggestions on how to capture Griffin. Future triple Oscar winner (1936, 1938, 1940, all for Best Supporting Actor) Walter Brennan is the "old man" (yet only 39 at the time) whose bicycle is stolen and can be spotted most clearly when the inquiry into the phenomenon is being held by the Iping police.

But most praiseworthy perhaps are the truly astounding effects of John P. Fulton, setting the standard for every "invisible entity" and ghost film to follow. Details into the process would require a book unto themselves, so perhaps it is best left to Fulton himself to describe them.

From *The American Cinematographer* (September 1934) and reprinted in the book *Universal Horrors*:

> The wire technique could not be used, for the clothes would look empty, and would hardly move naturally. So we had recourse to multiple printing…with variations. Most of these scenes involved other, normal characters, so we photographed these scenes in the normal manner, but without any trace of the invisible man. All of the action, of course, had to be carefully timed, as in any sort of double-exposure work. This negative was then developed in the normal manner.
>
> We used a completely black set…walled and floored with black velvet, to be as nearly non-reflective as possible. Our actor was garbed from head to foot in black velvet tights, with black gloves, and a black headpiece rather like a diver's helmet. Over this, he wore whatever

clothes might be required. This gave us a picture of the unsupported clothes moving around on a dead black field. From this negative, we made a print, and a duplicate negative, which we intensified to serve as mattes for printing.

The film was well received, with literary critic William Troy proclaiming, "Taken either as a technical exercise or as a sometimes profoundly moving retelling of the Frankenstein fable, it is one of the most rewarding of recent films." *Variety* was prescient in noting: "Well made and full of intentional and unintentional laughs. Should do well."

It's interesting to note that *The Invisible Man* and *King Kong* were both released in the same year. Despite sequels, remakes, and imitations, as well as improvements (or changes) in acting techniques and special-effects cinematography, the very charm of these two films continues to keep audiences amazed generation after generation.

ISLAND OF LOST SOULS (1933)
by Peter Christensen

Fifty-plus years ago, when I first watched this film, I had no idea of the shock that awaited me. After all, I'd seen most of the famous horror movies, and *Dracula, Frankenstein, The Wolf Man,* and *The Mummy* hadn't frightened me beyond the pleasure principle. This was in the early 1950s, a time when parents, quite rightly for the most part, saw no reason to monitor what their kids watched on TV—even if they were taking in a horror film late on a Saturday night. Although my parents hadn't seen *Island of Lost Souls,* they happily left me to it. The movie absolutely terrified me, and a half-century later, a recent viewing confirms that it has lost none of its potency.

Our first meaningful indication of just where the film's power and horror lie comes early on. Shipwreck victim Edward Parker (Richard Arlen) is rescued from the ocean by a ship heading for Moreau's island with a cargo of animals. Parker observes that one of the men on board has the ear of a dog. The audience isn't allowed to miss this fact either, since we get it in a potent closeup (there are many such closeups of makeup artist Wally Westmore's creations, almost literally shoving the monsters into our faces on occasion).

Moreau's island, as it turns out, is anything but a tropical paradise. Along with Parker, we come to learn that Moreau, played by Charles Laughton as an instantly detestable pudgy sadist, has been using his "House of Pain" to vivisect animals in an effort to create human beings out of them. With smug arrogance, Moreau openly acknowledges that his efforts to speed up evolution provide him with an opportunity to play God, a role for which he thinks himself fitted. The problem is that his surgery, performed without anesthetics, doesn't take. Despite the "Laws" which Moreau has given to his creatures—containing the supposedly rhetorical question "Are we not men?"—his creatures regress into beasts. Moreau, as God, has given his creations a set of commandments which parody those in the book of Exodus and which receive much the same treatment as those that God delivers to Moses. Moreau's whip can make the creatures obey for only so long, and when the revolt finally comes, it is uncontrollable.

Bela Lugosi plays the "Sayer of the Law" in makeup so hirsute as to make him virtually unrecognizable. This small fact, which has little interest on its own, may

The heavily disguised Bela Lugosi plays the Sayer of the Law.

suggest something about the direction in which Lugosi's career was going when he appeared in *Island of Lost Souls.* The actor's striking appearance and thick Hungarian accent, while ideally suited for his star-making turn as the otherworldly title character in *Dracula* (1931), took him out of the running for many other parts. He had turned down the role of the Monster in *Frankenstein* (1931) because he didn't care for the idea of appearing in makeup that masked his own identity. Two years later, Lugosi may have accepted this part in *Island,* despite its smallness and other disadvantages, simply because he (or his agent) may have understood this unfortunate truth.

Parker's presence on the island enables Moreau to take one further ugly step in his experiments. Parker is tempted into mating with Moreau's most successful experiment to date—Lota, the Panther Woman (Kathleen Burke). The word "bestiality" isn't mentioned, although reasonably attentive viewers will know precisely what's going on when Moreau puts his plan into action.

All ends well—or so it seems. Parker, his fiancée Ruth, and a doctor escape as the beast-men turn on Moreau and carry him to the House of Pain. His screams (we are spared any graphic imagery, leaving our fertile imaginations to do the work) tell us that his little empire has come to an end. As we get our last look at the island, we witness it being consumed in flames. The three escapees will return to civilization, but the idea of "civilization" should give the viewer pause, for the film leaves us with many issues to mull over as the credits roll.

What will the three think of the "creatures" who will surround them upon their return home? *Island* raises many questions about humanity's moral nature. It's fairly common for us to call certain people "animals" when they behave in socially unaccept-

Two manimals as rendered by Wally Westmore's makeup crew

able ways, but here again the film turns the figurative into the literal. The captain, who rescues Parker at sea before sending him to Moreau's island, conforms to our notions of a human "behaving like an animal," but what are we to make of those creatures who chant over and over again the words, "Are we not men?" Is the film suggesting that, when they regress, they are indeed acting exactly as humans do and are therefore human? We aren't given a specific answer to the question, but *Island* surely makes us ask it.

We also have to deal with the fact that Moreau makes it clear that he stands in for God. Do we dismiss this claim as megalomania, or is this is a genuine exploration of moral and theological issues? The film is loaded with images of prisons, and it seems to make the case that there are some prisons from which we cannot escape. We ourselves may be those prisons. Much of *Island*'s success lies in its willingness to deal with such complexity. It's true that the drunken doctor, at great risk to himself, redeems himself at the end and that Lota performs a selfless act. But, in the face of so much darkness, we might wonder if we can accept the conventional happy ending. Ultimately, if we assess it honestly, the film seems to confirm our lowest estimates of humanity and forces us to wonder if creation wasn't the cruelest of God's acts. The happy ending isn't something tacked on just to make us go home happy. It's there to make us think and wonder.

The picture gave great trouble to reviewers at the time of its release. Most of them didn't have any real idea of what it was about, and censors, both in America and in Britain (where it was simply banned), had a field day. By the standard of its time, it's a grisly film, but it seems at least possible that there were things other than its genuine horrific qualities that bothered viewers. H.G. Wells' 1896 novel *The Island of Doctor*

Moreau, upon which the film is based, was very much of its time in dealing with the issue of just how stable human nature really is. Stevenson's *The Strange Case of Dr. Jekyll and Mr. Hyde* (1886) is perhaps the most well-known instance, but such ideas also find their way into popular literature, with Conan Doyle's *The Hound of the Baskervilles* (1902) a notable example. When horror became the vogue in the 1930s, what greater horror could filmmakers explore than the possibility that we can create nothing worse than what we ourselves are?

Given *Island*'s initial response, which is still not as popular as other genre efforts of its time, it isn't surprising that its director, Erle C. Kenton, didn't become a star. He worked steadily as a film director until 1950, when he went into television, but his career was that of a journeyman. He directed a few other competent horror films including *Ghost of Frankenstein* (1942), *House of Frankenstein* (1944), and *House of Dracula* (1945), but the rest of his work, including five films with Abbott and Costello, is virtually forgotten. *Island of Lost Souls* is his masterpiece—a word which is appropriate—but it's the kind of masterpiece which may have relegated its creator to a career in mediocrity.

I WALKED WITH A ZOMBIE (1943)
by C.D. Ellefson

I Walked With a Zombie is a film whose breezy beginning and abrupt ending provide bookends for what is probably the most frightening and disturbing horror offering of the 1940s. Indeed, the decade was hardly the horror-lover's best era, with many pictures of the time falling into the noir or melodrama category. But *I Walked With a Zombie* is a horror movie in the true sense of the word. It also provided a blueprint for many horror features to come.

Zombie begins with a young nurse, Betsy (Frances Dee), being assigned her first nursing position on an island. Even though she is not told the details, she is game for the job. Her new employer, Paul Holland (Tom Conway), accompanies her on a ship to the island. He seems cold and distant, although polite. But she boldly presses on, excited by the trip. Her first night on the island plantation is punctuated by a frightening introduction to Mrs. Holland (Christine Gordon), who seemingly accosts her on the stairs of a private wing of the estate. Jessica Holland is to be Betsy's assignment, and our first vision of her is that of a menacing, advancing, animated corpse shambling from the darkness.

In the daylight, though, Jessica is a beautiful, semi-comatose patient, easy to care for and ambulate. Her doctor describes her as a "sleepwalker who can never be awakened," and vaguely blames her state on a "fever." Later we find out that Jessica and Mr. Holland's half-brother Wesley (James Ellison) were having an affair, and that Mr. Holland discovered this fact and became enraged. Both men believe that this is what has caused Jessica's illness. But the natives of the island believe differently. They believe Jessica is cursed with voodoo. Although the servants go about their care of the plantation and Jessica with great attention, there are mumblings of the bad luck the curse has brought to the island. Mrs. Rand (Edith Barrett), Wesley's mother, is a doctor on the island as well. She appears to believe in the straight medical diagnosis of Jessica, but in reality, she holds a dark secret that is quite the opposite. Betsy has

Darby Jones plays the guardian zombie Carrefour.

feelings and compassion for Mr. Holland, and wishes to cure Jessica, so he can be happy again. When experimental medical treatment fails, she turns to the natives of the island to try curing Jessica with voodoo. After leading her charge on a harrowing and frightening trip to the voodoo ceremonial site, we see what no one else has truly believed: Jessica is a *real* zombie.

I Walked With a Zombie has the usual horror themes running through it (superstition, the supernatural, things that go bump in the night), but the main underlying themes are the changing roles of men and women, science vs. magic, and the reparation of relations between races.

Christine Gordon plays Jessica with perfect deadpan, her face never moving a muscle. She is perfectly suited for the role, beautiful but blank. Oddly, she would never have a credited role after this. She represents the pre-war female, empty and beautiful, able to be led, completely dependent and subservient. Betsy and Mrs. Rand, however, show the changing roles of women. They are calm, intelligent, bold, and decisive, each in their own way. The men convey the confusion reminiscent of soldiers returning from WWII to find active and newly liberated women who had had to take over the workforce while the men were gone. No longer were women content to stay home, and men frequently looked to more "modern" women instead of the trophy wife that Jessica represents here. Medical science was also evolving quickly in the 1940s. Vaccinations were becoming available, and war injuries paved the way for a lot of new techniques and theories as well. But people were still accustomed to "old ways," and many still preferred a home remedy approach. Elders would say that if someone truly became a zombie, as in an animated corpse, there is not much that science can do for that person. At least, not without serious and unwanted repercussions, as we will be told in countless other genre efforts to follow. (And *still* that lesson will never be learned by anyone in a horror movie—until it is too late, of course.)

Finally, the relationship and interaction of the white civilians to the black natives of the island is particularly unusual for a movie of this era. The servants are servants, to be sure, and as usual are portrayed as finding pleasure in serving. But the interaction of the two societies is pleasant, and Betsy at one point describes a servant's sister's new baby as being beautiful, and that she is proud that he likes her. The native people of the island have the "solution" to Jessica's problem, ultimately saving her, albeit in "their way." These small things show the microscopic changes that were occurring in the world between races, and how the contributions of minorities were beginning to filter into mainstream society.

This may sound like a lot of content for what could pass as a cheesy horror movie, but *I Walked With a Zombie* is a standout in an otherwise bland era of horror. Val Lewton and Jacques Tourneur could be said to have kept the horror genre afloat in the film noir '40s. Not only did they collaborate on this film, clearly a horror masterpiece for the era, but they had previously teamed up for 1942's *Cat People*, and managed to make *The Leopard Man* in the same year as *I Walked With a Zombie*. Lewton would produce several more horror movies during the decade, and has had his '40s horror output immortalized in a special DVD box set collection released by Warner Bros. Whether he and Tourneur intended a running commentary on the changes WWII brought to human interaction and roles is uncertain. But clearly the trends in the world were beginning to affect the content of post-war films.

This early '40s horror film showed a sign of what was to come in the '50s; it was a pioneer of sorts for the future trend of science paranoia. The abrupt ending of *Zombie* is a standout as well; while not a happy one, it may be the only solution to Jessica's predicament. That being said, I found the ending to be rushed and lacking detail when compared with the rest of the film. (Perhaps the filmmakers were attempting a shocking ending, but although disturbing, it seemed as though they were not quite sure how to end it all.) However, personal regrets aside, Tourneur and Lewton do provide a true "horror movie ending" for what I would call the best genre film of the 1940s.

JACOB'S LADDER (1990)
by Kenneth Lund

Jacob Singer (Tim Robbins) is a veteran from the Vietnam War, working as a postman and living in New York with his girlfriend Jezebel (Elizabeth Peña). Prior to the war, he had a wife and three children, but one of the children, Gabriel (Macaulay Culkin), was killed in an accident, and Jacob no longer lives with his wife, Sarah (Patricia Kalember). While in Vietnam, Jacob was injured in combat during an incident he has never fully understood. Recently, however, Jacob has begun to suffer from

Jacob Singer (Tim Robbins) faces his own angels and demons.

strange hallucinations in which he is haunted by demon-like creatures. When he learns that his old army buddies are suffering from the same hallucinations, they suspect that they have been used as guinea pigs in a secret government experiment. Jacob will soon discover that nothing is what it seems to be.

I first saw *Jacob's Ladder* on TV in the mid-1990s and I clearly remember the feeling of confusion it left me with when I turned off the set. What had I just seen? Was it a Vietnam War movie, a government conspiracy thriller, or a horror movie? The brief glimpses of demonic imagery had me saying, "Did I just see that?" and the twist ending forced me to reconsider whatever interpretation I had concocted. I only knew I had to watch it again! I did pick up on some of the biblical symbolism, but I had the feeling of having only scratched the surface of the story, a sentiment that echoed my viewings of films such as Ingmar Bergman's *Persona* (1966) and David Lynch's *Eraserhead* (1977) and *Lost Highway* (1997).

Consider this a celebration of one of the greatest modern horror movies. While *Jacob's Ladder* was only a modest success at the box office compared to Adrian Lyne's previous hits, *Flashdance* (1983) and *Fatal Attraction* (1987), I would argue that it is his masterpiece. It has a moody and subtle soundtrack by Maurice Jarre, an engaging story with great depth and complexity, and a perfect cast with several actors who would later become big stars: Macaulay Culkin, Jason Alexander, Eriq La Salle, Ving Rhames, and the under-appreciated Pruitt Taylor Vince. Lyne combines these elements with flawless direction, lighting, camerawork, and cinematography.

Bruce Joel Rubin wrote the script for *Jacob's Ladder* back in the 1970s, but he could not find anyone to produce it until Lyne showed interest in the late '80s. According to Lyne's audio commentary and the documentary *Building Jacob's Ladder*, the script was changed in various important ways. Rubin envisioned the film's angels and demons as we think of them traditionally—angels with wings and demons with horns and pitchforks. Instead, Lyne elected to depict them as ordinary human characters. The angels are often shown in a warm light, giving the viewer a sense of safety and comfort when they are onscreen. The real shockers are the demons, their varied and horrific organic deformities shown only in brief flashes, so the viewer is never sure of what he/she just saw. Lyne realized early on that he would never be able to show audiences a demon that would be scary enough, so he gives us a hint and leaves it to our minds to fill in the blanks—a trick that I wish a lot of horror directors would consider before they throw CGI monsters and over-the-top special effects at the audience. Nothing can compete with the power of imagination.

What is the movie about? That is a question I have heard numerous times regarding *Jacob's Ladder*. Search anywhere, and one finds a multitude of explanations. Some argue it is about modern urban alienation, while others explain the story in Freudian terms, and there is plenty of evidence in the movie to validate both interpretations. One element that must be included in any analysis is the biblical references, which can help explain much of the story.

The only scenes in the movie that are "real" are the scenes in Vietnam where Jacob is wounded and the ending where he dies. Everything else takes place inside Jacob's head while he is dying. In this respect, the story is very much like Ambrose Bierce's classic short story "An Occurrence at Owl Creek Bridge."

The movie is best understood by starting with the key scene in the movie when Jacob's chiropractor, Louis (Danny Aiello), quotes Meister Eckhart (a 13th century German philosopher):

"Eckhart saw Hell too. He said the only thing that burns in Hell is the part of you that won't let go of life, your memories, your attachments. They burn them all away. But they're not punishing you, he said. They're freeing your soul. So, if you're frightened of dying and...and you're holding on, you'll see devils tearing your life away. But if you've made your peace, then the devils are really angels, freeing you from the earth." (In the beginning of the movie, we see Jezebel burning some of Jacob's pictures of his family, thereby acting accordingly.)

In the Bible, Jacob's Ladder is a ladder used by angels to move between levels of the afterlife. In the movie, Jacob's soul is in Hell (or Purgatory) trying to find a way to Heaven. Peña's Jezebel (the biblical Jezebel made King Ahab abandon his god, Jehovah, and worship her god, Baal, instead) is one of the demons symbolizing things which Jacob must let go. She is shown naked much of the time, and at the party we clearly get the message when she fornicates with another demon on the dance floor.

On the other hand, we feel very safe in the flashbacks where Jacob is with his family before his son Gabriel was killed. The flashbacks—first from the fever after the party and secondly after his visit to the hospital—occur when Jacob is close to dying in Vietnam. We want him to stay with his family, who are shown in an almost angelic light. The wife, Sarah, is depicted as the exact opposite of Jezebel's erotic character. Such imagery only adds to our appreciation of the movie.

My favorite part of the movie is the hospital scene—one of the most frightening I have ever encountered—which can be viewed as a descent into Hell and a forewarning of things to come if Jacob cannot "let go." Especially moving is how fiercely Jacob tries to convince the doctors (and himself) that he is not dead—that he really is alive! And as mentioned above, he awakens surrounded by his family—the memories and attachments that keep him alive.

After Louis' speech, Jacob finally realizes what he has to do. He goes back to his and Jezebel's apartment, finds his box of memories, and relives the day when Gabriel was killed. After Michael (Matt Craven), who worked as a chemist in Vietnam, reveals the truth about that fatal day in Vietnam and the nature of the experimental drug, Jacob takes a cab back to the apartment where he formerly lived with his family. The building is bathed in warm light, contrary to the dirty city Lyne has depicted so far; Jacob is finally freed from his earthly attachments and has forgiven himself for Gabe's death. Gabriel is waiting in the apartment. Hand in hand, Jacob and he ascend the ladder (a giant staircase) into Heaven, while the earthly Jacob dies in Vietnam.

Jacob's Ladder is one of my favorite films and one of the rare few I look forward to revisiting every year. Every time I watch it I find a new detail to think about, and while the 1990s were not the greatest decade for the horror genre, Lyne certainly gave it a good start. The use of a twist ending that forces the viewer to rethink the entire movie was not a new thing in horror (see *Carnival of Souls* [1962] for an early example), but *Jacob's Ladder* was one of the first for the modern era. It revisited a trend that would become very popular in the following years—most notably with director M. Night Shyamalan. Some critics may point out that the logic of the story is flawed—how can Jacob learn the truth about the experimental drug while being in a coma? I do not have the answer, but then again, who knows the logic of purgatory?

JAWS (1975)
by Mark J. Price

I can still hear the scream.

When the great white shark raised its head out of the water, revealing itself for the first time, the startled audience shrieked in unison. Knees buckled. Bodies recoiled. The entire room seemed to shudder. Never before had I witnessed such abject terror in a movie theater.

Neither had anyone else.

Filmgoers lined up in the summer of 1975 to scream and scream again. The movie *Jaws*, which grossed $260 million at the U.S. box office, ushered in the modern era of summer blockbusters, created an international sensation, and spawned a slew of inferior imitations.

It changed the movie industry, and it changed me. I was a young boy who lived on a freshwater lake in Ohio. And, suddenly, I was afraid to swim with bluegill and perch. But I wasn't afraid to see *Jaws* another 10 times that summer. Director Steven Spielberg's movie hooked me like no other film had before. All I wanted to do was talk about it, read about it, and, most importantly, see it again.

The suspenseful film is based loosely on Peter Benchley's best-selling novel, which I dutifully read that summer. Even as a child, I could tell that the source material wasn't as good as the movie. The book starts out well with a horrifying description of a shark attack, but then bogs down in a silly subplot about adultery. Spielberg wisely chose to

Police Chief Brody (Roy Scheider) confronts the deadly killer shark.

eliminate the soap-opera material to focus on the shark and its hunters. The changes that he and screenwriter Carl Gottlieb made, including a completely different ending, are major improvements.

Jaws may very well be the scariest PG-rated movie ever made. It escaped an R rating despite having several visceral sequences that made audiences gasp in 1975. The original advertisements, which warned that the movie "may be too intense for younger children," were not exaggerating. The film proved to be too intense for some adults as well.

Long before the shark appears on camera, tension is built through composer John Williams' Oscar-winning score. The primitive, churning theme that signals the shark's arrival is beautiful in its simplicity. Dread slowly creeps up on viewers as the music grows louder and more insistent. When the shark finally does attack, the moment is swift, fierce, and brutal. No one is safe. The dark monster gulps down men and women, young and old.

The great white is glimpsed only fleetingly in the first half of the movie. This turned out to be due to a happy accident. Problems with a mechanical shark (nicknamed "Bruce") caused long delays in the production and forced Spielberg to improvise. Instead of revealing too much too soon, Spielberg used shark point-of-view camera angles that thrust the viewer into the middle of the action.

According to Gottlieb's book *The Jaws Log*, a definitive chronicle of the making of the movie, production problems gave the cast extra time to develop roles and practice dialogue. The three lead actors—Roy Scheider as Amity Police Chief Martin Brody, Richard Dreyfuss as oceanographer Matt Hooper, and Robert Shaw as crusty sea captain Quint—had more time than usual to prepare, and it's apparent on film. Their realistic, three-dimensional performances give the movie its heart and soul.

A dramatic high point occurs when Spielberg halts the action so Shaw's character can deliver a moody, chilling soliloquy, in which he describes his experiences aboard the U.S.S. *Indianapolis* in WWII. The eerie tale, which explains Quint's motivation for hunting sharks, is completely hypnotic and psychologically unnerving. The carefully chosen words (scripted in part by Shaw himself) evoke as much horror as the killer shark that lurks beneath the ocean surface.

On virtually every level, *Jaws* succeeds. It teases, it jolts, it amuses, it terrifies. Spielberg plays the audience like a harpsichord. With the skillful editing of Oscar-winner Verna Fields, the film races along with the ease of a barrel skimming along waves.

For thrills and chills, movies don't get much better than *Jaws*. Critics loved it and crowds rushed to see it multiple times in 1975. According to the Internet Movie Database, the film became the first to shatter the $100 million mark and held all box-office records until *Star Wars* blasted off two years later.

Jaws grossed $470 million worldwide, and inspired a feeding frenzy of similar movies that tried to cash in on its success. Among them were *Mako* (1976), *Orca* (1977), *Tentacles* (1977), *Tintorera* (1977), *Barracuda* (1978), *Piranha* (1978), *Up from the Depths* (1979), and *Great White* (1981). It was only a matter of time before a sequel was made. Roy Scheider returned in 1978 for *Jaws 2*, a worthy follow-up, although Richard Dreyfuss and Robert Shaw were greatly missed. The inevitable second sequel, *Jaws 3-D* (1983), involves yet another shark on the loose, this time at a Florida sea park where Chief Brody's sons work. Surprisingly, the 3-D special effects weren't all that good, and the plot was so waterlogged that it barely stayed afloat. Audiences felt they had seen it all before, and, in fact, they had. The movie made a mere $45.5 million in the United States, less than half of the preceding film's take. Despite the diminishing returns, producers went ahead with the abomination that is *Jaws: The Revenge* (1987), a ludicrous, unintentionally hilarious bomb that effectively put a harpoon in the franchise.

But the original movie will never die. It lives on and on—in infinite reruns on cable channels and in best-selling DVD packages. I've lost track of how many times I've seen *Jaws*. If I had to guess, it would be at least 200. It's nice to know that the movie still has the power to shock. Every time I stumble across it on television, I stop what I'm doing and drift back to a terrifying world where killer sharks prey on New England tourists.

There's a certain scene that always gets to me. When the shark lifts its head out of the water and reveals itself for the first time, I always remember the startled audience from my childhood. I can still hear the scream.

JURASSIC PARK (1993)
by Lee Price

Like velociraptors stalking their prey, Hollywood producers descended on the high concept property of Michael Crichton's *Jurassic Park* before it was even published. They instinctively knew that millions would pay to see this plot: Imagine Disneyworld—but with real dinosaurs as the attractions. The thought of the potential worldwide audience was intoxicating. To quote Carl Denham in *King Kong*, "We're millionaires, boys. I'll share it with all of you!"

The core market was a built-in, predominantly male audience, ranging from little boys to little old men, all of them permanently arrested in the dinosaur phase that most boys quickly pass through. For better or worse, some of us never move on. Take me.

Let's hope the charging T-Rex is not as close as it appears.

In my mid-40s, I'm still dino-obsessed, unable to resist the call of any dino movie. Whether it features a tall guy in an allosaurus costume, an iguana tricked up with horns, or masterful animation by Willis O'Brien or Ray Harryhausen, I'll watch a dino movie any time, any place.

We dino fans treasure a handful of great dinosaur cinematic moments: From the flickering dawn of movie history, there's the impressively large *Gertie the Dinosaur* (1914), the first but hardly the last dino cartoon. Then there's the poetic brontosaur swimming out to sea in *The Lost World* (1925), the T. Rex that snarls and snaps at Fay Wray in *King Kong* (1933) as she lies pinned beneath a tree, the rhedosaurus lured by the lonesome call of the fog horn in *The Beast from 20,000 Fathoms* (1953), the first sight of the monster's head appearing over the hill in *Godzilla* (1954), the cowboys lassoing an allosaurus in *The Valley of Gwangi* (1969), etc. This is the stuff that our dreams are made of.

Then, from the early '70s to the early '90s, there was a painfully long drought.

I wanted Steven Spielberg to make a dinosaur movie from the time I first saw *Jaws* on opening day in a sweltering, packed theater in summer 1975. From the start, I instinctively knew that Spielberg loved dinosaurs and could make a great dinosaur movie. (I can only assume that dino fans have the dino equivalent of gay-dar—we can instantly spot a fellow dino fan.) Back in the early 1980s, I remember reading that Spielberg thought he would go for more of an Edgar Rice Burroughs' feel in his second Indiana Jones movie, and that raised my hopes. Burroughs loved dinosaurs! Perhaps Spielberg would do *Indiana Jones at the Earth's Core*? Or *Indiana Jones in the Land That Time Forgot*? But no such luck. Instead of fighting dinos, Indiana merely slaughtered members of the Kali-worshipping Thuggee cult and those ever-disposable Nazis in the sequels. And so the wait went on. *1941... The Color Purple... Empire of the Sun... Hook...* So much talent, and so few giant lizards.

Finally, in early 1990, we heard what all dino fans desperately wanted to hear when word leaked out that Spielberg would direct the movie version of Crichton's novel *Jurassic Park*. Then…three more years of waiting and rumors: Had he hired Ray Harryhausen as a consultant? Had Harryhausen left in a huff? Would Spielberg use puppets, or even a man in a suit, instead of state-of-the-art stop-motion animation?

Crichton's book was okay, but when Spielberg last tackled a horror-adventure-suspense movie (*Jaws*), he had taken wonderfully intuitive license with the story, improving it all the way. There was plenty of room for improvement on Crichton's novel, and I trusted Spielberg to do it.

The three-year wait was excruciating, but the movie finally opened, and… well, the best parts were everything that a full-blooded (warm or cold) dino fan could ever want. Granted, the 1933 *King Kong* remains the only true masterpiece in the dinosaur genre, but *Jurassic Park* was more than respectable with the dinosaurs themselves surpassing all expectations.

Today, I still appreciate *Jurassic Park*, primarily for three reasons: Spielberg's respectful awe when in the presence of dinosaurs, his extraordinary ability to compose a breathless action set piece, and the delightful onscreen teaming of Sam Neill and Laura Dern.

Cinematic dinosaurs mainly have a reputation for their skill at mass-scale destruction, but I sincerely hoped that Spielberg would also explore the otherworldly beauty of the dinos, an aspect sorely lacking in Crichton's book. Spielberg, aided by a team of f/x maestros (Dennis Muren, Stan Winston, Phil Tippet, and Michael Lantieri), didn't let me down. The two great reverential scenes both feature the brachiosaurs. The first comes just 20 minutes into the movie, when our scientist heroes, played by Neill and Dern, suddenly see the dinosaurs before them. Spielberg makes us wait through the reaction shots, before slowly tilting his camera up to reveal the tree-trunk legs and massive lower body, then stretching high into the sky to glimpse the peaceful little head, calmly munching on the tops of trees. It's perfectly edited, shot, and performed.

Much later, the movie briefly recaptures that feeling of Jurassic awe when Sam Neill and the kids wake up in a tree to a chorus of mooing brachiosaurs. The visual impact of the long necks rising over the treetops is impressive, but the artistic foley sound behind this scene is even better. Throughout the movie, the sound design is simply wonderful, filled with odd, mysterious sounds that add deep textures to the movie. Shortly after this, there's the gallimimus stampede, which looks like a Charles R. Knight painting come to life. (Knight was the great painter of prehistoric scenes that were reproduced in *National Geographic* and the *Time-Life* books of the 1960s, and decorated the halls of that national dino shrine, the American Museum of Natural History in New York City.)

But dino movies aren't all about cooing over the puppy-like vegetarian dinosaurs. Sooner or later, we have to get down to business, and *Jurassic Park* hits overdrive just about one hour in. The first T. Rex attack is one of the great dino moments in movie history, fully demonstrating Spielberg's mastery of choreographed action. It's his attention to the little details—the vibration on the surface of a cup of water, the steam from the T. Rex's nostrils fogging a window—that rivet this scene in the memory, not to mention the most memorable death scene in the movie. And then, to make our dino-lovin' hearts go all aflutter, Spielberg's team even inserts a Godzilla grace note into the T. Rex's majestic roar. It's perfect.

The velociraptors take over the final part of the movie, providing knowledgeable dino nerds with endless opportunities to nudge people and say, "Those are really *deinonychus*, you know." The raptors make superb master criminals, supplying the brains of the outfit in marked contrast to our earlier experiences with the brawn of T. Rex.

Is there a touch of 1938's *Bringing Up Baby* in the finale of the collapsing skeletons? I think so, just as so many of the set pieces are lightened with moments of welcome humor. As the unlikely action stars, Sam Neill and Laura Dern carry most of this humor with impressive comic timing. Above all, I completely accept that these two are really field scientists. They look and act like professionals in love with their chosen field of work. The scene that introduces the brachiosaurs is largely effective because of their expressions of undiluted amazement and delight. They look like real dino fans.

I'd love to dwell on the good points, but it's only fair to mention that a good half hour of the movie leaves me cringing. This isn't *Jaws*, which overcomes minor flaws to become a masterpiece of monster horror. Here the flaws are nearly impossible to ignore. John Williams' score oozes pomposity. There are more clunkers in the dialogue than there should be, especially whenever they start delving into traditional mad scientist "He meddled with things that man was meant to leave alone" territory, or Crichton's weird takes on chaos theory, stylishly mumbled by Jeff Goldblum.

But, worst of all, there are…the kids. This movie sorely tests the long-held assumption that Spielberg is a master at directing children. They add nothing, and they're not even particularly cute. Perhaps Spielberg attempted to make amends in the sequel, *The Lost World: Jurassic Park,* when he has the T. Rex devour a little boy and his dog, but it's too little, too late. He simply should have omitted the kids the first time around.

Since the release of *Jurassic Park* in 1993, there have been two sequels and a number of low-budget imitations. While Peter Jackson's 2005 *King Kong* redux offered up a healthy serving, the current generation is probably ripe for a new dino-spectacular. I can guarantee the core audience is still there, and still ravenous for more.

KING KONG (1933)
by Jake W.

He scaled the Empire State building in record time. He took down a Tyrannosaurus Rex single-handedly. He had a brief relationship with Fay Wray. He is one of the most memorable movie monsters in cinematic history. He's the big furry oaf known as Kong.

No one who has seen *King Kong* would deny that it defines "classic horror" and is nothing short of a truly brilliant and legendary motion picture. It was the first giant monster movie to combine sound with images when it was released in 1933 to America in the depths of the Great Depression. The movie-going public, fascinated by the film,

King Kong, Ann Darrow (Fay Wray), the Empire State Building, and biplanes

paid what little money they had to see it. They were not disappointed. *Kong* was an unbelievable hit that showed moviegoers things they had never seen (nor heard) before. It was the ultimate fantasy film, full of jaw-dropping action—just what the people needed to escape their problems.

The earlier films of *Kong*'s co-directors, Merian C. Cooper and Ernest B. Schoedsack, had also taken place in quite dangerous and primitive locations. Cooper had always wanted to do a picture about a giant ape, but had never known quite how to bring his crazy vision to life onscreen. He and friend/collaborator Schoedsack ended up hiring Willis H. O'Brien, who had been the first to master the technique of stop-motion animation. Prior to his involvement in *Kong*, O'Brien had been working on another project for RKO titled *Creation* which, due to its need of a much bigger budget, was eventually dropped by the studio and never finished. However, O'Brien's work on *Creation* was not wasted as many of the elements within it (stop-motion dinosaurs combined with real actors) were later used in *Kong*. After Cooper saw the stunning effects and effort O'Brien had put into the completed footage for *Creation*, he automatically knew this was the right man for the tricky challenge of bringing his giant ape to life. O'Brien and crew assembled an 18-inch puppet out of foam and fur over a bendable metal skeleton, eventually using four different models in the film.

The budget for *Kong* was somewhere around $670,000, substantially large for the time. Upon its release, the film shattered existing box-office records, grossing more in its opening weekend than any other movie in history. Pretty impressive considering there was a Depression going on, eh? People's curiosities were sparked, recognizing that it was something entirely different. Today, the film is studied and renowned by students and die-hard fans everywhere (myself definitely included). With the ever-improving CGI visual effects that Hollywood dishes out these days, I'm sure many younger viewers may not fully understand nor appreciate the impact of *Kong*. But what must be taken into consideration is the early state of cinema, the extensive effort that stop-motion animation takes, and how many different tricks were required to combine live actors in the same frame with the animated models, construct puppets, etc. According to Carlos Clarens' *An Illustrated History of the Horror Film*, "Each of Kong's steps would require a dozen different exposures, and 25 feet of film flashing on the screen for half a minute was the maximum result of a day's work." In this context, O'Brien's expressive work is nothing less than miraculous.

Another incredibly memorable aspect of the film is Fay Wray's performance as the beautiful and helpless Ann Darrow. Wray appeared in several horror classics including *Doctor X* (1932), *The Most Dangerous Game* (1932), and *The Vampire Bat* (1933). Out of her film roles, *King Kong* remains her most memorable and definitely proved that the gal had a powerful set of lungs.

The hugely successful movie spawned an immediate sequel, rushed out the same year, called *Son of Kong* (1933). Directed by Schoedsack, it was a much inferior film, featuring a giant, though certainly more cuddly, white gorilla. *Mighty Joe Young* (1949)—another Schoedsack effort—was a decent Kong-like film that featured Oscar-winning effects by O'Brien and his young protégé Ray Harryhausen. In 1962, Toho Studios imported Kong to take on their box office-trampling giant lizard in *King Kong vs. Godzilla*, followed by the even sillier *King Kong Escapes* (1967). There was even an ABC animated television series produced by Jules Bass and Arthur Rankin, Jr. in 1966. And of course, there are the big budget remakes in 1976 (not good) and 2005 (quite good).

Still, the 1933 classic remains the best, thanks to its groundbreaking effects and innovative, excellently paced fantasy storyline. *King Kong* is nothing short of amazing and is one of the most important films in cinematic history. I had the pleasure of viewing the original *Kong* years ago, and ever since, it has been one of my favorite films. I have always been a huge fan of stop-motion animation and to me, *King Kong* is the best use of that technique to this day. The film has countless memorable moments that are familiar to cinema fans everywhere, even if they have never seen the picture in its entirety—Kong fighting off biplanes atop the Empire State Building, Fay Wray screaming as an enormous hairy hand grabs her through the window, and of course, the famous final line: "It was beauty who killed the beast."

Personally, I think those pilots deserved a bit more credit, but that's just my sorry opinion.

THE LAST HOUSE ON THE LEFT (1972)
by Jason Herr

As a young un' of about six or seven years old, I remember strollin' with my Pops through the local mom-and-pop video store and always breaking away for a bit when I got near the horror section. Seeing the posters of John Carpenter's *The Thing*, Tobe Hooper's *The Texas Chain Saw Massacre*, Dario Argento's *Phenomena* (titled *Creepers* over here for the U.S. release), and William Lustig's *Maniac*—as well as the alluring box covers for films like Joe D'Amato's *Buio Omega* (under the *Buried Alive* title), Umberto Lenzi's *Cannibal Ferox* (as *Make Them Die Slowly*), and numerous Lucio Fulci films all beckoning me with promises of how horrible they were and how many countries they were banned in. I can honestly say that even at that tender age, before ever having seen such material, I knew I'd be a gorehead for life...

Among those exotic and enticing posters, I remember one the clearest—Wes Craven's *The Last House on the Left*. With all the gruesome imagery within eyeshot, it's strange that particular poster had such an impact on me. The artwork itself was very understated, especially compared to the skulls, Leatherfaces, roaches, and zombies so graphically prevalent in most of the horror poster designs. Instead, this one merely featured a print of a young lady in a nightgown lying in an outstretched hand, with a large house in the distance with some lightning, and the title of the film in the upper right-hand corner. No mutated, worm-spewing zombies, no chainsaw-wielding freaks, no hockey-masked psychos. So why did this particular poster grab me? No idea—but it's stuck with me clearly to this day.

Now, my family wasn't real big on horror films, so I didn't actually see *Last House* until I was about 20. I do recall seeing *Jaws* and a few other "lighter" horror films as a young buck, but it wasn't until the advent of *Saturday Nightmares* (a program on the USA cable network that showed horror films), pay-cable, and the then-booming video rental market that I began my foray into true splatter territory. (That, and my parents allowing me to have a TV in my bedroom.)

As much as the poster affected me when I was younger, *Last House* remained one of those films that I just kinda forgot about over the years—you know, the kind of film you always say you'll rent but never remember once you're at the store. I remember eventually seeing it on the shelf of another mom-and-pop video store that I used to frequent from time to time, and the box cover—though different from the poster that I recalled so well—brought back lots of memories. By this point in my "horror career," I knew about its notorious status as a shocking and graphic exploitation film, and this spurred me on to give it a go. Did it live up to the hype, and can it still manage to shock and repulse in this day and age of shot-on-video "extreme" gore films?

Suggested by Ingmar Bergman's 1960 film of rape and revenge, *The Virgin Spring*, Craven's film tells an updated but similar version of the story: Mari and Phyliss—two young girls, on their way to a rock concert in the city against Mari's parents' wishes—approach a guy about scorin' some pot for the "Bloodlust" show. Turns out he was the wrong guy to ask. Luring the naive teenagers with promises of primo weed, the girls are introduced to a quartet of escaped convicts—Krug Stillo (masterfully played by David Hess), Fred "Weasel" Podowski (Fred J. Lincoln, who would go on to become a semi-famous porn actor/director), Sadie (Jeramie Rain), and Junior Stillo (Marc Sheffler)—who decide to kidnap the girls and have a bit of "fun" with them. The gang takes the girls out to the woods and puts them through some pretty rigorous humiliation paces, before brutally raping and murdering both of them.

When the girls don't return home the next day, Mari's parents contact the local constabulary—a bumbling duo of Sheriff (Marshall Anker) and Deputy (Martin Kove, best known as the evil karate instructor "Kreese" in the smash-hit of 1984, *The Karate Kid*)—who begin to investigate the girls' disappearance. A stroke of bad luck for Krug and Company (their car craps out on them) leaves them stranded in the woods. After

Mari (Sandra Cassel) is brutally tortured by Krug and Company.

a bit of hiking, they end up at the house of a nice middle-aged couple who take them in, feed them, offer them shelter for the night—and just so happen to turn out to be Mari's parents. When Mari's mother notices Krug wearing a distinctive necklace that her daughter wore the night before, mom and dad put two-and-two together and decide to take the law into their own hands and deal out a little backwoods justice...

So now ya wanna know what the fuss is all about surrounding this film, right? Why are people still talking about this exploitation classic almost 35 years later? Is it really as "sick and twisted" as it's made out to be? Well given the general public's relative inexperience with this type of material—yeah—it's pretty rough stuff. Though the golden age of grindhouse and exploitation cinema was certainly hurtling ever nearer, this kind of material was relatively new in '72. I can imagine that this film really did shock a lot of people who might have unknowingly caught it at the theater. One part is the pacing, as *Last House* starts off very pleasantly, then quickly goes from bad to worse (to worse still) over the course of the picture. The other aspect is the graphic and brutal rape, torture, and murder scenes—something audiences didn't encounter very often in 1972—at least not portrayed as blatantly as in this film.

I think it would be safe to say that this, his first feature, is the ballsiest of any of Wes Craven's subsequent works. He has been a prolific genre presence since this initial work, and is arguably one of the most influential and important U.S. horror directors ever. His career spans such "classic" horror films as *The Hills Have Eyes* (1977), *A Nightmare on Elm Street* (1984), *The Serpent and the Rainbow* (1988), and one of the films that has been credited with horror's revival over the last 10 years: *Scream* (1996). But regardless of his large body of work, I personally believe *Last House* to be by far the strongest in terms of shock-value, and possibly even in regards to influence over similar films to come.

It's obvious that the ripples of *Last House* reached pretty far, spawning several rip-offs—in name, if not so much in content. There have been a slew of "Last House" films since the original—all trying to cash-in on the notoriety of Craven's shocker. Another David Hess vehicle, the 1977 Italian sleaze-thriller *Hitch-Hike*, was also released as *Hitch-Hike: Last House on the Left*. The super-low-budget 1977 snuff-themed *The Last House on Dead End Street* is another sadistic exploitation film that bought into the "*Last House*" hype. Others include *The Last House on the Beach* (1978), *The Last House on the Lake* (1979), *The House on the Edge of the Park* (1980—starring Hess in a similar role), and even the porno film, *The Last Whore House on the Left* (2004), directed by and starring original *Last House* co-star, Fred J. Lincoln. And that's not even mentioning the original *Last House*'s impact on jump-starting the whole rape/revenge genre—spawning such "nasty" films as *Thriller: A Cruel Picture* (1974) and *I Spit on Your Grave* (1978)—that thrives to this day.

Some will complain that some strange and disjointed humor appears too frequently, courtesy of the bumbling sheriff and deputy, and that much is true. I personally would have enjoyed the film without this added angle, but I don't feel it detracts from the overall impact. *Last House* continues to shock unsuspecting audiences, and I feel that its strong and realistic depiction of rape and abuse will continue to do so for a long while to come. Is it the most "shocking, disturbing, disgusting" film ever made?—not by a long shot. Does it have the power to repulse and sicken sensitive viewers?—absolutely.

A must-see for exploitation and "extreme" film fans as a stepping-stone into "harder" material, if not the be-all-end-all of shock-cinema.

MAD LOVE (1935)
by Christopher Philippo

Mad Love involves a romantic triangle of the Grand Guignol actress Yvonne (Frances Drake), her husband the concert pianist Stephen Orlac (Colin Clive), and a fan who lusts for her, the surgeon Dr. Gogol (Peter Lorre). Yvonne, though uninterested in Gogol, finds she must turn to him for help when her husband's hands are badly injured in a train wreck. Orlac becomes the recipient of a transplant, courtesy of newly executed knife thrower Rollo (Edward Brophy). Orlac's anxiety about the nature of his hands and Gogol's mad hope to "conquer love" drive the film to its stirring climax.

Over schedule and over budget, the film didn't do well when it was released. In a competitive year for horror movies, it was perceived—like *Freaks* before it—as *too* horrible and lost Metro-Goldwyn-Mayer (MGM) money. For decades, it was not shown on television. (That it had been relatively inaccessible may account for the numerous misstatements made about it in various reference materials. Jeremy Dyson states Gogol "devises a rather unlikely scheme to drive Clive mad by slipping on a pair of metal hands and going out and strangling people;" Phil Hardy reports that Gogol "conceives a diabolical plan to graft the hands of a knife-thrower guillotined for murder;" and Rod Mengham has Lorre playing the doctor in multiple film versions.)

Yet, over the years, appreciation has grown. Indeed, a number of critics from the 1970s on have found *Mad Love* a film to be admired, citing it as "one of the best Hollywood chillers," "the greatest hand movie of them all," and "one of Hollywood's greatest horror shows." Steve Haberman, in his DVD audio commentary, describes the film as

Dr. Gogol (Peter Lorre) tries to terrify Stephen Orlac into insanity.

a "catalogue of the many horrors that the audience had been enjoying for the last four years of cinemagoing." Charlie Chaplin, after seeing Lorre in *Mad Love*, called him "The Greatest Living Actor," a fact that was ballyhooed in the trailer for the film.

Maurice Renard's novel *Les Mains de Orlac* served as the literary source for the film. Renard was highly regarded in Europe and French-Canada, but little known elsewhere. The novel was first published in 1920, with an English version "translated and adapted" by Florence Crewe-Jones, appearing in 1929. Under the title *The Hands of Orlac*, and divided in two parts of 13 chapters each, "Portents" and "Crimes," it is a novel of apparently supernatural happenings.

Interest in and anxiety about the human body, medical science in general, and transplants specifically were subjects from the very beginning of cinema and literature. Could people be taken apart and put back together? Would recipients become like the donors? Georges Melies' *Conjuring a Lady at Robert Houdin's* (1896) involved a woman transforming into a skeleton, and *The Doctor's Experiment*, *The Monkey Man*, and *The Professor's Secret* (all 1908) all involved people acquiring characteristics of primates by glandular injection or transplant. In *The Thieving Hand* (1908), a beggar is rewarded for returning something by being brought a hand to replace his own missing one. The hand has a mind of its own—compulsively stealing—which lands him in jail. However, in jail the hand returns to its already imprisoned original owner and the good man is off the hook.

In adapting *Les Mains de Orlac*, many changes were made by screenwriters P.J. Wolfson and John L. Balderston; it is no more faithful to the original source material than

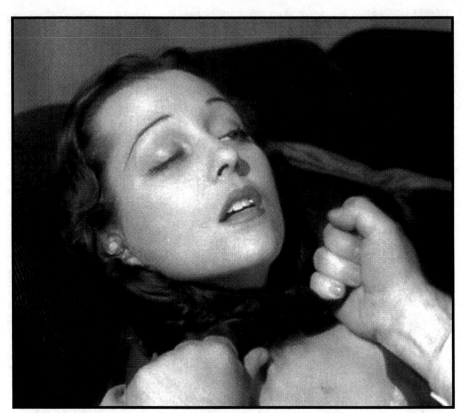

Dr. Gogol strangles Yvonne Orlac (Frances Drake) with her own hair.

Universal's *Dracula* or *Frankenstein* were to theirs—though some scenes are retained much as written, or used as inspiration. Adding a theme of "unhealthy sex" was adaptor Guy Endore, one that permeated his own novels. The Grand Guignol setting is unique to the film, though perhaps borne of a brief reference in the novel. Given the barest of mentions in the novel, but playing a larger role here, is the wax figure of Yvonne, which Gogol dubs "Galatea" (the stone sculpture created and loved by Pygmalion, which then came to life in his arms). Many find the comedic relief provided by the American journalist Reagan intrusive. However he does serve the plot well, and his presence is also a vestige from the novel, in which the journalist serves as the narrator/author.

As for the fantastic, which permeates so much of *The Hands of Orlac*, that is gone in fact but not in spirit. From Jeremy Dyson's *Bright Darkness: The Lost Art of the Supernatural Horror Film*: "[T]here is nothing overtly supernatural about *Mad Love*'s plot yet the film has a haunting, eerie quality [...] Some of this can be attributed to Dimitri Tiomkin's moody score and Lorre's genuinely creepy performance [...] but the bulk of the film's success lies, not surprisingly, considering Freund was directing, in its beautiful photography."

Peter Lorre was one of the best known horror men of the 1930s and '40s, following Bela Lugosi and Boris Karloff (both of whom he starred with in 1940's horror/comedy *You'll Find Out*). Peter Lorre agreed to be loaned out to MGM by Columbia Pictures' Harry Cohn in return for being given the opportunity to star in Columbia's production

Horror 101

of *Crime and Punishment* (1935) with his director of choice, Josef von Sternberg. *Mad Love* would be his first American film. (*Mad Love*'s title sequence echoes the introduction of Peter Lorre in his breakout film, Fritz Lang's *M* [1931], in which he also first appeared as a shadow, similarly dressed in a coat and hat.) Sadly, working on *Mad Love*, *Crime and Punishment*, and Alfred Hitchcock's *Secret Agent* (1936), one after another, may have been a contributing factor prompting Lorre's drug abuse problem.

As William K. Everson notes, "It's poetic justice, too, to see Colin Clive, the erstwhile Dr. Frankenstein, himself the victim of an enterprising Mad Doctor!" Like Frankenstein's creature whose reborn mortal is influenced by the evil brain of another human, Orlac's new hands possess something of their original blade-flinging owner. Clive also got to taste some of the extensive makeup Boris Karloff experienced as the Creature by way of the two-hour process by which his grafted hands were made to look alien and clumsy. Clive elaborated in a 1935 interview: "The finger joints were built up; the hands had to be almost a quarter larger than normal size. Then, around the wrists, where the surgeon has supposedly grafted them on to their new 'foundation,' ghastly scars were created...the experience of viewing one's own hands in this condition was in itself a shock. Often, I felt quite sick, and the real hands under this awful disguise ached with some unaccountable form of irritation. All day and every day I felt that I would give almost anything to be able to wash away the whole ghoulish mess and forget the rest of the picture."

Cut from *Mad Love* were a number of scenes, some at the script level, some after they were shot. None of them are known to survive, but enough is known about them that they may be described. Cut from the very beginning was a prefatory statement similar to the warning spoken by Edward Van Sloan at the beginning of Universal's *Frankenstein*. A minor scene of comic relief, wherein a man at the theater screams at the performance and is told he has a better scream than Yvonne's, also didn't make the final cut. One of the more horrific scenes omitted involved the operation that transplanted Rollo's hands to Orlac. Both the director and the star had some background in surgeries. According to Curt Siodmak, "Peter *really* had a sadistic streak. He liked to go watch operations in the hospital." The role of surgery in the movie was deemed important enough that Freund reportedly joined Lorre to spend a day observing surgery at the Lutheran Hospital.

Though not described as being part of a cut scene, there is a production still in Lorre's biography *The Lost One* by Stephen D. Youngkin, captioned "Fritz Lang takes anthropometric measurements of the plaster cast of Lorre's head from *Mad Love*, 1935." Given that there is no scene in the film involving a bust of Gogol, or his beheading, one wonders if perhaps there had been a nightmare sequence in which he lost his head to a guillotine, which may have been fitting for a man who'd watched such executions religiously, and who finally would have been due for an appointment with one himself.

Finally, as an example of how life often follows art, hand transplants would remain an element of speculative fiction until 1998 when the first (temporarily) successful one occurred. Appropriately enough, the operation occurred in France. The recipient was a New Zealander, Clint Hallam who, it turned out, had not been well screened; the hand was removed in 2001. A transplant that occurred in 1999 with a more careful screening process proved entirely successful, and it and further ones have been monitored at http://www.handtransplant.org. In 2006, a prosthetic hand capable of being moved by thought and that can feel heat and pressure was successfully attached. Mad, indeed!

MARTIN (1977)
by William S. Wilson

Created in the decade between *Night of the Living Dead* (1968) and *Dawn of the Dead* (1978), George A. Romero's *Martin* is a masterpiece of vampire cinema. While *Martin* hasn't received the same mainstream attention and critical success as the *Dead* pictures, it does further show Romero's penchant for creating thought-provoking horror films that deftly mix terror with social commentary.

Martin opens with the titular character Martin Madahas (John Amplas) riding alone on a train. A quiet, timid young man, Martin slowly creeps down a train car until he finds a door, picks the lock and enters the room. Once inside, Martin attacks the young female occupant, knocking her out with an injection and then bathing in and drinking her blood. Martin Madahas, you see, believes he is a vampire.

Arriving in Pennsylvania, Martin is met by his elder cousin Cuda Tata (Lincoln Maazel), a new caretaker who also devoutly believes the family allegations that Martin is really an 84-year-old vampire from Romania. Martin enters Cuda's household, adorned with both religious and vampire iconography, in middle class Braddock, Pennsylvania. Over time, Martin begins to ease into his new life and overcome his shyness. He starts a job delivering for Cuda's deli and, despite warnings from Cuda not to communicate with his granddaughter, forms a friendship with the young Christina (Christine Forrest). He also finds semi-acceptance within the community in two forms—a radio call-in show and a lonely housewife (Elyane Nadeau). The former dubs Martin "The Count" and allows listeners a chance to live vicariously through the "real life" exploits of a vampire. The latter uses Martin as a physical/sexual outlet, something he has never experienced before. But in spite of this, Martin can't eliminate his thirst for blood and, on dark moonlit nights, he ventures out to kill.

Romero often refers to *Martin* as his personal favorite and most realized work of his career, and it is easy to understand his affection. This film, much like *Night of the Living Dead*, takes an established horror category and gives it a new legend. The thing that sets *Martin* apart from other cinematic vampire outings is that it subverts the entire genre. Every cliché attached to vampire films up to this point is deconstructed.

Two scenes are pivotal in establishing this. Early on, when Martin arrives at Cuda's house, the standard weapons of vampire lore greet him. Garlic hangs from doors and crosses are affixed in every room. But Cuda is shocked when Martin actually casts a reflection. Martin confronts his cousin and these myths by taking a bite out of a bulb of garlic and placing a crucifix to his own face. "There isn't any magic," Martin informs him. Later, in one of the film's most memorable scenes, he attacks Cuda in a fog-covered playground, having donned a long black cape and sporting plastic fangs. Looking rather childlike as he prances around, Martin tells Cuda that "it's just a costume," once again denouncing the vampire tradition as we know it.

When Martin calls into the aforementioned radio show, he chastises the movies for not portraying vampires accurately. Yet, when he is preparing to attack victims, he visualizes a romanticized dream of his victim waiting with open arms on the other side. Martin himself possesses none of the known fantastic qualities of a vampire. He must drug his victims and cut them open with razor blades due to his distinct lack of fangs.

Martin Madahas (John Amplas) ... vampire or mental case?

This heavy stamp of screen vampires gone by allows Romero to construct a horror film with a twist. *Martin* offers up the question as to whether the character is truly an 84-year-old vampire or merely a young man with mental problems. Both scenarios are horrific and Romero's script is never specific as to Martin's true affliction, resulting in a far more challenging film for its audience. (For the record, in Paul Gagne's book *The Zombies That Ate Pittsburgh*, Romero states that both he and Amplas approached the character as a mentally unstable man.) Yet, despite the amount of time given to exploring the possibility that Martin may or may not be a true vampire, the film succeeds as a horror film. Every murder that audiences see Martin commit is appalling, yet somehow he remains a sympathetic character. Cuda, on the other hand, is clearly the villain, a man adhering to outdated ideas of mysticism. This dynamic allows Romero to insert doses of his trademark social commentary into the film, with the younger generation battling and dismissing their elders' values. "There is insanity in this family and you've got it," Christina yells at Cuda during an argument about Martin's alleged vampirism.

In addition to Romero's unique take on a standard genre, there are several other reasons why *Martin* is considered a classic today. First, this film marked Romero's return to horror filmmaking after a long period making sports documentaries. In fact, had the opportunity of *Martin* not presented itself, one could theorize that Romero might never have returned to the genre. Subsequently, several contemporary classics such as *Dawn of the Dead* or *Creepshow* (1982) might never have been made. Secondly, and more importantly from the horror film standpoint, *Martin* marks the first professional pairing of Romero with special effects man (and actor) Tom Savini. Romero dreamt up some new scenarios which Savini was able to work out to gain maximum impact on the screen. *Martin* can be seen as the test for their future symbiotic relationship. While the effects work is minimal, it allowed Savini to show Romero what he was capable of doing with limited funds and a lot of imagination. As most horror fans know, this pairing would set the makeup effects/gore standard with their very next collaboration (*Dawn*), forever changing the world of horror cinema.

Critically praised yet hurt by a rapid release, *Martin* is one of three films from a period of Romero's (1972-77) that regularly goes unnoticed. It is one of his works that fans eventually discover after having seen his zombie films countless times. That exact scenario happened with me when I finally saw *Martin* in the mid-'80s on video. The box, featuring the single striking image of a razor blade embossed with vampire fangs, drew me in. The film itself was a revelation. To me, Romero films, at the time, had been mainly about visceral shock, and it was interesting to get some additional dramatic material and social commentary. Today, *Martin* stands as my favorite film of Romero's filmography. Thankfully a series of DVD releases in the last few years have allowed fans to check out his masterpiece as well.

THE MASQUE OF THE RED DEATH (1964)
by Justin McKinney

Prince Prospero (Vincent Price) dabbles in the Dark Arts.

How a story of only 2,434 words can lay such solid foundation for a perfectly realized horror film is not only a testament to the colorful, carefully selected prose of a literary genius, but also to the ingenuity of director Roger Corman and his admirable cast and crew. Given twice his normal (though still low) budget, leftover sets from Peter Glenville's historical drama *Becket* (1964), a longer-than-usual shooting schedule (five weeks instead of his usual three), and a host of talents before and behind the camera, Corman managed to create his most accomplished work as a director with *The Masque of the Red Death*.

As visually sumptuous as it is intriguingly philosophical and literate, this is the most crucial film in the Corman oeuvre when it comes to bridging the gap between cult adoration and critical respectability. High praise indeed, especially since it shares company with seven other (mostly) impressive and beloved low-budget films in this Gothic series. Of these, *House of Usher* (1960) is filled to the rafters with progressive, subtle perversity while *The Pit and the Pendulum* (1961) slowly tightens its screws toward a truly thrilling climax. *Tales of Terror* (1962) branched out to tackle three different stories, *The Raven* (1963) introduced more visual effects and a sense of self-parody and *The Tomb of Ligeia* (1964) dared to spend some time outside castle walls. But of these, it is *Masque* that has best withstood the weathering of time. This is due in part to its stylish presentation and exquisite production values, but more significantly because the themes contained within, just like any good work of art, are so universal, thought-provoking and timeless.

Set in Italy in the 12th century, *Masque* opens on a wonderfully surreal note with a mysterious figure dressed in a crimson cloak, face obscured, sitting alone on a fog-en-shrouded hilltop flipping through a deck of tarot cards. When an elderly peasant woman stumbles upon him, he turns a white rose red and casually instructs her to go home to her impoverished village and inform everyone the day of their deliverance will come soon. In some instances, this deliverance will come in the form of death from the plague; in others, release from the evil, Satan-worshipping Prince Prospero's slavery.

In the role of the unwaveringly sadistic prince, the always impressive Vincent Price delivers one of his very best performances. Not only is Prospero one of the most thoroughly reprehensible characters Price ever got to play, but also the most intelligent, seductive, and dangerous of all his villains. So devoid of conscience is the suave prince that he almost mows over a toddler with his carriage, slaps a knight around, orders two men garroted, and burns down a village…and all during his first few minutes onscreen! When Prospero discovers the "red death" has started to infect the villagers, he hightails it back to the safety of his castle. Later, he decides to pass the time by hosting a lavish costume ball for a bunch of greedy, gluttonous, boozy noblemen and women, who are not above imitating animal noises and scrambling on the floor fighting over jewels at their host's whim.

Meanwhile, the peasants outside are dropping like flies and those who have man-aged to survive the plague will soon die at the foot of the castle when they demand mercy. Even a nobleman who shows up late on his invite gets the axe. No one in this film, regardless of class stature, is spared Prospero's wrath; in his universe everyone exists just to be toyed with, humiliated, corrupted, judged, and killed. Desiring some additional entertainment, Prospero abducts a beautiful, devout peasant girl named Fran-cesca (Jane Asher) and tries to corrupt her, first with his persuasive philosophizing, then by forcing her to chose which of the two men she loves will be executed—her father Ludovico (Nigel Green) or her lover Gino (David Weston). What he doesn't figure on is Francesca's refusal to break or compromise her beliefs and principles. Her will every bit as strong as his own, the two characters share a mutual admiration by the film's end when Death personified decides to crash the party.

Courtesy of the well-turned script by Charles Beaumont and R. Wright Campbell, several other peripheral characters effectively feed into the overall decadence and di-abolism. First is Juliana (Hazel Court), a regal woman who sweeps along the corridors in an almost dream-like trance while preparing for her upcoming "marriage" to Satan. Court's part is secondary in a way, yet Corman has afforded her the very best sequence in the entire film: a visually arresting nightmare sequence where she submits, body and soul, to her master. Shot through a hazy, wavering lens, the union is symbolized by having Court, wavering between absolute terror and overwhelming ecstasy, being murdered over and over again by a succession of costumed men. She wakes from her dream and proceeds to wander through four beautifully designed, colored, and photographed rooms into the ballroom, where a huge pendulum swings directly in front of the camera. The "marriage" then commences in a very unexpected way.

Also worked into the mix, though for some reason the species of amphibian has been changed for the film, is Poe's revenge tale "Hop-Frog." Alfredo (portrayed by notable British scene stealer Patrick Magee) is a snide, pompous nobleman obviously envious of Prospero's power and stature. When he slaps a diminutive female dancer for spilling some wine, the woman's lover, a dwarf named Hop Toad (Skip Martin), devises an ingenious plan for revenge. Coyly playing upon Alfredo's desire for distinction, admiration, and control in a situation where the nobleman is constantly playing second fiddle, Hop Toad convinces Alfredo to don an ape suit. The resulting scenes end up earning the clever little guy five gold pieces from Prospero for the "entertaining gesture!"

Just as important as the writing, direction, and performances is the crucial use of color in the film. The opening sequence is shot to appear almost black and white, with a single red rose providing the only vivid color—an effect very similar to a much-lauded use of color in Spielberg's *Schindler's List* (1993). Also, apart from the striking appearance of the death figure and the generally lavish costume design, much time is spent in four specific rooms, which seemingly take on a life of their own throughout the film. The rooms, identically designed but colored differently, start with the more vivid colors, like yellow and purple. At the core however is a black room, which is the perfect reflection of the souls and religious practices of the people who inhabit the castle. Several times, the camera pans through all four with unbroken takes—a striking, imaginative, almost psychedelic effect from gifted cinematographer Nicolas Roeg (who in a few years would become an acclaimed director himself).

Stripping away the decorative elements and boiling down the storyline to its most basic, we are left with more than a Gothic horror film with artistic leanings. A powerful study of basic human nature, *Masque* captures what it's like to be inherently human, set adrift in a world governed by corrupt forces and searching for higher purpose amongst casual everyday cruelties and injustice. It's a theme that defies space and time, and a place where fate—and humanity itself—can hang on a gesture, a word…or even the flip of a card.

THE MUMMY (1932)
by Matt Black

Universal Studios' horror classic *The Mummy* is the story of Egyptian High-Priest Im-Ho-Tep (Boris Karloff), and his undying love for the Pharaoh's daughter, Princess Anck-es-en-Amon. Devastated by the Princess' death, Im-Ho-Tep seeks to bring his lost love back to life by committing sacrilege and stealing the sacred Scroll of Thoth

Im-Ho-Tep/Ardath Bey (Boris Karloff)

from the Temple of Isis. But before he can revive his love, he is caught and condemned to "the nameless death," sealing his fate in this world and the next by being ritually embalmed alive.

Three thousand, seven hundred years pass. In 1921, Im-Ho-Tep's mummified body is uncovered by a team of British archaeologists who, upon unsealing his cursed tomb and reading from the ancient scroll found in a casket among the treasures of Im-Ho-Tep's burial chamber, accidentally bring the undead mummy back to life. Centuries may have passed, but Im-Ho-Tep still yearns for his lady love and plans to seek her out once again.

Another decade passes and a new British Museum expedition led by Frank Whemple (David Manners), son of Sir Joseph Whemple (Arthur Byron) who led the original 1921 excavation, is carrying out further research in the area. The expedition has been somewhat unsuccessful and is due to be abandoned when they are visited by the mysterious Ardath Bey, who leads them to the unearthed burial site of Princess Anck-es-en-Amon.

The findings of the expedition, including the Princess' sarcophagus, are moved to the Cairo Museum. Ardath Bey (whom we recognize as Im-Ho-Tep) follows and reads from the sacred scroll in an attempt to raise Anck-es-en-Amon from the dead, but instead discovers visiting dignitary's daughter Helen Grosvenor (Zita Johann) to be the reincarnated Princess. The film progresses into a love triangle from beyond the grave, as Frank falls for Helen and Im-Ho-Tep will stop at nothing to be reunited with his long lost love!

Following the success of Universal's other horror franchises, it's clear that the studio was eager to keep the momentum going with a vehicle to cater to Karloff's growing popularity as a horror icon. *The Mummy* is in fact Karloff's first horror film where he has any notable dialogue (his previous roles as Frankenstein's Monster and as Morgan in James Whale's *The Old Dark House* [1932] are both mute). As with *Frankenstein* (1931), Karloff plays his role as Im-Ho-Tep with a certain amount of empathy and human qualities, helping the film transcend the mere staggering monster-on-the-loose territory where the later Universal Mummy movies fall. Karloff was a master of quiet menace, great at working with makeup effects rather than simply hiding behind them. *The Mummy* is one of the best examples of this; Ardath Bey's deep unnerving voice and piercing eyes create an air of sinister discomfort, working in unison with Jack Pierce's fantastic makeup and Karl Freund's directorial style.

The Mummy is the directorial debut of Freund, a veteran German cinematographer who worked on many important silent films directed by Murnau (including *The Last Laugh* [1924]) and Lang (*Metropolis* [1927]), as well as the genre classics *Der Golem* (1920), Browning's *Dracula* (1931), and Robert Florey's *Murders in the Rue Morgue* (1932), so it is maybe inevitable that the film is imbued with a certain amount of stylization and atmosphere reminiscent of German Expressionist cinema. The film is visually creepy, yet also poetic and a shining example of the restrained "less is more" school of horror cinema later championed by Val Lewton, Jacques Tourneur, and Robert Wise. Although Karloff had spent countless hours in the makeup chair, only fleeting shots of the bandage-clad Mummy are shown early in the movie when he is first brought back to life; this minimalist and understated approach works to maximum effect.

It goes without saying Karloff (born William Henry Pratt) went on to star in further numerous landmark horror movies such as *Bride of Frankenstein* (1935), *The Tower of London* (1939), *The Body Snatcher* (1945), and *The Raven* (1963). Following *The Mummy*, his career spanned a further 37 years and earned him a place in the hearts of genre fans as a "Gentleman of Horror," alongside the likes of Bela Lugosi, Vincent Price, Christopher Lee, and Peter Cushing.

In addition to Karloff, *The Mummy* has a strong supporting cast. Leading lady Zita Johann had previously appeared in D.W. Griffiths' *The Struggle* (1931) and Howard Hawks' *Tiger Shark* (1932), but had a rather short lived career, only appearing in a further four films over the next three years, including the underestimated *The Sin of Nora Moran* (1933). Bizarrely enough, she had a minor role 50 years later in Sam Sherman's awful super-low-budget *Raiders of the Living Dead* (1986). David Manners and Edward Van Sloan, playing Frank Whemple and Dr. Muller, had previously appeared together in *Dracula* the year earlier playing Jonathan Harker and Van Helsing respectively. Manners made several more films up until 1936, including Edgar G. Ulmer's *The Black Cat* (1934) starring Karloff and Lugosi. A familiar face to fans of 1930s horror, character actor Van Sloan had also appeared as Dr. Waldman in *Frankenstein*. He went on to work in numerous films over the next 20 years or so, including *The Black Room* (1935), *Dracula's Daughter* (1936), and the serial *The Phantom Creeps* (1939).

Freund continued his work as a director making a further seven pictures within three years, including the horror classic *Mad Love* (1935) starring Peter Lorre as the insane Dr Gogol. He was, however, more prolific as a cinematographer, working on countless movies over the following 25 years including *The Great Ziegfeld* (1936), *Pride and Prejudice* (1940), *The Thin Man Goes Home* (1945), *Key Largo* (1948), and TV's *I Love Lucy* between 1951 and 1956.

Although not as monumentally popular among fans as Universal's other major horror icons of the time, *The Mummy* was a success and spawned a quartet of fun (if somewhat delayed) follow-ups of varying success: *The Mummy's Hand* (1940), *The Mummy's Tomb* (1942), *The Mummy's Ghost* (1944), and *The Mummy's Curse* (also 1944). It should be noted that these films aren't direct sequels, replacing the character of Im-Ho-Tep with a new Mummy by the name of Kharis, and while highly enjoyable in their own right (the best being *The Mummy's Hand*), they don't come close to the original film and its subtle qualities.

Even before the immortal image of Im-Ho-Tep first graced the silver screen and real life Egyptologists unearthed hidden treasures such as the tomb of Tutankhamun in the 1920s, mummies had been glimpsed in numerous movies (including several comedies) from the early years of cinema, including *The Mummy* (1911) and *The Egyptian Mummy* (1914). After Universal's success, the bandaged one became a source of comedy as well as horror, as in *We Want Our Mummy* (a 1939 Three Stooges comedy short) and *Abbott and Costello Meet The Mummy* (1955).

With the 75th Anniversary of the original *Mummy* here, I prefer to reflect on the days when Universal made great horror movies…movies that will continue, decade upon decade, to attract new generations of fans.

MYSTERY OF THE WAX MUSEUM (1933)
HOUSE OF WAX (1953)
by Doug Lamoreux

Any consideration of classic and influential horror films must include the ironic and wonderful *Mystery of the Wax Museum*. *Mystery* was groundbreaking; the first "modern" horror film. It has spawned, arguably, three remakes (one, *House of Wax*, we will discuss here as a classic itself) and inspired an uncounted number of lesser films.

The screenplay by Don Mullaly and Carl Erickson, based on a Charles S. Belden story, is admittedly convoluted and overwritten. *Mystery of the Wax Museum* tries too hard to be a mystery; any attempt to follow the twists and turns of the plot on the first viewing without a scorecard is an exercise in futility. Even with an overwritten script producing a potential handicap, *Mystery*, in the hands of director Michael Curtiz, leads to a rich and unforgettable experience for the viewer.

A genius sculptor, Ivan Igor (Lionel Atwill), runs a poorly attended wax museum in 1921 London. The business suffers because, rather than display murderers and their vicious acts, Igor is concerned only with creating displays of beauty, chief among them his masterpiece Marie Antoinette. His disreputable partner, Worth (Edwin Maxwell), makes known his intention to burn the museum down for insurance money. Amazingly, Worth then proceeds to do just that. A fight ensues as the museum goes up in flames around the combatants. Finally, the sculptor is left for dead amid the conflagration.

Contrary to what everyone believes, however, Igor does not die.

Twelve years later, Igor reopens his museum in New York City and makes good on his promise to recreate the beauty that was lost in the fire. Wheelchair bound, with horribly burned hands, Igor relies on an assistant, Professor Darcy (Arthur Edmund Carewe), to recreate his wax images. But all is not as it appears. Igor is insane and, with the help of the drug-addicted Darcy, restores his lost historical figures by murdering and

Lionel Atwill as the face and the face behind the mask—from *Mystery of the Wax Museum*

covering in wax individuals that resemble them. Further, while Igor is desperate to see his "children" reborn, his true obsession lies in finding Worth and exacting revenge by adding his ex-partner to the museum displays.

The story is driven by a 1930s cinema standard: a fast-talking reporter (Glenda Farrell) and her crusty but lovable editor (Frank McHugh), with whom she verbally jousts her way through the abounding plot twists and red-herrings of the picture. The damsel in distress, Charlotte (1930s scream queen Fay Wray), finds herself a target because of an unfortunate resemblance to Marie Antoinette. As a ranting Igor closes in on Charlotte, she pounds her fists into his face. To her horror—and our delight—Igor's face cracks and falls away. It, too, is made of wax and hides a monstrously scarred face beneath. Spurred on by the lady reporter, the police arrive in time to prevent Charlotte's immolation. Igor, shot during a thrilling fight, takes a high-fall into the bubbling vat of liquid wax below.

Atwill turns in a startling and memorable performance. While the dignified Englishman will always be remembered as a standout character actor throughout the horror films of the late '30s and early '40s, it should not be forgotten that he was a genuine star of numerous films. *Doctor X* (1932), *The Vampire Bat* (1933), and *Mystery of the Wax Museum* all featured Atwill devouring the scenery with menacing relish.

Wray, the heroine in jeopardy in all of Atwill's early fright films (and immortalized in the grip of a certain towering ape), delivers her shrieks on cue to raise the hairs on the back of the neck. Carewe, a sinister character actor from the early film shockers (*The Cat and the Canary* [1927], *Phantom of the Opera* [1925], *Doctor X*), is a standout as the addict/helpmate Darcy.

While not altogether true, it can be argued that *Mystery of the Wax Museum* is the first color horror film. Barrymore's *Dr. Jekyll and Mr. Hyde* (1920) featured tinted sequences. Chaney's *Phantom of the Opera* (1925) featured gorgeous color sequences wrapped by an otherwise black-and-white film. Technically speaking, *Doctor X* was the first terror film to be entirely shot in two-strip Technicolor. *Doctor X*, however, uses the process to little or no effect. Anecdotally, Warner/First National had a contractual commitment to the Technicolor Company that made filming *Doctor X* in color a necessary evil. In fact, other than initial engagements in New York and Los Angeles, the prints distributed to all other markets were in black and white.

Mystery of the Wax Museum, on the other hand, was designed for color and its prints were released that way. The two-strip Technicolor available at the time was far different from today's film color. Reds and greens are brilliant and beautiful, while other colors are muted. Still, with the fiery museum sequence and Atwill's twisted makeup, color adds immeasurably to the overall effect of the film. Images of the melting wax figures remain with the viewer long after the film is over.

On the lighter side, *Mystery* features inanities that, under Curtiz's direction, add rather than detract from the fun. Doors open and close by themselves, human eyes inexplicably peer out from beneath hoods and behind masks following frightened visitors about the museum (even when all of the museum staff are plainly accounted for), a morgue toe tag somehow makes it all the way to the museum showroom on opening day for no other reason than the script requiring a clue to be discovered, etc. All of this leads to chills and giggles. What more could one ask of a horror film?

What happened to *Mystery of the Wax Museum* following its initial theatrical release is as big a mystery as any contained within the film. Its last recorded public exhibition was in 1946 for Warner London's 20th Anniversary of Sound exhibition. That print, considered the last in existence, degenerated and was destroyed in 1954. From that point on, *Mystery* was considered a lost film. But thanks to the horror fans' bible, *Famous Monsters of Filmland* magazine, atmospheric stills from the picture kept it alive in the minds of horror enthusiasts, ensuring its status as a genre classic.

Legend has it, a copy of the film was eventually found in Jack Warner's personal vault. How, if, and when this happened is a source of controversy. William K. Everson's *Classics of the Horror Film* tells of an original 35mm color print discovered in the "very late '60s," while Calvin Thomas Beck's *Heroes of the Horrors* insists on an original negative found "around 1972." Both stories are thrown into question by the simple fact that current video prints of the film carry a copyright renewal date of 1960 by United Artists. (Why they would go to the effort to acquire the rights to a film thought not to exist causes one to wonder.) Whether portions of the story of its reemergence are apocryphal or not matters little. *Mystery of the Wax Museum* was lost, gained a delicious reputation during its absence, and eventually resurfaced to the disappointment of some and the delight of many.

Mystery of the Wax Museum was remade by Warner Bros. in 1953. Like its forerunner, *House of Wax* was a thrilling and innovative film. It made brilliant use of Warner Color at a time when most films and certainly the vast majority of American horror films were made in black and white. *House of Wax* debuted four years ahead of the first Gothic Hammer production and initiated a whole new way of looking at horror.

Vincent Price as the face and the face behind the mask—from *House of Wax*

Though not the first horror film shot in 3-D (that illustrious title belongs to Arch Oboler's tale of man-eating lions, *Bwana Devil* [1952]), *House of Wax* is undeniably one of the best. Despite a few brainless sequences existing only to exploit the process (a street barker with an endlessly thumping paddle and ball, for example), the eerie effectiveness of the 3-D wax museum bursting into flames cannot be overstated. Ironically, the film's director, Andre de Toth, had only one eye and was unable to experience the 3-D effect firsthand. Nevertheless, de Toth was a true believer in the process and had championed its use in films as early as the mid-1940s. It also should be noted that *House of Wax* was the first 3-D picture made with Stereophonic Sound and utilized 25 speakers at its Paramount Theater premiere in New York.

While telling virtually the same story, screenwriter Crane Wilbur (*The Bat* [1959], *Mysterious Island* [1961]) chose to eliminate the mystery aspects and instead tell a story of pure horror. The fast-talking reporter of the original is gone; likewise the subplot concerning the sculptor's ex-partner being a local criminal. In addition, the names of all the characters have needlessly been changed. Igor became Jarrod, Worth became Burke, etc. The most obvious change is considered by some a cheat. Rather than tell a modern story set in the present time, *House of Wax* is a period film (circa 1900). Complaints aside, it does work.

Otherwise, *House of Wax* is a true remake. Its storyline follows that of *Mystery of the Wax Museum* very closely indeed; a maneuver that is its salvation and, at the same time, its downfall. The highlights of one—the catastrophic museum fire, the stalking murderer, the climactic unmasking, and the villain's tumble into molten wax—are the highlights of the other. Likewise, the blunders of the original are repeated. Both feature an ineffectual police force unable to solve a mystery that is made evident to the audience almost immediately. (Though, to be fair, Frank Lovejoy and Dabs Greer made a better go at it than their forbearers.) Both give us a mad genius whose righthand man is a hopeless addict who eventually gives away the farm for a fix. Both feature a silly secondary character of an assistant sculptor, who is mute for no particular reason and capable only of recreating his own image in clay. And how, really, can either film visually recover from and/or surpass the stunning museum fire in their respective opening reels?

The most interesting aspect of a *Mystery/House* comparison is how absolutely similar the films are in plot and how diametrically opposed they are in theme. This is exemplified by the character of the mad sculptor in each. Atwill's Igor and Price's Jarrod are each driven by two obsessions. The least important is the second: the obsession they share to recreate their masterpiece, Marie Antoinette, and immortalize themselves through her. This is a bogus obsession, particularly in *House*, existing for the sole purpose of putting a damsel in distress for the closing reel. Their first obsession—the need for revenge—is far more compelling, believable, and is the key to the real difference between these films.

Igor, while definitely a murderer and certainly mad, is a man who has been terribly wronged. To the end he is heartbroken over his loss of the ability to create beauty. He wants revenge against one man, the partner who crippled him. Jarrod is, if insanity can be quantified, far madder. He has gone beyond heartbreak into bitterness and wants revenge upon the whole world. Consequently, Jarrod is a far less sympathetic character than Igor.

Compare the same scene in both films, when the sculptor examines the hands of a new assistant. Igor compares his own hands and laments, "Look at these claws. If I had those hands of yours, I would show you the meaning of what you're trying to do. All those beautiful things that were destroyed I could restore. It is a cruel irony that you people without souls have hands." Jarrod, on the other hand, merely seethes. "Mine were once like that. How I envy you." Jarrod, in fact, rages and hates all of humanity throughout the film. "Jarrod is dead," he tells Wallace, his new financial partner. "I'm a reincarnation." Later, he instructs an assistant to intensify the misery in a sculpture's face. "This fellow's been badly used by the world," he says with menace. "And he despises all the people in it."

The chronological order of the murders in each film reinforces this view. In *Mystery*, bodies have been disappearing for 18 months as the museum has been readied for its opening. Worth, the focus of Igor's rage, is his last victim. Igor screams his victory at the wax-covered corpse of his enemy. "For 12 years—12 awful years this terrible living dead man with the burnt hands and face has searched for this fiend. Now the account is closed." Jarrod, in comparison, murders his crippler first. His revenge on Burke is only a preamble to the mayhem he intends to exact upon the rest of the world.

Career-wise, *House of Wax* was both a boon and a boondoggle for Vincent Price. Its smash success made Price an instant horror film star. Ironically, it was at a time when horror films were out of vogue and few were produced. Thus Price became a household name for horror while, at the same time, putting himself out of work. With the sole exception of *The Mad Magician* (1954), Price was forced to tread water in supporting character roles for the next five years. It was not until Hammer exploded upon the scene that horror reemerged in American film. When it did, Vincent Price, the crown prince of horror, resurfaced with it. He starred in *The Fly* (1958) and the rest is history.

The rest of the cast is serviceable. Carolyn Jones (later Morticia Addams on television) is easy on the eyes…if not the ears. Charles Bronson (billed by his real name Charles Buchinski) surfaces in a role that wastes what talent he had, though Phyllis Kirk is an admirable replacement for Fay Wray in the scream department.

In considering two films so swollen with irony, both in their content and in the circumstances of their creation, ponder one last macabre anecdote: The first display pointed out to patrons on the opening night of the *House of Wax* is "Little Egypt, who danced at the Columbian Exposition in Chicago in 1893." Uncounted dozens of young women who traveled to the Windy City for that World's Fair were never heard from again. They fell victim to H.H. Holmes, also known as "Doctor Death," one of the worst real-life serial killers of all time. Many of his victims were stripped of flesh and their skeletons sold to hospitals for teaching displays. How appropriate.

A NIGHTMARE ON ELM STREET (1984)
by A.D. Gillott

In 1981, writer/director Wes Craven could have no idea that the script he had just completed, entitled *A Nightmare on Elm Street* (henceforth *ANOES*), would be such a phenomenal commercial success; a milestone horror movie that would define the decade, launch his career into the stratosphere (Craven had previously been associated only with low-budget horror such as 1972's *Last House on the Left* and 1977's *The Hills Have Eyes*), as well as kick off the acting careers of Heather Langenkamp and a then-unknown Johnny Depp. It would also lead to the creation of a globally recognized horror icon in the story's loathsome villain—Freddy Krueger—whose enduring appeal as a character has sustained six direct sequels to Craven's initial picture (seven including 2003's *Freddy vs. Jason*), spawned a short-lived television spin-off in the form of *Freddy's Nightmares* and whose image, to this day, can be found on a plethora of merchandise, everything from tee shirts and tattoos to comic books and videogames. Anybody and everybody knows Freddy…

Or do they? Therein lies one of the problems that newcomers to *ANOES* face, something to do with popularity and the old adage that "familiarity breeds contempt." Today, Freddy is an instantly recognizable name and image, whether we've actually seen any of the *Nightmare* series or not. Even children know him from the media, from MTV videos they've seen and the Halloween costumes they've probably worn, though they're far too young to have ever watched one of the movies. Time passes, the children grow up, and that's what Freddy is to them—a costume, a toy, a brand—he's not the boogeyman, he's fun old Uncle Freddy.

When these children at some point watch one (or all) of the *Nightmare* films, in some ways that image is solidified. As the series continued, and Freddy's popularity skyrocketed, he inevitably became the star, the single component that was consistent throughout the series, while the majority of the casts served only as disposable prey. Freddy became more visible, both physically (no longer a hideously burned creature swathed in shadows) and figuratively (in that the sequels have expanded on the original storyline to explain every detail about him). He no longer retains any of his mystique. By the sixth installment, *Freddy's Dead* (1991), he's all but indistinguishable from the creature in *ANOES*; instead he has become a quipping funnyman with an extravagant,

Nancy (Heather Langenkamp) is caught off guard sleeping in the bathtub.

comic way of dispatching his successive victims. In essence, the monster that is Freddy has been diluted, weakened. There's an element of practicality in this—as Freddy himself, Robert Englund, once noted: "If we had tried to top the primal horrors and gore in part one, we would have hit a ceiling very early on...There is not much more we could have done unless we had Freddy...go around decapitating babies; instead he turns you into a giant cockroach. There is a sense of humor which is almost Kafkaesque in the *Nightmare* films."

Whether readers are *Nightmare* virgins or confirmed fans, to fully appreciate this film we've got to mentally go back in time. Forget the sequels, the merchandise—they're gone. Now we're back on Craven's territory. Eyes drooping, sun setting, it's time to sleep. Let the nightmare begin afresh...

When the film was released in 1984, *ANOES* was something new and original. The concept is very astute; as Robert Shaye, producer of the movie and founder of the then fledgling New Line Cinema, said: "It was an original idea, dying in your dreams meant really dying. And four kids all had the same monster come to them while they slept...Here was the perfect common denominator. We all have to sleep." This takes the mechanics of an otherwise normal slasher picture and elevates it to something more psychologically disturbing. The killer is no longer a mere physical being; he has the ability to attack his prey mentally and at the point when they are at their most vulnerable. Nightmares, like dreams, have an elastic reality and Craven exploits this to great effect, such as when the wall, seemingly rubberized, indents behind Nancy as she sleeps and a hovering Krueger can be seen in its shape, ready to pounce. Or the way Freddy can impossibly stretch his arms, or appear both behind and in front of you within seconds. Just as there's no escape in the dreams, there's also no escape *from* the dreams, and this is the ultimate setting—it's not a haunted house or a patch of woods, places we can avoid and run from in reality; it's in our cozy beds in our quiet suburban homestead, or the sly nap at work or school—the killer is inescapable.

For a film to blur the boundaries of reality and fantasy was not, at the time, an overused concept, and Craven's execution of this is extremely subtle—it takes but a single flutter of a character's eyelids and that's it, they're in Freddy's domain. It's not always noticeable at first to the audience, which is intentional, putting us in the shoes of the dreamer, who doesn't yet know that he/she has finally succumbed to sleep. Slowly, the revelation comes. Surreal moments and the elements that are identifiably nightmarish allow the tension to build as we, along with the character, know that the beast is somewhere, waiting, ready to psychologically torture us before striking with his wicked blades. And Craven doesn't skimp on the gore, though it never reaches laughable excess. In the bloodbath of Tina's infamous demise and "ceiling crawl," for example, the lurid neon blue lighting of the scene and the black splashes of blood are very reminiscent of some of the Italian *giallos*—gripping, haunting, instantly memorable.

Then there's Freddy himself. He's not loquacious here, though sometimes he displays a black, cruel wit. Aside from an explanation that he was a child-murderer and that he met justice at the hands of the children's parents, there's no real history to Krueger. At best, Craven intimates that a more raw, cosmic evil may reside in this entity (a theme that he develops more thoroughly in *Wes Craven's New Nightmare* [1994]) through the speech delivered by Nancy's high school English teacher as Nancy fights to stay awake: "What is seen is not always real...According to Shakespeare there was something operating in nature, perhaps inside human nature itself, that was rotten—a 'canker' as he put it..."

Revisit the opening scene of the film. Seeing the loving way Fred constructs and tenderly caresses his glove, the blades becoming an extension of himself, points to the sadism of the character, his ecstasy in causing the pain and deaths of others. And these "others" are society's most innocent and fragile—children. Furthermore, this hints at something else—that Krueger was a pedophile. Explicitly, the film states only that he was a child killer, but the fact that he takes such sensual pleasure in his killings implies more. In fact, Englund recalls: "Wes wrote the most evil, corrupt thing he could think of. Originally, that meant Freddy was a child molester." This was changed, Englund goes on to state, because at the time of filming, a child molestation scandal broke and Craven did not want to be accused of exploiting a terrible situation.

On the subject of Englund, his contribution into the creation of Freddy cannot be understated, as much of what makes Freddy so menacing in this film is given through Englund's jaunty, swaggering performance. The character in the initial *Nightmare* is a virtually unknown predator, so Englund's decision to put so much into sheer body language was a masterstroke, as it also separated his character from other stalkers that populated slasher films of the day. "The stance was just trying to be as far away from any kind of monster or Frankenstein walk; I decided to put in a bit of cockiness, sexuality, and threat." The glove too, being such a unique weapon, was used to good effect; Craven often announces its presence through a series of teeth-setting, metallic scratching sounds long before it is made visible. Englund took the initiative and "played" the glove, taking inspiration from Klaus Kinski's performance in Werner Herzog's *Nosferatu* (1979): "He had very long fingernails, and that is where I got the idea how to act with the glove and the long blades on it."

In all, these elements—the hideous killer, the concept so ripe for a fertile imagination to pick up and run with, and the psychological nature of the horror—are what make the movie formidable. Even today it still retains that initial, primal power to get under the skin and into the mind. The sequels may have diluted the idea, but when given the due respect and consideration it warrants, *A Nightmare on Elm Street* remains a unique and frightening experience, well deserving of its accolades, its popularity, and its status as a true horror classic.

NIGHT OF THE DEMON (1957)
(aka CURSE OF THE DEMON)
by Chris Benedict

Mr. Bobo the Clown, aka devil-worshiping Karswell (Niall MacGinnis), entertains the neighborhood children.

Jacques Tourneur's *Night of the Demon* examines the conflict between reason and superstition. The questions it asks are multifaceted, as are the answers it provides. Tourneur intended to omit the demon of the title, preferring not to show it at all. A veteran of the Val Lewton school of horror filmmaking, he preferred to let the audience's imagination fill in the blanks. The insertion of the demon—at the insistence of the producers— particularly at the beginning of the film, almost undoes the movie.

The puppet demon... love him or hate him!

Although based on "Casting the Runes" by M.R. James, the film (scripted by Charles Bennett and Hal E. Chester) is actually closer to a tale by H.P. Lovecraft. As in a typical Lovecraft story, the plot involves determined academics gradually drawing aside the curtain of prosaic reality only to find utter chaos beneath. In this, the insertion of an undeniably tangible demon has some justification. If we open the door, we can see in. The film's visual obsession with geometry has no parallel in the original story, but it was one of Lovecraft's dominant themes. In any event, this may be the first flowering of Lovecraft's influence in cinema, though it would be a reach to say its influence in the horror genre is largely due to this movie. While always famous, the movie hasn't always been easy to see.

Night begins with a montage of Stonehenge, suggesting that Britain's pre-Christian past is Satanic, and that Christian and Pagan magic are at odds. It's worth noting that Tourneur is a Christian filmmaker (as evidenced by *Stars in My Crown* [1950]). So here we have a film about superstition by a believer in one kind of supernatural world.

We are then introduced to Professor Harrington (Maurice Denham), driving to a rendezvous with Julian Karswell (Niall MacGinnis). Trees play a significant role throughout, placing panicked characters in the darkest part of the forest whenever supernatural forces are pursuing them. Harrington is one such panicked character. Karswell has called...something...to terrorize the professor, who implores him to call it off. At the outset, Tourneur is pitting contradictions against one other. Karswell's library is where he is most often seen in his own home. The architecture of Karswell's home is neo-classical. The shape of the space is round, but the floor is rectilinear—geometric shapes in the shot play an important thematic role in *Night of the Demon*. Karswell's study suggests a place of classical order, but it is appointed with the paraphernalia of the occult.

Karswell is our villain, but he is also the most sympathetic character. Based in part on Aleister Crowley, he is later presented as a clown and a mama's boy, a decided departure from M.R. James's story. Dr. Kumar, one of the scientists, articulates the film's attitude towards him: "[The Devil] is most dangerous…when he's being pleasant."

Harrington's demise at the hands of the demon follows, and there's no denying that the demon itself is a striking visual. We first see it as an amorphous cloud, perhaps tearing the veil between its own reality and our own. Then we see its silhouette, backlit by fire and smoke. Eventually, we get a closeup. As special effects go, it's among the best of its era.

We meet the film's ostensible hero, Professor Holden (Dana Andrews), on an airplane. We also meet Professor Harrington's niece, Joanna (Peggy Cummings). Holden's arrival at Heathrow provides a visual counterpoint to his personality. An arch skeptic, we first see him in settings where superstition has been banished. Heathrow is a thoroughly modern space, with straight lines and bright lights surrounding Holden as he holds court with the press. Holden outlines a hardcore skepticism that admits no possibility of the breath of other worlds. "All good scientists are from Missouri," he says a little later in the film, "they should continually be saying 'show me.'" "And if you are shown?" his colleague asks. "Then I'll look twice."

Holden's first encounter with Karswell takes place in a bastion of reason: The library at the British Museum. Like Karswell's library, the space of the library is round. Just as Professor Harrington approached Karswell's manor through an iron gate, so Holden approaches the museum through a similar gate. And when Holden is seen entering the rotunda, it is in an overhead shot in which he seems to be entering a maze. Holden is henceforth framed by different geometries. The railings at the museum, for example, are rectilinear shapes violated by curves. These are echoed later in the film by planks and panels of a door drawn with wards against hexes.

Holden is introduced to Joanna at her uncle's funeral. She then meets Holden at his hotel where she tries to convince him that there are dark forces behind her uncle's death. The movie sets her up as an alternate protagonist and as a different kind of rationalist. She bristles at Holden's condescension and asserts her own intellect when she announces that she, too, has studied psychology. This sets her up as a direct parallel to Holden, one who is more open to the face value of the evidence.

One side effect of presenting the demon so early is that it presents Holden as pigheadedly hidebound—the audience already knows what's behind everything, and because we know, Holden seems willfully dense. This is a striking contrast to Joanna. She's a kindergarten teacher who chides Holden at one point that, "You can learn a lot from children. They believe in things in the dark until we tell them it's not so. Maybe we've been fooling them." Ms. Harrington trusts her senses more than Holden does, and comes to the correct conclusions sooner.

Tourneur offers another visual repetition as Holden and Joanna approach Karswell's estate in the next scene, the composition echoing Holden's approach to the British Museum. Karswell is in his element in this sequence, indulging in a flair for the theatrical as Bobo the Magnificent, entertaining the village children and later conjuring a windstorm for Holden's benefit. The object of Holden and Joanna's visit is a rare book, which is emblematic of one of the movie's minor themes: Writing has power. Holden punctures this notion earlier: "Runic symbols are one of the oldest forms of alphabet…They're supposed to have magic powers. They don't." In the context of the movie, he's dead wrong.

The sequence at Karswell's children's party also introduces Karswell's mother (Athene Seyler), who attempts to mediate between Karswell and Holden. Both dismiss her: Karswell considers her a fool, Holden thinks her a pawn of her son. Mrs. Karswell's attempts to dissuade Holden become fundamental to the plot in the second half of the movie, culminating in a séance where Joanna is convinced of her uncle's presence while Holden is convinced he's witnessing theater. It does provide Holden with the key that unlocks his skepticism with the film's most famous line: "It's in the trees! It's coming." Mrs. Karswell is a foil for Karswell himself in a scene where he laments that he's just as trapped as his followers, and is just as vulnerable to the forces they have unleashed.

The film's other plotline is the investigation of Rand Hobart, suspected of murder in relation to Karswell's cult. This investigation takes Holden to Hobart's family and rural community, away from the ivory tower of the academy and into a world of superstition and ignorance. Here, we find out that Holden himself has been marked for death by a mysterious parchment that has been passed to him.

Both plotlines come to a head when Holden finally examines Rand Hobart (Brian Wilde). Hobart, like Holden, was marked by the parchment. Unlike Holden, he knew what awaited him, and passed it back. Hobart repeats the line, "It's in the trees," which is the evidence that Holden needs to peek behind the veil of perceived reality. What follows is a final battle of wits in which Holden must return the parchment to Karswell without him knowing about it. The irony of all of this is that Holden arrives at superstitious belief through reason and investigation, though even at the end, he remains incredulous about Karswell's ultimate fate. "Maybe it's best *not* to know," he tells Joanna.

Night of the Demon's influence was modest, but the works that *do* reflect its presence are a distinguished bunch: *The Innocents* (1961) and *The Haunting* (1963) (the latter directed by fellow Lewton alum Robert Wise), as well as *Night*'s thematic twin, Sidney Hayers' *Burn, Witch, Burn* (aka *Night of the Eagle* [1962]). The film gained a different kind of fame as one of the 13 movies mentioned in "Science Fiction Double Feature" in *The Rocky Horror Picture Show* (1975). It gets the song's best lyrics, to boot:

"Dana Andrews said prunes,
Gave him the runes,
And passing them took lots of skill…"

NIGHT OF THE LIVING DEAD (1968)
by Jimmy Seiersen

Night of the Living Dead begins with Barbra and her brother Johnny arriving at a cemetery to visit their father's grave. Johnny teases Barbra for being afraid. A man is walking at the cemetery and gets closer and closer to them. Without warning, he attacks Johnny, who moments later lies lifeless on the ground. Barbra flees to a nearby house. Not long thereafter, a man named Ben also arrives. More and more "ghouls" start to gather around the house, forcing Ben and Barbra to barricade themselves. They soon learn that other people are hiding in the house's cellar. The debate within the small group soon rages as to which place is safer: the cellar, where they have only one, fairly strong door to protect (but no other alternate exit), or the more exposed ground floor, where they can escape if necessary.

The first ghoul (Bill Hinzman [Heinzman in film credits]) attacks Johnny and Barbra.

After the success of movies like *It Came from Outer Space* (1953), *Godzilla* (1954), and *Creature from the Black Lagoon* (1954), there were numerous low-budget monster/creature movies being made in the 1950s and '60s. Most of them had silly scripts, bad special effects, and terrible acting. While some of them were entertaining (*The Giant Gila Monster* [1959] and *Attack of the Giant Leeches* [1959]), they were hardly what you would call high-quality cinema.

In June 1967, George A. Romero started shooting his first feature-length film, and the result of his efforts would make him famous. It was, in several ways, a variant on these earlier creature features, but this featured a monster which had not been seen before: the flesh-eating zombie. Zombie movies had been around for quite some time already, with *White Zombie* (1932) often credited as the first. But these older movies featured zombies that were merely slaves to their voodoo master. All that changed with *Night of the Living Dead*. Romero's zombies had no master, no one controlling them, and they were hungry for human flesh.

However, it wasn't just the nature of the zombies that set the movie apart from its low-budget horror counterparts. The movie had stronger characterizations and performances than the one-dimensional characters horror audiences were used to, and emotionally it was a very dark film, not as fun as many of the monster movies that preceded it. The minimal special effects were great for the budget, and featured gore to a higher extent than what was the norm at the time. Romero explains: "There was no MPAA or rating board at that point, so there was no panel of experts issuing dictates or reviewing films saying 'You can leave this in but you have to take that out.' But there was this unwritten law which said you had to sort of stand back and be polite and just show the shadow and not show the knife entering flesh. I guess from having been weaned on EC comic books and things like that, I thought, why hasn't anyone done it?

I didn't think we were breaking down barriers…" Other important influences for *Night of the Living Dead* include Herk Harvey's film *Carnival of Souls* (1962) and Richard Matheson's vampire novel *I am Legend*.

Because of the low budget ($114,000), the filmmakers had to be quite inventive in the special effects department. Some zombies were actually mannequins with clay in their face and ping-pong balls for eyes. (The "upstairs" zombie was made by Romero himself.) Additionally, some of the crew members were cast in roles to save money. For example, producers Russell W. Streiner and Karl Hardman are seen as Johnny and Harry, respectively. Near the end of the movie, we can see Streiner's aunt as a zombie in a nightgown.

Upon its initial and subsequent releases, the movie made $30,000,000 world-wide.

Though *Night of the Living Dead* initially received some criticism for its violence, it also received praise from American film critic Rex Reed and the famous French movie magazine *Cahiers du Cinéma*. Roger Ebert liked the film itself, but decried the fact that young children were allowed to see it. Today, it's seen as one of the great classics of the horror genre. In the U.S. in 1999, The National Film Preservation Board inducted the film into the National Film Registry. It also sits at #93 on the American Film Institute's list, "100 Years, 100 Thrills."

Night of the Living Dead has generated three sequels to date, all directed by Romero: *Dawn of the Dead* (1978), *Day of the Dead* (1985), and *Land of the Dead* (2005). The original movie has also been remade twice, in 1990 and 2006. The first was directed by f/x maestro Tom Savini, with Romero updating the original script. The two had, of course, collaborated previously, with Savini famously contributing the memorable special effects to Romero's *Dawn* and *Day*. The 2006 version is a 3-D movie entitled, oddly enough, *Night of the Living Dead 3D*, directed by Jeff Broadstreet.

In articulating my own thoughts, I find both the beginning and ending of the film very ironic. The first scene is a classic: Johnny says his famous line "They're coming to get you, Barbra," in a strange and creepy voice, following up with "Look, there's one of them now!" referring to the older man walking in the cemetery. What neither Johnny nor Barbra knows is that the man is one of the living dead that hungers for human flesh. Johnny is right in his assessment that the man *is* "one of them"—even if he doesn't know it…yet.

Another strong scene is toward the end, when the little Cooper girl has turned into a zombie and kills her own mother. In my opinion, this is the strongest scene in the movie and Romero showed real guts (pardon the expression) by pushing the barriers of what one could show in American horror movies at the time. One could argue that movies could do without extreme scenes like that, but here it's a brutal and effective way of showing how emotionless these zombies are. The movie wouldn't be the same without it.

Several different messages/social commentaries have been read into the movie. Many people felt, especially with its bleak ending, that *Night of the Living Dead* was a comment on racism. However, according to the filmmakers, this was unintentional. While the movie is historically the first horror movie with an African-American (Duane Jones) in a leading role, Jones was not chosen for his race, but because he was simply the best actor for the role. Other viewers saw connections to the war in Vietnam. For myself, when I saw the movie for the first time, I saw it as a reflection of people's universal inability to cooperate. Quoted in *Short Cuts: The Horror Genre*, George Romero himself said: "It came out of the anger of the times. No one was gleeful at the way that the world was going, so these political themes were addressed in the film. The zombies could be the dead in Vietnam, the consequences of our mistakes in the past, you name it…"

The fact that Romero did not have a huge budget to work with was probably the reason for much of the outside information coming from TV and radio broadcasts. In my opinion, this serves as an advantage, as it adds a realistic touch. Isn't this the way most people would get their information if something like this were to happen in real life? And while shooting the movie in black and white was a budgetary decision, it gives the movie its documentary-like feel, echoing the evening newscasts of the '60s. In addition, attentive audience members will notice that several scenes are shot diagonally, a subtle but effective way to increase the unsettling mood.

I also find the characters more realistic than in many movies. Often, I find people annoyed by Barbra's catatonia, her inability to *do something*. But in an extreme situation like this, like it or not, some people are going to be in a state of shock and not be in the best psychological shape.

With *Night*, the filmmakers took what little they had and managed to make a movie that feels very real, one that still impresses new viewers today. Ahead of its time in many ways, this little independent film, shot outside Romero's native Pittsburgh, led the charge for what was to become the horror genre's modern age.

NOSFERATU: A SYMPHONY OF HORROR (1922)
by Andreas Charalambous

There are times when a product or brand emerges that defines a particular culture and commands instant recognition—McDonald's, the iPod, Coca Cola, etc. While it might seem an odd device to discuss branding and marketing when the subject at hand is a silent film from the dawn of horror cinema, F.W. Murnau's classic *Nosferatu: A Symphony of Horror* is based on one such instantly recognizable image. The antagonist in the film originates from a pivotal literary text containing a character that did for the horror genre what Mickey Mouse did for cartoons and Superman did for comic books. I am of course referring to Bram Stoker's *Dracula*.

Since the creation of *Nosferatu*, there have been countless films featuring Count Dracula, but it was not always this easy to commit the Prince of Darkness to celluloid. Murnau was involved in a bitter legal battle with Bram Stoker's widow in order to create the world's first Dracula film—one in which he had no success. The Stoker estate continually refused to grant Murnau permission to adapt the popular novel to the screen. In order to sidestep this legal obstacle, the determined director performed some rudimentary (if transparent) name and plot substitutions. Count Dracula became Count Orlock, England became Germany, and the production of a seminal silent horror film was underway.

Modern viewers approaching *Nosferatu* for the first time will find few surprises, as it closely follows Stoker's now familiar novel (in some instances, to the word). However, I would recommend this film as one of *the* original examples of vampire cinema.

Count Orlock's (Max Schreck) presence is represented by shadowy cinematography.

Although most who have seen any *Dracula* movie through the ages will instantly recognize the plot, I implore the viewer to bear a few things in mind before dismissing it as a redundant viewing experience.

Firstly, it is important to remember that this is indeed the first interpretation of *Dracula*. Considering cinema was a fairly new medium and photographic technology very crude, audiences cannot help but admire Murnau's efforts. Secondly, this was a real labor of love for its creator. Not only did he risk the wrath of the authorities in its creation, but ultimately laid the foundations for Stoker's novel to become a success. Ironically, it was only after *Nosferatu* had been viewed by the theater-going masses that the undead Count's name captured the public's imagination, leading to wave after wave of cliché-riddled *Dracula* films and products. One wonders what state the *Dracula* franchise would be in today had it not been for the appearance of its Teutonic predecessor?

As mentioned previously, the plot is fairly familiar to fans of the genre, but the real pleasures are to be found in marveling at the way it was made and the beauty of its symbolism and photography.

Having made clear that the storyline is nothing not seen in one form or another in later *Dracula* films, let us examine the film itself (keep an eye out for the "similarities"). Murnau's effort starts in the director's homeland, Germany—Bremen (or Wisborg, depending on which version you're watching) to be precise. Hutter (Gustav Von Wangenheim), a real estate agent, is assigned by his employer to travel to a remote castle in the Carpathian Mountains to meet with a prospective buyer. As he travels by horse-drawn coach, he makes a stop at a local inn, where all its inhabitants express their fear and discomfort when Hutter explains his business. Dismissing their warnings of vampirism as sheer superstition, Hutter is determined to complete his mission, and when the driver of the coach refuses to take him to the castle, the Count sends his own transportation. Upon meeting the Count and sealing the deal, Hutter realizes that not all is as it seems and attempts to cut his stay with his host short to race back to Bremen. Unfortunately, Hutter is held at the castle against his will and witnesses firsthand that his enigmatic client is indeed something much more sinister. Eventually, the Count sets sail for his new home. The ship's cargo? A stack of coffins. Hutter makes his escape and races to return to Bremen before the Count.

The arrival of Orlock and his coffins in Bremen coincides with a devastating outbreak of the plague. The townsfolk come to the conclusion that there may be a connection to this with the Count. Hutter's beloved, Ellen (in whom the Count has expressed an interest) learns of the Count's sinister behavioral patterns and reaches the conclusion that he is indeed a vampire. She discovers that the only way to stop a vampire is for a good woman to distract him so that he stays out of his coffin past the first cock's crow. Her sacrifice not only saves the town but also gives rise to the buried sexuality in Stoker's tale. This also marked the first time in history, literary or otherwise, that the rays of the sun would prove lethal to a vampire.

As Bela Lugosi and Christopher Lee would later timelessly portray the "legitimate" Dracula onscreen, both with merit, Max Schreck bought an equally influential portrayal of the Count. His Orlock is a sinister rodent-like creature—complete with pointed ears, rat-like fangs and spindly long fingers—who creeps around in the darkness of night. Although this film contained extreme plagiarism of the original novel, the manner in which it was filmed, highlighting the stunning visuals, was an unusual and pioneering effort considering how new a medium cinema was in the 1920s. Filmed in the same gloriously artistic wave of German Expressionism as *Das Cabinet des Dr. Caligari* (1920), Fritz Lang's *Metropolis* (1927), and *M* (1931), this film is an absolute pleasure to view. Sharp-angled scenery and shots of sinister shadows abound. (One shot of the Count's shadow creeping against a wall, and another of the Count's rigid form rising from a coffin have become iconic to horror cinema imagery.)

Nosferatu announced the swinging of artistic momentum from Romanticism to Expressionism, with the clear presence of the macabre, the sinister, and the Gothic. As Orlock's vampire represented the positioning between life and death, love and murder, so too this film positions itself between art and moving image. Although the tale would eventually be given a modern manifestation in Werner Herzog's *Nosferatu: Phantom der Nacht* (1979) with Klaus Kinski as the Count, it is one of those films, such as Hitchcock's *Psycho* (1960), which one can only imagine enjoying in the glory of black and white (or in this case, sepia). There is something about the warm tones and the flicker of the picture which make the viewer appreciate that they are watching a piece of cinematic art and history.

But again, this was almost not the case.

According to cinema history, following the release of *Nosferatu*, the Stoker estate once again sought legal action, which almost resulted in the very extinction of the film. It was effectively withdrawn from distribution, and nearly all existing prints were destroyed. Luckily for fans of cinema (horror and otherwise) a few copies survived, but at a price. There are countless available versions which differ in length—ranging from comparatively short running times of just over one hour to slightly longer versions which run to a respectable 94 minutes. The difference in duration is accountable by whichever of the varying rescued reels were used for print transfer. Similarly, there is variation in the orchestral scores that accompany this silent film, ranging from Hans Erdmann's original score to more modern compositions.

In the climactic scene, Count Orlock dissolves to nothingness in the rays of the sun. It would have been a true tragedy had the same thing happened to this film. Cinema history would be a poorer place had this worthy classic not survived for today's and future generations.

THE OMEN (1976)
by Anish Jethmalani

Damien (Harvey Stephens) is not safe to be around.

Ahhh...Satan! How could anyone possibly think of not including Lucifer himself as a subject of a horror film? Well, that's just quite devilish if you ask me. Fascination with the Antichrist has been at the center of myths, tales, folklore, novels, and even the Bible itself for years, decades, even centuries. In 1976, director Richard Donner, producer Harvey Bernhard, and screenwriter David Seltzer took this fascination and made it into a blockbuster called *The Omen*. The resulting film had amazing direction, acting, music, and a story with enough clever, bloody, gut-spilling deaths to scare the holy you-know-what out of you.

Seltzer's script for *The Omen* was loosely based on the writings of Revelations in the New Testament of the Bible, where the end of time and the rise of the Antichrist are depicted. The concept was not a new one at the time, coming hot on the heels of a cycle of films in the 1970s centering around demonic children, including *Rosemary's Baby* (1968), *I Don't Want To Be Born* (1975), *To the Devil a Daughter* (1976), and of course, *The Exorcist* (1973).

Okay, so if you don't know the story of *The Omen*...you're going straight to Hell...how dare you!?   Well, it goes something like this: While in Italy, influential American diplomat Robert Thorn (Gregory Peck) learns that the baby born to his wife Katherine (Lee Remick) has died. When informed of this, Robert quickly agrees to adopt another child who was, coincidentally, born at the exact same time after its *mother* died. No one, the priest assures him, will ever know the real truth. Not even, as we learn, the Thorns.

See, fact is, the legitimate child of Robert and Katherine was actually murdered by a group of fanatical disciples who look after the new child, Damien (Harvey Stephens), with a careful eye to make sure that his, ahem...mission is carried out. Damien, as it turns out, was born of a jackal—yup, a jackal. Unaware of "their" child's true lineage, Robert and Katherine Thorn raise Damien, living as a normal family. However, a series of strange and increasingly horrifying occurrences begin to inform us that Damien is *not* safe to be around. As Damien grows older, various individuals approach the Thorns to persuade them to see the light before it's too late. Robert begins to learn the painful truth about Damien, and who/what his child really is, and he must make a very difficult decision before the rest of the world suffers Damien's wrath.

When I first saw *The Omen* at the age of 10 (I was raised Hindu, so there was no problem with seeing the movie in terms of my age—it's *all* fiction anyway according to Hinduism...couldn't happen...right?), I was fascinated and horrified at the same time. Sure, I was a kid, but regardless, Jerry Goldsmith's haunting theme sent a chill up my spine every time I heard it. This soundtrack, which won veteran Goldsmith his one and only Oscar for Original Score, is perhaps the centerpiece of the film. The dark choral Latin chant, which has lyrics such as "We drink the blood, we eat the flesh" and "Hail, Satan!" is enough to drive anyone insane, keeping his/her eyes above the covers to make sure no one is around. I, of course, could not stand to listen to that music too much without it doing me serious harm...believe you me. Of course, watching a young nanny hang herself at Damien's festive birthday party, a priest speared by the forces of evil in the middle of a churchyard, and a man getting decapitated by a sheet of glass (which is hands down, the best death scene in the film) could also account for a certain 10-year-old boy screaming in the middle of the night.

Seeing the film several times over the years has always had the same effect on me. Even over time, the movie still has a way of creeping up on us and making us feel a bit disturbed. In addition to Goldsmith's overwhelming score, what makes this film unique from its religion-themed brethren is its combination of great acting and Donner's subtle camera angles. From the still camera shot of Damien and his parents sitting in the car before arriving at church (after which the kid goes ballistic, realizing he's in a holy place) to the scene at the zoo (where the presence of the evil child drives the baboons nuts), Donner displays a real knack for keeping things quiet and still and/or loud and violent, depending on what the onscreen action calls for.

Screenwriter David Seltzer created *The Omen* after producer Harvey Bernhard hired him to create a story based on the symbolism characterized in Revelations. One passage introduced the infamous "Number of the Beast," 666, which in the film is the birthmark on young Damien's scalp. When Bernhard secured the talents of veteran TV director Richard Donner (who would also go on to direct *Superman* [1978] and the *Lethal Weapon* franchise) and legendary actors Gregory Peck and Lee Remick in the pivotal roles of the Thorns, he had already won half the battle. Donner proceeded to cast four-year-old Harvey Stephens in the pivotal role of Damien after encouraging the youth to beat him up during the audition, which Stephens did with such force that he managed to hit Donner's testicles in the process.

A series of suspicious events occurred during the filming of *The Omen*, which led some to believe that project was "cursed," including: The plane for scriptwriter David Seltzer was struck by lightning; Richard Donner's hotel was bombed by the Provisional IRA; after Gregory Peck canceled a flight to Israel, the chartered plane crashed, killing all on board (a group of Japanese businessmen); a warden at the safari park used in the "crazy baboon" scene was attacked and killed by a tiger the day after the crew left; and on the first day of shooting, several principal members of the crew survived a head-on car crash.

When the film was finally released, the impact far exceeded the industry's expectations. Audience members were indeed terrified. As a gimmick to enhance publicity (which producers of the 2006 remake would also use), signs were posted outside of the first screening notifying audience members that they had just watched the movie on the sixth day of the sixth month in the year 1976. Reviewers were lukewarm, with Roger Ebert from *The Chicago Sun-Times* saying that "As long as movies like *The Omen* are merely scaring us, they're fun in a portentous sort of way" while *The New York Times'* Richard Eder opined: "It is a dreadfully silly film, which is not to say that it is totally bad." But the resounding success of the movie, with its very healthy $48 million at the box office, spawned three sequels: *Damien: Omen II* (1978), *The Final Conflict* (1981, later subtitled *Omen III*), and a made-for-television movie entitled *Omen IV: The Awakening* (1991). Although all were individually good, none of them could really hold up to the original in my opinion. In addition, each of the films had a novel (or novelization) associated with it. (There was also an *Omen V* novel, but no screen version followed.)

The Omen remake in 2006, starring Liev Schreiber and Julia Stiles, opened to mixed reviews with many critics yawning it off, saying that nothing's really new here. In other words, if it's not broke, don't fix it! In a rather tired marketing stunt to promote the film, the opening was scheduled for the sixth day of the sixth month of the sixth year, 6/6/06, (marking one of the few times in history where a calendar date dictated a film's greenlighting and release).

The Omen's legacy continues to last even today as Damien's character has reappeared in everything from an episode of TV's *South Park* to the subject of a song by rapper DMX. And here's a little something to keep fans up at night: According to wikipedia.com, "An American study of Attention-Deficit Hyperactivity Disorder (ADHD) carried out by the Duke University School of Medicine in the 1990s reported that boys called Damien were six times more likely to suffer from the disorder than average." Now, if that's not scary, I don't know what is.

As a film, *The Omen* holds its own as one of the classics of the horror genre. Years after its debut in theaters, it continues to horrify parents and give them pause before cursing out their children ever again.

ONIBABA (1964)
by Denise T. LoRusso

Nobuko Otowa plays the Mother, here in full demon regalia.

The *susuki* [Japanese silver grass] looms high above the heads of two lost soldiers, camouflaging them in a sea of waving blades of grass. Laboring their way through, desperate for any refuge that the grass will provide from the heat of high summer, they take solace in the cool stillness of the ground. Without warning, a spear pierces through the grass into the chests of the men. Two women, one old, one young, emerge and stare at their prey, straining to discern any remaining glimmer of life. Finding none, the women work furiously to disrobe the men of their armor and weaponry. Dragging the bodies to the edge of a deep, black hole, they deposit their quarry.

Thus is the manner in which a mother and her daughter-in-law eke out an existence after one of the many Japanese feudal wars calls the village men to action: Ambushing weary samurai, then bartering their ill-gotten gain for millet and other supplies. When a local man returns after deserting the army, he informs the women that their son/husband has died. At first, grief-stricken, the young widow's passions are soon aroused by the virile, younger man. Enraged by the wanton lust of the young pair, the older woman sets out to teach her daughter-in-law a lesson from Hell.

Onibaba's title translates to "demon woman," or "demon hag," and is premised in Buddhist folklore. Indeed, there are many demons in the *susuki* grass. Demons of lust, resentment, rage, and more. This beautifully imagined cult classic reminds us that millions of dollars and a host of fancy effects aren't necessary to make a timeless masterpiece. Made in 1964, this captivating, black and white film provides a terrifying glimpse of what life might have been like in medieval Japan.

Hauntingly beautiful, yet at the same time claustrophobic, the grass provides the perfect killing ground. Vitally aware of its importance, writer/director Kaneto Shindo searched throughout his native Japan for just the right field. Many were too small to realize his expansive vision, while still others had vestiges of modern civilization in the way of summer cottages, electrical wiring, and the like. Finally, an assistant told him about an area in the Chiba prefecture. The Nagato River runs through part of Chiba's Inba Swamp, and this bit of luck provided the perfect shooting location. The life-giving water was vital for the women in our story. Shindo had at last found his *susuki* field, so integral to his story, indeed, a character unto itself.

Interviewed on the *Onibaba* Criterion/Janus DVD, Shindo speaks about the rigors and hardships faced by the cast and crew while making the film. It was his philosophy that they all be sequestered at the location so as to "unify their minds." He had the crew construct pre-fab buildings in which they all lived. Sweltering heat, unrelenting insects, and flooding often plagued the set. In all, the endeavor took about three months to complete. All that time, the cast and crew remained on location (due in part, no doubt, to the fact they wouldn't be paid until filming was completed!).

Along with Nobuko Otowa (who plays the "Mother" character), Shindo and another partner created their own production company, *Kindai Eiga Kyokai*. This allowed Shindo to make the film exactly as he wanted, without interference from the Japanese film industry's strict censorship. It's a good thing, too, as we might not have had the brutally honest portrayal of human nature, specifically its sexuality, which serves as the driving force in the film. Shindo wanted to show sex as a basis for human existence, not just for the satisfaction of lust ("sexual desire within the soul," according to the director). He manages to infuse his film with sexual tension that plays out in the destruction of the triangular relationship of its characters. Even the *susuki* grass undulates with the imagery of carnal desires, waving frantically as the tension increases. Shindo uses the sounds of pigeons cooing to represent the young woman's kindling desire, mounting to an explosion of Hikaru Hayashi's frenetic, percussive jazz-like score, accentuated with a samurai scream, as her desire reaches its crescendo.

The interaction between the two female characters is one of the most intense relationships I have ever seen depicted onscreen. Mother and Wife are both strong and capable. They have to be to survive in their time. Sweat glistens on their face. They behave fiercely, eat fiercely, performing everything with an unrelenting rage. But we know nothing else about them. What were they like before the war tore their world asunder? Would they have been capable of killing so easily before poverty drove them to it? According to Shindo, in the time of the film (known as The Warring States Period of Japan), women of their social class had very little stature. The women's names are never even *mentioned* in the film. They are simply "Mother" and "Wife of Kichi," the lost son. I can't help but think about the women they used to be. Were they soft and tender, nurturing and loving? One can only wonder.

As I watch the events unfold in this film, it's obvious to me that Shindo is protesting the futility of war. Certainly those that are murdered by the women are part of the warring class, responsible for all the ills in the women's world: the reason their men are gone, the reason they can't farm their land, the reason for their killing.

Later, a passing samurai general speaks about the cruelty he himself has inflicted in war. He wears the terrifying mask of an *oni*, or demon. He claims the mask protects his beautiful face from injury on the battlefield. A plan soon ignites in the older woman's mind, combining this demonic visage and the young woman's natural fear of Hell. This *oni* mask is the single most identifiable icon of this great film. Horrific, yet at the same time hypnotic, the viewer cannot look away from its beauty/ugliness. Wikipedia. org reports that the demon mask inspired William Friedkin to use a similar design for subliminal shots of a white-faced demon, commonly known as Pazuzu (or "Captain Howdy"), in his 1973 film, *The Exorcist.*

Then there is the Hole, the black abyss, used to dispose of the murdered samurai. It symbolizes the very Hell the old woman talks about. Playing a pivotal role in the film, it proved to be a difficult task for the construction crew. Shindo tells us that no less than five pits had to be dug because each kept filling with water from the swamp. Finally the fifth was maintained with scaffolding, cement, wire, and netting. I am fascinated by the meticulousness that Shindo took with this and every aspect of the film. His attention to detail is so evident in the brilliant cinematography, breathing life into this amazing film. Choosing black and white over the more traditionally used color at that time, Shindo captures every nuance of the characters and their milieu. His prowling, predatory camera scrutinizes every detail, every move, often in closeup. Cinematographer Kiyomi Kuroda's efforts would be rewarded with the Tokyo critics' prestigious "Blue Ribbon Award" in 1965.

So you may be wondering, is *Onibaba*'s inclusion herein a mistake in editing? Is it really a horror film? A resounding yes! This film explores the depraved lengths one will go to survive, the horror of the dark side of human nature. Add to this the wonderfully eerie set piece of the hideous demon mask, which can only be removed by wrenching off the tender flesh of its wearer. (It's been rumored that Shindo created the facial trauma of the mask wearer to mimic the horrific likenesses of the survivors of the nuclear bombs dropped in Hiroshima and Nagasaki.)

Onibaba is one of those films that pulls audiences in with the first frame, and leaves them breathless by the last. As the voyeuristic camera floats above the reeds, and finds the Hole, hearts will start to pound. Vague feelings of unease will start to overtake the viewer. The Hole, the sea of grass, the *taiko* drumbeat, these all portend of things to come. For any discerning horror aficionado, it doesn't get any better than this.

PEEPING TOM (1960)
by Will Harvard

The year 1960 was a defining year in horror, and greatly influenced what horror films could be and what the public perceived of them. In the 1930s and '40s, horror was primarily composed of 19th-century book adaptations, such as *Dracula* and *Frankenstein* (both 1931), or myths and legends like *The Mummy* (1932) or *The Wolf Man* (1941). In the 1950s, in addition to the monsters of the previous two decades, films featuring invaders from space (such as *Invasion of the Body Snatchers* [1956]) became popular, many of which were in reality thinly-veiled cold war propaganda. Around 1960, the idea that horror could come, not from the Gothic or the supernatural realms, nor even from space, but rather from within the *natural* world started to become explored. Many look at Alfred Hitchcock's *Psycho* (1960) as the defining moment of this shift, with its depiction of the cross-dressing, mother-obsessed serial killer Norman Bates, and certainly *Psycho* deserves much credit in the development of modern horror. Yet, many remain unaware of a similar film, released the same year in Great Britain, called *Peeping Tom*.

Director Michael Powell's film opens with a shot of a camera lens, then segues into footage taken from the point of view of a camera that the owner has hidden in his coat. We see him solicit sex from a prostitute. The prostitute leads him (and us) up a flight of stairs as the camera rolls, slowly building the tension and dread. Finally, the prostitute and he go into a small room where she begins to take off her clothes. The prostitute turns around, and with terror in her eyes, finally realizes what is about to happen. She screams, but it is too late. As the footage ends, we have met the film's first victim. And our "hero" is her killer.

Peeping Tom tells the story of Mark Lewis (Carl Boehm), a deranged cameraman and aspiring director, who films his victims as they die, watching the footage later in his small apartment. His weapon of choice is not a machete or an axe, but his camera itself. Mark has put a spike on one leg of his tripod, which he uses to stab his victims to death. To make the murders even more frightening, however, he has a placed a mirror on the camera as well, so his victims are forced to watch themselves as they die.

The viewer is now given a glimpse into Mark's world. Mark is a quiet, mild-mannered man with few friends. His entire life appears to be devoted to his work and his hobby, both of which happen to be filmmaking. He lives in a small apartment in an old renovated house, of which he is the landlord. His is a very quiet, ordinary life, except for the fact that he is often driven to kill.

Much like Norman Bates from *Psycho*, who faced years of debasement at the hands of his mother, Mark has suffered from debilitating parental abuse as well. As the film progresses, we learn that Mark's father was a scientist obsessed with fear. In order to gain a wider knowledge of his favorite subject, Mark's father would often subject his son to horrific experiments, such as dropping lizards on the young boy as he slept, and filming his terrified reactions. (It is interesting to note that Mark has kept his father's footage in his collection, along with his own murders.)

Despite the hardships that Mark has faced in his life, which have probably directly led to his crimes, his life begins to look up when a birthday party is held at the apartment complex. Walking up the stairs to retreat into his apartment as usual, the birthday girl, Helen Stephens (Anna Massey), asks him if he would like a slice of cake. The two begin to strike up a conversation, and they quickly become friends. Helen explains that she lives with her blind mother (Maxine Audley) in the floor below Mark. Mark reveals that he is, in fact, the landlord for the building, which greatly surprises Helen. Perhaps pitying Mark, Helen begins to have a romantic relationship with him. She enjoys Mark's pleasant, quiet demeanor even if he is a bit peculiar. But she remains unaware that, beneath his mild-mannered exterior, there lurks a psychopathic murderer waiting for his next victim.

Even though Mark makes a valid attempt to lead a normal life, he cannot rid himself of his murderous impulses. In one of the movie's most infamous scenes, Mark playfully sets up an "after hours" screen test for an actress/stand-in, Vivian (Moira Shearer), on the set of the film they are both working on. At first Vivian enjoys the game with Mark, reveling in the pretense that she is the star. But soon the game takes a dangerous turn, as Mark becomes more threatening, asking her disturbing questions. He takes the cover off

The perverse Mark Lewis (Carl Boehm) holds his instrument of murder, his camera.

his tripod to reveal the gleaming spike. As he moves closer to his victim, he informs her (and us) that the mirror on his camera will allow her to watch her own death. Later, in a particularly macabre moment, Vivian's body is discovered (while the movie-within-the-movie's cameras are rolling) on the set stuffed into a large trunk.

Other murders follow, including Helen's mother, a suspicious blind woman unable to realize the danger until Mark has placed the spike into her neck. In the film's climax, on the run from the police, Mark retreats to his apartment to relive his latest murder onscreen. When Helen comes into his room, Mark quickly removes the film from the projector and hides it in a container. Helen, curious as to what Mark is hiding from her, begs him to show her the film. After much persistence, Mark finally gives in. As she witnesses Vivian's final moments onscreen, the frightened Helen asks Mark if the film is fake, or is indeed real. Mark leans close and confirms her worst fear. Just then, the police arrive outside Mark's apartment. Realizing there is no escape, Mark secures his camera to the wall and, with his last breath, films his own suicide.

Despite its recognized status as a classic and influential film, *Peeping Tom* still exists in relative obscurity. When *Peeping Tom* first hit cinemas in Britain, it was a groundbreaking horror film, and the critics responded in the same way they did to other groundbreaking horror films, such as *Night of the Living Dead* (1968) and *The Texas Chain Saw Massacre* (1974): They trashed it as a "sick" movie with little or no redeeming qualities. All three films were unlike anything anyone had seen at the time, and the critics did not know how to handle the film. Derek Hill wrote in his review for *The Tribune*, "The only really satisfactory way to dispose of *Peeping Tom* would be to shovel it up and flush it swiftly down the nearest sewer. Even then the stench would remain." (Powell-Pressburger.org). In many ways, *Psycho* also faced a similar problem the same year as Powell's film. However, a major difference lies in what happened to the careers of the films' directors. Whereas Tobe Hooper, George A. Romero, and Alfred Hitchcock all became more popular due to their respective films, Michael Powell saw his career all but finished.

Perhaps the key difference lies in how the directors were perceived at the times of the films' releases. For both Hooper and Romero, presenting their debut work, there were no pre-existing expectations. Hitchcock, on the other hand, was already identified with darker films, although with *Psycho* this was taken to its extreme. Michael Powell, however, was known much more as a family director, associated with films such as *The Thief of Bagdad* (1940), *The Life and Death of Colonel Blimp* (1943), and *The Red Shoes* (1948). A director of this ilk was not supposed to direct such "vile trash." Powell managed to make only a few other theatrical efforts, and never again achieved the level of respect prior to *Peeping Tom*'s release. As for the film itself, it was pulled from theaters and shelved, seemingly destined for complete oblivion when it found its savior in director Martin Scorsese, whose love for the film (and Powell's work in general) led him on a crusade to rescue this lost gem of horror.

Unlike, say, Norman Bates, few today would recognize the name "Mark Lewis" as one of the greatest villains in horror film history, and Mark's exploits have not become part of our culture. Unfortunately, many people refuse to watch an "old" movie, and *Peeping Tom* is an *ancient* 45-plus years old. I first became aware of the existence of this film through my love of *Psycho*, having heard that my favorite film had a "British cousin" so to speak. Happily, thanks to Turner Classic Movies, I recently completed a task that I, along with numerous other fans, have spent years trying to accomplish. I finally saw *Peeping Tom*.

PHANTASM (1979)
by Michael Vario

In 1979, the horror movie scene was starting to boom. *Halloween* (1978) had come out only a few months earlier and blown horror fans away. When television commercials started running for a new release called *Phantasm*, my friends and I were immediately grabbed by the image of a flying silver sphere. But when we finally saw the film, it was more like a nightmare set to celluloid, surreal in its imagery and often nonlinear in its storytelling. Yet it still had the jump scares and gore we were looking for. The story left many things unexplained, but it didn't matter because this was one scary movie.

As *Phantasm* begins, a couple are making out behind a gravestone in Morningside Cemetery. The woman, in a lavender-colored dress, pulls out a knife and kills the man. The dead man is Tommy. His two best friends, Jody (a musician) and Reggie (an ice cream man), are seen attending his funeral. Having recently lost his parents, Jody visits his parents' crypt inside the mortuary where he encounters the towering, gray-haired mortician referred to only as the Tall Man (Angus Scrimm). Meanwhile, Jody's younger brother Mike, having covertly followed him to the funeral, is spooked in the cemetery by small, dark shapes that scuttle just out of sight behind the headstones. After

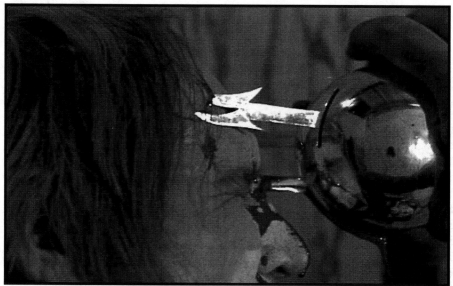

The flying silver sphere finds its target in the caretaker (Ken Jones).

the interment, when everyone else has gone, Mike spies the Tall Man lifting Tommy's coffin with superhuman strength and putting it back in the hearse. The supernatural, other-dimensional, shape-shifting nightmare continues.

Obviously, it is difficult to convey the feeling of the film through a synopsis of the plot, as it is impossible to describe the movie without using words like "surreal" and "dreamlike." Often, *Phantasm* abandons traditional narrative structure with dream sequences and nightmare imagery.

The film was written and directed by Don Coscarelli (*The Beastmaster* [1982], *Bubba Ho-Tep* [2002]), who was 23 years old when he started shooting *Phantasm*. In the 2005 documentary *Phantasmagoria*, Coscarelli discusses what prompted him to make *Phantasm*. He had previously done two low-budget films, one of which included a small jump scare in a Halloween scene. He was so thrilled seeing the audience jump that he decided to make a full-length horror film, one that he would pack with scares. Rather than the more traditional horror films popular at the time, he wanted to make it more dreamlike, incorporating elements from surreal cinema, citing the Luis Buñuel 1929 film *Un Chien Andalou* as an influence.

With a production budget of $300,000, the movie was made over the course of two years, often filming on weekends to save on equipment rental costs, with most of the cast made up of actors who had worked on Coscarelli's two earlier efforts. Kate Coscarelli, Don's mother, did makeup, set design, and production design. Coscarelli's and Bannister's parents filled in as extras, while neighborhood children played the dwarves.

Phantasm was filmed at various locations around California. The cemetery scenes were shot in Chatsworth Park, while the interior of the mortuary was shot on a set constructed in a warehouse also in Chatsworth. The Dunsmuir mansion in Oakland served as the exterior of the mortuary. As shot, the first cut was over three hours long, so a lot of footage (including alternate endings) needed to be trimmed. Some of this would find its way to DVD as deleted scenes, and much of it was eventually used in the third sequel, *Phantasm IV: Oblivion* (1998).

The film struck a chord with horror fans, grossing $12 million in U.S. ticket sales, as well as reaching many others through TV and home video over the years. As a result of its growing cult status, Coscarelli was persuaded to make a sequel, *Phantasm II*, released in 1988. Produced by Universal Pictures, the budget was three million dollars, 10 times that of the original. Unfortunately, it bombed at the box office, earning only seven million dollars, thus sealing its fate as the only *Phantasm* film to be produced by a major studio. Coscarelli eventually followed up with two direct-to-video sequels, *Phantasm III: Lord of the Dead* (1994) and the aforementioned *Phantasm IV: Oblivion*. In 2005, New Line Cinema bought the rights to remake *Phantasm,* while also mentioning the possibility of producing another sequel.

While not always a favorite of fans of more traditional horror narratives, *Phantasm* has always had a large group of followers with whom its surreal storytelling resonated. Over the years the film has reached cult status and has received recognition in the world of horror. It was named #25 on the Bravo list of "100 Scariest Movie Moments," as well as #10 on Film Threat's "13 Scariest Horror Films Ever" and #10 on E! Online's list of "Top 10 Horror Films." Obviously, that little flying chrome sphere with the nasty surprises left quite an impression on a few folks out there.

THE PHANTOM OF THE OPERA (1925)
by Preston B. Collins (with Aaron Christensen)

Aaron Christensen: So, my man, you've just watched Lon Chaney's *The Phantom of the Opera* for the first time in years. What'd you think?

Preston B. Collins: Loved it. I've got one of those 50 DVD packs that has a bunch of B-and-C flicks, along with a couple good old ones like *Nosferatu, Night of the Living Dead, Carnival of Souls*, stuff like that. Ah, public domain.

AC: Just as an FYI for serious fans, the Image/Milestone 2-disc DVD is the one to grab. It's got an outstanding audio commentary by Scott MacQueen about the film's troubled genesis and the picture has been beautifully restored.

PBC: You know, the first time I saw *Phantom*, it was at a screening at the public library. I think I was about seven, just getting into monster movies.

AC: That must have been cool. Did it scare you?

PBC: I don't remember being *scared*, really. The unmasking scene was cool. Actually, the final scene with the mob all falling upon him, *that* freaked me out. I don't think I'd ever seen that kind of violence depicted onscreen before. I thought, "Wow, they just keep hitting him. He looked bad enough before, what's he gotta look like after all that?" I remember later trying to impress one of the older kids by blustering, "Yeah, man, they should have shown that scene close up!" He just looked at me like I was a weirdo and walked away.

AC: Way to go. Did you get beaten up after school?

PBC: Well, yes. But not for that. (laughs)

AC: By the time I saw the film for the first time, I had seen the unmasking scene about a billion times on various horror-themed TV specials, so it didn't really have the full impact. Like the *Psycho* shower scene, some moments become iconic and familiar.

Erik (Lon Chaney) is unmasked by Christine (Mary Philbin).

Still, I was struck by how we the audience see Erik unmasked first, and then we think, "Oh man, now he's going to turn around…"

PBC: It's a double scare. We get spooked and jump back, then eagerly lean back in to see how Christine's going to react. David J. Skal describes the unmasking as "verging on visual rape, with Erik's bulging bald head and stiff carriage giving him the aspect of a ruined penis that can no longer seduce, only repulse the beloved."

AC: Dude, come on. I'm eating over here. I'll go along with the visual rape thing, but a *ruined penis*? I've heard Chaney was going for a skull-like image. That's why he did the thing with the wires pulling his nose back and bulging his eyes, which I imagine hurt like a bugger. *Phantom*'s cinematographer, Charles Van Enger, reported that Chaney would sometimes "bleed like hell" from the devices. The man *suffered* for his art.

PBC: What's interesting is when people say, "There'll never be another Lon Chaney," they're more right than they know. These days, a film actor wouldn't be allowed to design and apply his own makeup, someone like Rick Baker or KNB would come in.

AC: Right, but Chaney's career was so much more than just a bunch of makeup stunts. Watching something like *Phantom* or 1923's *Hunchback of Notre Dame* and then seeing him in *The Unknown* (1927), where he plays the armless knife thrower, you see what a masterful and versatile actor he was.

PBC: Good call on *The Unknown*. I wish more people would see that film, some amazing moments there. Thank heaven for DVD. What's hilarious is that most people, when you mention *Phantom* today, they think you're talking about the Broadway musical. (singing) Bummmm-bah-bah-bah-bahhhhh.

AC: I know! The musical portrays the Phantom as some unfortunate, misunderstood romantic hero. I mean, yes, he is misunderstood and unfortunate, but he's also twisted with anger and hatred at the world that has reduced him to living in an underground lair beneath the Paris Opera House. He's a *monster*, folks. He's not looking for pity, he's looking for revenge.

PBC: ...and a little love. (laughs) The other thing that really sets this version apart from the later films is that, like in Gaston Leroux's original novel, Chaney's Erik was *born* this way, so he's been dealing with society's disgust his entire life. The later versions seem to all be regular guys who had acid or something thrown on them, and their vengeance is directed towards the one who wronged them. Erik is angry at *everyone*, including God himself. Not that other Phantom performances aren't fine. I mean, Claude Rains is terrific in the 1943 Universal remake and Herbert Lom does well with what he has to work with in Hammer's 1962 version.

AC: Yes, although Rains is doing the *Invisible Man* thing again, doing the majority of the acting with his voice. Chaney uses his entire body as a tool, not having the opportunity to vocalize.

PBC: I love the scene where he enters the masked ball as "The Red Death." You *know* that's Chaney in there. And the burst of color works really well for the scene. I found that as delightfully shocking as the unmasking. Take that, *Wizard of Oz*! Tell you what, though, the Christine character (Mary Philbin) is one of the most annoying chicks I've ever seen on film. All she does, throughout the entire picture, is ignore every single instruction that Erik gives her, betraying his every confidence. He tells her, "Don't tell anyone about me, don't kiss anyone else, don't take the mask off..." And she's like, "Sure, no problem. Tell, kiss, unmask. Got it." I coulda killed her.

AC: Well, now that you mention it, it is a bit of a one-horse show, as the rest of the characters are far less fascinating.

PBC: It's no wonder that Chaney runs away with the film. His performance is breathtaking: tender, and loving one minute, a snarling, vengeful beast the next. The romantic lead? Norman Kerry? What a dud. Chaney has more charisma in his little fingernail. Which is I guess why Chaney is a legend and Kerry is "ol' what's-his-name." There's one other person who doesn't get nearly as much press as he deserves, and that's Carl Laemmle, Sr. He produced both of Chaney's big spectaculars, *Phantom* and *Hunchback*, at Universal and gave them the budget required to create opulence.

AC: We also don't hear much about the director, Rupert Julian. (My God, does MacQueen tear into him on the Image DVD commentary.) Granted, he mostly worked in the silent era as an actor and director, and he only did two other obscure films in the horror genre, *The Creaking Stairs* (1919) and *The Cat Creeps* (1930). *An Illustrated History of the Horror Film* states that Edward Sedgewick eventually replaced Julian and completed the shooting, and that, in fact, Chaney directed many of his own scenes.

PBC: It really is Chaney's show, his and art director Charles D. Hall.

AC: This is one of those films I wish I had a time machine, to travel back to 1925. Can you imagine what that must have been like for a first time audience, watching the unmasking scene, the chandelier falling, the masked ball with Chaney striding down the stairs in red on the big screen?

PBC: That reminds me of my favorite moment. When the mob has cornered Erik and he turns around to face them...

AC: Yes!!!

PBC: And he raises up his fist and they all just freeze in their tracks, completely awestruck. Then he opens his hand to reveal…nothing at all. What did they think he had, a bomb? A grenade? No, they knew in their hearts that he had nothing, and yet they were arrested by the sheer force of his will. It is his last moment of triumph, and he goes down laughing at them. There's a chilling quality to it, as though he has somehow won. Of course, then they proceed to kill him and toss him in the Seine.

AC: That's the power of Chaney. It's funny you mention that scene, because when he turns around, I always draw back in my seat. "Oh jeez, what's he going to do now?" Great stuff. It's no wonder the film has survived all these years. The funny thing is that when all the films were being assigned for this project, *Phantom* was the last one chosen. Thanks for picking up the ball, by the way.

PBC: No worries, mate. I suppose the problem is trying to say something that hasn't already been said before. Plus the sad fact that the majority of today's horror fans aren't all that keen on the older films, especially from the silent era. But Chaney's Erik isn't some stuffy old curio. Sitting down with the film this last time, I was surprised again and again by the subtler things that Chaney does, in addition to the flamboyant moments. I hope younger viewers are willing to take a chance, as well as more experienced fans who haven't sat down with it in a while. It really does deserve its place at the table of great horror films, or at least, great performances.

AC: Amen, brother.

PLAN 9 FROM OUTER SPACE (1959)
by Patrick Mathewes

Our narrator Criswell makes some transparent predictions ("We are all interested in the future, for that is where you and I are going to spend the rest of our lives."), then delivers some equally vague hints as to what the film may be about. As Criswell continues to narrate off-screen, we are introduced to a grieving old man (Bela Lugosi) at his wife's funeral. As the mourners leave the cemetery, the wife (Vampira) rises from the dead and kills two gravediggers. The old man meets a fatal accident shortly after that and is laid to rest in the same cemetery. After his funeral, two of the mourners discover the corpses of the gravediggers and the police are called in. The police, led by Inspector Clay (Tor Johnson), proceed to investigate the murders. Clay's investigation and life are cut short by another appearance of the Ghoul Woman, now accompanied by her recently deceased husband. Meanwhile over Hollywood, flying saucers are spotted…

As the above paragraph indicates, *Plan 9 from Outer Space* has a complex, bizarre narrative that is not easily summarized. In the documentary, *Flying Saucers Over Hollywood: The Plan 9 Companion* (1992), fan Brad Linaweaver describes the film as having "…so many framing devices that it's like a bunch of Chinese boxes…you disappear into the thickets of commentary and you forget there was ever a story line. It's a confidence trick." Ed Wood was indeed pulling off a sort of con. Beginning with a few minutes of footage he had already shot of Bela Lugosi before Lugosi's untimely death, he structured a film story around what was available. To flesh out the footage, Lugosi was doubled by Wood's chiropractor using one of the late star's Dracula capes, careful to keep his face covered whenever he was onscreen.

Reanimated Tor Johnson and Vampira haunt the graveyards.

As if that wasn't enough, Wood also had to deal with a minuscule budget (which didn't allow for adequate special effects or retakes) and interference from the Southern Baptists who had put up most of the funds. Uncomfortable with the film's subject, they insisted that the working title of "Grave Robbers from Outer Space" be changed, and further demanded that Wood and his cast be baptized into the church. Wood persevered and completed *Plan 9* in four to seven days (accounts vary), shoddy f/x and all.

There are many cheap effects and gaffes that helped earn the film the reputation of "Worst Film of All Time" in Harry and Michael Medved's book, *The Golden Turkey Awards*. The gravestones in the cemetery are obviously cardboard and have a tendency to wobble and fall down, while the trees cast shadows on the "sky." When Lugosi exits the screen for his fatal meeting with a passing car, the frame freezes, and although the sound effects of a scream and screeching brakes indicate what happened, his shadow can still be plainly seen on the ground. Within scenes, there are frequent shifts from night to day, and there is always a cloud-filled daytime sky through the viewport in the saucer, even when scenes take place at night. It is admittedly an easy film to laugh at, thanks to Wood's frequently odd decisions as director and writer, as well as the eccentric performances from a cast of primarily amateur actors. But believe it or not, other things going are going on here.

In his essay on the film in *Cult Movies*, Danny Peary convincingly argues that Wood is only putting up a "crazy façade" so that he can get away with making a subversive movie. The movie is openly critical of the American military, implying that they routinely cover up events, yet *Plan 9 from Outer Space* was made in one of the most conservative eras in U.S. history. Certainly, no other sci-fi/horror films of the '50s were taking such a bold stance and presenting it so matter-of-factly.

I view the film as an early artifact of Pop Surrealism, a modern art movement that places pop icons into traditional styles. In *Plan 9*, Wood incorporated his love of serials and old monster movies, from the Flash Gordon-inspired alien garb to the appearance of the ghouls and the presence of the original Dracula himself, hearkening back to the Universal horror films of the '30s. He also utilized TV personalities Criswell and Vampira, as well as the recent craze for flying saucers. With his collage method of integrating pop culture into his works, Wood anticipated filmmakers (such as Quentin Tarantino) who frequently rework the films they love from the past into their own pictures.

Those who dismiss Wood as a totally incompetent filmmaker have not watched *Plan 9* closely enough. The infamously cheap flying saucers are not paper plates or pie tins as many claim, but model kits purchased from a local toy store. The film is often derided for having the saucer being clearly *square* in shape when characters approach it on the ground, but that square base can actually be seen on the miniature saucers as they land in the graveyard. In sequences of the saucers soaring over Hollywood and in combat with the military, Wood gives a clear indication of what is going on and blends stock with original footage to tell his story. As a testimony to Wood's editing skill, this sequence, which has narration in the film, works just as well if played back completely silent. In a pre-digital age, the strings manipulating the saucers could not be erased, but with a little suspension of disbelief it's an effective sequence.

Apart from *Plan 9*, Ed Wood also brought his offbeat sensibilities to a handful of other memorable films, including *Glen or Glenda* (1953), *Bride of the Monster* (1955), and *Night of the Ghouls* (1959). *Plan 9* did nothing to improve his standing in Hollywood and his productions got increasingly cheaper. He eventually ended up cranking out "adult" paperbacks and screenplays for low-budget porn features. Even in his hack work, Wood remained true to his basic interests, often incorporating transvestites and ghouls into his plots. *Necromania: A Tale of Weird Love* (1971) even played with the idea of necrophilia and had two characters having sex in a coffin to overcome their hang-ups. His writing is still used as the basis for new films, perhaps most successfully in *I Woke Up Early the Day I Died* (1998), filmed from Wood's unadulterated screenplay with Billy Zane, Ron Perlman, and Christina Ricci.

As far as the *Plan 9* players go, most of Bela Lugosi's classics date from the early '30s, but as the decade continued a series of bad career decisions and an unshakable accent resulted in fewer and fewer roles offered until he found his way into the low-budget studios.

Tor Johnson had a successful career as a wrestler and appeared in bit parts in close to 20 films before Wood "discovered" him and cast him as the creature Lobo in *Bride of the Monster*, a role he returned to in *Night of the Ghouls*. Other than his films for Wood, Johnson is best known for his titular role as *The Beast of Yucca Flats* (1961), and as the basis for a best-selling latex Halloween mask modeled after his appearance as a zombie in *Plan 9*.

Vampira began her career as Maila Nurmi and adopted her more famous pseudonym when she began appearing as the host of a local TV horror show. She became an international celebrity, even though her show was only broadcast in the Los Angeles area. Her distinctive look (inspired by the cartoons of Charles Addams) and her campy intros to schlocky horror films predated Elvira by several decades. Her most recent role was a bit part in *I Woke Up Early the Day I Died*.

Plan 9 had no immediate impact upon other films since it was barely even released. It was only later, when it was sold to television and became a frequent late night staple, that the magic began. As a result of these off-hour encounters, voters chose it as the "Worst Film of All Time" in 1980 for the Medved book, which in turn enticed even more viewers to seek it out. In 1992, Rudolph Grey published *Nightmare of Ecstasy: The Life and Art of Edward D. Wood, Jr.*, which was adapted into the screenplay for Tim Burton's loving biopic, *Ed Wood* (1994).

Those works have all brought more fans into contact with Wood's odd, heartfelt films, and today more people know who he was than at any point in his lifetime. *Plan 9* alone has inspired t-shirts, posters, comics, masks, model kits, soundtrack albums, and even a stage musical, as well as an ongoing interest in bad cinema. It also helped restore Bela Lugosi's reputation, who had fallen into obscurity when it was made, as a long-standing horror icon.

POLTERGEIST (1982)
by Amanda Rose

Steven (Craig T. Nelson) battles ghostly special effects.

A childhood obsession, I watched *Poltergeist* on VHS over and over until I could recite it word perfect. When released, it earned $76,600,000 in box-office receipts in the U.S. alone, making it the fifth highest grossing movie of that year. Obviously, it wasn't only me who saw something special in this supernatural tale. Just why is *Poltergeist* so fondly remembered by so many?

With Tobe Hooper at the helm, one might be expecting an ultra-brutal portrayal—with lashings of female hysteria—of that Hollywood horror staple: The Haunted House. However, the overwhelming influence on *Poltergeist*, drowning out Hooper with signature motifs and devices, is producer Steven Spielberg (who co-wrote the screenplay). Here is a wondrous yarn that seamlessly blends humor, drama, and chills; a child is our main focus, with childhood fears explored. Add an enchanting score of lullaby simplicity from Jerry Goldsmith, a talented ensemble cast, special effects that continue to hold up today, and it's not difficult to see how something exceptional came to be.

From the opening credits, it's obvious this isn't traditional haunted house fare; no Gothic mansion, tales of murders, or offers of a cash prize for spending the night. Instead the camera sweeps over an All-American neighborhood; kids playing on their bikes, white picket fences. Normality. This is where you or I could live.

This feeling of "they're just like us" is compounded as we meet the Freelings: Father Steven (Craig T. Nelson) watching football with buddies while sparring with his neighbor; mother Diane (JoBeth Williams) keeping house; the kids—Dana, Robbie, and Carol Anne (Dominique Dunne, Oliver Robins, Heather O'Rourke)—arguing at the breakfast table whilst slipping waffles to their dog. They're a real family.

The first indication that something isn't quite right comes at night, after Steven has fallen asleep in front of the TV. Carol Anne approaches the snowy screen, answering questions we cannot hear, awakening the family with her frustrated cries to "Talk louder!" The next night Carol Anne is again drawn to the television as her family sleeps. Suddenly, a force shoots from the television into the wall, rocking the whole house and awakening the family. Carol Anne informs them, and us: "They're here."

Not long after, Diane, Steven, and Carol Anne are delighted by astounding acts of chairs balancing and moving. However the playful games of the "TV People" take a sudden turn for the sinister when Carol Anne is sucked into their dimension (following some distraction tactics in the form of a gnarled tree's attack on Robbie). As the family searches around the house and in the outdoor swimming pool, shell-shocked Robbie hears his sister's disembodied cry for her Mommy…coming from the TV.

The ghostly goings-on within the house step up a notch or 50. In Robbie and Carol Anne's bedroom, objects now move at will, lights flash; in short, the room is *alive*. Bewildered, the Freelings call in a trio of paranormal investigators, led by Dr. Lesh (Beatrice Straight). The scene where they attempt to contact Carol Anne is by turns wondrous, exhilarating, and terrifying. It's testament to Williams' acting abilities that the only special effect needed to communicate Carol Anne's spirit rushing through her is a wind machine. It's a moment of goose bump proportions, particularly for any parents watching.

That night, we are treated to the goriest part of a film otherwise devoid of blood and guts. As Marty (Marty Casella) makes his way into the kitchen for a snack, his flashlight illuminates a steak on the counter that suddenly erupts spewing maggots. Nauseous, he runs to the sink to splash his face with water…but doesn't stop there. Marty pokes his finger into a cut that has appeared on his cheek, then proceeds to literally rip his face off, the meaty lumps of flesh and blood dropping onto the white porcelain of the sink. Not until the bones of his face and jaw are visible and his eyeball is dropping out of its socket does the image flash back to normal, with Marty looking in stunned bewilderment at his reflection.

Before we meet Tangina (Zelda Rubenstein), a medium brought in by Dr. Lesh, there is a mundane, yet significant exchange between Steven and his boss, Mr. Teague (James Karen). It is revealed that the whole neighborhood where the family resides was built upon a cemetery that was relocated. Despite Teague's assertion that "It's not ancient tribal burial ground. It's just…people," Steven is uneasy (although not altogether joining the dots that seem obvious to us).

While all the performances are uniformly strong, Rubenstein commands the screen with authority despite her unconventional appearance and vocal pitch. She makes it clear she is capable of reading Steven's skeptical mind, then speaks of "The Beast," a malevolent force that is holding onto Carol Anne as a lure to keep other spirits away from "the light." But she has a plan: They're going in after Carol Anne.

The debate over how much of the film Hooper actually directed rages on to this day. At the time of filming, Spielberg was under an exclusivity contract to direct *E.T: The Extra-Terrestrial* (1982) and so, officially, could not direct *Poltergeist*. Yet any aficionado of Spielberg's work will recognize his overwhelming influence throughout, from the themes to specific shots to the use of music. Spielberg seems to either defend Hooper or coyly infer that the direction is his own, depending on the occasion. My personal feeling is that *Poltergeist* just *feels* like a Spielberg and doesn't bear any trademark indications of Hooper's involvement. However, the bottom line is that whomever is really responsible for this trip into suburban family horror, it's a hell of a ride.

Rumors of a "*Poltergeist* curse" began when principal actors from the films began meeting the grim reaper either during or shortly after filming. Dominique Dunne (who played eldest daughter Dana) was brutally murdered by her estranged boyfriend after *Poltergeist* wrapped. Julian Beck (Rev. Kane) left this mortal coil before *Poltergeist II: The Other Side* (1986) opened, with co-star Will Sampson (Taylor) passing away the year after its release. Perhaps most tragically of all, Heather O'Rourke (Carol Anne) died during the filming of *Poltergeist III* (1988) at the age of 12 (stand-ins were used to complete her scenes). However, can we really credit four deaths, however untimely, to a curse when they span a six-year period? Would it be churlish to suggest that perhaps marketing and spin are actually at the bottom of our supposed curse? As they say, there's no such thing as bad publicity…

PROFONDO ROSSO (1975)
(aka DEEP RED)
by Thierry Wybauw

Marcus Daly (David Hemmings) faces his demons.

Horror 101

Born September 7, 1940, the son of Salvatore Argento, *Maestro* Dario Argento's passions for horror-filmmaking were first introduced through hair-raising, bedtime-story versions of Italian folk tales as told by family members.

Argento started his film career as a movie critic for the daily *Paese Sera*. As such, writing came as normal for him as red is the color of blood, and it didn't take long before he stepped onto the path of writing screenplays. As he worked his way up the ranks, one of his big breaks came at the age of 20 when he (alongside another budding legend of Italian cinema, Bernardo Bertolucci) co-wrote the screen story for Sergio Leone's epic Spaghetti Western, *Once Upon a Time in the West* (1968).

Three years later, he would write the screenplay for his directorial debut, *The Bird with the Crystal Plumage* (1969), the first of his "animal trilogy" (followed by *Four Flies on Grey Velvet* and *The Cat o' Nine Tails*, both released in 1971, all produced by his father Salvatore). Argento has been quoted as saying that the reason he ended up taking the directing into his own hands was "out of fear that another director might rape my screenplay." In doing so, he produced a series of critically acclaimed, box-office hits with audiences worldwide, which would soon rank him among the icons of top-notch horror directors.

These films would also mark his first steps into the *giallo*/horror industry. This unique film genre was originated and later popularized by Italian directors such as Mario Bava (and later Argento). Distinctive characteristics include murder scenes featuring explicit bloodshed and violence, artistic camerawork imbedded in extraordinary color-schemes, and bizarre, psychedelic sound-scores. *Gialli* also often includes copious rafts of nudity and explicit sex.

Several years later, after a stint doing some directing for Italian television, Argento revisited his favorite genre in 1975 with *Profondo Rosso* (aka *Deep Red*). Considered by many as his masterpiece, the film is unequivocally a "magnum-opus" in his personal career, and for the *giallo* genre overall.

At a parapsychology conference in Rome, psychic Helga Ulman (Macha Meril), displays the power of telepathic logic. That evening, she senses the twisted thoughts of an audience member. The observer-killer's murderous spirit reveals that they have killed before and will afresh.

Later on that night, the psychic's instincts become fact.

Marcus Daly (David Hemmings), an English jazz pianist living in Rome, walks towards his home accompanied by his friend Carlo (Gabriele Lavia). They hear the distressing screams of Helga, and running to her aid, discover the agonizing, hatchet-hewn aftermath of the psychic's slaughter. Fascinated by the conundrum, and assisted by the local paparazzi Gianna (Daria Nicolodi), Marcus cannot rest until he unravels the answers to this dark riddle…

With the screenplay for *Profondo Rosso*, co-scripted by Bernardino Zapponi, Argento specifically set out to create fundamental horror, using elements that his viewers could identify with. For example, the fear of a shotgun held at point blank is beyond the realm of most people's personal experiences. Therefore, Argento reasoned, it becomes quite difficult to relate to such a sensation, and the fear generated does not resonate on a visceral level. However, excessive heat and/or being burned is another story, as nearly everyone has been burned by hot water at some point in his or her life. When Argento puts these identifiable sensations onscreen—as in the memorable scene where a woman

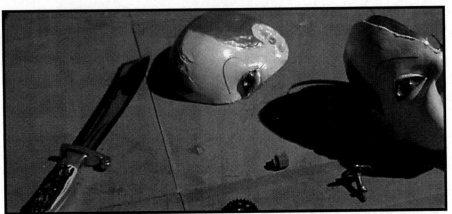
Disturbing images populate Dario Argento's cinematic world.

is scalded to death—it becomes a reality in the viewer's mind, translating into vivid, emotional, recognizable pain.

Argento also introduced a different approach of storytelling from previous films, using new empirical camera angles and disturbing scenes. This new maneuver insured that audiences wouldn't have time to relax. As said by Bernardino Zapponi: "There has to be this continuous evil discomfort which is essential to a thriller!" All throughout *Profondo Rosso*, such discomforts are featured. There's a mysterious little kid, a haunting puppet, an eccentric children's song, and the vigorous psychedelic soundtrack of Goblin. Fear and tension were assured!

Argento's mastery as a writer/director also lies in the power of playing with his audience. By serving them up a puzzle/mystery, the viewer naturally has the desire to solve the riddle while watching, to put the pieces back together. As the film progresses, however, Argento hands out a hodgepodge of information little by little, mystifying the observers such that they are unable to decipher this cryptogram. All the clues, while legitimate, are distributed so unobtrusively (and in such strategic places) that it becomes nearly impossible to spot the tree through the thick forest.

Visually, *Profondo Rosso* is also a standout example of Argento's artistic *modus operandi*. Each little square of the film is filled with his stunning eye for detail, emerging as what is known as the "Argentorian" style. These elements include daring camera angles, prodigious scene-lattice, exceptional closeup work of the murders from the killer's perspective, and inventively composed, artistically framed shots laid out with a deliberate use of color. (Trivia: When the killer's black leather gloved hands appear onscreen in Argento's films, they're always the director's own hands!)

Argento's skillful originality in creating detailed sets reaches yet another level in *Profondo Rosso*: Many of the people in the backgrounds don't even move, serving as living statues. Influenced by a book he had bought on the artist Edward Hopper, Argento decided to exactly reconstruct Hopper's famous bar painting, "Nighthawks," as a set within his movie. Furthermore, viewers should keep an eagle eye on the "hallway of paintings" scene 19 minutes into the movie, a typical example of how Argento loves to fool with his audience. It all works impeccably.

The memorable *Profondo Rosso* soundtrack, as performed by Goblin, was not actually the first score commissioned. Argento had originally hired Italian composer

Giorgio Gaslini, but upon listening to the submitted tracks, Argento felt that Gaslini hadn't captured the right spirit. The director's female lead, Daria Nicolodi, introduced Argento to a young group from the St. Cecilia's Music Conservatory in Rome, the progressive rock band Oliver. After hearing a track of their debut album (recorded under the label-imposed name "Cherry Five"), Argento enthusiastically handed them the project.

Goblin's music with charismatic front man Claudio Simonetti, including the sound-tracks for Argento's *Profondo Rosso* and *Suspiria,* influenced the music for many other films (John Carpenter was clearly influenced when he created the music score to *Halloween* [1978]). With its embryonic and innovative psychedelic rock stylings, Goblin added a nonconformist, avant garde sound within the thriller/*giallo* genre. Their score for *Profondo Rosso* spent a remarkable 15 weeks at #1 on Italian album charts, going on to sell over three million copies.

The outstanding acting performances are also worth noting. David Hemmings is outstanding as Marcus, doggedly pursuing a mystery that seems to have no answer, a conscious nod to his most famous role as the photographer in Michelangelo Antonioni's *Blowup* (1966). Working up until his death in 2003, Hemmings appeared in the cult Jane Fonda film *Barbarella* (1968), *Gladiator* (2000), *Spy Game* (2001), *Gangs of New York* (2002), and scores of TV roles. As a director throughout the 1980s, he also directed extensively for television programs including *The A-Team* and *Airwolf,* in which he also played the role of Dr. Charles Henry Moffett.

In her first major screen role, Daria Nicolodi was cast as the reporter-cum-amateur sleuth in Argento's *Profondo Rosso*, and in the process, became romantically entangled with the young filmmaker. She would co-write the screenplay to Argento's next film, *Suspiria* (1977), loosely based on her grandmother's experiences with the occult. Her long-time relationship with Argento (despite many rumors to the contrary, they have never been married) also yielded the couple's two daughters, Fiore and Asia, who would both be seen in their father's films. Nicolodi would go on to appear in several other Argento projects, such as *Inferno* (1980), *Tenebrae* (1982), *Phenomena* (1984), as well as *Opera* (1988). Nicolodi is currently slated to return to the screen along with daughter Asia in the final film of Argento's "Three Mothers" trilogy (of which *Suspiria* and *Inferno* make up the first two chapters), titled *The Mother of Tears.*

Profondo Rosso, in addition to being a brutal/violent mystery-thriller in its own right, went on to inspire countless international directors within the thriller-horror genre, eventually evolving into the American slasher genre of the '80s. It was a film that so upset film censors with its excessive blood and violence that, upon its initial release, its running time was cut by almost an hour in some countries! Nevertheless, *Profondo Rosso* has survived throughout the years and remains still a cutting-edge classic.

PSYCHO (1960)
by Zane Younger

On June 16, 1960, Alfred Hitchcock's *Psycho* was released in the United States. It was an instant sensation, eventually generating $50,000,000 worldwide. Part of the film's initial success can be attributed to its ingenious marketing scheme, which restricted people from entering the theater once the movie had started. On the surface, this policy

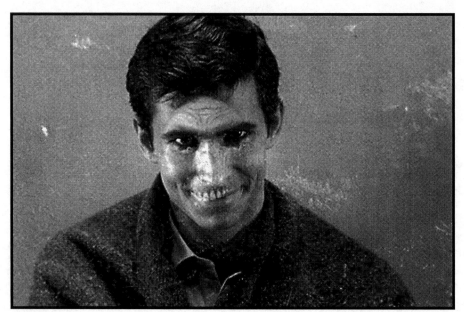
Norman Bates (Anthony Perkins) superimposed over Mother, in his final shot. The super-imposed moment is so quick that viewers often miss the merger of mother and son.

merely seemed as though Hitchcock wanted people to see it from start to finish. But more importantly, the scheme was designed to protect the film's renowned plot twists. Audiences were shocked by the envelope-pushing sexuality and violence, in particular the infamous "shower scene," in which our leading character is shockingly bumped off less than halfway through the film. After the film's release, Alfred Hitchcock received an angry letter from the father of a girl who refused to have a bath after seeing *Les Diaboliques* (1955), and now refused to shower after seeing his film. Hitchcock sent a note back simply saying, "Send her to the dry cleaners."

The film begins with Marion (Janet Leigh) stealing $40,000 from her employer's client so she and her lover, Sam (John Gavin), can finally get married. On the run, she pulls into the out-of-the-way Bates Motel where she meets the young, handsome Nor-man Bates (Anthony Perkins). Following some awkward conversation with her host, Marion returns to her room to take a shower. While she rubs soap over her shoulders, a shadowy figure enters the room behind her, creeps up, pulls back the shower curtain, and then proceeds to stab Ms. Crane to death. (The sound of the knife penetrating the flesh is actually the sound of a knife stabbing a casaba melon and the blood was Bosco chocolate syrup.)

As modern day viewers, we can only *imagine* the shock this must have had on the unsuspecting moviegoers of 1960. We followed Marion Crane from the beginning of the film, and now she lies slain on the floor of the bathroom with her blood circling in the drain. (Hitchcock anonymously purchased the rights to Robert Bloch's novel for only $9,000, then reportedly bought up as many copies of the novel as he could to keep the movie's plot a secret.) From the ominous Bates House on the hill, we hear Norman yelling, "Mother, oh god, Mother! Blood, blood!" before running to the scene of the crime. Apparently, Norman's mother is the killer and, as we watch, Norman cleans up the scene, eventually dumping Marion's body and car into a nearby swamp. Worried about her sister, Lila Crane (Vera Miles) tries to track Marion down, ultimately leading to *Psycho*'s immortal twist ending.

In a prolonged denouement, it is revealed that Norman killed his mother and her lover years ago, but his mother stayed with him in his mind…and his cellar. He committed all the murders dressed in her clothes, often having two-way conversations with her. Norman is committed to an asylum. The final image of the film is a trick shot, with the skull of Norman's mother superimposed on his face. Because it is transparent, some viewers miss the skull entirely.

It was the right film at the right time, and represented a huge shift in horror films. In fact most people consider it the biggest step towards what is now known as "modern" horror, paving the way for such unrelenting films as *Rosemary's Baby* (1968), *Night of the Living Dead* (1968), *The Exorcist* (1973), and *The Texas Chain Saw Massacre* (1974). The open sexuality in the opening scene, the gruesome murders, and the idea of a transsexual serial killer were things not usually seen in cinema before *Psycho*. One of the reasons Alfred Hitchcock filmed *Psycho* in black and white was he thought it would be too gory in color. However, Hitchcock was insistent on the elements of realism throughout the film. The lingerie worn by Marion Crane in the movie was not "made to order" but bought off the rack from clothing stores. Hitchcock wanted female viewers to identify the lingerie and thus add to the mystique of realism. And, at the insistence of screenwriter Joseph Stefano, it was also the first American film ever to show a toilet flushing onscreen.

One would be remiss without mentioning one of *Psycho*'s most effective and enduring traits: the memorable and distinctive score by Bernard Herrmann, with its now-famous screeching violins. Having been copied and parodied in countless films that followed, it is easily the most recognizable tune from any horror movie.

Psycho's influence is seen in many films, including *Dressed to Kill* (1980), *The Silence of the Lambs* (1991), and the slasher movement spawned by *Halloween* (1978) and *Friday the 13th* (1980). Eventually, in the blood-soaked environment that it had helped to create 23 years earlier, the time seemed right for a sequel. In 1983, *Psycho II* was released, with Anthony Perkins and Vera Miles returning in their original roles. The film, directed by Richard Franklin and scripted by Tom Holland, was received relatively well with audiences and critics, resulting in a medium-sized hit. Three years after that, with franchise horror in full swing, it seemed fitting to have a trilogy, so *Psycho III* (1986) was released, with Perkins in the director's chair as well as reprising his most familiar role. However, the third time was *not* the charm; the movie was a critical flop and died at the box office. Two made-for-TV sequels followed, but the biggest indignity was to come in 1998 when director Gus Van Sant infamously remade *Psycho* shot-for-shot with Vince Vaughn standing in Norman's (and Mother's) shoes.

Happily, the original's reputation remains untarnished. When I first picked up the movie from the video store, I already knew the surprise ending and the shower scene from the usual "Top Scariest Movie Moments" TV specials around Halloween time. However, that didn't stop me from enjoying the movie overall and the detective/staircase sequence scared the hell out of me! I've watched it a few times since, and although it fails to generate the same scare factor on repeat viewings, it's hard not to marvel at the technical brilliance of the shower scene and Alfred Hitchcock's wonderful directing.

The film became an instant classic, and remains one of my all-time favorite movies. With the success of *Psycho*, Hitchcock's name continued to be (and still remains) forever linked with the concepts of fear, suspense, and murder—despite the fact that his horror output is actually rather limited, his last real genre offering being *Frenzy* (1972). With *Psycho* Hitchcock created a seminal film, getting everything just right. By way of proof, just think of how many verbal touchstones the film has created: Bates Motel; Norman Bates; psycho; shower scene; or just imitating Herrmann's distinctive "Eeee-eeee-eeee-eeee!" musical stings.

With *Psycho*, Hitch definitely got it right.

RE-ANIMATOR (1985)
by Dave Kosanke

1985 was a banner year for horror films, especially those featuring zombies. For starters, we were witness to George Romero's long awaited return to his "Dead" opus with *Day of the Dead,* which was followed by Dan O'Bannon's own spin on the Romero mythos, *The Return of the Living Dead.* However the crowning jewel out of that pesky bunch (and the entire year for that matter) was Stuart Gordon's *Re-Animator.* Yet for all its glory, *Re-Animator* was one of the last truly great films to emerge from that decade. Herbert West's reagent may have been able to revive the dead, but it couldn't jumpstart a genre that was soon to be on a slab of its own.

The prolific H.P. Lovecraft wrote a series of six stories based around the exploits of Herbert West, a crazed scientist patterned after the likes of Dr. Frankenstein. Screenwriter Dennis Paoli wove Lovecraft's basic scenario into a script befitting a feature-length movie. The challenge of adapting Lovecraft to the screen was a difficult chore, since past efforts (including AIP's *The Haunted Palace* [1963], and *The Dunwich Horror* [1970]) had proved less than satisfactory.

Script in hand, Paoli approached another relative newcomer, Stuart Gordon, to helm the project. (The two had cut their respective writing/directing teeth together on the 1979 TV film, *Bleacher Bums*.) Working with producer Brian Yuzna, this talented trio would put their names on the horror map and prove to be a force to be reckoned with for years. The result of their collaborative efforts (true to Lovecraft or not) was a winner in every category. Gordon took Paoli's material and spiced it up with ample amounts of sex and violence, which, while unfortunately alienating some die-hard Lovecraft fans, pleased jaded horror nuts to no end.

Dr. Herbert West (Jeffrey Combs) is introduced wrestling with one Dr. Gruber, gore spraying from Gruber's eyeballs, as West's colleagues stand around in shock. This hilariously messy episode immediately sets the mood, propelling us into the next 90 minutes of pure insanity. West moves onward to Miskatonic University (Lovecraft's literary stomping ground) where he enlists the aid of college student Dan Cain (Bruce Abbott). Reluctant at first, Cain soon sees the magic that West's glow-in-the-dark green reagent formula can produce; namely animating the dead into a lifelike state. To further complicate matters, Cain's girlfriend Meg (Barbara Crampton) is the daughter of the university dean (Robert Sampson). After being accidentally gored by a recently reanimated corpse, the dean becomes one of West's experiments, much to Meg's dismay. West's professional rival, Dr. Carl Hill (David Gale), not only attempts to steal Meg

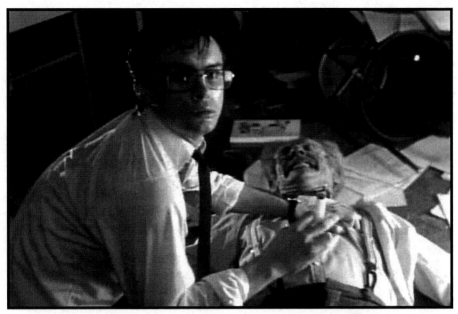

Herbert West (Jeffrey Combs), meddling in things that man should leave alone

from Dan, but he goes after West's reagent as well. Things get progressively worse, the end result best summed up by *Texas Chain Saw Massacre*'s tag line: "Who will survive and what will be left of them?"

Outrageous story aside, a big element of *Re-Animator*'s success is its strong ensemble of actors fleshing out Paoli and Gordon's vivid, black comic script. Everyone brings something to the table: Crampton's Meg is the emotional core, also providing an ample dose of sex appeal. Combs, Sampson, and Gale invoke equal parts madness, hate, jealously, and heroism, with Abbott the personification of innocence corrupted.

Yet the one factor which places *Re-Animator* above all others is the mayhem dished out by the characters and brought to life by the talented effects group of John Buechler, Tony Doublin, and John Naulin. These geniuses pulled off some wonderful sequences. How about a cadaver getting a bone saw plunged through its chest? Who can forget the flying, screeching dead/alive cat Rufus? ("Don't expect it to tango, it has a broken back.") How about strangulation by large intestine? Or maybe a cavalcade of zombies with shotgunned faces, burnt skin, or "one meatball run over by a semi!" Yet if there is one sequence that will remain in infamy throughout the annals of horrordom, it would be the sight of Barbara Crampton laying naked, spread-eagled, on an operating table about to be given oral gratification by a decapitated head! Truly depraved madness of this sort doesn't happen often, but *Re-Animator* dished it out in spades.

Released under the banner of Charles Band's Empire Pictures, *Re-Animator* was chock full of gleeful gore, making it difficult to secure an R rating. According to Gordon, "We actually submitted the film [to the MPAA], just to see what they would say, and they told us that we would have to cut everything after the second reel. If we'd done everything they 'suggested,' there would have been about half an hour of film left." The film eventually went out unrated. While this move assured horror fans that the goods would be delivered, it virtually guaranteed that the film wouldn't be a blockbuster in its theatrical run. Luckily, the burgeoning cable television and videocassette market embraced *Re-Animator* wholeheartedly, and the film was able to recoup its modest budget of about one million dollars.

HBO was where I first witnessed Herbert West's outrageous acts of science. I was privy to the uncut, full-strength version and squealed like a gleeful pig upon seeing this twisted gem. This was the type of gonzo, anything-goes cinema I had craved. Elite Entertainment would eventually unleash the ultimate laserdisc version of Gordon's film, complete with audio commentaries, extended footage, and a deleted dream sequence previously unavailable in *any* video version! When DVDs hit the market in the late '90s, Elite reissued this version, followed by a two-disc Millennium edition that added even more to the mix and stands today as the definitive release.

For the film's 1990 sequel, *Bride of Re-Animator,* producer Brian Yuzna stepped into the director's chair, with Combs, Abbott, and Gale returning in their respective roles. Yuzna would try milking the syringe years later with *Beyond Re-Animator* (2003), shifting the action to an insane asylum.

While *Re-Animator should* have carried the entire horror genre on its back and proclaimed to the world, "Let us witness the birth of undiluted horror served up with plentiful doses of gore the likes of which we never experienced before," sadly, that wasn't the case. As the '80s wore on, the MPAA tightened the belt on filmmakers willing to go the extra mile, castrating imagination in favor of the almighty dollar. Once-great directors and craftsmen like Tobe Hooper, John Carpenter, and Wes Craven were saddled with lackluster projects. The *Nightmare on Elm Street, Halloween, Friday the 13th* and *Texas Chain Saw Massacre* franchises aimed to please fans, but instead insulted them with lame humor, hokey stories, and bloated special effects.

We can't recreate 1985, nor should we try. However, the simple reason why the films spawned in the wake of *Re-Animator* failed to capture its magic is that too many people tried to emulate, rather than *create,* something original. The visionary creative spark of Gordon, Yuzna, Paoli, or even Lovecraft himself wasn't manufactured or produced under the ceiling of big-budget honchos. Instead, their visions were realized by playing by their own rules, and offering apologies to *no one.* Even if we are still suffering from far too many weak-kneed efforts, we can always remember that for 90 minutes back in 1985, *Re-Animator* showed us just how good bringing the dead back to life can be.

REPULSION (1965)
by Brian Huddleston

In *1001 Movies You Have to See Before You Die*, Jonathan Rosenbaum declares, "Roman Polanski's first film in English is still his scariest and most disturbing—not only for its evocations of sexual panic but also because his masterful use of sound puts the audience's imagination to work in numerous ways." As he would demonstrate time and again in his genre efforts, Polanski isn't necessarily interested in showing the viewer specifically what happens, but in creating a mood of disorientation, often through hallucinatory means. For the Polish-born director, the themes of isolation and claustrophobia are deadly tools that he wields like a first-class surgeon, cutting to the marrow of our most primal fears.

Carole (Catherine Deneuve) slowly slips into madness.

Established early on is Carole's (Catherine Deneuve in an astonishing performance, at once fragile and feral) revulsion of the opposite sex. When potential suitor Colin (John Fraser) extends a kindly kiss of goodbye to smooth things over between them, Carole runs free from his car and immediately washes her mouth out, wiping his kiss from her mouth in complete disgust. At home, she openly opposes her sister Hélène's (Yvonne Furneaux) affair with the gruff (and married) Michael (Ian Hendry). Hélène doesn't like Carole's "sticking her nose where it doesn't belong" and demands that she butt out. Carole covertly expresses her distaste for Michael, angrily eyeing the straight razor he shaves his filthy face with. Later she will throw his bathroom toiletries in the trash so she doesn't have to look at them. When confronted by Hélène over this action, Carole replies, "They don't belong there."

As Carole is walking to get lunch, she is again met by Colin. Colin is presented as a caring (if a bit overzealous), slightly self-centered man, keenly interested in Carole and in developing a deeper, more "meaningful" relationship. It is Colin who is the first witness to Carole's decaying mental state. She reluctantly agrees to have supper with him, but as she crosses the street to meet him at the restaurant, she sees a peculiar crack in the sidewalk pavement and becomes transfixed with it for hours. Angry at having been stood up, Colin sets out to find Carole and finds her sitting on a bench, lost in a void he cannot penetrate.

We are provided with early scenes of Carole at work as a beautician's assistant, staring vacantly into space rather than painting a client's nails. The salon where she is employed is quite posh, catering to a wealthy clientele. As her world unravels, Carole will begin to miss work. When she does manage to punch in, she injures one of the salon's most prestigious clients, bloodying her finger with a nail clipper. As a result, Carole is sent home, and her (and the viewer's) nightmare really begins.

The script hints, but never makes explicit, that Carole's downfall may have started as a result of Hélène's indifference. It's obvious Carole is unstable and highly dependent on Hélène in many ways, but as her sister is so involved in Michael, she neglects her "duties" as Carole's caretaker. When Hélène agrees to go on a holiday with Michael, Carole is left alone to fend against the demons that will soon hold sway over her fragile mind.

Polanski uses the confines of an apartment (illustrating the nightmarish state of Carole's mind) to the greatest advantage, deliberately fixing on light that glimmers ever so discreetly from within massive dark. We often simply see the light focus on Carole's face while her eyes flit nervously around, searching for the creeps in the night. Polanski allows his viewers to follow Carole into her mental "cracks," combining intense popping sounds on the soundtrack with visuals of large fissures appearing along the apartment walls. These vivid metaphors for Carole's crumbling sanity are combined with macabre images of decay which, in addition to evoking an emotional reaction, cleverly indicate the passage of time. Polanski trains his camera on grotesqueries such as potatoes growing stalks and the decomposing remains of the skinned rabbit Hélène was preparing to cook for Michael. These images are instrumental in Polanski's design to creep out the viewer, setting the stage for the nightmarish events yet to come.

Adding to the suspense and unease is the lingering unpaid rent for Hélène and Carole's apartment. Hélène has given clear instructions for Carole to deliver the balance due to their overbearing landlord. But as inertia takes hold of Carole's existence, the money sits on the dresser, the phones go unanswered, and the viewer is helpless to do anything but watch…and wait.

After not seeing Carole for days, Colin is so distraught that he goes to her apartment and smashes in the door. Disturbed by his brazen intrusion, she responds with a stunning burst of unexpected (and lethal) violence. She then nails the damaged door shut and retreats, safe again for the time being. Or so she thinks.

Throughout the film, Polanski opens up Carole's nightmares for us to bear witness to through startling imagery. In addition to the ever-widening cracks, men's ghastly hands now emerge from within the walls to grab her. The apartment takes on the guise of darkened catacombs as Carole tries to find her way out of a madness that seems to never end. Her horrors culminate in shocking scenes of violation that are made all the more devastating and surreal by Polanski violently cutting off the soundtrack. Carole finds herself raped again and again in her dreams, all shot in suffocating silence. A faceless man forces himself on her, Carole unable to break free from his grasp. Does this man represent someone from Carole's past? Is this man the reason Carole is such a mess? Polanski never tips his hand. This phantom could represent a memory of abuse, a deep-seeded phobia, or even, as unsettling as it sounds, some twisted fantasy on her part. What is established is that this specter is a vital threat that Carole cannot escape: A resident of her mind that she cannot elude nor control, given free rein to use her as he/it will.

Soon the landlord (in the leering, sweating form of Patrick Wymark), infuriated by Hélène's delayed payment, comes to the apartment looking for answers as to why the green isn't in his hands by now. When his loud cries of anger get no response, he breaks through the barricaded door to find the apartment a complete mess. Carole, not well at all by this time, manages to present the money to him, but the landlord has a steeper, more personal payment in mind. With Carole wearing only her nightgown, the degenerate landlord drools over her legs, becoming increasingly overwhelmed with lust. After failing to sway her with husky-voiced propositions, he plunges on top of her, with Carole barely able to press him off. Finding no alternative in her fragile mind, Carole slices the landlord repeatedly with the razor blade (using Michael's ugly "male" weapon against her assailant).

Hélène and Michael return home the next day, encountering the horrifying wreckage of the apartment as well as three lives: two corpses and Carole locked in an advanced stage of shock. Hélène sees the result of her "abandonment," what it has caused, and what will now remain.

Polanski closes the film with an enigmatic image: a family photograph containing two sisters and their parents. Three of the four are smiling into the camera with certain joy, while one girl stares into a place of which the others know nothing. They are blissfully unaware; free from the abyss that has captured the girl's gaze. A cold deadness in her eyes shows a haunted look of fear staring into ever nearing oblivion.

Repulsion may be rooted in the fear that Polanski experienced in his homeland as the Nazi regime began to rise. Miraculously surviving capture and execution (thanks to a farmer kind enough to hide him in a cow stall), perhaps the gripping paranoia at the heart of *Repulsion* stems from these childhood horrors. Ironically, in his 1984 autobiography, Polanski writes that he and co-writer Gerard Brach regarded *Repulsion* "mainly as a means to an end"—namely, a commercial success to enable them to finance their next, non-horror offering, *Cul-de-sac* (1966). Pauline Kael would describe the film as clinical Grand Guignol, with Polanski's camera fondling the horrors. "Undeniably skillful and effective, all right—excruciatingly tense and frightening. But is it entertaining?" Audiences apparently thought so, as the film was an enormous hit and launched Polanski's career in the U.S. It is a mark of his formidable talents that he not only adapted to commercial requirements, but achieved a chilling and memorable film in the process.

THE RETURN OF THE LIVING DEAD (1985)
by Brett Harrison

In 1968, writer John Russo and Pittsburgh-based director (and wearer of the world's largest pair of spectacles) George Romero rewrote the rules of horror with their seminal, groundbreaking zombie film *Night of the Living Dead*. Following the runaway success of this ghoulish tale of reanimated flesh-eating corpses, Russo parted company with Romero over a dispute regarding the creative direction of possible sequels. Eventually, the two reached a settlement whereby Russo retained the right to use the words "Living Dead" in the title of any of his future projects, whilst Romero's sequels would only use the suffix "Dead."

By the mid '70s, Russo had set about writing a sequel to *Night of the Living Dead*, entitled *The Return of the Living Dead*. Meanwhile, Romero was busy setting the wheels in motion for *his* follow-up, collaborating with creepy Italian horror auteur Dario

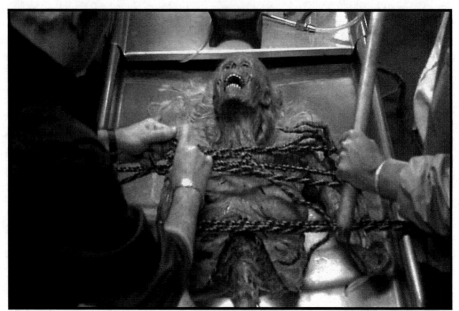

The chatty half-corpse was created by animatronics maestro Tony Gardner.

Argento. Romero released his movie, the gore-drenched *Dawn of the Dead*, to critical acclaim in 1978, but despite Russo selling the movie rights to his book the following year, *The Return of the Living Dead* was passed from studio to studio. It was to be several years before the project finally clawed its way out of development hell.

The early '80s saw Russo finally back on track, with top genre scribe Dan O'Bannon not only preparing the screenplay but also helming the film. Tobe (*Texas Chain Saw Massacre*) Hooper, who was originally slated to direct, had dropped out in favor of another project (most likely to start work on *Lifeforce* [1985]. Ironic, since that eventual clunker was co-written by—yes, you guessed it—Dan O'Bannon!)

O'Bannon's directorial debut eventually hit screens in 1985—the same year as Romero released his third "Dead" movie, *Day of the Dead*. But where Romero presented a deadly serious tale of scientific and military conflict against an apocalyptic backdrop, O'Bannon delivered a decidedly different take on the undead genre, packing in as much black humor as he did blood-red gore. Opening with the claim that "the events portrayed in this film are all true" and "the names are real names of real people and real organizations," O'Bannon quickly establishes the movie's outrageous tone. Although this was a horror comedy, it was never going to be a parody that mocked the genre. Rather, it would be respectful of its horror roots, both acknowledging and deriving its humor from the absurdity of the premise.

Frank (James Karen) and his nephew Freddy (Thom Mathews) are employees working the July 4th weekend at the Uneeda Medical Supply warehouse. When Freddy asks his uncle "What's the weirdest thing you ever saw in here?" Frank replies cryptically: "Did you see that movie *Night of the Living Dead*?"

According to old Frank, the film was actually based on a true case, but the filmmakers, in an effort to avoid being sued, changed all the facts around. Apparently, what actually happened was that an accidental spill of experimental chemical 245-Trioxin resulted in the reanimation of corpses at a hospital morgue. The army cleared up the mess, and sealed the bodies in special airtight containers. However, to quote Frank, "in a typical army f**k-up, the transportation department got the orders crossed." The bodies ended up at the Uneeda Medical Supplies center, where they have remained ever since, untouched in the basement.

Frank takes Freddy to see the canisters, lifting the lid on one to reveal the zombie within. "Do these things leak?" inquires Freddy, and in a miscalculated show of patriotism, Frank slaps one of them proclaiming, "Hell no, these things were made by the U.S. Army Corps of Engineers." The canister immediately springs a leak and sprays toxic gas into their faces, knocking them both out.

When they regain consciousness, the canister is minus one mouldy corpse. Realizing that perhaps matters are beyond their control, they decide to call their boss Burt (Clu Gulager).

Burt arrives, and fearing legal action, decides that it would be prudent to handle matters themselves. They open the body-storage door and attempt to deal with a more-than-lively corpse within, first slamming a pickax through its skull, and when that fails to quiet it down, dismembering it with a bone saw. Desperate to destroy all evidence of the contamination, Burt cajoles old pal Ernie Kaltenbrunner (Don Calfa), the local mortician and owner of a crematorium, into assisting him with the disposal of any evidence. They burn the body parts, but in doing so release a cloud of gas into the atmosphere. A storm builds, and acid rain pours from the sky—landing on the cemetery in which Freddy's friends are partying. Before long, the maggot-infested inhabitants of the boneyard are crawling to the surface—and they're hungry...for brains!

O'Bannon's razor-sharp script delivers the goods in both the horror and comedy departments, succeeding in blending these genres where many others have failed. But this really comes as no surprise to fans of his work; O'Bannon had previously written the brilliantly funny *Dark Star* (1974), the absolutely bloody terrifying *Alien* (1979), and the darkly humorous *Dead & Buried* (1981). However, much of the film's success can also be attributed to the anarchic approach. Just like *Return*'s rebellious gang of punks, O'Bannon dispenses with the established rules of the genre, presenting viewers with an effective EC comic-influenced directorial style and a refreshing new take on the zombie mythos.

In O'Bannon's movie, corpses don't walk—they run! Not only that, but they can think and talk too, making escape from the dead much harder than in Romero's zombieverse. (Gone are the days when you could throw a custard pie in the face of a zombie and walk away laughing!) Furthermore, a bullet in the brain doesn't seem to stop these critters—only total dismemberment or incineration will do. On a plus point, victims do not automatically join the ranks of the undead; only those exposed to 245-Trioxin are reanimated.

The top notch undead/gore effects are well handled by makeup wiz William Munns and animatronics maestro Tony Gardner. The movie delivers two of the greatest cinematic zombies of all time in the form of the gloopy "Tar Man," who escapes from the breached canister, and the chatty "half-corpse," who informs the survivors that it eats brains to relieve the pain of being dead.

Despite the movie's comedy content, the overall pervading atmosphere of *The Return of the Living Dead* is one of hopelessness, nihilism, and chaos, accentuated further by its marvelous punk rock soundtrack. Where Romero only dabbled in the downbeat (more so in *Night* than in *Dawn* or *Day*, both of which allowed some characters to escape death), O'Bannon goes whole hog, refusing to offer a light at the end of the tunnel for any of his characters (save for the blinding light of an atomic blast!).

The cast is excellent on the whole, with only a few members of the punk gang giving wooden performances. However, since Linnea Quigley is so memorable as death-obsessed punk hottie Trash, I am willing to forgive the less-than-stellar acting from her co-stars. Trash loves nothing more than to take her clothes off, regaling audiences on and offscreen with a full-frontal striptease atop a tomb in the creepy cemetery. Nice work, Linnea!

As a 17 year old obsessed with horror, I caught the movie on its original release in my local fleapit cinema and loved every bloody minute of it. I bought it ASAP on video, and it has remained a favorite of mine ever since. It seems that I am not alone in thinking this film is the bee's knees, as it has spawned four sequels thus far. Unfortunately, only *Return of the Living Dead 3* (1993) has come anywhere close to matching the unhinged genius of the original.

Dan O'Bannon has only directed one other film since his zombie masterpiece of '85 (a fairly well received adaptation of H.P. Lovecraft's "The Case of Charles Dexter Ward" called *The Resurrected* [1992]), and even O'Bannon screenplays seem to be a rare occurrence these days. But even if he never returns to the director's chair, the sheer magnificence of *The Return of the Living Dead* is enough to guarantee him an enduring place in the hearts of horror fans worldwide.

RINGU (1998)
by Jason Herr

One afternoon in 2001, married Dreamworks executives Walter Parkes and Laurie MacDonald were visited at home by a fellow colleague. In his hand, he carried a videocassette, one that he insisted they watch at their earliest opportunity. The contents turned out to be an inventive and terrifying flick called *Ringu*, which centered on a cursed videotape and a vengeful ghost, directed by a largely unknown Japanese director named Hideo Nakata. As the film climaxed with a long-haired female specter crawling out of a television, the duo realized that they had encountered something very special. Dreamworks immediately forked over more than $1,000,000 for the remake rights.

Asian horror/thrillers had been popular among film geeks for years, but no one thought they would work abroad. They were regarded as too cryptic, too weird, too dark. But this departure from tradition turned out to be the perfect sell for Stateside audiences. Opening in October 2002, *The Ring* ended up with a domestic haul of $129 million in North America and almost $250 million worldwide. It was only a matter of time before U.S. remakes of *Ju-on: The Grudge, Dark Water,* and *Pulse (Kairo)* began to hit theaters and the original films (and their brethren) would flood the local Blockbuster shelves.

Though perhaps not the best of all Asian horror cinema, the impact that *Ringu* had in terms of bringing Asian horror cinema the recognition that it currently enjoys is undeniable. Prior to the release of *The Ring*, most mainstream filmgoers viewed Japan as the land of cheesy samurai films and rampaging guy-in-a-suit monster flicks. When

Sadako (Rie Inou), famous for her straight hair and bulging eye

American horror audiences witnessed *The Ring*, and even more importantly, when they learned that this extremely original ghost story was a remake of a Japanese film—the floodgates burst open for the acceptance of Asian horror.

That is not to say that there weren't worthwhile Asian horror films prior to *Ringu*. On the contrary, Asia has been kicking out plenty of horror-related films since the 1960s and before. Films such as *Onibaba* and *Kwaidan* (both 1964) show as much filmmaking prowess as any classic American horror film of the time. The problem was—no one seemed to be interested in these films outside of their respective countries, other than a few diehard world cinema fans. *Ringu*'s importance lies not only in the film itself, but also in its influence on Western audiences—opening mainstream viewers' eyes to Asian horror.

For my money, *Ringu* (based on the bestselling novel by Koji Suzuki) is essential viewing for horror fans looking to expand their horizons outside the typical U.S. theatrical releases. Few films are as universal and truly frightening. Eschewing both the "blood-'n'-guts" and the "teenybopper" stylings prevalent during the late '90s era of horror films (at least here in the States), *Ringu* brought something *different* to the table—strong storyline, slow-build pacing, and an original concept that was completely unique to most horror viewers.

Playing on both the traditional ghost story and man's inherent fear of technology, the horrifying hook of *Ringu* is simplicity itself: A cursed videotape causes the death of anyone who watches it seven days after viewing. Reporter Asakawa Reiko (Matsushima Nanako) is embroiled in the investigation of this urban legend when a group of teenagers (one of whom is her niece) end up dead under strange circumstances after a trip to a cabin. Suspicions about the kids' deaths lead Reiko to believe that the cursed tape may be responsible, and the search is on for the tape and the answers to the mystery.

After finding and viewing the tape (which is filled with strange and surreal images), Reiko becomes infected by the curse and now has one week to solve the puzzle and save her own life.

Director Hideo Nakata infuses *Ringu* with tension and mystery instead of graphic gore and overbearing special effects. I'm personally a fan of gory exploitation films, but I can appreciate the slow-burn horror thrillers as well. Though the plot is often confusing and somewhat convoluted, *Ringu* accomplishes what it sets out to do—to assault its audience with psychological scares and a deep sense of dread rather than only employ the typical "jump" moments prevalent in other films. Though there are a number of creepy visuals and set pieces, the film competently minimizes the blatant use of horror clichés, instead proving that the "less-is-more" concept can be very effective if handled correctly.

Unfortunately, as original as this film is/was, there have been numerous Asian horror films since *Ringu*'s release that feature the "scary-girl-with-long-black-hair"—so many in fact that it seems to have spawned its own subgenre (and that's not even counting the original's own sequels, remakes, and *sequels* to remakes). Of the few that I've seen, none measure up to the intensity of *Ringu*; just another example of the relentless bastardization of an original concept, a practice all too prevalent in the film industry.

For those looking for hardcore gore and sleaze (which the Japanese also do quite well, by the way), *Ringu* is going to be a miss. However, for horror fans looking for something a little different, or even for more jaded horror fans that can handle a slower pace, *Ringu* is one to keep an eye out for.

ROSEMARY'S BABY (1968)
by Richard Sparks

Rosemary's Baby has so many caveats tucked into its concept that it's easy to pick and choose which to apply to one's own lifestyle: Don't live in an apartment building. Don't pretend you're in a soap opera. Don't marry an actor. We could also add, don't let Vidal Sassoon do your hair, don't dream (at least not about Satan), and don't drink anything Ruth Gordon hands you. Gee, maybe it's best to just stay in Nebraska, pull up the covers, and never venture into the big city. Not that there aren't some good scares in the Midwest. But at the time *Rosemary's Baby* was released, *In Cold Blood* had already been made. Hmm, come to think of it, maybe it's not safe to live anywhere.

When was the last time you saw *Rosemary's Baby*? It's time you treated yourself again, or perhaps for the first time. Roman Polanski's film adaptation of Ira Levin's book remains reliably creepy, despite its plot device—Satan needs to spawn, preferably with a willowy blonde—having been used and re-used endlessly, most recently in an episode of *7th Heaven* (though I doubt that was Aaron Spelling's intention or that anyone noticed but me). The film is as effective as it is because Polanski gets all the details right. For example, I'm sure there really was a time in history when a between-gigs New York actor who had made only one TV commercial ("Discover the Swingin' World of Yamaha") and his non-working wife could get an apartment in the Dakota. But that's not all the director nails. He knows that floor tiles crack and are left unrepaired, that laundry rooms are usually in badly lit basements, and that walls of apartments are thin, so very, very thin. The movie is also revolutionary within the horror genre in that

Sometimes a game of Scrabble tells the truth!

nothing happens, and it happens a lot: People stand in doorways, they walk down halls, they make polite conversation, and they make coffee. This attention to small detail in the service of malevolence is what gives any good soap opera its power to unnerve. And, let's face it, *Rosemary's Baby* is good soap opera.

The movie opens with a young married couple, Guy and Rosemary Woodhouse (John Cassavetes and Mia Farrow), being shown an apartment in the Dakota, here re-named the Bramford, which I'm sure the rental agent appreciated after the movie turned out to be a huge hit. After all, how many Satanist applicants can one turn down before starting to suspect oneself of religious bias? Soon after the Woodhouses move in, it becomes clear that they have been targeted for friendship by Minnie and Roman, the elderly eccentrics down the hall (Ruth Gordon and Sidney Blackmer). That's only the beginning of the creepiness. Not long after, Guy is hanging with the old folks on a regular basis, and not long after that, his sluggish career takes off. Meanwhile, his wife has started to have very disturbing dreams in which she is being defiled by some animalistic entity. Or *are* they dreams? (A phone call to Gena Rowlands might have cleared things up real quick.)

As time goes on, the now pregnant Rosemary finds herself more or less the football that is being tossed around among an assortment of odd-duck fringe figures in her life. (I always imagined Satan's minions would be a little better looking than this, didn't you? Oh well, at least they don't eat bugs like that Renfield guy.) Then this happens, and then that happens, the little monster is born and everyone shouts "Hail Adrian!" at a really stiff cocktail party, and the credits roll. There are a few other plot points worth mentioning, such as a couple of convenient deaths, one suspicious case of spontaneous blindness, a husband who engages in some brokered *Indecent Proposal*-type activities with the Antichrist, a baby-faced Charles Grodin as a duplicitous gyno, and liberal use of something called "United Mental Force" (united, but not unionized, thank goodness). This movie will also have audiences wondering just how cadaverous a gal can look before her friends actually, oh I don't know, *call the cops?* And get a load of the opening song. ("Love Theme from *Rosemary's Baby*"? Could there really be such a thing?) It's "sung" by Farrow herself, and it will make viewers appreciate that she stuck to acting and adopting kids. Oh, and keep an ear out for someone in the cast who uses the "actress accent," someone, by the way, who happens to not be from England and who also happens to not be Audrey Hepburn. Busted, Mia!

Rosemary's Baby was released in June 1968, only a year after the Summer of Love, the zenith of hippiedom, which only goes to show that horror has no season. The film fits nicely as the second entry in director Roman Polanski's paranoiac trilogy concerning the downsides of apartment dwelling, with the first being *Repulsion* (1965) and the third *The Tenant* (1976). (I highly recommend these films as well. If *Rosemary's Baby* is a soap opera, then *Repulsion* is a mental health documentary and *The Tenant* is a Marx Brothers horror movie.) The key player behind *Rosemary's Baby* was hipster lady-killer Robert Evans who handpicked Polanski for the task, and it was Evans' first big hit for Paramount. Movie rights to the novel had been obtained by schlockmeister William Castle (*The Tingler, House on Haunted Hill, 13 Ghosts*) who planned to direct. But Evans, being above schlock, said he would only greenlight the film if Polanski directed. (This coming from the man who would make *Love Story*.) This was too bad because the mind reels imagining what the gimmick-mad Castle would have done with it—horned baby dolls falling from the theater ceiling? Or an exorcist in the lobby for expectant newlyweds?

Along with terrific box office, *Rosemary's Baby* also did well at the Academy Awards. Polanski was nominated for his screenplay and Ruth Gordon won for Best Supporting Actress. I like to think she won for the way she said "pregnant" ("preg-uh-nunt"), but it was probably something else. It's interesting to note that for the lead roles Polanski originally wanted Tuesday Weld and Robert Redford. I don't know how much that casting would have changed the movie, but I can't help but think that it wouldn't have felt as New Yorky. Maybe kind of Wisconsiny.

The "cursed" movie also had its fair share of bitter coincidences attached. John Lennon would, years later, be slain in the courtyard of the Dakota, the same courtyard shown in the opening sequence. One year after the film's release, Christopher Komeda, the composer for *Rosemary's Baby,* died of head injuries sustained in an accident, and Polanski's pregnant bride, Sharon Tate, was murdered by the Manson family, who scrawled "Helter Skelter" on the walls of the murder scene, ironically the title of a Beatles song. Additionally, producer William Castle was hospitalized with a nearly lethal case of kidney stones. Death of another kind visited Farrow when she received on set—as well as on the verge of stardom—divorce papers from then-husband Frank Sinatra. (Unexpected? I mean, what could those two have possibly talked about?)

This last thing isn't coincidental, but it is bitter. I'm referring to the sequel, 1976's TV movie *Look What's Happened to Rosemary's Baby.* I've never seen it, but apparently it's all about how a son can disappoint his dad when he doesn't continue in the family business. It would seem the horror community finds it execrable, although Ruth Gordon reprises her role from the original. Maybe she did it for the fans, but I'm guessing the producers tempted her with Knicks floor tickets.

All kidding aside, which is difficult for me, *Rosemary's Baby* must be given its due. With no special effects and very few locations, Roman Polanski created a thoroughly chilling atmosphere of dread. It just goes to show that the fire made by rubbing sticks together can still burn your feet. After a recent viewing of the film, I was struck by its simplicity, which was really innovation. A few movies that *Rosemary's Baby* paved the path for include *The Exorcist* (1973), *It's Alive* (1974), *The Omen* (1976), and my favorite, *Xtro* (1983). I'm even going to throw in 1979's *Alien*, because that movie's restraint in revealing the face of its monster is similar to Polanski's full-on refusal to show us anything at all. And those are just the titles that immediately come to mind.

So what to conclude? We live in a post-*Rosemary's* world, where just a few caveats apply: Don't wander into traffic. Don't bother with a second opinion. Don't worry about the "undertaste."

SCREAM (1996)
by Mark Easteadt

Stuart (Matthew Lilliard), left; Billy (Skeet Ulrich), right

In November 1996, I was walking out of a Counting Crows concert in Manhattan, and outside a street team was handing out tickets to an advanced screening of a new horror film called *Scream*. As a general movie buff, I had read a bit about it, but knew little except that Drew Barrymore was one of the stars. Two weeks later, I am in a theater packed with young people waiting for the film to start. Just as the opening credits began to roll, one person several rows in front of me caught my eye. It was the back of his silver-haired head in a sea of teens and 20-somethings that made him stand out. But then the movie began and I forgot all about him.

With pulse pounding, holding my breath, I watched as the only big-name star was literally gutted and hung from a tree for her parents to find before the film was even

10 minutes old. It was then that I thought, "If this filmmaker is willing to brutally kill off the big-money names right off the bat, what else would he be willing to do? What am I in for?" As it turns out, the filmmaker in question was willing (and able) to both lovingly honor and hilariously eviscerate the genre that had made him.

A hundred or so minutes later, the lights came up, the silver-haired gentleman stood up, turned around. . . who could it be? The man had just deliciously tortured me with a funny, scary, exhilarating film—none other than Wes Craven himself. That was the night I became a true horror fan. Thanks, Mr. Craven.

That was my introduction to *Scream*. The film centers on the character of Sydney Prescott (Neve Campbell), a high schooler whose mom was murdered a year earlier. Now, she's being stalked by a masked killer armed with a sharp knife (and an unusually vast knowledge of horror movies), who has just killed two of her classmates. As the bodies pile up and the tension mounts, a town curfew is set and a big party is planned. Can Sydney, along with the help of tabloid reporter Gale Weathers (Courtney Cox) and bumbling deputy Dewey (David Arquette), find out what is going on before it is too late?

Scream came along at a time when the horror genre had been floundering, lost in a glut of tired sequels and mostly uninspired originals. On the surface, it too seemed to fit the mold of other *Halloween* and *Friday the 13th* rip-offs—a masked killer stalks a nubile group of teens. This is where we expect all the clichés to start, with familiarity breeding contempt. Instead, we enter a movie world where the characters are as aware of those well-worn conventions as the audience. In fact, many of the films where these clichés originate are directly referenced. *Scream* was actually so bold as to give a list of the "rules" of horror movies so that the audience could play along and try to spot them.

Randy (Jamie Kennedy), the requisite film nerd, highlights many of the obvious clichés: 1) Simplicity—if the plot is too convoluted the audience won't follow it; 2) Everybody's a suspect—use as many red herrings as possible to throw the audience off the scent; and 3) The supposedly dead killer *always* comes back for one more scare.

How to survive a horror film? Just remember that sex equals death (only the virgin survives to the final reel); Just say no (if you drink alcohol or do drugs, you will die); and never, *ever* say, "I'll be right back" (because you won't).

Of course, if *Scream* had merely acknowledged the clichés of the genre, it probably would not have gone on to gross $100 million domestically. The real draw of *Scream* is that while it winks at the audience and invites them to be a part of the fun, it then pulls the rug out from under them by breaking the rules it has just set up. Rather than being simple, the plot involves two killers, including one that had been previously exonerated. Almost everyone who drinks and drugs makes it out alive. It is one of the killers that voices the dreaded, "I'll be right back." And the kicker—the heroine/"final girl" has sex minutes before she survives the bloody climax.

It is this messing with the rules that makes *Scream* so hard to classify. Is it an homage to past horror films (particularly the slasher films of the late '70s and '80s)? Is it a satire or parody of those same films? The answer seems to be yes on all counts. It is one of the rare films that succeeds both as a genre film and as a film that pokes fun at the genre (a great, lesser-known example of this exists in the mutant/big bug genre, *Tremors* [1990]). In *Scream*'s case, this means we are both in on the joke and being scared at the same time. Critics and audiences alike seemed to enjoy the sensation of being invited to the party, then sucker punched repeatedly before it was all over.

The next 10 years saw a slew of substandard copycats, ranging from the just average *I Know What You Did Last Summer* (1997) to the abysmal *Valentine* (2001). Regrettably, it is this overabundance of wannabe self-aware teen horrors that have hurt *Scream*'s legacy. Instead of acknowledging the innovative and accomplished work of Craven and screenwriter Kevin Williamson, work that almost single-handedly reinvigorated the horror genre in the mid-'90s, horror fans now scornfully affiliate it with its sub-par descendants (which would not have existed if *Scream* did not pave the way.)

It can even be tempting to lump in *Scream*'s two sequels with the other swill that followed, as it is certainly a textbook case of diminishing returns with *Scream 2* (1997) and *Scream 3* (2000). While *Scream 2* has some good fun with the tropes of "sequelitis" that afflicted many slasher films from the '80s, *Scream 3* cannot seem to pull itself above the clichés it is trying so hard to mock. And, as is so often the case by the third in a series, *Scream 3* is a mere shadow of the first. While they are enjoyable as a whole story, only the original *Scream* will stand the test of time to become a horror classic and innovator.

With *Scream*, Wes Craven became one of the few directors around to release iconic horror films in three separate decades. He began his career with the grueling exploitation classic *The Last House on the Left* (1972), made everyone afraid to go to sleep with *A Nightmare on Elm Street* (1984), and brought the audience into the picture with *Scream*. Does he have one more classic in him for this decade?

Who knows, but I for one will be there whenever Wes Craven asks, "Do you like scary movies?"

SE7EN (1995)
by Michelle Trudel

Stop and think for a moment—can you name the Seven Deadly Sins? I couldn't, and I was raised Catholic. Obviously, my parents were not all that concerned with the guilt/punishment aspects of that religion—not so for "John Doe's" mommy and daddy, but we'll get to that.

David Fincher's dark and disturbing *Se7en* is the story of a maniac on a mission, and the two seemingly mismatched detectives, who are always one step behind and have no idea what they've gotten themselves into—until it's too late. One of the first characters we meet is the *city* where the story unfolds—a dark, rainy, decaying urban landscape that sets a grim tone from the outset. It is wet, cold, violent, ugly. And the rain, always the rain—disorienting in a way—people can't always see where they are... Interestingly, the location goes unnamed throughout; we could be in any inner city in America.

Veteran homicide detective Lt. William Somerset (Morgan Freeman) is burned out and on the verge of retirement. He uses the rhythm of a metronome to quiet his brain before sleep because he's simply seen too much, and is perhaps too human to do battle with the demons of the city any longer. We get clued-in to his inherent decency early on when his chief concern at a murder scene is, "Did the kid see it?" Detective David Mills (Brad Pitt), Somerset's cocky, ambitious, somewhat homophobic, and inexperi-

John Doe (Kevin Spacey) turns himself in to the police.

enced replacement, shows up and before long, the two are in the thick of a serial killer's ingeniously constructed, frighteningly methodical lesson plan.

A sadistic murderer calling himself John Doe sets out to "teach" a sinful society a lesson. Using the Seven Deadly Sins as his guide, he tortures and murders his carefully selected victims, leaving behind grotesque scenes of suffering as well as clues that lead to his next "sermon."

Our first glimpse of John Doe's handiwork comes in the form of an obese man in a dark, cockroach-infested kitchen, dead, his face buried in a plate of spaghetti. Mills' first thought: "Fat Boy had a heart attack?" Nope. Somerset points out that the victim's hands and feet, hidden from view, are tied with wire. And it gets better. We learn that this man ate himself to death. Or rather, was *forced* to eat, and *continue* eating until his innards burst. The question hangs in the air: Why would someone take the time to do this unless the act had meaning?

Next up, a high-powered attorney, forced to carve a pound of flesh from his own body, bleeds out on the floor of his office, the word GREED scrawled in blood on the carpet.

Are these two crimes related? They don't seem to be, until…

Somerset is called back to the autopsy lab and is given a jar containing some out-of-the-ordinary little extras taken from the obese man's stomach. He revisits the crime scene and discovers what we've all been waiting for—the word *Gluttony* is painted in grease on the kitchen wall next to a note that reads: "*Long is the way, and hard, that out of hell leads up to light*." Somerset recognizes the quote from *Paradise Lost*, and tells his captain (played by the fabulously crotchety R. Lee Ermey) to expect five more related killings. "He's preaching," says Somerset. *Pride, Lust, Envy, Sloth,* and *Wrath* remain. We can name them now and can only imagine what's to come.

"Have you ever seen anything like this?" asks Mills. As an audience, we are as much in the dark as Somerset and Mills—we don't see the crimes happen, we only see the aftermath, a brilliant choice on Fincher's part. We see what this killer is capable of, but not his *face*. (The first time I saw *Se7en* in the theater, I found myself scanning the darkness, looking at the anonymous moviegoers seated around me and thinking, my God, any one of these faceless people could be a John Doe, a psychotic person, a sick murderer...)

In the midst of the ugliness, we meet Mills' wife Tracy (Gwyneth Paltrow), who invites Somerset home for an evening meal. We're allowed a moment of calm, and the two detectives actually begin to get to know each other as people. Somerset and Mills' adversarial relationship is forever changed thanks to Tracy, and we like her for it.

But it just keeps raining.

Our mysterious killer is inventive and vicious—so much so that I remember feeling both extreme dread and giddy excitement as my mind raced to put together what the next crime scene could possibly look like—how could someone use the concepts of *Pride* or *Envy* or *Sloth* as an inspiration for another horribly sadistic murder?

Somerset and Mills do their homework (with Mills doing the *Cliff's Notes* version throughout), and not only find their way to the next crime scene (the unbelievable *Sloth*—demonstrating Doe's merciless nature, as well as his terrifying *patience*), but by a stroke of good luck they arrive literally at our killer's doorstep. One amazing chase sequence later (a chase that saw Pitt injured during filming, hence the cast he wears in later scenes), and we begin to understand the depth of John Doe's obsession. His living quarters are filled with thousands of notebooks, all filled with stream-of-consciousness ramblings on the evils of society (*"What sick ridiculous puppets we are... we are not what was intended"*), as well as evidence of his horrific crimes. In a jar we see the left hand of our Sloth victim; in a makeshift darkroom, photos documenting the deaths of our Gluttony and Greed victims, shots of a prostitute (a potential victim?), and several recently developed pictures of...Detective Mills. *But not a single fingerprint is to be found!*

And while the good guys are busy trying to nail him, the bad guy is still out there being, well, bad. Really bad.

John Doe's sermon on *Lust* is beyond anything I could have imagined—brutal doesn't describe it—and Fincher ups the ante by only showing us glimpses—once again, he lets our minds do the rest. We also get a special treat here with an appearance by the always slightly off-kilter Leland Orser as our killer's hapless collaborator.

More rain. Doe's call to 911 ("I've gone and done it again.") brings us to a beautiful model's apartment and a little lesson on *Pride*. And just when you think you can't possibly take in another grotesque display of butchery...

John Doe walks into the police station covered in blood, and *turns himself in*. Our Mr. Doe has a face now, and he looks an awful lot like Kevin f**king *Spacey*. Uh-huh. That extraordinary actor with the benign Everyman look is the fiend—and how smart Spacey was to insist that his name not be in the opening credits. This simple gesture serves the film perfectly, and I applaud him for it.

The conclusion to *Se7en* is as shocking as the rest of the film, although we shouldn't be surprised. As Somerset tells Mills, "If John Doe's head splits open and a UFO should fly out, I want you to have expected it." But we don't expect what Fincher gives us. The good guys have the bad guy shackled, they're in an open field with police helicopters circling and *the sun is shining*. What could possibly go wrong? Well, the answer to that, if you're Detective Somerset, is *everything*. Here's my only beef with the movie: Why wouldn't a veteran cop like Somerset, who's seen the worst of the worst, be able to keep his cool once he realized Doe's true intentions? He doesn't follow his own counsel, which seems slightly unrealistic to me.

But what a joy to watch a horror movie that actually horrifies—good actors do that. *Se7en* would not be as much a part of popular culture as it is without the masterful performances of Freeman, Pitt, and Spacey. And Andrew Kevin Walker's screenplay (written while he was an employee at Tower Records) is nothing less than twisted genius.

Then there's David Fincher himself. If we take nothing else from his work on *Se7en*, one thing is obvious: *Details matter*. John Doe's notebooks are all real and took a crew two months and $15,000 to create. The photos, shot by Melodie McDaniel, were meticulously distressed to achieve their grungy, realistic look. Fincher's atmosphere pervades everything; the flashlight beams cutting through the dark, the sense of decay, the attention to every set, every prop, every piece of furniture… Even the gritty, shaky opening credit sequence with its mind-bending collage of images—bloody fingers, razors, needles—all set to Coil's remix of Nine Inch Nails' "Closer." The tone is set for us and it ain't pretty.

Watch this film 20 times and one will see something new each time. And even after nearly that many viewings, I still have a very physical reaction—this movie has *smells* and *tastes*—I get itchy visiting this grimy place. Detail, detail. Brilliant. When I watch *Se7en* I feel respected as an audience member, and I'm grateful.

THE 7ᵀᴴ VOYAGE OF SINBAD (1958)
by Eric Fraisher Hayes

Seven minutes into 1958's *The 7th Voyage of Sinbad*, a 30-foot tall Cyclops dominates the screen. And in that instant, a new age dawned. Yes, colossal creatures previously existed on film, but when this mythological vision emerged from the sorcerer's cave, giant monsters joined the world of widescreen Technicolor spectacles. The 1950s were an era of looking toward the future, and with this picture, monster movies announced that they too would be a part of it.

Producer Charles H. Schneer (*It Came from Beneath the Sea* [1955], *20 Million Miles to Earth* [1957]) traveled the studio circuit armed with a series of Ray Harryhausen's sketches based on the Arabian Nights. Eventually, Columbia Pictures agreed to the project with the condition that the movie be made in color. Harryhausen had never attempted to bring his stop-motion talents to a color picture. Although initially hesitant, Harryhausen went to work trying to find a way to make the transition. After a year of tests, he adapted his stop-motion animation process (dubbed "Dynamation") to the world of Technicolor.

The picture opens with Sinbad and his men lost at sea, desperately looking for dry land where they can find food and fresh water. Through a blinding night fog, Sinbad spies an island. With his apparent bionic night vision, matinee idol hair and clean-shaven square jaw, it is immediately established that Sinbad is this movie's Captain Kirk; able to do what no other man can do and look good doing it. The next morning, Sinbad and his

The sword-fighting skeleton, one of the marvels created by Ray Harryhausen

crew row ashore and discover an unusual looking cave. But before they have a chance to investigate, Sokurah the Magician emerges from its mouth, clutching a magic lamp as he flees from a giant Cyclops. While Sinbad and his men battle with the monster, Sokurah summons the genie of the lamp to provide an escape. The Cyclops is subdued, but during the escape, the magician loses his grasp of the lamp. As the men reach the ship, they look back to see the Cyclops fishing the lamp out of the sea.

Back in Bagdad, Sokurah repeatedly appeals to the Caliph for a ship to return to Colossa to retrieve his magic lamp. His pleas fall on deaf ears as all prepare for the pending marriage of Sinbad and Princess Parisa. But the night before the wedding, the princess has mysteriously shrunk to the size of a Pez dispenser. When Sinbad rushes to her bedside, he realizes his wedding night plans have changed…drastically. The magician says he can restore the princess to her original size with the help of a piece of eggshell from a gigantic two-headed bird known as the Roc. Of course, the only place the Roc can be found is…drum roll please…the island of Colossa. With little choice left, Sinbad agrees to round up a crew. He is about to embark on his perilous seventh voyage!

Under the direction of Nathan Juran (*20 Million Miles to Earth*, *Attack of the 50 Foot Woman* [1958], and *The Deadly Mantis* [1957]) and stirringly scored by Bernard Herrmann, *The 7th Voyage of Sinbad* spins an enchanting tale. Kerwin Mathews in the title role is about as Anglo-Saxon as can be, but proves surprisingly adept at acting opposite invisible partners. Three quarters of Mathews' screen time is shared either with giant monsters or his tiny princess, all of which were added in post-production. Kathryn Grant, the soon-to-be Mrs. Bing Crosby and future mother of a gaggle of Minute Maid-lovin' little Crosbys, is radiantly, if not terminally, optimistic regardless of her stature. Torin Thatcher with his heavy accent and intense stare finds a near perfect balance between menace and good-natured geniality. His Sokurah seems to be constantly inviting people to dinner, withholding the news that they are on the menu. Richard Eyer as the Genie receives prominent billing, which often confused me. Was he the kid that Jerry Mathers beat out for the role of the Beave or something? Doing a little research, I found that Eyer had an extensive television career during the 1950s and also played the title role in the 1957 film *The Invisible Boy*, which cashed-in on the popularity of *Forbidden Planet* (1956). Eyer retired from his child star film/TV career in the 1960s. He is currently a third grade teacher in Bishop, California.

Made for less than a million dollars, *The 7th Voyage of Sinbad* grossed over six million dollars in its initial release, a great success for Harryhausen and Schneer. In the years that followed, this team created a series of epic pictures that included *The Three Worlds of Gulliver* (1960), *Mysterious Island* (1961), and *Jason and the Argonauts* (1963). All told, Ray Harryhausen and Charles H. Schneer made 12 films together, including two more Sinbad installments, *The Golden Voyage of Sinbad* (1974) and *Sinbad and the Eye of the Tiger* (1977).

Although I have only recognized it recently, the importance of this film to me personally cannot be underestimated. For years, I have been doing "dinosaur" impersonations. I even have listed it under the "special skills" section of my acting resumé, and from time to time, I have been asked to give a demonstration at auditions. During the process of digging into this film, I realized that I had in fact been attempting to channel the Cyclops from *7th Voyage* all these years. All of the elements—the way I shift my weight back on my haunches, thrust my chest forward, rear back my arms and slide my glance from side-to-side in an attempt to capture a sense of the strange and the menacing—are directly from the 7th minute of *The 7th Voyage of Sinbad*.

Ultimately, the film's true stars are Ray Harryhausen and Bernard Herrmann. As fantastic as the animation is, it constitutes less than a quarter of the picture. Herrmann's stirring musical score carries the rest. Every twist and turn of the story is propelled by his strings and winds, another great turn in a phenomenal career.

However, Harryhausen's animated creations are unforgettably vivid and every frame of film for which they appear reflects the subtle humanity of their creator's hand. Harryhausen's work on this film had a profound impact on the shape of cinema. *The 7th Voyage of Sinbad* took the team of Schneer and Harryhausen from science fiction B-movies to the world of the mainstream hit and, more importantly, inspired a generation of animators who have gone on to bring us the CGI spectacles of today.

THE SHINING (1980)
by Rob Dennehy

What do fans look for in a horror film? Is it suspense that makes the hair on the back of your neck stand up? A plot that makes you wonder, "What if I was in that situation?" Perhaps it's characters that we can identify with, or maybe it's just all about the blood and gore. When watching *The Shining*, we get a little bit of everything. The film contains violence, great characters, atmosphere, suspense, and one of the finest performances (by Jack Nicholson) in the horror film canon. Upon its release in 1980, it quickly gained critical acclaim, box-office success, and was hailed an instant classic.

All work and no play makes Wendy (Shelley Duvall) a little nervous.

In an interview with Michel Ciment, Stanley Kubrick discussed his interest in directing *The Shining*. "I've always been interested in ESP and the paranormal. But *The Shining* didn't originate from any particular desire to do a film about this. The manuscript of the novel was sent to me by John Calley, of Warner Bros. I thought it was one of the most ingenious and exciting stories of the genre I had read. It seemed to strike an extraordinary balance between the psychological and the supernatural in such a way as to lead you to think that the supernatural would eventually be explained by the psychological: 'Jack must be imagining these things because he's crazy.' This allowed you to suspend your doubt of the supernatural until you were so thoroughly into the story that you could accept it almost without noticing."

Initially scheduled to be filmed in 17 weeks, Kubrick's notorious penchant for perfection resulted in an exhausting 11-month shoot. Understandably, this took its toll on the cast and crew. Shelley Duvall revealed to Roger Ebert, "[It was] almost unbearable. Jack Nicholson's character had to be crazy and angry all the time. And my character had to cry 12 hours a day, all day long, the last nine months straight, five or six days a week. After all that work, hardly anyone even criticized my performance. The reviews were all about Kubrick, like I wasn't there."

The Shining follows an unemployed, recovering alcoholic named Jack Torrance (Nicholson) who agrees to be the winter caretaker for the Overlook Hotel. Jack's wife Wendy (Duvall) and son Danny (Danny Lloyd) accompany him to the hotel, located deep in the Colorado mountains.

Shortly after meeting Danny, we find out he has a very special talent. He possesses psychic abilities that allow him to see things that haven't happened yet, things that happened a long time ago, or things that are currently happening elsewhere. This ability, which he utilizes through his imaginary friend "Tony," becomes more active while staying at the Overlook. During the introductory tour of the hotel, Danny meets a cook by the name of Dick Halloran (Scatman Crothers) who also possesses the same unique skill. Halloran calls their mutual gift "shining." Over a dish of ice cream, Halloran tells Danny that the Overlook also has a certain "shine" to it.

Once alone in the hotel, everything proceeds smoothly for the Torrances. Jack works on his book, Wendy cooks away in the kitchen, and Danny rides his Big Wheel all over the place. Unfortunately, cabin fever and a case of writer's block soon set in, and it's at this point the viewer senses that Jack may not be up to the next several months. One quietly unnerving scene shows him endlessly throwing a tennis ball against a wall instead of writing or taking a walk with his wife and son.

Early on, we learn that the former Overlook caretaker, Delbert Grady, went crazy, murdering his wife and twin daughters. In what is possibly the film's most terrifying scene, Danny rides his Big Wheel down a long passage. At the end of the hallway, Danny encounters the twin girls who invite him to "Come play with us...forever and ever and ever and ever..." As they repeat the words, Danny has a vision of the twins' bloody corpses, with gore smeared all over the walls. This bit has always freaked me out and remains one of the more memorable sequences.

But the ghosts of the Overlook have not solely targeted Danny. Jack continues his downward spiral, seeing visions of a beautiful naked woman in a bathtub, a friendly bartender, and a waiter who spills a drink all over him. This waiter turns out to be none other than Delbert Grady, the former caretaker. Grady suggests to Jack that he should "correct" his wife and son, the way Grady corrected his family. Jack, now totally insane, takes a liking to Grady's suggestion.

At this point, it is worth noting that Stanley Kubrick's take on Stephen King's novel has been frowned upon by some as being "unfaithful." One interesting change is the film's use of the labyrinthian hedge maze as opposed to the novel's menacing topiary animals. Kubrick quickly realized that filming the moving topiary would be next to impossible and made the decision to use a hedge maze instead. King himself was not enthralled with the film version of his bestselling novel. "I'd admired Kubrick for a long time and had great expectations for the project, but I was deeply disappointed in the end result. Parts of the film are chilling, charged with a relentlessly claustrophobic terror, but others fall flat. The real problem is that Kubrick set out to make a horror movie with no apparent understanding of the genre." (*Playboy*, June 1983)

I, for one, disagree with this assessment. One of the many things that make *The Shining* great is Kubrick's tremendous sense of claustrophobic isolation. As the film progresses, we are sucked into the world of the Torrance family and the Overlook Hotel. The moody musical score is very well done, and the extensive use of Steadicam shots (brilliantly realized by cinematographer John Alcott) only adds to the mystique and allure of the film.

Additionally, the stellar dialogue by Kubrick and co-writer Diane Johnson is peppered with memorable quotes that have been uttered and re-uttered over the years by legions of horror fans. My favorite of these occurs late in the film when Wendy discovers the literary effort Jack has been diligently working on: "*All work and no play makes Jack a dull boy,*" typed repeatedly onto dozens and dozens of pages. While Wendy quietly freaks out, Jack appears behind her, asking if she likes it. Slowly pursuing her across the room, Jack utters the immortal words: "Wendy... Darling... Light of my life... You didn't let me finish my sentence. I said, I'm not going to hurt you. I'm just going to bash your brains in. I'm going to bash them right the f**k in." Thankfully, Wendy is carrying a baseball bat at the time and is able to knock her husband unconscious, then drag him into the pantry, locking him inside. But the Overlook spirits have great power and offer to release Jack on one condition: He must kill his wife and son. Jack enthusiastically agrees.

As Jack tries to break into the bathroom where his wife and son have taken refuge, Wendy and Danny try to escape out the window, but only Danny is able to fit. As he breaks down the bathroom door with his ax, Jack spews another legendary piece of dialogue, one that could be considered the shining (ha-ha) moment of the film. Pausing in his efforts, Jack sticks his head in the door and intones with maniacal glee, "Heeeeeere's... Johnny!"

At this point, intuitively feeling that the family is in trouble, Halloran arrives on the noisy Snowcat, then further makes his presence known by calling out to the deserted hotel for anyone who might be within shouting distance. All of a sudden, Jack appears out of nowhere and strikes Halloran in the chest with the ax, killing him instantly. The film's final minutes are some of the most suspenseful in cinema history.

The Shining has always mystified me, and even though I've seen it more than a dozen times, it always manages to induce the same awe-inspiring reaction. Kubrick's chilling picture is one of the greatest horror films ever made, a timeless classic and a must-see for fans of the horror genre.

SHIVERS (1975)
(aka THEY CAME FROM WITHIN)
by Streebo Majic

From the bloody stages of the Grand Guignol theater to the silver screen's most recent psychological thriller, two schools of thought in horror exist: to show or not to show. When David Cronenberg gave us *Shivers*, he showed us everything we were afraid of and made us afraid to ever look again.

Cronenberg's feature debut (known initially as *The Parasite Murders* in Canada and *They Came from Within* in the United States) tells the story of Dr. Roger St. Luc as he fights a parasitic infestation threatening the idyllic and plastic world of Starliner Towers. After a TV commercial introduces us to this self-contained paradise complete with tennis courts, restaurants, medical clinics, shopping malls, and an indoor pool, we follow a starry-eyed young couple as they tour the apartment complex. This picturesque mood is shattered as the scene suddenly shifts to witness a brutal attack on a beautiful young girl. As we watch helplessly, an old man strangles her, slices her open, then slits his own throat from ear to ear.

In that moment, we are baptized into the visceral, existential, and philosophically challenging world of David Cronenberg.

Shivers follows the lives of Nicholas Tudor (Allan Migicovsky), who embraces the transformation brought about by the parasites, and Dr. Roger St. Luc (Paul Hampton), the resident physician that resists the infestation. St. Luc discovers that the parasites have been created by his mentor Dr. Hobbs, the same man who murdered the girl in the film's opening. Hobbs created the parasites as an alternative to organ transplant, designing them to replace a diseased or damaged organ and assume its functions within the host body. In his notes, Hobbs elaborates on his philosophy, describing the parasites as "a combination of aphrodisiac and venereal disease that will hopefully turn the world into one big, beautiful mindless orgy."

St. Luc learns that Hobbs killed the young woman in an attempt to prevent the spread of the parasites. However, he remains unaware that she has already passed the "infection" to her lovers, which include Nicholas Tudor.

Some of the most disturbing moments in *Shivers* come courtesy of Tudor's acceptance of his transformation; he stalks the towers, leaving bloody slime trails in his wake. At night, Tudor lays in bed, his chest bared as he hyperventilates in orgasmic fashion and whispers to the crawling lumps beneath the flesh of his stomach. "Come on. Come on. Here, boy. You and me, we're gonna make us friends." This scene features work by noted makeup expert Joe Blasco, who managed to create the disturbing effect (using bladders) of the parasites moving under Tudor's skin.

Cronenberg's recurring themes of pansexuality become apparent as Starliner Tower is overtaken by the parasites. The parasites pass from victim to victim through various orifices, usually via the mouth. The carriers ravish sexually everything in their path including men, women, children, and the elderly. In Cronenberg's world, no one is spared the plagues of the flesh.

Dr. St. Luc tries to escape the building with Nurse Forsythe (Lynn Lowry) in tow. After Forsythe succumbs to the parasites, she tries to seduce St. Luc by recounting a dream: "I found myself making love to a strange man. He's old and he's dying and he smells bad and I find him repulsive. But then he tells me that everything is erotic. That everything is sexual. You know what I mean? He tells me that old flesh is erotic flesh. That disease is the love of two alien kinds of creatures for each other. That even dying is an act of eroticism. That talking is sexual. That breathing is sexual. That even to physically exist is sexual."

In one of the most effective scenes predating the zombie wave of the '70s, the doctor is herded into the swimming pool of the tower by swarms of shambling, drooling parasite carriers. No longer able to resist, St. Luc's mask of resistance melts away as Forsythe administers the parasitic kiss, replaced with a look of painful, inevitable acceptance. Later, a caravan of automobiles files out of the parking garage, with St. Luc and Forsythe leading the train of cars. A radio broadcast plays over the credits, informing us of allegations of citywide sexual assaults, spreading from the vicinity of Starliner Island and out into the world.

The product of a strict Catholic upbringing, I was taught that premarital sex was a sin, drugs and alcohol were bad, etc. Absolutely forbidden to watch horror films, my limited early experiences consisted of staring at video box covers or surreptitiously watching them at a friend's house. However, even hearing about Cronenberg's work made an imprint on me, just from the sheer outrageousness of the concepts: *Scanners* featured a man's head exploding, *The Fly* was about a man turning into a fly, *Shivers* had parasites invading people, etc.

With time, I managed to see every Cronenberg film…except for *Shivers*. Until the DVD release, my only exposure to the film came from production photos in a reference

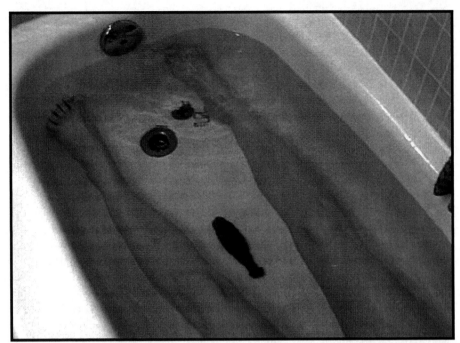

As one of David Cronenberg's phallic parasites crawls from the drain in search of a new host, the film's sexual imagery is quite obvious.

book on horror movies. Two images resonated strongest, that of Barbara Steele's legs spread in a bathtub with a small parasite crawling from the drain, and the subsequent photo of Ms. Steele writhing in agony. These photos embodied everything that was terrifying about Cronenberg. They showed a woman at her most vulnerable, naked in the bath, apparently being attacked by a small phallic parasite (it didn't take much imagination to guess where that nasty thing had crawled into). They showed a filmmaker that knew no boundaries or taboos, one who was willing to attack anywhere, one who represented everything my parents never wanted me to see. I had to see more.

Early in his search for funding, the Canadian Film Development Corporation and Cinepix showed interest in Cronenberg's script, but not the director himself as his experience up to that point only consisted of the short art films, *Stereo* (1969) and *Crimes of the Future* (1970). Refusing to sell his script, Cronenberg traveled to California to talk to Roger Corman. Despite never meeting with the legendary producer/director, he learned a valuable lesson from Corman's New World Pictures: there were ways to make *any* film with limited funding.

Cinepix eventually agreed to fund the film with Cronenberg as director, then surrounded him with seasoned professionals, including line producer Ivan Reitman, who would go on to helm the successful comedies *Meatballs* (1979), *Stripes* (1981), and *Ghostbusters* (1984). The addition of cult horror icon Barbara Steele, as well as the nymph-like Lowry, who had appeared in George A. Romero's *The Crazies* (1973), bolstered the less-than-seasoned cast.

In *The Directors: David Cronenberg*, Cronenberg states that, "the movie cost I think $385,000. I think it made five million dollars. It was the first film the CFDC ever invested in that actually made money back, but it almost brought them down. It almost caused them to be dissolved because there was an article written...saying this movie is obscene and hideous and an atrocity and you should know about it because you paid for it, you the tax payer."

Shivers introduced the world to Cronenberg's type of "body horror," full of gory, oozing detail. We encounter his recurring theme of "the human body as destiny" and the various ways to subvert human destiny by transforming it, often through destructive or "perverted" means. His transformed characters are always liberated in some sense, casting off their material concerns in a return to their pre-material primal urges.

Controversy would become a recurring theme for Cronenberg, as his films present themes so challenging, so disturbing, that few who watch them feel comforted. *In Long Live the New Flesh: The Films of David Cronenberg*, he remarks that, "the phrase 'biological horror' refers to the fact that my films are very body conscious. They're very conscious of physical existence as a living organism, rather than other horror films or science fiction films that are very technologically oriented or are concerned with the supernatural. I've never been religious in the sense that there was a God, that there was an external structure, a universal cosmic that was imposed upon human beings. I really did always feel that we have created our own universe and therefore what is wrong with it also comes from us. My world view is human-centered as opposed to centered outside humanity. I think that naturally leads you to the feeling that if you're dealing with horror, then it might also be human-centered. It comes from men. The idea is that you carry the seeds of your own destruction with you, always, and that they can erupt at any time. There is no defense against it. There is no escape from it, and I find that scarier."

David Cronenberg's fans expect him to deliver the unimaginable and to present paradigm-shifting themes. We rely on him to provide us with unexpected imagery and situations that make us feel uneasy at work, disturbed at play, and troubled in love. And, once we overcome our initial revulsion, we come back and love him all the more for it.

THE SILENCE OF THE LAMBS (1991)
by A.D. Gillott

Up until the 1990s, the "psychological thriller" had more or less become a forgotten horror subgenre, having had its heyday during Hitchcock's tenure as the maestro of the field. The shedding of censorship fetters during the '70s had given way to a more visually explicit style of filmmaking that, with revolutions in technical special effects, would dominate the horror of the '80s. Yet since then it is a genre that has burgeoned, carrying horror into new territory. After the slasher boom and before the *Scream* renaissance, films like David Fincher's *Se7en* (1995) showed that serial killers were once again in vogue. But these weren't the old-fashioned, mask-wearing, babysitter-slaughtering boogeymen from horror's past. These were new devils, based very much on the serial murderers and psychopaths of reality, with authentic psychoses and *modus operandi*. And the movie that started it off, the one that is still the benchmark to which these others aspire? The one and only: *The Silence of the Lambs*.

What makes *Silence* so unique is not just its gripping, suspense-ridden plot with ingenious twists and turns. The movie is set up to revolve around three perfectly believ-

Deadly psychopath Hannibal Lecter (Anthony Hopkins)

able main characters—Clarice Starling (Jodie Foster), a trainee in the FBI, and not one but *two* deadly psychopaths; the one, Hannibal Lecter (Anthony Hopkins), being used to capture the other, Jame "Buffalo Bill" Gumb (Ted Levine). Three main characters and a brilliant, layered narrative—this was no small feat for a director to tackle. In fact, on paper, it must have sounded crazy rather than revolutionary. *Silence*'s director, Jonathan Demme, thought so too, and almost passed up the opportunity to take on the project. It wasn't until he read Thomas Harris' source novel and talked to screenwriter Ted Tally that he understood its potential.

It is to Demme's credit that he recognized the inherent horror in the script: "One of the great things…is its genre base. It's a suspense movie with a female protagonist who's never in sexual peril. It's a slasher movie that's devoid not only of slasher scenes, but of the anticipation of them." This recognition informs Demme's method of directing and is evident throughout. With this new style of a more realistic serial killer, Demme employs a more reserved, old-fashioned series of implied horror techniques—rather than the all-out *hack 'n'slash* of the '80s—yet he never allows the film to become an anemic action movie or a simple police procedural. It still has its moments of pique and when they come, they're all the more shocking because they're unexpected. By focusing on the narrative and not overdosing on bloodthirsty scenes throughout, the viewer hasn't become desensitized or detached from the experience, apathetic of the gore.

For instance, a particularly grisly scene witnesses Lecter bludgeoning a prison guard to death with his own truncheon, sweeping the baton majestically to the strains of Bach's "Goldberg Variations," visibly demonstrating his power and animal ferocity. Yet Demme is still restrained—we never see the blows being delivered or the victim—knowing that it would have been unnecessary and ultimately less brutal if we had.

Moments like this are rare in the movie. Instead there is an adept, quiet creation of tension throughout, with Demme often relying on the old tricks of allowing the viewer to conjure his/her own demons, adroitly playing with our expectations. Take, for example, Lecter's introduction: As Clarice and the facility's head, Dr. Chilton (Anthony Heald, in a wonderfully arrogant, preening turn), sweep through countless corridors and gates, Chilton describes one particularly vicious attack a prior "guest" encountered at Lecter's hands. A photograph is handed to her—we never see it and we don't have to—Foster allows us to see the revulsion and vulnerability on Starling's face. There's also some subtle imagery at work: a descent down numerous stairways, leading into the bowels of the facility—a metaphoric hell for Clarice, surrounded by other cells populated by the insane, a reflection of Dante's *Inferno* with its tiers of hell filled with the ranks of the damned. There's even a splash of red light in the static moment between her and Chilton, compounding the Mephisthophelean imagery.

It's at this point the film undercuts us, as by this time we're expecting an eight-foot powerhouse, Lucifer himself. What we see is a balding, middle-aged man of average stature, polite, poised, graceful, and quiet. But as Starling's interview proceeds we realize that the rug has been pulled from under us again, a reversal of a reversal. For something commanding and preternatural exists about this man, utterly deadly and ruthless, yet at the same time creepily playful, with a powerful intelligence radiating from his mesmerizing gaze. This comes courtesy of a combination of elements, including Harris' superlative characterization (supposedly based partly on the American serial killer/cannibal, Albert Fish) and Tally's fine script. But most of all, there is the absolutely canny, bravura turn by Hopkins, whose performance would so dominate the film that he would go on to win an Oscar for Best Actor despite having little more than 16 minutes of screen time in total.

Like Satan in Milton's *Paradise Lost,* Lecter is an anti-hero—irresistibly charming but recognizably an intimidating fiend too, weaving a spell that continually enthralls the viewer. As veteran horror maestro John Carpenter comments: "Someone like Hannibal Lecter is…interesting…because he combines this brilliant mind with an absolutely horrifying monster." Hopkins' strength in the part is made all the more amazing for the fact that he was not the first actor to play Lecter; it is usually the first actor who inhabits a role to be considered the best. Brian Cox gave a sinister, understated performance as the taciturn doctor in Michael Mann's excellent *Manhunter* (1986), an adaptation of the first in Harris' Lecter series, *Red Dragon. Manhunter* went almost unnoticed at the time, receiving poor box-office returns, but it has since become something of a cult favorite in itself, particularly after the success of *Silence.*

Lecter remains perhaps the most memorable of the three main characters, and inevitably became something of the pin-up for the '90s horror fan, though it is a shrewd decision that Demme stuck with Harris' story and did not feel compelled to overuse him—all three of the main characters are integral to the movie, and he never lets the others become marginalized. For the few instances that the camera leaves our protagonist, it is to focus on "Buffalo Bill." Levine gives a haunting performance, one in the style of some of cinema's classic monsters in that it is a sympathetic portrayal of a disturbed mind, adding a depth to a character that could easily have become a caricature, a standard villain. There are moments where his humanity is touching, and others where the cool and calculating cruelty of his actions is equally terrifying.

It is, however, Starling who is the main focus of the movie, an astute move given that she could have easily been overshadowed by either of these standout villains.

Demme accomplishes this so well with a daring choice of cinematic style—in the sequences involving Clarice we often see a subjective, roaming point-of-view shot, as if watching the events unfold through her eyes. We clearly see how this woman has to function within a close-knit male environment like the FBI and the world in general. (Note the palpable awkwardness as she walks into a mortuary filled with all male cops, their glances suggesting how she is alternately judged either as an inferior, competition to be scorned, or a sexual object, all based on her gender alone). Consequently, we protectively draw her to us, and in caring so deeply we feel it all the more when she is facing peril.

This is all aided by Foster's terrific Oscar-winning performance, wonderfully nuanced and textured, evolving and changing constantly in response to the situations she faces. At the beginning, for example, we see that although she is loath to entertain Chilton's advances to obtain an interview with Lecter alone, she later flirts and flatters him, using her femininity. Curiously, it is the monster himself, Lecter, who chastises her affectations when she tries to cozen him. "Hmmm…that is rather *slippery* of you, Agent Starling." We see the hurt and recoil on Foster's face and, from that moment, the "*quid pro quo*" game is begun. This, too, is part of the magnetism of the movie, as scriptwriter Tally describes it: "…that strange sexual power struggle, that chess game between this young woman and this man—this monster."

This is what sets *The Silence of the Lambs* apart—the savvy decision to make all three of the main players believable, human characters. Putting this to the backdrop of such a gripping, intelligent plot, with oodles of clever cinematic style to sound the depths of this many-layered narrative, it elevates what would otherwise be just another police manhunt yarn into a brilliantly suspenseful horror classic, cranking up the tension to dizzying heights. So do yourself a favor and watch *Silence* tonight. Better yet, invite an old friend to view it with you…they might just be in time for dinner—glass of Chianti, anyone?

THE SIXTH SENSE (1999)
by Seth Pearce

"I see dead people."

Cole Sear's plaintive, whispered confession is now one of the most familiar snatches of dialogue in modern film, etched in the psyche of pop culture, and for good reason. This tour-de-force ghost story became an instant classic upon its release in the late summer of 1999, eventually heralded as not just as a superior horror movie, but one of the best movies (in any genre) of all time. By the end of its initial U.S. theatrical run, the film had earned nearly $300 million, become one of the top-10 grossing films in history, and been nominated for six Academy Awards, including Best Picture and Best Director for Hollywood newcomer M. Night Shyamalan.

Some may argue that this film is more appropriately placed in the thriller genre. To these hair-splitters I ask, how many supernatural thrillers are there? At its core, *The Sixth Sense* remains a ghost story, perhaps the oldest form of horror there is in human culture. Long before serial killers and mutant monsters, man feared predators and the spirits. Horror movies are made to scare and ghosts are at the core of our primal fears; thus, this *is* a horror movie.

Cole (Haley Joel Osment) turns away from a reccent accident victim.

The brilliantly written script can be divided into five components: Introduction, Act I, Act II, Act III, and Coda. In this way, Shyamalan's writing is a throwback to when movies' narrative structures still resembled stage plays, each segment opening with a scene-setting introduction shot and concluding with a fade to black. (Akira Kurosawa used the same narrative technique in 1954's *Seven Samurai* and, in more ways than one, Shyamalan's filmmaking process shows similarities to the legendary director.) In the landscape of MTV-influenced writing and cinematography, the more traditional *Sixth Sense* is a welcome change. This structure allows Shyamalan to drop "revelation bombs" on us, then afford us the chance to catch our collective breath and ponder their implications.

In the Introduction, we meet the first of our principal characters, Dr. Malcolm Crowe (Bruce Willis), a child psychologist of the finest order. However, we quickly learn that even those at the top of their field are not immune to making mistakes. Former patient Vincent Grey (Donnie Wahlberg) visits revenge upon Malcolm for failing to help him, launching into a vague and deliriously psychotic tirade. At the conclusion of his dysphoric spray, Grey shoots his former doctor in the guts and then shoots himself.

Act I begins with Crowe attempting to make amends for his failure by taking up the case of Cole Sear (Haley Joel Osment), a troubled young boy with similar symptoms to

Malcolm's attacker. The film is structured in a third-person limited, in that the audience knows only what Malcolm knows, and we follow the story from his perspective. How can he help Cole? What is Cole's secret? Cole's overworked, over-stressed single mother (Toni Collette) is also obsessed with learning how to help Cole. Act I concludes with a secret told to Dr. Crowe in confidence: Cole sees ghosts. And he is terrified of them.

Act II shifts gears. The film changes to a third-person limited that now follows Cole; we see the ghosts as he sees them, giving us brief glimpses of the hell of Cole's daily life. Malcolm struggles to find a way to help, but does not believe in his patient's specters. However, in reviewing the case recordings of Vincent Grey, Dr. Crowe discovers a terrified voice begging for its life (where there should only be Vincent alone in the room). The kicker is the voice is in Spanish, a language we must conclude Grey does not speak. Crowe certainly comes to that conclusion and makes up his mind to help Cole.

With this, hope comes to a tense and bleak story. Act III centers on Cole's attempts to implement Crowe's radical advice: to try helping the visiting spirits. The terrifying appearance of a sick young girl's ghost is the film's crescendo, marking Cole's transformation from cursed to gifted. Though audiences might not guess it from her heart-stopping entrance, young Kira comes to Cole for help, needing him to reveal the truth of her death to her father. Cole, accompanied by Crowe, travels to Kira's funeral. There, at the young ghost's direction, he provides proof that Kira's own mother was the cause of her death! (Ironically, this heart-wrenching reveal ultimately becomes the *least* important to the overall plot, as we soon see, yet that does nothing to diminish its shock and tragedy.)

The Coda offers a three-part resolution. We see Cole's improved social adjustment, and with it, the conclusion of Cole and Malcolm's doctor/patient relationship. Cole shares his secret with his mother and finds acceptance. However, the film's coup-de-grace is the mind-blowing bombshell that Dr. Malcolm Crowe is actually…dead. Throughout the film, he has been, in fact, a ghost who needed Cole's help as much as Cole needed his. A superlative montage of previous scenes confirms this fact, revealing that our hero was killed by his attacker in the Introduction. It is this twist that elevates a wonderfully told story into a masterpiece. *The Sixth Sense* is one of a handful of films that is truly a different film from the first viewing to the second.

The conspiratorial air on the set while shooting helped preserve this massive secret for the film's theatrical release, as well as creating phenomenal media buzz. Once it came out, the word of mouth was beyond belief, with the twist ending carefully guarded by the growing legion of fans. I consider myself fortunate that even though I did not see *The Sixth Sense* until its video release, the reveal of Malcolm's death had not been ruined for me. I am just as grateful that the cast and crew of this movie were so meticulous in their creative process, manufacturing a set of rules and sticking to them. The insertion of clues throughout as to the true nature of the film makes repeat viewings especially rewarding. Indeed, for some, this movie is even better the second time. Not many pictures can make such a boast. I have watched it maybe 10 times now, picking up some new information or perspective with every viewing.

Shyamalan's masterfully original screenplay is the heart of the film, but just as important are its eyes. Tak Fujimoto's cinematography is brilliant, combining excellent point of view (POV), alternating hand-held with stable tracking, and employing organic-feeling, non-centered framing. His tendency towards the long take, repositioning the camera during the shot (rather than using multiple takes cut together), is a testament to his planning and patience. Fujimoto's use of POV, instructing the audiences to view the world from the perspective of Dr. Crowe at the beginning of Act I, is one example of cerebral influence within camera technique. The camera is not just our eyes; it provides the director with a means to reveal information, provide instruction and facilitate empathy with our characters. The pace and action of this film is one of slow take, set-up and quick-cutting/panning action, creating a push/pull effect that is subtle yet effective. With so many ghost stories prone to using "quick motion combined with a blast of sound" to produce scares, it's nice to see something more creative.

The small but brilliant cast accentuates the organic feel and realism. Bruce Willis is the star, but he brilliantly defers to his youthful onscreen colleague. Willis has in the past shown the ability to transcend his action hero typecasting in such films as *Pulp Fiction* (1994) and *Twelve Monkeys* (1995). In *The Sixth Sense* he goes even further. His stillness and attentive listening are essential, allowing the audience to focus on Cole. Happily, Osment does not disappoint. His Best Supporting Actor nomination is testament to a riveting, second-to-none performance. Indeed, if not for Osment's skill, all the film's aforementioned brilliance could have been flushed straight down the crapper. Also nominated for a statuette was Toni Collette's portrayal of Cole's distraught mother. Collette's Philly accent is excellent (especially when one considers she is Australian) and her frustrated, overbearing mothering is wonderfully augmented with flashes of anger and deep compassion.

The Sixth Sense is an excellent movie *and* an excellent ghost story. The horror genre is better for its inclusion. This is a horror movie for the general public and not just the fan; tense and gripping but without excessive violence and gore. Like *Rosemary's Baby* (1968) or *The Blair Witch Project* (1999), it reinforces the notion that the power of the imagination can be more frightening than a bucket of blood. Also, its technical and performance proficiency has helped it to garner the adoration of the film educated. Oftentimes, films that are considered good horror movies are not well shot or acted. (In fact, no other genre as regularly tolerates such deficiencies.) When looking at a picture designed to scare, one's analysis might indeed start with the "goosebump factor," but perhaps that shouldn't be the sole criteria for success. Fortunately, there are filmmakers like M. Night Shyamalan who understand this and seek not just to make the audience jump, but to satisfy all the elements of quality performance art.

THE STEPFORD WIVES (1975)
by Robie Gelpi

There's no doubt about it—people love to get scared. Amusement parks and haunted houses are proof positive of people's desire to be frightened. Getting our adrenaline pumped up by a thrilling, scary experience is not a passing trend, but a worldwide, popular pastime event. There is a reason why scary movies have fascinated audiences for years. From the moment the silent *Nosferatu* (1922) and Lon Chaney's *Phantom of the Opera* (1925) debuted in movie theaters, followed by the original *Dracula* and *Frankenstein* in the 1930s, our love affair with horror films began. It is a love-hate relationship that has lasted for a long time—we suffer through every second of the terrifying experience, but then we anticipate watching it again and again. All kinds of

Joanna (Katharine Ross) and her vacant eyes reveal the truth.

horror films exist: Slashers, ghost stories, vampires, werewolves, and many others. But for me, none are more interesting than those that take place in a realistic setting that the audience can recognize...one that looks alarmingly like home.

Based on Ira Levin's highly popular novel, *The Stepford Wives* clearly stands as one of the most successful attempts at presenting horror in a straightforward manner. There are no supernatural forces at play here and the setting is suburban America, not a remote village in an unfamiliar foreign country. For years, horror films took viewers to exotic locations, unnerving them with a variety of wacky characters and larger-than-life situations. By contrast, *The Stepford Wives* is a great example of the direction horror took in the years following the release of Alfred Hitchcock's *Psycho*. Like that groundbreaking 1960 movie, Levin's story (ably adapted by William Goldman) brings horror into our comfort zone, into the humdrum of our daily lives. It was a trend that became more and more popular, and I think Levin, as he did with *Rosemary's Baby*, effectively took advantage of viewers' growing realization that our biggest nightmares emanate from the horrors supplied by a natural, realistic environment.

For the uninitiated, this film adaptation of Levin's chilling story is about a typical American family that moves to a quiet upper class neighborhood of Stepford, Connecticut. Having strived economically and now able to improve their living conditions, the family chooses to move away from the hectic, often threatening life of the city, where crime has escalated constantly. The town of Stepford is the archetypical safe heaven we often dream about but few people are able to find. But the town's seemly hushed exterior hides an unexpectedly dark, sinister secret, one that touches the very core of humanity. Without the digital wizardry of modern ventures like *What Lies Beneath* (2000) and *The Devil's Backbone* (2001), the film manages to create a slow-burn crescendo that climaxes with a truly distressing, excruciating, and nihilistic finale.

The Stepford Wives is one of the most unsettling films ever made, achieving most of its bone-chilling effects by suggestive camerawork and very little exposition. British director Bryan Forbes and screenwriter Goldman smartly expand the psychological undertones of the original text, while staying very close to Levin's original intentions. This film is undeniably one of the most successful adaptations of a book of this type, and becomes a great example of how well horror mixes with social commentary. Having only flirted with the horror genre once before (*Séance on a Wet Afternoon* [1964]), the successful dramatic director demonstrates an uncanny ability to display the presence of evil underneath the ostensibly ordinary facade of daily life. Although not in the category of directors like Hitchcock and David Lynch, director Forbes seems to understand the old adagio that suggestion is a more powerful tool than anything shown on the screen. His understated way of introducing the audience to peculiar behavior provides a cinematic force difficult to ignore.

From a technical standpoint alone, this is a remarkable work. First off, it does not use special effects to enhance the gloomy atmosphere; instead the eerie ambiance is achieved by careful editing and intelligent use of negative space. One has to recognize how important the overall *look* is to the movie as a whole—without the careful organization of images it would have been difficult to achieve the desired unnerving effect. Mostly told from the perspective of the main character Joanna (the mother/wife of a family), *Stepford Wives* effectively forces the viewer to become part of the action. The chilling bits of information we do gain (that Joanna is not privy to) only heighten our sense of dread. No longer passive observers, we are gradually, seductively pulled inside the story.

One of the most notable visual aspects is Forbes' use of light and shadows, manipulating dark and bright spaces to hypnotic effect. *Stepford*'s first half is bright and sunny, with the movie becoming darker as the story progresses. This technique also effectively creates anticipation and excitement; throughout, the locale becomes more forbidding, slowly conditioning the viewer for the macabre climax to come.

From a directorial point of view, this is a brilliant exercise in minimalism. Forbes somehow manages to break away from the cinematic techniques of the time. Multiple viewings reveal an astonishing and original movie that even today dazzles the eye and stimulates the intellect within its simple milieu. As hinted before, the story revolves around a timeless theme, which most people undoubtedly will find interesting. It deals, more or less, with the dark side of the American dream. Here, the idyllic suburban life is a metaphor for the tyranny of the majority: Assimilate or be considered an enemy against the status quo—a message that continues to be relevant 30 years later.

As much as I like what Forbes does with the material, I have to admit that much of *The Stepford Wives'* success relies on Katharine Ross' empathic, controlled performance as the "trophy wife" exposed to situations that she cannot understand. She's superb as an unfulfilled, independently minded woman who becomes more resolute in finding an explanation to the strange events she is witnessing. Although primarily remembered today for her roles in films like *The Graduate* (1967) and *Butch Cassidy and the Sun-*

dance Kid (1969), *The Stepford Wives* provided Ross with one of the best roles of her career. The waves of emotions registered on her face are priceless every time a piece of the puzzle unravels. Her fully developed characterization greatly emphasizes the ambivalent nature of the story, keeping us guessing whether she is truly seeing abnormal behavior or simply being paranoid. That element of uncertainty is what ultimately transforms this chiller into a heart-pounding tragedy.

Critics, movie buffs, and the general public alike have somehow neglected *The Stepford Wives*, despite the fact that the title has become a part of American jargon. Most people remain unaware of its influence and excellence. Even after three decades, it remains *the* 1970s American film that best combines chills with social satire, a textbook lesson in how to effectively tell this kind of story. Photographed in a frighteningly antiseptic manner by Enrique Bravo and Owen Roizman, and scored with Michael Small's spine-tingling music, it remains an absolute must for horror film lovers and serious students of the power of cinema.

My first encounter with *The Stepford Wives* was on a rainy night (before infomercials took over late night TV) almost 20 years ago. Once it was released on VHS and I could finally watch the film without intrusive commercial interruptions, I came to appreciate the carefully constructed storyline and the marvelous way in which the film builds up to its smashing and unexpected climax. Also, after multiple viewings, I was able to notice the black comic moments within the storyline. Once you know the punch line, the film's wicked and clever sense of humor is on full display to be savored.

A classic that certainly deserves more attention, *The Stepford Wives* is available on DVD (Paramount and Anchor Bay), and can now be rediscovered by a new generation of moviegoers. Though it currently remains underappreciated, I remain hopeful the film will soon be reevaluated by the critical mass.

SUSPIRIA (1977)
by Nick Brown

From the moment it begins, *Suspiria*'s dazzling array of colors, intoxicating musical score, and inspired direction assures audiences they are not in for just another horror film. Dario Argento's hallucinogenic nightmare is in a class all its own—aside from its follow-up, *Inferno* (1980), there's no other film quite like this one. Writing for Anchor Bay upon the U.K. DVD release, Travis Crawford remarks that *Suspiria* is a "full throttle sensory assault," and while such a claim may sound pretentious, that is not the case here. The pumping soundtrack, courtesy of Argento's house band Goblin, interacts brilliantly with the color scheme, lighting, and bizarre set-design. Every sequence in the film is beautiful in its presentation and is given extra intensity courtesy of the attention to detail. Crawford goes on to state that *Suspiria* is the most widely seen Italian horror film, and it has served as a gateway to a wealth of European horror for many fans.

One of the first foreign horrors I'd ever sat down to watch, my interest had been sparked by vivid descriptions of the film's three central set-piece murders. Reviewers often remark that Argento gets better upon repeat viewings, and while *Suspiria* definitely made a impression on me the first time I saw it, my overall esteem has indeed grown stronger with every subsequent viewing. Each time I see it, I discover something that I'd never noticed before. While aspects such as the humming lights and marvelous

Another beautiful female dies horribly at the hands of Argento.

stained glass windows hit you instantly, it is Argento's exquisite attention to smaller details (such as the fact that the door handles in the dance academy are head-height for the actresses) that continues to spark further interest.

Beyond the bizarre tone seen throughout *Suspiria*, Argento provided the film with a remarkable cast. The lead role of Suzy Bannion is inhabited by a young Jessica Harper, whose performance for Brian De Palma in *Phantom of the Paradise* (1974) impressed Argento so much that he gave her the lead role. Harper manages to deliver her performance with just the right amount of boldness and naivety, and she does well at embodying the childish mentality of the students at the academy. More interesting are the performers in the matriarchal roles. Joan Bennett, an American actress who worked prolifically throughout the 1930s and 1940s under the direction of heavyweights such as George Cukor and Fritz Lang, takes the central role of Madame Blanc. Joining her at the top of the film's hierarchy is Alida Valli, an Italian actress who broke into American films (as 'Valli') with Alfred Hitchcock's *The Paradine Case* (1947) and most notably had a lead role in the classic *The Third Man* (1949). She would go on to star in *Eyes Without a Face* (1959), then work with the great Mario Bava on *Lisa and the Devil* (1973). Bennett and Valli are only in supporting roles, but they lead from the rear and provide two strong female characters. Stefania Casini stands out as Suzy's classmate, and every cult fan on the planet will instantly recognize Udo Kier, who was given his small role because he "really, really wanted to be in *Suspiria*."

Purely in terms of style, *Suspiria* is almost impossible to criticize. Everything appears completely alien to the world we inhabit. Argento is reported to have based his look on Disney classics, and the rich vein of childish dialogue and naivety among the central characters absurdly complements this visual design. Argento depicts every sequence with great care and attention to detail, but his strikingly original touches, such as his devilish use of lighting, are really what make the film what it is. Often, the bright hues feel superfluous to what is immediately going on with the story—but the way that they exist in their own right, aside from any element of the plot, helps to create the nightmare world that Argento uses so effectively in *Suspiria*.

With its main influence seemingly Lewis Carroll's *Alice in Wonderland*, the story follows a classic fairytale set-up as we follow a young girl traveling into an ominous world of mystery and witchcraft. The film even starts with a voiceover explaining the basic situation while the title credits run, an obvious nod to its fairytale styling.

Suspiria is famous (or more properly, *infamous*) for its trio of gratuitous and unique murder scenes. The first one appears less than 10 minutes after the opening credits, and at this point, it becomes clear that Argento will not be holding anything back. With a sequence that is the cinematic equivalent of being slapped in the face, the viewer sees a young woman stabbed repeatedly, and then thrown through a stained glass skylight with a noose around her neck, the falling glass killing her friend in the process. The sequence is violent and grisly, but it's offset by the beautiful way in which it is filmed. Because Argento has perfectly orchestrated the atmosphere around the killing, there is no need to feel guilty about enjoying seeing the young victim heinously lacerated by the unknown assailant's blade. The fact is, the scene is *beautiful*, despite what it depicts.

Argento's orchestration hits a high during the next murder sequence, as we are treated to a blackly comic scene that is as brilliantly realized as it is unexpected and bizarre. A blind man and his dog stand in the middle of a town square. Meanwhile, Goblin's menacing soundtrack screams "Witch!" and the director makes his audience believe that the danger is approaching from above by way of a swooping camera movement from the top of the screen. All of this takes place seconds before the guide dog sinks its teeth into its master's neck, leaving the viewer distracted, disoriented, and shocked in one clean strike.

The third and final absurd death scene is more simplistic than the other two, but nonetheless effective. Inside the dance academy, a central character is chased through a top window, where she is greeted by a room stocked full of razor wire!

While it continually impresses on a stylish level, we must admit that the film largely lacks substance. Personally, however, I don't see this as a problem in the slightest. With *Vertigo* (1958), the great Alfred Hitchcock proved that a film can be successful without finding a balance between style and substance, and Argento proves it again with *Suspiria*. If there is a defining thematic point to *Suspiria*, it's hidden beneath a mass of glowing lights, huge stained glass windows and ceilings full of maggots; and in the end, this doesn't matter at all. As he often did in the '70s and '80s, Argento provides his audience with exactly what they came to see, and I find it difficult to criticize him for that. The film features several nods to fascinating ideas such as the hierarchy of a witch's coven and the implications of a young girl lost in a world she doesn't understand. But all of these things are secondary to the hallucinogenic visuals and hypnotic atmosphere, and I wouldn't have it any other way.

Suspiria may not be one of the most influential pictures ever made, but to me this is a testament to its enduring originality. Fellow filmmakers understand that it is one of a kind, and the fact that the lavish style pioneered within is not often copied ensures that *Suspiria* isn't easy to forget. Dario Argento's masterpiece is important for me personally, as it introduced me to a world of cinema's hidden pleasures. With that in mind, I implore everyone who hasn't seen it, and considers themself a fan of horror, to rectify the problem immediately.

THE TERMINATOR (1984)
by Mikey Diablo

The Terminator is the quintessential robot stalker story of the last 20 years. Released in 1984, the picture captivated critics and moviegoers alike with its special effects, intriguing characters, and intelligent, well-written storyline. Pitting a singular-minded robot against a singular-minded human with the fate of humanity lying in the balance, this whirlwind tour-de-force combined horror and sci-fi elements with breathtaking action sequences. Not bad for a film from an unproven director and featuring an actor known more for his bulging biceps than his acting chops.

Foremost amongst its many assets, *The Terminator* sports a brilliantly simple yet original plotline: Sarah Connor is just an ordinary girl. She has a thankless job waiting tables and seems to have the usual cares and needs of any other working class 20-something. Little does she know, she is the key to saving the human race. Sarah's life or death holds with it the balance of the future. If Sarah dies, Skynet (an all-powerful artificial intelligence) and its robot forces will triumph—all humans will be eradicated. If she lives, the human resistance (led by her unborn son, John) will prevail. From this future, two warriors have returned to find Sarah; one to protect, the other to, well, terminate.

Any discussion of *The Terminator* has to begin with what has become its calling card, the hulking Austrian whose evil robotic monotone sent shivers down film fans' backs: Arnold Schwarzenegger. Despite his prowess on the bodybuilding circuit and appearing in *Hercules in New York* (1970), *Conan the Barbarian* (1982), and *Conan the Destroyer* (1984), the seven-time Mr. Olympia was hardly a household name in Hollywood's eyes. Following his triumphant turn in *Terminator*, "Ah-nold" became a fixture in action blockbusters, eventually becoming one of the most popular and powerful figures in the film industry. While often a liability in other films, Schwarzenegger's wooden tone, heavy Teutonic accent, and complete lack of emotion were ideal for the killer android. His portrayal, featuring a creepy baseline voice, proved thoroughly disturbing, unsettling, and timeless. Without his magnetic presence as the title character, one wonders whether this movie could have stood the test of time. (Ironically, Schwarzenegger was originally considered for the Kyle Reese "hero" character, later played by Michael Biehn.)

As impressive as our title character is, the most important piece of this revolutionary cinematic puzzle is James Cameron, whose filmmaking career began in 1978 with the 12-minute short film, *Xenogenesis*. After serving as serving as art director on 1980's *Battle Beyond the Stars* for Roger Corman's New World Pictures, he was tapped to direct *Piranha II: The Spawning* (1981). While this low-budget movie wasn't exactly

The killer android (Arnold Schwarzenegger) stalks his prey.

the kind Cameron envisioned for himself, it certainly provided a valuable first step into the world of directing. Cameron encountered many obstacles during production, not the least of which being that producer Ed Carlin wasn't interested in any rookie director's "concept." Cameron's original cut was brutally hacked apart and re-edited to suit Carlin's desires. However, the sleepless nights following this traumatic experience would ultimately yield the first seeds of *Terminator*. Inspired by a dream of an assassin from the future, Cameron set to work and, with the help of producer Gail Ann Hurd, he polished his script into arguably his best ever. (Heavy praise indeed when one considers 1997's *Titanic,* one of the most celebrated works to ever hit the screen, lay in his future.)

After being shopped around quite a bit, *The Terminator* finally found backing with Hemdale Pictures. The resulting movie showcased all of Cameron's talents as a filmmaker, oozing tension and action set pieces that fall directly into the audience's lap. (When the police department's reception desk is hit head on by the T-800, it feels like the car is coming through the screen.) Additionally, the film showcases Cameron's ability for depicting extreme situations peopled with realistic characters. Sarah Connor's plight is so engrossing because she is someone with whom we can identify. She is our neighbor, the lady behind us in line at the grocery store, or our waitress. Cameron's uncanny knack for this quality appears in almost all of his films, including *Aliens* (1986), *The Abyss* (1989), *Terminator 2: Judgment Day* (1991), and *True Lies* (1994).

Rounding out the cast are Michael Biehn and Linda Hamilton. While neither may be governors or Academy Award winners, their importance to *The Terminator*'s success cannot be understated. Without them, the intensity of the movie would be lost, and the final impact dull and unappealing. As the representative of the human resistance, it was important that Biehn embody the "rebel with a heart," the ultimate human side. Because of the action-packed nature of the picture, his contributions often go unrecognized, which is a shame. As Kyle Reese, Biehn manages to craft a fully believable character within a fantastic and insane scenario, a testament to his acting abilities. He would go on to appear in several other memorable onscreen endeavors, including Johnny Ringo in the 1993 Neo-Western *Tombstone*, as well as *Aliens* and *The Abyss* under Cameron. Likewise, Hamilton's grounded, human emotions elevate the production from simply being a "chase movie." Her Sarah is realistic, vulnerable, and resourceful. Her convincing portrayal plays nicely against all the onscreen testosterone. But by the time *T2: Judgment Day* rolled around, it wasn't just Schwarzenegger's physique that folks were talking about. Hamilton's transformation from everyday lady to gun-toting zealot was, for many, a revelation. Her other efforts include *Children of the Corn* (1984), *Dante's Peak* (1997), and television's *Beauty and the Beast*.

While the talent involved in this movie is undebatable, one thing just might be: Many people might question its status as a horror film. As cinema has progressed and become more prolific, so has the need to categorize it. For many fans, as soon as a film shows any element of science fiction, it cannot be a horror movie. I would ask such people to re-watch *The Terminator*, imagining Schwarzenegger's guns replaced by machetes. *Voila*, a bona-fide slasher movie emerges. Despite being thrilling movies in their own right, *T2: Judgment Day* and *Terminator 3: Rise of the Machines* (2003) have sadly clouded what the original did so well. Focusing more on explosions and special effects, the sequels are seemingly content to wow their audiences rather than scare them, becoming less about saving a damsel in distress and more about changing the future through manipulation of events. At the end of the day, while Kyle Reese may have come from the morally decaying future, his role in *The Terminator* is to protect Sarah Connor…from a monster.

Boiled down to its core, *The Terminator* is essentially one big chase scene that ratchets the tension higher and higher. To simply write this movie off as an exercise in sci-fi/action is absurd. From the opening sequence where a hoodlum (an unknown Bill Paxton) literally loses his heart, to the police station massacre, to its chase-through-shadowy-corridors finale, *The Terminator* works almost exclusively on the principles of a horror movie. Regrettably, because the popular sequels do not subscribe to these same principles, people forget where the original's bio-mechanical heart belongs.

The success of *The Terminator* and its sequels effectively changed modern cinema. With its sledge-fisted robotic arm, it smashed through three separate genres—horror, action and science fiction—inspiring a new generation of filmmakers with its use of breakneck thrills, character-driven storytelling, and good old-fashioned blood and guts. James Cameron went on to become, in his own words, "King of the World," and Schwarzenegger's resulting stardom contributed in no small part to his becoming governor of California in 2003. The film itself became the flagship for one of the most successful franchises in Hollywood history. This marriage of horror and science fiction is not historically unique, but rarely has it been executed with such daring and verve.

When thinking back to this movie, fans everywhere can still feel the hairs on the back of their necks stand up when they hear, "I'll be back."

THE TEXAS CHAIN SAW MASSACRE (1974)
by Andrew Haubert

Leatherface puts his victim Pam (Teri McMinn) on a hook.

Sally Hardesty (Marilyn Burns), her paraplegic brother Franklin (Paul A. Partain), and three of their friends travel to rural Texas to check on the final remains of their grandfather, after it is reported that a series of bizarre grave robberies have occurred at the cemetery where he was buried. The youths are relieved to learn the remains of their relatives have been undisturbed, but their relief is short lived when they come across a local residence which contains one of most macabre settings in the annals of time. What appears to be a quiet farmhouse is actually the slaughterhouse for a family of barbaric cannibals, who butcher any unfortunate soul that happens to get lost on the backroads of their chunk of Texas. Inside awaits furniture made from human remains and a 300-plus pound man, who knows nothing but murder. While certainly not the brains of the Sawyer clan, the often childlike Leatherface (Gunnar Hansen) is certainly the most menacing member of the family. Wearing a mask formed from skin flayed off the faces of previous victims, Leatherface turns the teens' innocent search for gasoline into a bloodbath while wielding many weapons of butchery—most famously his iconic chainsaw.

I cannot even attempt to hide my bias for *The Texas Chain Saw Massacre*. I consider it the greatest horror film ever made. The fact is, Tobe Hooper's masterpiece disturbed me to the point that I felt like I had been emotionally scarred. That night I had trouble sleeping, and I heard Sally's screams from the dinner scene in my head for days afterward. The last film to have that kind of effect on me had been *Jaws* (1975), when I was five years old. However, unlike when I first saw Spielberg's movie, I was no longer a child who had never seen a legitimate horror flick; I was a college sophomore, and a seasoned veteran of the horror genre.

I am not the only one to be deeply affected by their first viewing of this film either. Unleashed upon unsuspecting audiences in 1974, *The Texas Chain Saw Massacre* became an overnight sensation and an instant horror classic. According to the documentary *Texas Chainsaw Massacre: The Shocking Truth* (2000), most of the crew considered the film doomed to become an obscure box-office failure. Instead, so many people ended up passing through the turnstiles that for years it was one of the most profitable films ever released. One might ask why so many people were seeing this movie, and the simple answer is that the film was very effective at scaring its viewers.

However, many of these souls walked away believing they had just experienced the most explicitly violent film ever produced. *The Texas Chain Saw Massacre* was said to be so brutal that it was banned in several European countries, most famously in the United Kingdom where the uncut version was not available until 1999. Yet the explicit brutality viewers claimed to have witnessed was just an illusion attained through quick editing, a grinding score, and discordant sound effects. Tobe Hooper has often claimed that he was actually attempting to attain a PG-rating for the film, and if the viewer pays close attention, they will be surprised to see very little onscreen blood.

In 1974, Austin native Hooper and his almost exclusively Texas-born cast and crew set out to make *The Texas Chain Saw Massacre*, based on the real-life killings of Ed Gein, a cannibalistic killer responsible for the grisly murders of several people in the 1950s. Despite its eventual success, the production was nearly shut down dozens of times for lack of money. In order to keep within the budget, many principal cast and crew members sold portions of their prearranged salaries for stock in future profits. Unfortunately, their contracts only entitled them to profits received by the production company, Vortex Films, while the distribution companies (including Bryanston Distributing, a well-known front for organized crime, and another company that quickly went out of business) enjoyed the bigger profits. Needless to say, most involved in the production walked away monetarily slighted, but better educated for future filmmaking experiences.

The Texas Chain Saw Massacre instantly cemented Hooper's icon status within the horror genre. Throughout the next two decades, however, the director's career would endure its fair share of ups and downs. In 1977, *Eaten Alive*, his long awaited follow-up, was released. The film reunited several key members from *The Texas Chain Saw Massacre*—including star Marilyn Burns in the female lead and writer/producer Kim Henkel—but the film encountered mixed reviews, sporadic distribution, and a so-so take at the box office (a pattern recurrent throughout Hooper's career). In 1979, he rebounded with the acclaimed made-for-television adaptation of Stephen King's *Salem's Lot*, followed by *The Funhouse* (1981), one of the last worthwhile slasher films. But, while *The Texas Chain Saw Massacre* is undoubtedly Hooper's best film, his most successful film financially was *Poltergeist* (1982), for which he was handpicked to direct by filmmaking icon Steven Spielberg (who also produced).

Hooper never again matched the success he experienced in his first decade of filmmaking. His output has ranged from cult favorites (*Lifeforce* [1985], *The Texas*

Chainsaw Massacre 2, [1986], and *Spontaneous Combustion* [1990]) to complete failures (*Night Terrors* [1993], *The Mangler* [1995], and *Crocodile* [2000]). Despite mixed results since 1982, Hooper made a recent resurgence in the 21st century with his remake of the exploitation classic, *The Toolbox Murders* (2005).

While *The Texas Chain Saw Massacre* elevated Tobe Hooper's status within the genre and created a horror icon in Leatherface, the film's most lasting impact has probably been the manner in which it changed horror film distribution. Romero's *Night of the Living Dead* (1968) and Craven's *The Last House on the Left* (1972) were undeniably influential in raising the level of violence on film, but it was the success of *The Texas Chain Saw Massacre* that opened the doors for grindhouse horror within U.S. theaters.

The Texas Chain Saw Massacre is a true classic of the genre. From the deceptive editing to the jarring sound effects, few directors have been able to put as disturbing a scene on film as the infamous "dinner scene." In this viewer's opinion, when it comes to gritty horror movies, there's not one that can surpass it. The film echoes in one's brain for days and continues to haunt us for weeks, no matter where we go.

Just be careful where you try to run, as you'll want to stay away from the back roads.

THEM! (1954)
by Linda Townsend

A plane flies overhead, searching the desert after reports of a child seen wandering alone. The little girl is spotted walking, clutching a doll, eyes staring in shock. What has happened to her? Where has she come from? The investigation into the child's origins leads to a ruined camper by the side of the road, its occupants missing. The only clues are strange prints left in the sand and stranger noises heard in the desert wind. Farther down the road, another mystery, another destroyed building. But this time a body is also discovered, the battered corpse containing enough formic acid to kill 20 men.

The investigation into the attacks reveals the discovery of giant mutated ants, apparently created when the U.S. government detonated an atomic bomb in the sands of New Mexico nine years earlier. This fantastic mutation, caused by "lingering atomic radiation," represents a new breed of pest: a savage ant colony where the smallest warrior is nine feet in length. New Mexico policeman Ben Peterson (James Whitmore) and FBI agent Robert Graham (James Arness) team with the Doctors Harold Medford (Edmund Gwenn) and lovely Pat Medford (Joan Weldon) to neutralize the colony, only to learn that two new Queens have hatched, flown away under the radar, and probably started new colonies elsewhere in the continental United States. If these ant colonies aren't destroyed quickly, Dr. Medford predicts that mankind will become an extinct species within a calendar year. The race is then on, stretching from the deserts of New Mexico to the sewers of Los Angeles, to try to destroy the mutated horrors before they can lay waste to the planet.

This cautionary tale of the dangerous use of atomic weapons and their unfathomable aftermath boasts a very strong script (by Russell S. Hughes and Ted Sherdeman, story by George Worthing Yates) and a wealth of convincing performances, all expertly guided by the hand of director Gordon Douglas.

Puny humans (Joan Weldon, James Arness) face off with *Them!* in the desert.

Them! was the first of the "big bug" movies, and was the biggest moneymaker for Warner Bros. in the year of its release. It was nominated for an Academy Award for Special Effects and won the Motion Picture Sound Editors' Golden Reel Award for Best Sound Editing. Originally slated to be shot in color, the nervous studio cut the budget (two days before shooting began), and the film had to be made in black and white (although the film's title has been colored red). The black and white photography may have worked to director Douglas' advantage, as he manages to build an impressively stark and eerie atmosphere. Beginning the film in the wind-scoured desert landscape, Douglas proceeds to fill the screen with intriguing elements—the girl found in a near catatonic state, the ruined camper and store, a mutilated body, the strange noises carried on the wind. To add to the suspense, the script doesn't reveal the ants until nearly halfway through and when we finally do see them, we only half glimpse the creatures during a desert storm. (The ants were achieved with full-size mechanical models, and their screeching cries and fierce jaw-pincers combine to create an unsettling nemesis for their human foes.)

Them! was also scheduled to be released in 3-D, though this idea was eventually scrapped for budgetary reasons as well. Some obvious elements of the 3-D effects, such as the ants having extreme closeups and filming the flamethrowers shooting straight into the camera lens, still remain evident. If audiences watch closely they will see cameo appearances by Leonard Nimoy (*Star Trek*), playing an Air Force Sergeant, and Fess Parker (*Daniel Boone*), playing Alan Crotty, who has the unfortunate experience of sighting ant-shaped UFOs. He's left in the mental hospital as a deranged psychotic, as per the suggestion put to his doctor by the FBI. Is this the prototype for the poor innocent caught in a cover-up?

Often considered the best big-bug movie ever made, the film served as the inspiration for many "nuclear monster" movies to come, and spawned countless imitators. *Them!* essentially charted out a common blueprint for the formulas the imitators would follow—the staunch military defenders of law and order, the technical assistance from a scientist savant, and the mutated monsters heading for a major civilian area wreaking mass destruction in their wake. *Them!* introduced the 1950s to its singular obsession with rampaging atomically revived and/or mutated monsters. The genre would soon run the gamut with a plethora of mutated creatures, including *It Came from Beneath the Sea* (1955), *Tarantula* (1955), *The Deadly Mantis*, *The Monster That Challenged the World*, *The Black Scorpion*, *Beginning of the End*, *Attack of the Crab Monsters* (all 1957), and *Attack of the Giant Leeches* (1959), just to name a few.

Even today we can still see its influence on modern monster movies. From the storm-drain sequence in 1991's *Terminator 2* to the modern big-bug movies *Starship Troopers* (1997) and *Eight Legged Freaks* (2002), all pay homage in one way or another to *Them!* It obviously had a big influence on James Cameron's *Aliens* (1986) as well. (Witness the catatonic little girl holding her broken doll, the underground battles with the monsters, flamethrowers burning up the nest, etc.)

One of the great things about the ever-growing DVD market is that it allows these classic films to be available for home viewing right along with the current blockbusters. Recently, releases of those great little sci-fi flicks that I enjoyed as a child have become plentiful, the very films that began my life-long enjoyment of movies. I have fond memories of those childhood days spent watching every sci-fi/horror flick on TV, and *Them!* is right up there at the top of the list. From the catatonic little girl waking up and screaming "Them! Them!" to the horrific death of Sgt. Ben Peterson and the tense claustrophobic firefight in the sewers of L.A., it's the perfect blend of horror and humor, action and drama, all of which holds the viewer's attention until the climactic ending. I've watched this movie over and over and never tired of it.

The 1950s was the decade where science fiction movies reigned supreme and *Them!* is definitely a classic from that period. One might think that a movie made more than 50 years ago would seem positively antique by today's standards, but *Them!* holds up remarkably well. One of the most influential films of its time, it deals with fears of the atomic age and the "what if" scenario of how our continued testing and use of nuclear arms would affect Mother Nature. This is essential viewing and a worthy addition to anyone's collection.

THE THING FROM ANOTHER WORLD (1951)
THE THING (1982)
by James Blackford

The premise of the short story "Who Goes There?" by science fiction author John W. Campbell Jr. (originally written under the pen name Don A. Stuart) screams cinematic potential. It's a gruesome tale in which a group of researchers in the Antarctic happen across an alien spaceship that has been buried in the ice for a few million years. Ecstatic with their new find, the intrepid scientists set to thawing out the alien vessel and having a poke around inside. Unfortunately, in all the excitement, they fail to consider the risks involved in their bold behavior. Lo and behold, the ship turns out to be occupied by a

The Thing (James Arness) is electrocuted into oblivion by the military.

hideous, malevolent extraterrestrial capable of assuming the shape of any lifeform it consumes and hellbent on wreaking havoc the world over…

Unsurprisingly, such great monster movie fodder was not left untouched by Hollywood producers. Campbell's pulp classic has more than lived up to its potential by providing fans with two bonafide classics of the sci-fi/horror genre.

In 1951, Howard Hawks presided over the first adaptation for RKO Pictures, entitled *The Thing from Another World*, which deviated markedly from its source material. Rather than a shape-shifting alien creature, The Thing (played by James Arness) is presented as a monstrous hybrid of human and vegetable that must feed on blood to survive. Although Hawks' long time editor Christian Nyby is officially credited as director, it has widely been acknowledged (even by Nyby) that Hawks oversaw the day-to-day shooting.

Thirty years later, cult horror director John Carpenter gave us his interpretation of Campbell's story, dubbed simply *The Thing*. In spite of his admitted affection for the Hawks' film, Carpenter chose to stay closer to the source material; in the remake, as in the original text, the menace is a merciless, ever-evolving monstrosity that infiltrates the base causing hysteria, paranoia, and death. Carpenter also explored considerably more explicit horror terrain than the '51 model, employing hardcore splatter and animatronic special effects to show the alien in its spectacular throes of metamorphosis.

In examining what makes both versions of *The Thing* classics of the horror genre, I have avoided making the following analysis and comparison evaluative. It seems pointless and unfair to make qualitative judgments when comparing two films from such diverse eras, especially when they approach the subject matter so differently. For contemporary audiences, Carpenter's effort—with its superior visual effects and more realistic acting—will probably seem scarier and more effective. However, not only was Hawks working in a vastly different industrial context in 1951 with far less technology at his disposal, he was approaching the Campbell story with different aims. Therefore, I have focused instead on three key elements that will give significant insight into both the cinematic *form* and thematic/intellectual *content* of each individual film, while also illuminating the differences and similarities of both.

With regards to film form and visual style, *The Thing from Another World* adheres to the conventions of "classical Hollywood realist representation." In the archetypical classical text, dialogue tends to drive the narrative and shape the picture's meaning while "film style" (the shots, editing, and *mise-en-scene*) act as a secondary element, one that reinforces the narrative, giving it a spatial and temporal context. In the Hawks film there is no attempt to create an explicit visual aesthetic; instead the formal qualities are governed by the demands of the story. The viewer is invited to become immersed in the world of the story without consciously reflecting on the formal construction of the images and representation of space.

The opening sequence of the '51 *Thing* serves as a fine example of these formal conventions at work. We see a clear example of classical Hollywood narration: An establishing medium shot (a building with a sign above the doors reading "Officers Club: Anchorage, Alaska") introduces the "world" space, within which a series of closer static shots are cut together. In this mode of classical cinematic representation, film style and editing become almost invisible, encouraging total unconscious immersion in the film-text without reflection on the formal properties of the sequence.

The Thing from Another World was made in an entirely different era of cinema from *The Thing*. If the former is to be viewed as a fine example of classical Hollywood realist narration and style, then the latter must be considered in its post-classical, post "New Hollywood" context. By 1982, Hollywood films could be more explicitly stylized, allowing directors more freedom to create a visual aesthetic. Also, technical advancements (such as the Steadicam) meant that cameras could be more mobile. Consequently we see a much freer, faster editing technique, as well as a wider variety of camera angles and elaborate set design. While the remake does utilize the classical mode of storytelling with a dialogue-driven narrative, it is built primarily around set pieces, in which film style becomes a more prominent means of signifying causality and creating meaning. For example, think of the lengthy sequence in which MacReady (Kurt Russell) and Dr. Copper (Richard Dysart) explore the Norwegian's burnt-out camp. There is little dialogue; instead, the sequence is narrated solely with images and Ennio Morricone's music: A uniquely cinematic means of communication through purely visual and aural means—a flowing mode of narration freed from the spoken word.

Although the later film diverges from its precursor in many respects, Carpenter shows his admiration by paying homage to several of the original production's most memorable images. For starters, the opening titles, in which the words "The Thing" appear to burn onto the screen, are a careful recreation of the effect used in the original's credits. Also, when MacReady's group watch the video recording of the Norwegians discovering the alien vessel, the onscreen images of the men encircling the frozen saucer strongly recall similar shots from the Hawks film.

In terms of narrative and thematic content, *The Thing from Another World* and *The Thing* also occupy considerably different realms. While the former is ostensibly a sci-fi/horror film, it deals with the horror elements of the narrative in a self-consciously perfunctory way; the main protagonists seem barely flustered by the presence of the alien monster which itself occupies little screen time. Instead, the director seems more interested in the symbolic possibilities of the narrative. Hawks posits the alien characteristics of the Thing—an asexual "intellectual carrot" totally devoid of all emotions—against the intuitive male group (and its lone female) bonded by pragmatism, mutual respect, and solidarity (the director's usual thematic trope). In the narrative, the "primitive" human values of respect, humanity, and camaraderie overcome the alien's inhuman intellectualism. There is a clear opposition between a positive value system represented by the military and led by Captain Hendry (Kenneth Tobey) against the dangerous values of progress, intellectualism, and scientific inquiry represented in human form by Dr. Carrington (Robert Cornthwaite) and in alien form by the Thing itself.

Such symbolism of course betrays a reactionary ideology when considered in light of the socio-political context of 1950s America's phobia of Communism. The alien is presented as a horrific "other," a dangerous threat to the values of the American home while Dr. Carrington, the human representation of intellectualism, is depicted as a dangerous liberal, inhuman and foolish in his attempts to communicate with the Thing. The positive American values of rugged individualism, pragmatism, and camaraderie succeed in fending off the impending threat. Normality is restored by the film's conclusion, which ends with a call to arms for all Americans to be on guard against the alien (i.e. Communist) threat, courtesy of Scotty's famous broadcast to "keep watching the skies."

In *The Thing,* Carpenter is concerned with an entirely different set of narrative and thematic possibilities. Most obviously, the remake stresses the horror elements that the Hawks film downplays, in particular gruesome special effects and gore. Carpenter reveals an obsession with corporeality and physical mutability, to the extent that the violent special effects structure the rhythm of his film—the spectacle of gore and the corruption of the body become the main thematic thrust of narrative. The bloodshed is lovingly filmed with an unflinching camera; it seems the director demands that the viewer be both disgusted by what he shows and amazed by the craftsmanship involved in mounting such cinematic brutality. Certainly, the extremities of Rob Bottin's gruesome special effects are what many viewers remember the film for.

Carpenter also diverges from his forbearer's model with regard to his depiction of the Antarctic troupe. Hawks depicted a harmonious, self-reliant community bonded by a shared ideology and united (with the exception of the vilified Dr. Carrington) in the fight against the invasive enemy. The update, on the other hand, portrays the team as a community of isolated, dope-smoking misfits incapable of communicating with one another. MacReady, the "hero," is an alcoholic loner who for reasons of self-preservation assumes the role of reluctant leader—against the will of his colleagues.

In Hawks' version the alien is always external; it resides outside of the group and the security and stability that the group represents. By contrast, the alien is *internal* to the group in the later film; it is the source of its paranoia and the reason for the group's disintegration. Rather than an outside threat, alien to the self, the Thing becomes a signifier for everything that threatens the integrity of the self from within. For Carpenter, the Thing represents our own paranoia, our own unconscious desires, and our own fragility.

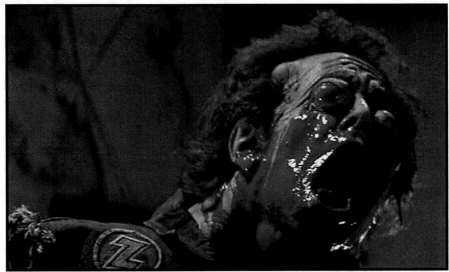

Rob Bottin's special effects highlight John Carpenter's *The Thing.*

Bearing these aspects in mind, we can deduce that the '82 film betrays an ideology quite at odds with the elder model. While *The Thing from Another World* implies a credo focused on an idealized America built upon the principles of respect, humanity, and camaraderie, the remake offers a bleak vision where this idealized force for good is fractured and failing. The latter picture can be seen as a nihilistic critique of the reactionary ideology of the original; America is not idealized but rather is a society in conflict and crisis. Crucial to this nihilism is the dark and ambiguous conclusion in which MacReady is left to freeze to death while the Thing quite possibly lives on. Normality is not restored. Everything is not okay.

In their own ways, both *The Thing from Another World* and *The Thing* are firmly established as genre classics. But largely, the films find favor with different audience demographics. Despite its lowbrow cultural signifiers (sci-fi picture, monster movie), *The Thing from Another World* has garnered acclaim from mainstream critics and film scholars, perhaps largely due to its association with Hawks—one of the key classical Hollywood auteurs. In fact, the film quite literally entered the official canon of all-time classics in 2001 when the U.S. Library of Congress deemed it "culturally significant" and selected it for preservation in the National Film Registry. *The Thing*, on the other hand, has to some extent been disregarded by the mainstream critics, earning its cult status among a younger audience of gorehounds impressed by Bottin's visceral special effects.

This pervading attitude of cultural significance goes some way towards explaining the vastly different contexts within which I initially encountered the two pictures. I first saw *The Thing* as a young teenager, hungry for the sensationalist thrills that a salacious gory cult classic could offer. I rented out a beaten-up copy from the local video library, turned the lights down, and prepared to be grossed out and entertained. I was after a forbidden fruit—an *"objet d'gore,"* if you will—and Carpenter's flick certainly delivered. Several years later, as a young man attending a Film Studies course at university, I saw *The Thing from Another World* as part of a Howard Hawks retrospective. It was introduced and discussed by scholars—authorities on Hawks—in attendance. Within this context, the 1951 movie was unashamedly presented as a "work of art"—worthy of close analysis and created by one of the geniuses of the Hollywood system. Of course, *The Thing from Another World* has not *always* been held in such high esteem; its cultural meaning and value has changed with the passing of time and the changing of the critical landscape. However, at the time of this writing, mainstream critics and scholars alike still largely hold the original effort in higher esteem than they do the remake.

Personally, as a horror fan and someone who takes a critical stance when watching film, I believe it unfair that, in some quarters, *The Thing* resides in the shadow of its precursor. Carpenter's effort succeeds in different ways, on different levels—it works as a visceral, exciting horror film with awe-inspiring visual effects that still impress (and repulse) today. I find myself asking the question, have critics dismissed the more "modern" offering merely because of its lowbrow subject matter, its apparent sensationalism? Perhaps the grotesqueness of the remake, its unashamed wallowing in lowbrow gore, proved too much of an affront to critics and scholars bound to fairly bourgeois notions of taste and value. Certainly it is the more conservative/elitist schools of film-thought that have found Carpenter's film less satisfactory, namely broadsheet reviewers, academics—those who carry "cultural capital" and shape the canon. Genre enthusiasts and gorehounds have loved the film for years. To quote Robin Wood, "What the critic demands, as at least a precondition to according a film serious attention, is not so much evidence of a genuine creative impulse…as a set of external signifiers that advertise the film as a 'work of art'."

Historically, such elitist distinctions of taste have ensured the canonisation of "respectable" forms of culture and the dismissal of so-called disreputable "low" culture. Rather than the earlier film being far superior than the remake, it seems more likely that, the "politics of taste" have led to the canonization of *The Thing from Another World* and the neglect of *The Thing* among mainstream critics and so-called scholars. But I say, who needs taste anyway? In my eyes, if horror fans avoid "their" standards of accomplishment and value and hold true to our own, then we're doing all right. Those of us who truly appreciate horror cinema (a culture outside of the boring, homogenized world of "legitimate" culture) know this. We have our own code of accomplishment and significance, and by those standards, both *Thing*s stand shoulder to shoulder—giants of the sci-fi/horror canon.

THE UNINVITED (1944)
by Craig G. Watson

On the bleak and wave-battered cliffs of England's Cornish coast stands an old Georgian house. The empty windows stare out into the cold, gray Atlantic and gulls circle above, cutting the air with mournful cries. No one has lived in the house for many years, for it was once the scene of a terrible tragedy—an event so powerful that the restless spirits of those involved still linger to this day. In the nearby village, the locals know the house as "Cliff End," but few know of the unseen things that walk its dusty rooms, waiting to drive away uninvited guests.

Such was the captivating locale created by Irish writer and historian Dorothy Mac-Ardle in her 1941 novel *Uneasy Freehold*. The novel soon found its way to America

Stella (Gail Russell) and Rick Fitzgerald (Ray Milland)

where it was re-titled *The Uninvited*. In 1944, three years after the book's release, the story found its way to the screen under the wing of director Lewis Allen. In the movie adaptation, the house once known as "Cliff End" became the enchanting "Windward."

Although the movie wasn't a huge success at the time of release, today *The Uninvited* is widely recognized as a classic in its own right, one of the first serious attempts by Hollywood to portray a haunted house on the silver screen.

The plot involves a young businessman and aspiring musician by the name of Rick Fitzgerald and his sister Pamela. One morning while taking their dog Bobby for a walk along the peaceful Cornish beaches, the pair stumble upon the deserted Windward house and are immediately captivated by it. Pamela soon convinces her brother that they should buy the property and retire for a simpler life on the coast.

The house belongs to the stiff old Commander Beech who lives in the nearby village with his naive and beautiful granddaughter, Stella Meredith. With some reluctance the Commander sells the house to the Fitzgeralds and they move in with their strict but jovial housekeeper, Lizzie Flynn. This is when the fun really begins, for it seems that there are other occupants of Windward house intent on causing sleepless nights.

The first signs of the haunting are mild enough: the Fitzgeralds are awoken in the middle of the night by the mournful, disembodied sound of a woman crying from somewhere in the house; the floral scent of mimosa lingers in the air and the old painting studio, with its broad vista of the Atlantic, always seems cold and oppressive. Even the dog refuses to ascend the stairs and eventually runs away altogether.

These innocent phenomena take a much more sinister turn when Rick develops a blossoming romance with Stella Meredith. Windward house formerly belonged to Stella's mother, Mary Meredith, and a tragic history of jealousy, betrayal, and murder seems to be the cause of the troubled spirits that linger there. Rick realizes that the restless souls will never be finished with Stella until the dark history of the house is uncovered and old grievances are put to rest.

Here, in the clever unraveling of the house's history, lies the strength of *The Uninvited*. The viewer is whisked along with the Fitzgeralds' excitement as they uncover the mystery, but the script always seems to be one step ahead—delightfully revealing new twists and turns with each scene. The threads of the plot are intricately woven by screenwriter Dodie Smith. Add a haunting background score by Victor Young (whose theme for *The Uninvited*—"Stella by Starlight"—has become a favorite composition among pianists worldwide) and we have all the elements for a supernatural classic.

The final ingredient for the success of *The Uninvited* comes from great performances by the cast. Ray Milland is charming and hilariously self-deprecating as Rick (Milland went on to win the Best Actor Academy Award in 1945 for *The Lost Weekend*). Ruth Hussey is convincing as his well-grounded sister Pamela, and Cornelia Otis Skinner is sinister and enthralling as the secretive Miss Holloway.

But above all, it is the luminous Gail Russell as Stella Meredith who steals the show and the viewers' hearts. In a tragic twist, shortly after the filming *The Uninvited*, Russell spiraled down into addictive alcoholism from which she never recovered. Fueled by studio pressures and a terrible stage fright that seemed to be calmed only by drinking, she died of alcohol-related illness in August 1961. She was just 36 years of age.

I first watched *The Uninvited* in the bright, sunlit living room of my home in North Carolina, with my cat avidly watching birds through the window and the groundskeeper running a gas-powered hedge-trimmer nearby—admittedly not the best setting in which to enjoy a ghost story. I was already a jaded veteran of countless ghost movies and an aspiring writer, so I knew all the literary tricks and plot-devices of haunted house movies. It was going to take a lot to satisfy me.

But as *The Uninvited* played I felt a certain growing delight. As the characters travel through the light-hearted days and uneasy nights in Windward house, I began to realize that despite its shadows and thick atmosphere, *The Uninvited* is at heart a *feel good* movie. It offers up scares and comfort in equal measure. The dialogue is sharp and witty, the special effects are reticent but impressive, and the story unfolds to a neat and charming resolution.

As the end credits rolled after that first viewing, I caught myself smiling. Unlike modern horror movies—which seem bent on leaving the viewer feeling somehow dirty and depressed—*The Uninvited* left me feeling as sunny inside as the day was outside. Even today, after many more viewings, it still leaves me feeling joyful.

I'm not the only one whose life *The Uninvited* has touched in this way. Wherever one finds mention of the movie, praise abounds. The Windward house has found its way into the heart of many a horror movie fan and *The Uninvited* has secured its rightful place as one of the most popular ghost stories ever to appear on the silver screen.

VIDEODROME (1983)
by Dave Kosanke

James Woods is Max Renn, who works for independent cable station Civic TV. He seeks out some softcore pornography as a possible acquisition, but isn't satisfied. "It's soft. I'm looking for something that will break through…something *tough*."

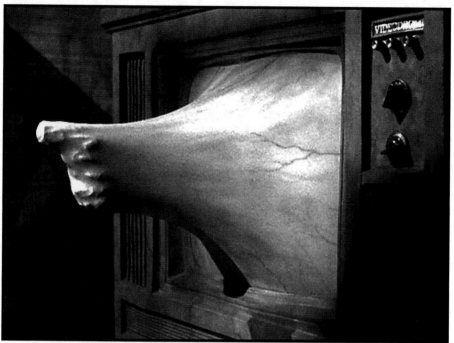
Tumors create video hallucinations of the new flesh.

He finds the answer with Videodrome, via a weak satellite signal broadcast from Malaysia (as we are initially led to believe) courtesy of his co-worker Harlan (Peter Dvorsky). Videodrome presents nothing but scenes of sadistic torture and violence. Renn becomes obsessed, to the point where he starts hallucinating. The signal generates tumors in his brain, which turn him into a literal killing machine. He soon comes into contact with Spectacular Optical, headed by Barry Convex (Les Carlson), who wants Videodrome to introduce the world to the "new flesh." Max Renn will become the first to see the operation through to the end.

Videodrome is a complex, multi-layered journey through one man's vision of a (possible) future. Unleashed in 1983 on an unsuspecting public, David Cronenberg's film challenged audiences and critics alike. Based upon an old story Cronenberg had gestating entitled "Network of Blood," it became (pardon the pun) fleshed out when he decided to take the concept further as a one-person-perspective film. That perspective belongs to Max Renn, who changes before our very eyes (along with the characters around him). In an interview with *Fangoria*'s David Everitt, Cronenberg stated, "I had always wanted to make a movie that is subjective, in the sense of a first person movie. As Max's reality changes, the reality on the screen changes, with no shift of vision." This unique ploy certainly helped confuse audience members not used to such devious techniques, especially within the confines of horror cinema. As a teenager, I myself was caught off guard on my initial viewing of *Videodrome* on cable TV (considering the themes raised within the film itself, seeing it on cable or videocassette seemed ideal—even over theatrical screenings).

With the passing of time, the messages and themes presented within the film seem to resonate even stronger in the two decades since its release. Today's fickle TV audience does demand more, something "tougher," perhaps best exemplified on the reality TV shows and other types of "entertainment" such as *Fear Factor* that push the limit of taste to the extreme. Cinema itself has become harder lately, nowhere more evident than within the horror genre's newfound love of "torture movies." The basic gist of *Videodrome* lies specifically within the context of the snuff film: violence and murder being filmed for real. The snuff idea was originally born out of the Manson family crimes of 1969 when stories persisted of them filming some of their heinous murders. This idea (naturally) trickled into the film world, and horror movies were fertile ground for this type of lurid material, be it with inferior junk like *Snuff* (1976) or superior efforts like *Cannibal Holocaust* (1980). Even the mainstream world has dabbled in the snuff subject matter with *52 Pick-Up* (1986) and *8MM* (1999), albeit with decidedly mixed results.

The suggestion that TV can physically transform us into fleshy, murderous beings programmed like a videocassette (just open us up, insert tape, and press Play) certainly has it origins planted firmly in David Cronenberg's brain. His theme of "body politics" has been evident in basically everything he has done (with 1977's *Fast Company* the biggest stretch), especially prior to *Videodrome* where his track record reads as follows: *Shivers* (later retitled *They Came from Within* for the U.S. [1975]), *Rabid* (1977), *The Brood* (1979), and *Scanners* (1981). The idea of *internal*, rather than external, horror would prove to be a Cronenberg standard. Max Renn's search for harsh material could also reflect some horror fans who become dissatisfied with current tastes and decide to delve deeper within the genre to get their next fix of over-the-top violence, sex, and/or gore.

Clearly *Videodrome* has so much going for it story-wise, the ideas presented within its 89 minutes (uncut version) could fuel a dozen or so other films. It is to Cronenberg's credit that the film never becomes too bogged down under its own weight, managing to confound and delight viewers at every turn. Cronenberg states, "I don't mind ambivalence or ambiguity in a film—in fact, I think it's necessary—but confusion is never necessary." ("The Image as Virus," Tim Lucas, excerpted from *The Shape of Rage: The Films of David Cronenberg*).

While the gripping screenplay by Cronenberg is the fuel, the fire comes from the excellent cast who play out the actions rather convincingly. James Woods is wonderful as Max Renn, giving the character the right amount of naiveté, determination, and edginess so that we don't ever feel disconnected from him, but rather *become him,* since the film is viewed from his perspective. Debbie Harry (lead singer of Blondie) comes up a winner as Max's desire of obsession, Nikki Brand, who succumbs to the Videodrome signal as well. Her character was so vital to preview audiences, who felt her abrupt disappearance from the film was a mistake, Cronenberg shot additional scenes with her, culminating in the powerful climax where Max sees her image on a television set as she instructs him in the ways of the new flesh.

Videodrome would be hard to duplicate or even emulate within the horror genre, so it should come as no surprise that no single vision since has even come close to Cronenberg's. In fact, it is safe to say that Cronenberg himself is a genre, dubbed "Cronenbergian" by some for lack of a better word. Incidentally, perhaps because of *Videodrome*'s excessive weirdness (and/or failure at the box office), Cronenberg would next choose to delve into the works of other screenwriters. His immediate follow-ups, in the form of Jeffrey Boam's adaptation of Stephen King's *The Dead Zone* (1983), followed by the 1986 remake of *The Fly* (for which Cronenberg would share a screenplay credit with Charles Edward Pogue), cemented the Canadian director into the mainstream consciousness.

Faced with spectacular visions (realized by f/x whiz kids Rick Baker, Bill Sturgeon, and Steve Johnson) such as cancerous tumors causing a man's head to crumble internally, a grotesque fleshy hand gun, a globular television set that can be plunged into, and yet another cathode ray tube riddled with human viscera, the viewer isn't being exposed to the normal cookie cutter horror hokum. It is precisely this type of confrontational experience that renders *Videodrome* a true anomaly in the paradox of the horror film. In fact, simply labeling it horror seems a disservice, since it crosses too many boundaries to belong to any one genre. All too often these searing visions are kept under lock and key by fearful studios worried that they won't make a profit from such head-scratching ideas. I give Universal Studios all the praise in the world for daring to take on such an oddball film as *Videodrome*. Too many people tend to look down on the more adventurous productions that go before the light of a projector, but for every 25 embarrassments, to be able to witness and experience *one* golden gem like *Videodrome* makes it all worth it.

VILLAGE OF THE DAMNED (1960)
by Mark Allan Gunnells

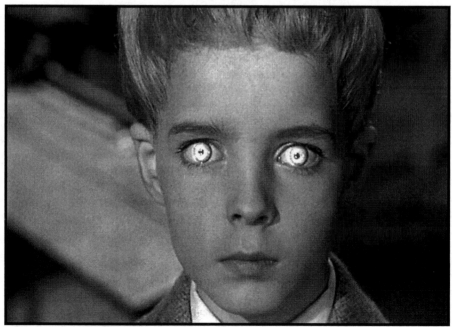

David (Martin Stephens), the leader of the alien children

I am afraid of children.

It's not a typical phobia—I'm not even sure if the APA has a term for it—but it is one I have suffered from all my adult life. Children seem incomprehensible to me, strange creatures whose thoughts and motivations are a complete mystery. I sometimes suspect that parents, though they do not talk about it, look at their children with a mixture of affection and distrust. After all, children are little strangers that have come into their parents' homes. Despite the fact that you raise a child, you can never really have control over who (or what) that child will become.

In this age of "family values" rhetoric, my views on the matter of children may be unpopular and somewhat treasonous, but I do not believe that I am alone. If we look at the history of film over the years, we'll see that the theme of children-as-instruments-of-evil is one that has been often explored. From *The Bad Seed* (1956) to *The Exorcist* (1973) to *The Omen* (1976) to *Children of the Corn* (1984), the "evil child" has long been a staple of the horror genre.

One of the best examples of this subgenre is *Village of the Damned*, director Wolf Rilla's adaptation of John Wyndam's novel, *The Midwich Cuckoos* (1957). Produced in 1960, with a terrific script by Rilla, Stirling Silliphant, and producer Ronald Kinnoch (as George Barclay), *Village of the Damned* is a superb exercise in fear and oppression. In the way of good fiction, the movie uses fantasy elements and extreme situations to perfectly capture everything about children that makes me uneasy when I'm asked to baby-sit for friends and family.

The film opens with an establishing shot of the peaceful village of Midwich. It is not an extended shot, nothing that overstays its welcome. It's just a quick glimpse to establish the very bucolic normalcy of the place before introducing the more otherworldly elements of the story.

It doesn't take long for the bizarre and unearthly to start invading the quiet village. The citizens of Midwich have their routine existence interrupted when everyone in the village suddenly loses consciousness. In the midst of day-to-day activities—making phone calls, ironing the laundry, cleaning house, working—everyone simply falls down into a deep sleep.

This unusual occurrence might have gone undetected by the rest of the world except that Professor Gordon Zellaby (the excellent George Sanders) passes out while on the phone with his brother-in-law, Major Alan Bernard (Michael Gwynn), abruptly cutting off their conversation in mid-sentence. Bernard, worried about his inability to reconnect with his sister's husband, decides to go to Midwich to check on things. What he discovers is that no one can enter the village's town limits without falling into a coma. The military sends out officers and scientists in an attempt to discern what is causing the phenomenon, but while they are all still struggling for an explanation, everyone in Midwich simply wakes up.

And that's when the real fun begins.

Some months later, life in Midwich having returned to normal, Gordon's wife Anthea (Hammer veteran Barbara Shelley) gives her husband some good news: they are going to have a child. However, Gordon quickly realizes that things are not as happy as they seem when he discovers from Dr. Willers (Laurence Naismith) that a lot of other women in the town are also pregnant. In fact, *all* the women in the village that are capable of becoming pregnant are pregnant.

This is the point when the film really begins to use its supernatural storyline as a metaphor for some real fears. The husband of one of the pregnant women has just returned from an extended stay overseas, which means he cannot possibly be the father of the child. His wife insists there has been no other, and yet the fact of her pregnancy remains, as indisputable as it is inexplicable.

There is a saying that goes, "How do you know who your father is? Because your mother told you so." In a day and age when men often raise children only to find out years later that they are not the biological fathers, the concerns explored in *Village of the Damned* seem more relevant than ever. I suspect that many men look at their children with a nagging voice in the back of their minds saying, "Is it really mine?" Sometimes these fears are baseless, other times not, but the fear is there all the same.

In the film, Anthea becomes distraught when she learns that the child she carries is probably not the result of her and her husband's love for one another. A young girl, who swears she is a virgin, attempts suicide. Watching this portion of the film, I could not help but think of the plight of women who conceive a child through an act of rape. They have a living being inside of them, a being that is connected to them in the most intimate way, and yet they also carry the knowledge that the child was created from humiliation, violence and pain, which means in some ways the child will always be a reminder of a traumatic experience. Can a woman truly love a child that reminds her of the worst moment of her life?

After the Midwich children are born, they grow rapidly. They are all similar in appearance and demeanor. White-haired with strange eyes, they are oddly detached and emotionless, possessing seemingly unlimited intelligence. It also becomes apparent early on that they are capable of things which human children should not be. They possess the ability to read people's minds and to control people's actions.

Anthea attempts to make an emotional connection with her son David (a commanding performance by young Martin Stephens), but he resists, treating her with chilly indifference. This causes Anthea much pain. I would imagine many parents feel rejected by their offspring, especially when they hit their teenage years. Children often rebel and pull away from their parents, shunning familial affection. This can leave parents feeling as if they don't know their own children.

Eventually the youngsters of *Village of the Damned* begin using their powers to commit murder. A motorist who almost runs over one of the clan is forced to drive his car into a wall. The brother of the motorist plans to kill the children, but is instead forced to shoot himself. The military is ready to take action, but Gordon convinces them to isolate the alien youth and allow him to try to teach them proper human behavior. This attempt ultimately fails in the most explosive manner. The final scenes, with Gordon struggling to maintain the image of a brick wall in his mind as the children try to break it down, are intense and exciting yet stunning in their simplicity.

I would imagine that parents of delinquent and criminal juveniles often feel helpless in the face of their offspring's behavior. It is a common misperception that young people who commit crimes come from parents that are either neglectful or criminal themselves, but that is not always the case. Sometimes criminals come from good homes with decent parents. What sends these children down the wrong path is anyone's guess, but I believe parents of these types of children must fear their own progeny.

A huge hit upon its release, an inevitable sequel appeared three years later. *Children of the Damned* (1963) revisits similar terrain, and while an effective thriller, it doesn't come close to the impact of the original. And the less said about John Carpenter's pointless 1995 remake, the better.

Village of the Damned stands out to me as a classic horror film not just because of its well-executed chills and eerie atmosphere, but because there is a deeper truth that lies below the surface. To me, what separates a good horror film from a great horror film is the ability to reflect society's fears through a veneer of fantasy. I believe *Village of the Damned* manages this splendidly. It takes parents' worst nightmares and places them in the safe confines of fiction.

When I sit down and pop *Village of the Damned* in the player, I can enjoy it for the expertly crafted film it is, but I am also aware that the film is feeding my phobia.

I am afraid of children.

WAR OF THE WORLDS (1953)
by Cheryl Melville

The 1950s definitely served as a golden feast for science fiction on the silver screen, and *War of the Worlds* is deservedly among the elite on any list of luminary cinematic efforts. Audiences lapped up all the monsters, aliens, and disaster films Hollywood was prepared to produce. By the latter half of the decade, there was an overflow of second-rate and oftentimes downright silly beasties menacing drive-ins everywhere. However, prior to the flood, there were quite a few notable films unveiled, including *The Day the Earth Stood Still* (1951), *When Worlds Collide* (1951), and *This Island Earth* (1955). Joining these jewels in the sci-fi crown is this mini-epic by director Byron Haskin and legendary producer George Pal, which took audiences by storm and sealed its popularity in the genre. With a budget of only $2,000,000, a mere $600,000 was spent on the live-action scenes. The remaining funds were spent on the extensive and elaborate special effects overseen by Gordon Jennings, who was ultimately rewarded with an Academy Award for his team's efforts. (The film also scored nominations for Film Editing and Sound).

Orson Welles shocked listeners back in 1938 with his Halloween radio broadcast about aliens attacking the earth. Panic swept the nation when rapt listening audiences took the radio drama, styled as a series of news bulletins, for the real article. In 1953, after earlier stalled attempts by Cecil B. DeMille and Alfred Hitchcock, *War of the Worlds* hit the big screen and filmgoers were awed by what they saw. The thrilling storyline gleaned from H.G. Wells' novel (updated from its Victorian setting to the then-modern day setting of the Cold War '50s) and the screenwriting talents of Barré Lyndon combined to bring the story to the screen in an intelligent and concise fashion.

War of the Worlds opens calmly enough with the dulcet-toned narration of veteran actor Sir Cedric Hardwicke introducing the audience to the underlying plot: Mars has always fascinated mankind and back in Roman days Mars was hailed as the God of War.

Following this, we are witness to a meteorite crashing to earth one starry evening near a small township outside Los Angeles. (Note: This is the first motion picture to film on the newly completed Harbor Freeway in L.A. known as "The Stack" before it opened in 1953.) Curious spectators who witness the event set out to investigate what has dropped from the sky. The next night, the so-called meteorite begins to take on a life of its own; instead of a dormant piece of rock from space, the visitors quickly reveal their true identity. These are nothing less than invincible war machines from

The swan-like Martian ship wreaks havoc on the helpless humans below.

Mars, intent on eradicating everything in their paths with devastating death rays. (The ray's onscreen effects were accomplished by double-exposing the sparks from burning welding wire.) No mortal weaponry can match the ingenuity of the Martians' technical superiority. The military is defenseless, with even a last-ditch atomic bomb failing to have any effect on the extraterrestrial interlopers.

Will mankind survive an all-out attack from creatures from another planet? Finally when all seems lost, and our heroes' fate seems sealed as they cower in the ruins of a church, the bright green swan-like Martian crafts inexplicably begin to plummet earthward. As the bewildered protagonists (as well as we, the bewildered audience members) look on, Hardwicke's reassuring voiceover informs us: "The Martians had no resistance to the bacteria in our atmosphere to which we have long since become immune. Once they had breathed our air, germs, which no longer affect us, began to kill them. The end came swiftly. All over the world, their machines began to stop and fall. After all that men could do had failed, the Martians were destroyed and humanity was saved by the littlest things, which God, in His wisdom, had put upon this Earth." The human race is once again safe…for now.

However, part of the film's lasting impact is that it does not only concern itself with invasion issues, but more importantly, it boldly dares to question human creation and its worth. Witness a memorable exchange between Pastor Dr. Matthew Collins (Lewis Martin) and his niece Sylvia Van Buren (Ann Robinson) just before he takes a fateful walk to greet the Martians:

> Pastor: I think we have to try and make them understand we mean them no harm. They're living creatures out there.
> Sylvia: They're not human. Dr. Forrester says they're some kind of advanced civilization.
> Pastor: If they're more advanced than us, they should be nearer to the Creator for that reason.

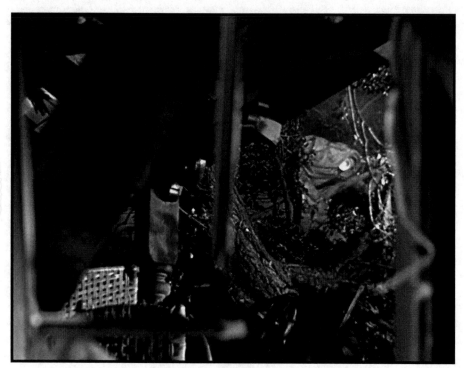
A Martian monster appears lurking at the farmhouse.

War of the Worlds hits pitch-perfect marks in practically every department: production, acting, effects, script, and so on. The gorgeous Technicolor adds dramatically to the film's overall style. One can hardly imagine watching it in black and white, as the stunning visuals by Jennings and cinematographer George Burns would be lost. Another aspect that deserves to be pointed out is the streamlined continuity of the plot, with everything falling cohesively into place. Rather than boring scenes of exposition leading up to the action, Lyndon's script allows the onscreen chaos to develop the characters for us. Haskin's direction captivates the audience's utmost attention, leading to the ultimate success of the production. From the onset, the film's pace is such that I didn't dare take my eyes off the screen. *War of the Worlds* has stayed in my memory since the first time I watched it.

In addition to the breathtaking visuals, the film packs a sonic impact as well. The memorable hum of the Martian ships was created by recording three electric guitars, then playing the tape backward. The vulnerable three-eyed Martian's screams are the result of a microphone scraping along dry ice combined with a woman's scream played in reverse.

But as any sci-fi fan will say, no true classic survives on glitzy special effects alone. Without a strong human element, this film could not have survived the march of time. Originally, Orson Welles was approached to make an appearance, which he instantly declined. Instead the two main cast members were relative newcomers, Gene Barry and Ann Robinson, who make a very likeable couple. Producer Pal knew he didn't need legitimate "stars," that the real attractions would be his floating weapons of mass destruction. Barry and Robinson's post-*Worlds* appearances were primarily limited to the small screen; by far their most memorable onscreen performances remain *War of the Worlds*. Sharp-eyed fans would see them again (in minor roles) toward the conclusion of Steven Spielberg's 2005 remake.

No science fiction fan's movie collection would be complete without a copy of the original *War of the Worlds*. It's an essential inclusion and a superior movie, one that immediately shows audiences what makes classic sci-fi/horror films so magical and why new generations keep coming back for more.

WESTWORLD (1973)
by Thierry Wybauw

Many film directors throughout the past century have tried to impress audiences with their automatons; machines which, by means of mechanical, pneumatic, hydraulic, or electronic devices, are able to perform acts imitating the human body. We can find many vicious onscreen automatons, droids, cyborgs, and robots going berserk with Fritz Lang's notorious "Maschinian-Mensch" in *Metropolis* (1927), an early example; followed by *The Day the Earth Stood Still* (1951), *Forbidden Planet* (1956), *The Terminator* (1984), *RoboCop* (1987), and *Tetsuo: The Iron Man* (1989), among others. Terrifying killer machines that cannot be stopped…even by those who created them.

From his very early years, Michael Crichton managed to build an impressive resume: Harvard-educated medical doctor, novelist, screenwriter, TV/film producer, and director. Indicative of his background, many of his novels contain a medical or scientific setting and have provided ample cinematic material, including *The Andromeda Strain* (1971), *The Terminal Man* (1974), *Jurassic Park* (1993), and *The Lost World: Jurassic Park* (1997).

In the '70s, Crichton had the idea for a novel called *Westworld*. However, during its development stages, it became clear to him that his story possessed elements that would be better explored in a visual medium and turned it into a screenplay. MGM studios acquisitioned the script and entrusted the production (at a scanty budget of one million dollars) to Crichton. In 1973, Crichton's directorial debut would hit the big screen.

"Delos: The vacation of the future, today." For a mere $1,000 a day, tourists are given access to Delos' complex of three resorts: Westworld, a recreation of the 1880s American frontier, a lawless society filled with guns and action; Romanworld, the lusty, decadent delights of Pompeii, for a traveller who wants to experience the sensual relaxed morality of the Imperial Roman Empire; and Medievalworld, a reconstructed 13th-century Europe, a world of chivalry, combat, and romance.

Chicago businessmen Peter Martin (Richard Benjamin) and John Blane (James Brolin) book a two-week leisure trip into Westworld. In a perfect replica of frontier boondocks, they live out their fantasies, having the time of their lives in saloon fights, bank robberies, quick-draw contests (with gunslinger Yul Brynner, dressed in his *The Magnificent Seven* duds), and even spending the night with the local gin mill harlots. The gimmick is that all of their brawling, six-shooting, dance hall companions, along with the other citizens of the town, are life-sized, state-of-the-art, computer-engineered robots. All are under the safe guidance of a controlled/monitored environment.

But, of course, something goes wrong. And a gun-slinging fantasy becomes a horrifying reality.

Crichton realized from the start that he faced certain challenges. In addition to pre-production difficulties (the full cast for the movie was assembled less than 48 hours before principal shooting commenced), the film's meager financial state became an overshadowing burden. Crichton and his producers discovered that working with such a minimal quantum, it would be impossible to bring their futuristic vision to light, and they requested an additional $250,000 from MGM. Even so, Crichton and crew were forced to economize where possible, resorting to innovative, ingenious solutions.

Art director Herman Blumenthal was given a budget of only $75,000 to create 20 sets, spreading over a mere 200,000 square feet. To prevail over his pecuniary purse, Blumenthal's dexterous mind would be put to the test to accomplish his task; renting and repainting sets, reorganizing decors so they could be used in multiple scenes, etc. For example, one single underground corridor was filmed nine times using six different lighting designs. The medieval stairway, as well as the hotel room, became diversiform in multiple scenes by changing camera-angles. One of Blumenthal's most adroit tricks was the scene involving the hovercraft. Only half the interior was built and later mirrored (via optical printer) to create the illusion of the other half.

With several dozen camera set-ups a day, Crichton and his crew completed filming in less than 30 days. However, the decors and sets never look cheap. On the contrary, they come off rather convincing and the movie itself has a sophisticated look. Reasoning that the onscreen characters represent the imagery of the classic adventure films, Crichton elected to shoot in an orthodox optical style. The direction is steady and aboveboard overall, without fancy camera tricks or angles. As Crichton himself relates, "The strangeness of the story would, in fact, be emphasized by conventional shooting, rather than by a photographic style which kept saying to the viewer: Isn't this odd?"

Within his tight and solid dramatic scenario, Crichton elects not to explicitly explain the true nature of the malfunction, i.e. what causes the androids to run wild. The exact reasons why the androids target their human quarry, or how the androids bypass the safety feature of their guns that prevent them from hurting humans, are never spelled out. Instead, Crichton only offers a typical technology-gone-wild quote (by one of the underground-control technicians): "We aren't dealing with ordinary machines here. These are highly complicated pieces of equipment, almost as complicated as living organisms. In some cases they've been designed by other computers. We don't know exactly how they work!" Additionally, why the control room doors lock shut remains a mystery, as does the resulting humidity problem. Crichton should have perhaps taken a closer look at these vague areas, but he ably distracts his viewers from the tenuous technicalities by focusing on the killer robot scenario. And here, he absolutely delivers the thrills and chills.

Crichton's dialogue cleverly mixes technological jargon with the main characters' comic banter. Brolin's one-liner philosophy after they've spent their night with the local girls-of-pleasures is one for the history books: "Machines are the servant of man." One little sentence that applies both to the terrifying scenario played out onscreen as well as behind the scenes. (*Westworld* was the first feature film to use 2-D computer-generated imagery, today commonly known as CGI. Interestingly, the first use of 3-D CGI is found in its sequel, *Futureworld* [1976], which featured a computer-generated hand and face.)

The soundtrack orchestrated by Fred Karlin ventures occasionally into a creepy surrealistic mood, as heard in the night repair/reorganization scenes, and later during

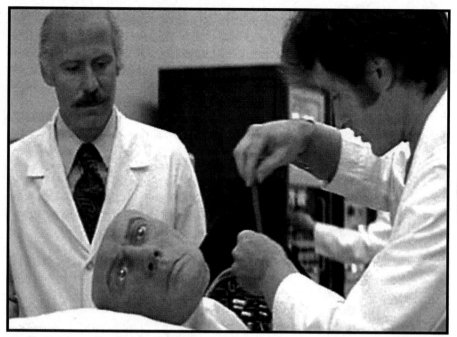

Technicians attend to the Gunslinger's (Yul Brynner) circuit-fried android body.

the Gunslinger's dogged pursuit of his human prey. The alliance of consonance and illumination blend perfectly, building up tension that locks the audience in their seats. By contrast, Karlin also underscores Crichton's homage towards the old Westerns, featuring rollicking country tunes that highlight the comic aspects (the saloon fight is a prime example).

The cast grounds the film's more fantastic elements with credible and well-rounded characters. Brolin and Benjamin seem to having as much fun as kids on a Disneyland rollercoaster, particularly in the first shot of whiskey and saloon fight scenes. Their excitement toward the project reflects onscreen, and it's a pleasure to see how well the duo fit together. Benjamin, primarily known for comedy, might be familiar from his roles in *Love at First Bite* (1979) and *Saturday the 14th* (1981). Brolin, by contrast, has appeared in a host of sci-fi/horror offerings, including *Fantastic Voyage* (1966), *The Boston Strangler* (1968), *The Car* (1977), *Capricorn One* (1978), and *The Amityville Horror* (1979).

However, *Westworld* is dominated by Yul Brynner's presence as the circuit-fried crazy Gunslinger. His solid, steady, and perfectly controlled performance as the ruthless outcast is cold and merciless, hypnotic and flawless. Witness the awe-inspiring first second he steps into the picture. Despite being fitted with painful silver contact lenses, Brynner added the little character trait of not blinking his eyes once throughout the whole movie, collaborating with Crichton to create a disconcertingly inhuman look. As the actor explains in the film's original press material, "I would try to think how Chris (Brynner's character from *The Magnificent Seven*) would behave if he were a highly developed machine, and I tried to make him even more evil with my eyes!"

Brynner's unbalanced droid remains the film's greatest asset. His performance would have a far-reaching impact, including serving as the inspiration for another memorable psycho killer, John Carpenter's *Halloween* monster Michael Myers. As Carpenter once commented in an interview, "I wanted to raise the Myers character up to a mythical status, make him human but almost like a force, a force that never will be stopped, one that can't be denied. Like Yul Brynner's character, the robot, the killer robot that couldn't be destroyed." Brynner's turn would also influence Arnold Schwarzenegger's killer cyborg in the 1984 box-office hit, *The Terminator*.

After an austere battle to control his project, Crichton still hadn't a clue how audiences would react, so MGM decided to hold a sneak preview to collect opinions. Opinions they got, with 100 percent of the audience rating the film between "good" and "excellent." *Westworld* collected $2 million dollars in its first week of showing, even more impressive when one considers that the film was only screened in three cities: Chicago, Detroit and Cleveland. It would go on to become a hit with audiences worldwide, establishing itself as a touchstone in the world of essential sci-fi/horror that still manages to impress today.

WHAT EVER HAPPENED TO BABY JANE? (1962)
by Robert Gannon

In a genre of cinema often thought of as nothing more than an assortment of monsters, murders, and mayhem, the deteriorating relationship between two sisters might seem an odd choice for a horror film. However, to call *What Ever Happened to Baby Jane?* a simple tale of two sisters would be a grave injustice to a truly disturbing film. Lukas Heller's screenplay highlights the destructive nature of the entertainment industry, focusing in on two dramatically different former celebrities who happen to be sisters. While some stars will be recognized with the eternal success and reverie of a Blanche Hudson, many others will spiral into a cycle of abuse and self-loathing like Baby Jane.

Baby Jane Hudson (Bette Davis) became a great success in the world of vaudeville as a child, packing theaters and selling life-size dolls in her image, all the while acting like an ungrateful brat to her family and fans. Blanche Hudson (Joan Crawford) doesn't receive her chance at success until later in life, where her prestige as a movie star, combined with grace and humility, enables her to negotiate an equal contract for her less talented, much-maligned sister. Unfortunately for Blanche, her career is ended by a crippling car accident at her own mansion, paralyzing her from the waist down. Baby Jane is forced to take care of her sister and accept the blame for the accident. However, when Blanche decides to sell her mansion and place Baby Jane under psychiatric care, Jane's mental condition begins to deteriorate rapidly. Incensed by the arrival of Blanche's films to television, she begins to abuse her sister by denying her food, privacy, and contact with the outside world. Baby Jane decides to prove that she was the real star by reviving her stage act and letting her sister have no part in her new pursuit. With Jane focusing solely on her relationship with pianist Edwin Flagg (Victor Buono), Blanche is left to fight for her freedom any way she can.

What Ever Happened to Baby Jane? originated from the novel of the same name by Henry Farrell, and was almost not made at all. Robert Aldrich, already involved as producer and director, sent Joan Crawford to meet with Bette Davis, suggesting the novel had the perfect part for both actors. What seemed to the three of them to be an

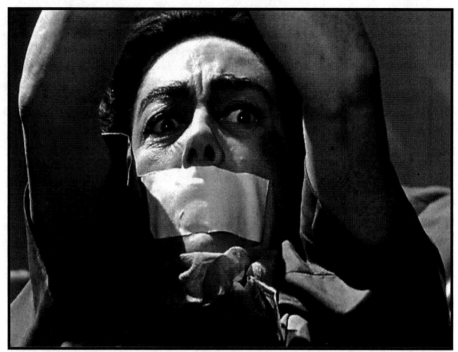

Blanche (Joan Crawford) becomes the victim of her insane sister Baby Jane. This movie initiated the subgenre of "horror hags" running amok.

easily financed project turned into a huge challenge. No studio wanted to pay, feeling that the aging stars would not draw any business. As a result, Bette Davis and Joan Crawford had to agree to significant pay cuts just to get *Baby Jane* made; they would have the last laugh, though, as the agreement gave them both a percentage of the profits from the enormously successful feature. It also garnered critical recognition, including five Academy Awards nominations (with Norma Koch bringing home the Oscar for her costume design), two BAFTA Award Nominations, and two Golden Globe nominations. Interestingly enough, it was the use of two older, established actors that helped launch a new subgenre of horror, that of the "Psycho-biddy," characterized by the use of older actresses in peril, a subgenre that became highly popular in the 1960s and '70s.

I was first introduced to *What Ever Happened to Baby Jane?* because of my work in theater. When I decided that I wanted to learn how to do more character-oriented work, a friend recommended the film solely for Bette Davis' performance. Upon watching, I understood why it was beneficial from a performance perspective, but was upset to learn that so many people believed the sole defining feature to be Davis' turn. My recent viewings of the movie confirmed exactly what I thought: Yes, the performances—all of them, not just Bette, Joan, and Victor—are universally excellent, but what makes them so great is the smart technical design that defines every character in the film.

One of the most significant yet ignored aspects of *What Ever Happened to Baby Jane?* is the original score by Frank De Vol. The core essence of the music is Baby Jane's trademark song, "I've Written a Letter to Daddy." While the song itself appears in its original form more than once in the film, every aspect of the score is either a continuation or a variation of this number. Each character in the film has his/her own theme music that defines his/her personality. Blanche, the former Hollywood star, is accompanied by rich orchestrations of strings and winds to create the highly emotional, evocative style of melodrama based on the basic key and arrangement of "Letter." As her situation becomes more desperate, the transitions become more erratic, the tempo increases, and the style matches the isolation she feels in her own home. Baby Jane, slowly losing her grip on reality, is marked with highly percussive, heavy, sharp, repetitive patterns of demented vaudevillian vamping. Every time she mimics Blanche or inflicts a new torture upon her sister, the music swells up to a chilling crescendo of mental distress. Finally, playing off Victor Buono's sheer size and presence, De Vol creates a bumbling, bouncing comedic anthem tagging pianist Flagg with a natural naivety surrounding his involvement with the Hudson sisters. As the characters become more involved with each other, the score combines the three distinct themes and trademark song to create a disturbing, penetrating sense of unease. While traditional orchestral scoring is used to supplement onscreen events, De Vol composed music that truly helped create a psychologically disturbing film, with traces of the songs ingrained in the collective psyche of the viewers.

Perhaps the most important aspect behind the success of the film was the actual on-and-offscreen tension between Davis and Crawford. Even though it would be nice to believe that the immense talent of these two screen stars would be enough to create the palpable tension inherent in every scene, the fact remains that these two actors just did not get along. The rivalry is even believed to have resulted in physical injuries to both players. In the infamous scene where Baby Jane attacks Blanche, Crawford was actually kicked, requiring stitches from Davis' blow. Davis would later claim that, in retaliation, Crawford put weights in her pockets for the scenes where Baby Jane carried Blanche around her room; Crawford denied these rumors, but did admit that she intentionally made it difficult for Davis to move her about. These two actors had such strong differences in opinions of what this project should be, it created the necessary tension to truly capture the desperate relationship between the Hudson sisters.

While some may not initially think *What Ever Happened to Baby Jane?* a "true" horror effort, this is easily one of the most terrifying pictures I have seen. The most disturbing aspect is watching the deterioration of a person whose success peaked far too early in life. The vindictive, hateful things that come from the mind of Baby Jane are some of the most alarming scenes ever captured onscreen. Watching Blanche pulled farther and farther away from the outside world with every new scene ratchets up the tension to unbearable levels. Worst of all, the small cast and limited sets make it feel like we are in the room with Blanche and Baby Jane, a silent witness to the dreadful events in their lives. Combined with tight camera work, the viewer feels like they can actually see what the characters are thinking.

What Ever Happened to Baby Jane? is by no means a traditional horror outing, but the more character-based storytelling, supplemented with smart design and performances, easily make it essential viewing for any fan of the genre. It just goes to show that perhaps one of the most frightful things of all is the destruction of a mind.

WHITE ZOMBIE (1932)
by Danny Fuller

Two Americans, Madeline (Madge Bellamy) and Neil (John Harron), come to Haiti to get married at Charles Beaumont's (Robert Frazer) sugar plantation. As Charles is an acquaintance they have only recently met, the couple does not suspect that Charles is in love with Madeline and will do anything to possess her.

In an early scene, Neil and Madeline are riding on a moonlit road. As they bear witness to a strange sight—a burial in the middle of the road—they meet up with "Murder" Legendre (Bela Lugosi). A very curious and bizarre man, he fixes Madeline with a hypnotic stare. As the pair's coach leaves, Legendre steals her scarf.

Charles first tries to talk Madeline into leaving Neil for him. When this fails, he enlists the help of voodoo zombie master Legendre. Legendre gives Charles a potion that will turn Madeline into a zombie. (The zombies in this film are not the modern undead zombies, but are people in a hypnotic trance.) Charles realizes that possessing a lifeless beauty is not as great as he originally thought. He tries to get Legendre to reverse the spell, but the magician has other plans, double-crossing Charles and keeping Madeline for himself.

White Zombie is the original zombie movie, a far cry from the flesh-chomping gorefests spawned by George A. Romero and peers. The result of a tight, 11-day shoot with a budget of only $50,000, the film was independently produced by siblings Edward and Victor Halperin, with Victor directing. The horror floodgates were just opening in 1932, after the commercial success of three studio releases (Universal's *Frankenstein* and *Dracula*, and Paramount's *Dr. Jekyll and Mr. Hyde*) created a desire for further tales of terror and the macabre. However, unlike other horror films of the era, *White Zombie* did not evolve from a literary source, but was instead the original invention of its screenwriter, Garnett Weston. While most of the horror films of the early 1930s originated from European stories, Weston's script was inspired by stories of voodoo rituals in Haiti passed along during the United States' occupation in the early 20th century. Inexperienced and uncertain Americans feared these voodoo rituals, and *White Zombie* was able to capitalize on (and profit from) these fears.

It is a low-budget movie where the sum is better than the parts, though Lugosi is majestic as Legendre. His hypnotic eyes, dignified persona, and grand gestures mystify the audience whenever he is onscreen. Similar to his turn as Dracula, Mr. Lugosi seems to represent pure evil, his character analogous to Satan himself. In contrast, Madge Bellamy is enchanting as the young and innocent Madeline. Her large eyes allow her to look very haunting and lifeless after her transformation into a zombie. Unfortunately, the rest of the acting in the movie remains sub-par. Most of the cast, veterans of the silent era, display a tendency to overact. The most interesting of the film's other main characters is Charles, who seems heavily inspired by F.W. Murnau's 1926 classic *Faust*. In Murnau's film, Faust makes a deal with the evil Mephisto, just as Charles makes a similar deal with Legendre in *White Zombie*. Both characters realize the error of their ways and strive for redemption by the end of the film.

The set backdrops were painted, giving the film the Expressionistic look popular from the silent horror film era. Lines of dialogue tend to be short due to the expense

Murder Legendre (Bela Lugosi) provides a sinister presence.

of adding sound in the early 1930s. This preference of Halperin's to let the images do the talking also lends the picture its haunting, silent movie feel. The musical score by Guy Bevier (and an uncredited Xavier Cugat!) is a mix of classical music and voodoo chanting. While eerie in small doses, it does get a little repetitive by the end of the film. Luckily, it is not used often.

The movie's horrific images remain scary to this day. A prime example is the opening scene that features the local Haitians digging graves in the middle of the road to prevent their loved ones from being dug up and turned into zombies. In addition, Bellamy's performance as Madeline is a plus. Her huge eyes are very sad when she is in the zombie trance, and her white dresses and blonde hair make a nice contrast to the dark sets, giving her the look of an innocent damsel in distress. The finest and most gruesome sequence by far is the sugar mill scene. The only sound is the creaking of the gears as blank-faced zombies run the mill like a human conveyer belt. The camera shows the inside of the big sugar cane grinder, then pans out to a zombie falling into the pit. The scene is made all the more ghastly because the audience does *not* see the zombie being ground up. Instead, one is left to imagine what horrors occur among the cane and husks, and with the suspicion that this probably isn't the first (nor the last) time that this has happened.

Like many horror movies of its time, *White Zombie* capitalized on Americans' fear of foreigners and immigration. The movie's plot revolves around innocent Americans traveling abroad and being threatened by a malevolent non-American. It is interesting to contrast the film with Romero's zombie picture, *Night of the Living Dead* (1968), which was made during a period of social unrest in the United States, due to the Vietnam

War and the Civil Rights Movement. By this point in time, Americans also harbored fear of internal threats, as Romero uses the concept that even your next-door neighbor could now be the enemy.

Overall, *White Zombie* is a must-see film which has generated quite the cult following. Fans of the movie include singer/songwriter-cum-horror film writer/director Rob Zombie, who named his late '80s/early '90s rock band after the film. On the whole, people tend to either love the movie (for its fantastic atmosphere and Lugosi's spellbinding performance) or hate it (due to the poor acting and stagy look). Critics, both upon its release and today, have had mixed views of it as well. *White Zombie* is one of my all time favorite horror movies. I am a big fan of zombie films and was trying to get a historical view of the evolution of the subgenre. Upon viewing it for the first time, I was blown away by the Expressionist imagery, the sugar mill scene, and Lugosi's great performance.

Victor Halperin would go on to make another zombie movie, also produced by brother Edward, *Revolt of the Zombies* (1936). Lacking the visually appealing backdrops that made *White Zombie* so special, this is extremely poorly made movie which I cannot recommend viewing. Despite the fact that Lugosi never appears in the film, Halperin shamelessly uses inserts of the actor's hypnotic eyes from the earlier film when Armand Louque (future Academy Award winner Dean Jagger), the zombie master, hypnotizes people. Without the majestic Bela, *Revolt* falls flat. Halperin would direct several other horror films in his career, including *Supernatural* (1933) and *Torture Ship* (1939), but none come close to the overall quality of *White Zombie*.

Sadly, this movie has not been very well preserved. Even the best existing versions still contain ragged splices and missing dialogue. Fortunately, the roughness of the movie actually adds to its spooky ambiance. While it is a public domain film, I recommend getting the Roan Group's version of the film on DVD, which currently stands as the best restoration of the film. With superior sound and visual quality, it also includes a wonderful commentary by Gary Don Rhodes, as well as two interviews with Bela Lugosi (one from the 1930s, the other a 1951 shipboard interview). Although the interviews have nothing to do with *White Zombie*, they are nice touch and a must-see for Lugosi fans.

THE WICKER MAN (1973)
by C. Austin

The Wicker Man follows the story of Sergeant Howie (magnificently portrayed by Edward Woodward), a virginal Scottish police officer and a staunch Christian—something which becomes his defining character trait. He receives a letter purportedly from a concerned resident of an obscure farming community located on Summerisle, which we discover is an isolated isle roughly a week away from the mainland by rowboat. The letter informs Howie that a young girl by the name of Rowan Morrison has vanished and implores him to look for the girl. Through a sense of duty and morality, Howie travels by seaplane to the island to conduct a search, but his investigations lead him to uncover something far more sinister about the apparently peaceful people of the island and the charismatic Lord Summerisle, played by Christopher Lee in one of the best performances in his distinguished career.

Summerisle (Christopher Lee), Sgt. Howie (Edward Woodward) and the Wicker Man

Religion is a subject that evokes many different thoughts and feelings for many people. For some, it is a guiding light to shape their lives. For others, it represents basic ideals by which to live, and for still others, it is nothing more than a collection of fables. Ironically, perhaps the most prominent recurring theme in examining the religions of the world is conflict; whether it is the internal struggle between good and evil or the external rivalry between the followers of different faiths (which has acted as a catalyst in virtually every major event in human history, from the Crusades to World War II to the modern day "War on Terror"). While religious beliefs inherently seem to represent an intrinsic good, it is inarguable that the *acts* carried out in the name of religion are often far from it.

The 1970s proved to be a most interesting period. The relaxed, free-loving, and experimental attitudes of the previous decade had begun to fade, with the negative aspects of the hedonistic lifestyles that had been fondly embraced slowly coming to light. Throughout the United Kingdom, Continental Europe, and the United States, where the population had so lovingly attached itself to "hippie culture," the painful, harmful, and all-too-real after-effects of the age left many people seriously ill, depressed, or even dead. It is perhaps then no shock that religion, which had been suppressed by the young masses in the previous decade, once again rose to prominence in the 1970s, offering followers a new way to live their lives away from the "past evils" of the 1960s.

It was during this time that a British preacher famously referred to Charles Manson, who himself had embraced hippie culture, as an Angel of Death, sent by the Lord to kill the immoral evil from within. A shocking and frankly ludicrous suggestion given the facts of the Manson case, but it would be one which nonetheless resonated strongly amongst the Western populous subscribing to a new morality. The following years witnessed a substantial increase in attendance of religious ceremonies and a profound willingness to embrace the Christian Lord God. With the huge shift from the late '60s to the early '70s, it was only natural that the cinematic medium would reflect the contemporary culture. Thus were born numerous religious-themed horror films, many of which would center on the subject of conflict, perhaps alluding to the conflict between '60s and '70s youth culture. Undoubtedly, the film that would become the most successful and significant of this era was William Friedkin's *The Exorcist* (1973). But released the same year, we find one of the most overlooked and interesting movies of the era: Robin Hardy's *The Wicker Man*.

The Wicker Man's conflict occurs between the Church of England, represented by the character of Sergeant Howie, and the pagan people of the remote Summerisle, headed by Christopher Lee's imposing character of Lord Summerisle. With similarity to actual written history, the clash between the two vastly differing religious structures bears a strong resemblance to the same power struggles between Paganism and Christianity that occurred centuries beforehand, when Christianity first found its way to Europe. In essence, Summerisle is a community lost in the wilderness of time, existing on an archaic belief system but with clear knowledge of what they term as "alternate religions." *The Wicker Man* serves as a product of its time, taking on board the strong religious opinions of the Protestant masses and counterbalancing them with a religion that many Protestants had grown to fear. Most interestingly, the film could be seen as a direct comparison (or even competition) between the authoritarian, new-morality of the 1970s in the form of Howie's staunchly Christian views and the fun-loving, free-loving hedonistic 1960s as seen in the Pagan beliefs of Summerisle.

The film itself is little short of a masterstroke of low-budget filmmaking. From the splendid performances to the unusual and enchanting soundtrack, the luscious and surprisingly vibrant cinematography to Anthony Shaffer's intricate, finely detailed screenplay (based on his own novel), there is very little about *The Wicker Man* that doesn't exude the exquisite perfection that we all hope to encounter when watching a movie. Director Hardy turned an almost doomed production (British Lion studios would go bankrupt shortly after completion) made on a shoe-string budget (Christopher Lee has said that he himself worked for free) into one of the most original, mesmerizing movies in the history of cinema.

I find that the picture's finest aspect is the way in which a second viewing changes one's very perception of what occurs. At first glance, the film seems almost like a kooky, bizarre drama crossed with a warped musical, which is perhaps not too far from the truth. However, *The Wicker Man*'s real power lies in the way in which it works as a retrospective horror movie, where knowledge of what *will* happen allows one to fully appreciate the ominous situations and the significant and terrifying aspects of several key points. For example, unaware of Howie's fate, the seductive, nude dance of Willow (Britt Ekland, although much of the dance was performed by a body double) seems bizarre and almost avant garde in its peculiar nature. However, further knowledge allows one to appreciate the explicit importance of this one scene—Willow is testing Howie's religious beliefs and claims, ascertaining for Lord Summerisle the poor Sergeant's suitability for his appointment with the Wicker Man.

One of the most intriguing aspects of *The Wicker Man* is the use of music. While little explanation has been offered for the often bizarre and eerily enchanting songs that the residents of Summerisle sporadically sing, it could perhaps be seen as a further comparison between Christianity and the Pagan attitudes of the islanders. Christians have always expressed their admiration of God in songs, with hymns dating back centuries offered up as part of their regular worship and an outward, open expression of their belief system. The islanders too sing about their beliefs, but instead focus on the parts of their religion considered to be most important. The very nature of their free-loving society, driven by phallic symbols, is captured perfectly in the famous "May Pole Song" which tells of their beliefs in reincarnation and evolution of life through nature and conception. "The Landlord's Daughter" is also indicative of their earthy values as an entire public house bursts into song, praising Willow's sexual appeal in a manner suggesting her promiscuity.

Today, two versions of *The Wicker Man* currently exist. The 1973 theatrical version which Christopher Lee describes as "a shadow of the film we made," and an extended version, which features newly discovered material spliced into the theatrical version in order to elaborate and clarify the viewing experience. Unfortunately, the added footage has yet to be restored, and is of poor visual quality in the current DVD version (although purists will undoubtedly find much of the added footage crucial to the development of the film). Christopher Lee and Robin Hardy have also said in interviews that much more film was shot, but due to the initial troubles in releasing a film made by a bankrupt studio, this resulted in the loss of many scenes. A commonly heard rumor is that several reels of the film are to be found buried under the M3 motorway in London, England.

The Wicker Man is not a film that can be described with any great degree of aptitude. It is a film to experience, over and over and over again. So much is learned on subsequent viewings that each time it feels almost as if we are watching a whole new movie. *The Wicker Man* becomes an unforgettable horror experience, a musing on theological diversity, and a thinly veiled history lesson all in one.

WITCHFINDER GENERAL (1968)
(aka THE CONQUEROR WORM)
by Mark McCormac

It is the Year of Our Lord 1645. England is experiencing a very bloody Civil War. Oliver Cromwell and his parliamentary party followers, known as the Roundheads, are fighting for outright power of England with the Royalists, whose loyalties lie with King Charles, keeping alive his now-weakened Monarchy. This amalgam of events is seen by the more unscrupulous characters in society as license to abuse the law and take advantage of the public's fears. A license to take whatever benefits they choose, be they financial or sexual.

One such person is the titular Witchfinder General, Matthew Hopkins (Vincent Price). A lawyer by trade, his day job is to roam his apportioned district, East Anglia, seeking out and gaining confessions from suspected witches in whatever manner he sees fit. Whether by torture or dunking in the local river, Hopkins usually gets his confessions. The fear-torn locals are only too pleased to help out, throwing accusations of witchcraft at one another, hoping to deflect any such implications from themselves. The fate of the accused is to be hanged or burned alive if they are guilty. And what if they are innocent? Well, if they happen to drown in the river while strapped to the dunking

Matthew Hopkins (Vincent Price) is evil personified.

chair, then of course the charges are dropped against the newly deceased. Either way, once a charge has been made, the accused is damned. After his men throw three people into the moat as a witchcraft test, Hopkins is heard to calmly say, "They swim. The mark of Satan is upon them. They must hang." Of course, the fact that Hopkins is paid for each witch he burns (as opposed to a fixed salary) only adds to his greed. As his terrifying reputation spreads through the country, there are plenty of candidates for his witch burnings, with Hopkins acting on even the weakest of accusations, or sometimes none at all. Lives are destroyed until Hopkins' reign of terror can be challenged

It might seem hard to believe now, but fledgling director Michael Reeves initially wanted Donald Pleasence to play Matthew Hopkins. But American International Pictures, the American distributor and co-financier of the film, insisted that Vincent Price play the title character and Reeves grudgingly accepted. Much as I like Pleasence, I think it would have been a much lesser film without Price. So, "Well done!" to AIP, for Price's performance is one of the few occasions in his latter career where he plays his role without any hint of camp. The renowned actor's ability to balance between dry charm and cold-blooded ruthlessness makes the film's final impact all the more striking, with Price's pageboy hairstyle lending him a look of innocence that belies his evil intentions.

Reeves, it would seem, was not a fan of Price. One anecdote follows that while filming a scene involving the dunking of the witches, Reeves asked the veteran not to roll his eyes and wave his hands so much. Price replied, "You know, young man, I have made 87 films. What have you done?" Reeves sharply retorted, "Well, I've made two *good ones.*" A brave thing to say to such a fine and respected actor, and as much as his witty reply didn't have much basis in fact, Price saw the funny side and laughed heartily. Reeves had been the darling of the new wave of British horror directors and much was expected of him. Despite the roughness of his earlier low-budget works like *The She-Beast* (1966) and *The Sorcerers* (1967), his budding style shone through. *Witchfinder General* proved to be his masterwork. However, it also was his last film, as Reeves tragically died soon after from a barbiturate overdose (at the very young age of 23) during pre-production for *The Oblong Box*. With Price again as its star, *The Oblong Box* would eventually be directed in 1969 by Gordon Hessler of *Scream and Scream Again* (1970) fame.

Ian Ogilvy had long been an associate of Reeves, appearing in *The She Beast* and *The Sorcerers*, and was the director's personal choice for the part of Richard Marshall. His performance is admirable, as he instills a respectful trust in his character. We know he will fight until the bitter end for justice to be served, a rarity in those desperate and troubled times.

Hilary Heath is the epitome of an "English Rose." A fair-haired shining beauty, her innocence is etched on her face, and as such she was an excellent choice for Sarah. Although her role is small, her story is the very essence of the film, taking us from her innocence, beyond her first sexual experience, and through her journey to learning life's harsh lessons. Her screams caught in freeze-frame over the end credits will long remain in the casual viewer's memory, her corruption complete.

Witchfinder General's other great performance is oddly enough from the Norfolk countryside. Never has scenery been put to such good use in a horror film, literally living and breathing with a character all of its own. With ethereal fog-filled forests mixed with deadly silences (broken only by the distant cawing of crows), it has a leaden sense of foreboding and dread building from the first scene that never lets up. Much credit must also be given to the stunning cinematography of John Coquillon and the wonderfully evocative music of Paul Ferris. Both romantic and poignant, Ferris' score was sadly replaced in the U.S. version (known there as *The Conqueror Worm*) with one composed by Kendall Schmidt.

The film inspired other similar-themed ventures like Tigon's *Blood on Satan's Claw* (1971), directed by Piers Haggard, and Michael Armstrong's *Mark of the Devil* (1970), both of which used ideas from Reeves' epic and come highly recommended. When *Witchfinder General* was originally in production, alternate versions of certain scenes were filmed to cater to the more lenient foreign markets. The remastered print available in the U.K. is the full export version, which includes more explicit scenes of torture and sex. However, these restored scenes are of fairly poor print quality and can be quite easily recognized in the present cut of the film (possibly detracting from one's overall enjoyment).

Witchfinder General will always remain a standard bearer for the British Horror Film, a beacon of light that confronted controversial topics and succeeded in making us think. In its own unique way, while it may titillate its viewers with crude violence and bare breasts, it nevertheless brings home a sense that we are catching a glimpse of England's horrific history, a glimpse that is both breathtaking and unforgettable.

THE WOLF MAN (1941)
by Denise T. LoRusso

Familiar to legions of horror fans, the words "Even a man who is pure in heart..." foreshadow the nightmare to come in Universal Studios' iconic horror film, *The Wolf Man*. Produced/directed by George Waggner in 1941, this howling good black-and-white film introduced audiences to a character that stands alongside Frankenstein's Monster and Dracula as one of the "Unholy Three," the most recognized of the Universal monsters.

The Wolf Man boasts a believable script and wonderful performances. Heading the cast is Lon Chaney, Jr., the brooding lycanthrope; Claude Rains, his unrelenting father; Evelyn Ankers as the beautiful local girl; and Ralph Bellamy as the stubborn constable. Bela Lugosi makes a brief appearance as the tortured Gypsy fortune-teller Bela (the ill-fated first werewolf). The Russian stage actress Maria Ouspenskaya plays his Gypsy mother Maleva, and it is her gravitas-filled presence that anchors the film's more fantastic scenes.

Writer Curt Siodmak researched European folklore on the werewolf legend, but it was his fertile imagination that gave us some of the cinematic truths about werewolves. After Larry admits to Maleva that he was bitten by the werewolf, she utters, "Whoever is bitten by a werewolf, and lives, becomes a werewolf himself." That's pure Siodmak, along with the great poems in the film, shape-shifting under the full moon (surprisingly, no full moon is ever seen in the movie!), pentagram markings, and the lycanthrope's vulnerability to silver. What's remarkable is that these concepts have since taken root as real, old-world folklore.

Our tragic tale takes place in the quaint Welsh village of Llanwelly. (This information comes courtesy of Tom Weaver's commentary on *The Wolf Man Legacy Edition* DVD. The film itself makes no mention of the locale.) Sir John Talbot (Rains) is lord of the manor of Talbot Castle where dense, fog-shrouded woodlands and moors surround the vast estate. After 18 years in America, his son Larry (Chaney) returns home upon the accidental hunting death of Larry's older brother. While at a Gypsy carnival, Larry is unsuccessful in trying to save a local woman from a wolf attack. He bludgeons the beast with a silver-handled walking stick (mounted in the shape of a wolf), but he is bitten in the melee. At first nervously dismissing the idea of becoming a werewolf as a "witch's tale," Larry soon is fearful and confused. He becomes convinced of his fate when he awakens one morning with mud on his feet, paw prints on the carpet, and unable to remember the previous night's events. When the news that a young woman has been brutally murdered by a wild animal reaches Larry, he is tormented with the knowledge that he has become a savage beast with the lust to kill. With increasing desperation he tries to get help. The film concludes in a stunning, tragic climax.

According to Weaver, Siodmak's original script was titled *Destiny.* Instead of Talbot, Larry's last name was Gill, an American mechanic installing a telescope in Talbot Castle. The original script placed more emphasis on Larry's *psyche* rather than on the possibility that he was shape-shifting. This aspect was made deliberately ambiguous to the viewer as to whether Larry was really a werewolf or just believed it to the point of "running around on all fours baying at the moon" (classic-horror.com). The beast was

Lon Chaney, Jr. as both the Wolf Man and Lawrence Talbot

not to be shown except in mirrors or reflections in water because the audience was not supposed to know whether Larry was really changing into a wolf, or if it were all in his mind. Poor doomed Larry! His tragic plea for help goes unanswered. This victimized hero storyline can be seen in later werewolf films such as *I Was a Teenage Werewolf* (1957) and *An American Werewolf in London* (1981). It's one of the major reasons why this film works. We can all imagine ourselves in poor Larry's "paws"!

The film is neither gory nor bloody, but as with many fine horror films, what *isn't* seen is much more effective in scaring us silly! Though filmed entirely on the Universal back lot, the thick forest, filled with old gnarled trees, provides the perfect backdrop for the werewolf's prowl, dense fog hugging the forest floor. Rarely has a fog machine been put to better use, and the whole film is drenched in a creepy atmosphere. We can almost feel the drenching mist on *our* feet and smell the damp, musty air. What a perfect setting for the blood-curdling howl of the beast! The frenetic and moody score really heightens the tension and atmosphere.

Classic-horror.com purports that the motion picture-censoring body of the time would not allow the werewolf to look "too bestial." Man-to-wolf transformations weren't allowed either. That's why we only see shots of Larry's legs and feet as he transforms into the creature. Curiously, wolf-to-man *was* allowed and we see this process twice in the film. These scenes were created using a time-intensive technique known as "lap-dissolves": Chaney would get made-up a little, a few camera shots were taken, he would get made-up a little more, and additional shots were taken, and so on. Chaney often claimed that he would have to sit perfectly still for hours upon hours, once for 22 hours! Weaver doubts this, though, and contends that the transformation involved three cameras "spotting" Chaney and exacting his position. That way he could take breaks between camera shots.

Chaney's werewolf is bi-pedal, crouching low behind fog-laden brush, just waiting for the chance to lunge at his next victim. Those wolf feet were really molded slip-on boots designed to keep Chaney's foot from laying flat. The wolf's front paws were actually gloves, fitting well up Chaney's arm.

Jack Pierce, makeup master and the father of the most famous Universal monsters, was responsible for Chaney's transformation. Working "out of the kit," Pierce used materials such as yak hair, collodion, spirit gum, stranded kelp, and cotton, with the complete process taking up to six hours. I can't imagine a scarier, more convincing beast than Pierce's werewolf. He originally created the concept for Universal's *Werewolf of London* (1935), but star Henry Hull refused to wear the full makeup, necessitating a subtler look.

Having grown up in the '50s and '60s, I was glued to the TV. Saturday mornings and weekday evenings the local station would play all the old horror movies. I remember poring over the *TV Guide* looking for movies with the description *melodrama* (the term for what we now call "horror"). I remember watching *The Wolf Man* many times within those years, *always* captivated at how Chaney could display so much pathos in his human form juxtaposed with his ferocious, soulless beast. For me, Chaney really *does* become a howling beast. As hard as I try, I can't see Chaney's real face under the makeup—an unnerving but delicious thrill!

Alas, only death could set our poor Larry free from the curse of the pentagram, but as the sequels proved, death is only temporary in monster movies. *The Wolf Man* spawned four follow-ups, and Chaney played the reluctant werewolf in all: *Frankenstein Meets the Wolf Man* (1943), *House of Frankenstein* (1944), *House of Dracula* (1945), and *Abbott and Costello Meet Frankenstein* (1948). Lon Chaney always said of his portrayal of *The Wolf Man* that he made it his own. "He was my baby!" Even though Chaney is the only actor ever to have portrayed all four classic Universal monsters (Dracula, Frankenstein's Monster, the Wolf Man, and the Mummy), *The Wolf Man* was always his favorite role.

What makes this old monster movie a standout? It remains genuinely scary. Watch it on a cold-rainy autumn night, or in the middle of a sunlit summer day, it will still have the same terrorizing impact. Every time I see this film I am always amazed at its ability to raise the hairs on the back of my neck. The movie produces a pure adrenaline rush for a horror devotee. I think it represents the best of the post-'30s heyday of monster-mania, meant to be watched through the ages. Indeed, a classic.

CONTRIBUTORS

Nile Arena (*Blood and Black Lace*) shares a birthday with icons Vincent Price and Christopher Lee, which might account for his passion for horror movies. Originally from Bloomington, Indiana, Nile is currently an actor and student at the Chicago College of Performing Arts.

C. Austin (*The Wicker Man*) is a 23-year-old technical writer of Celtic descent from England. He has been an avid movie fan for several years and also enjoys video games and sports, mostly football (soccer), ice hockey and rugby.

Don Bapst (*Les Diaboliques, Friday the 13th*) is the author of several novels and plays, including his own Grand Guignol, *The Horror*. A regular contributor to *blue*, Don has written for dozens of publications and is currently at work on editing his short psychological thriller, *A Haunted House*. (donbapst.com)

Fawn Bartosch (*Henry: Portrait of a Serial Killer*) is the estranged daughter of a Samoan chief. She escaped from Utah at birth, immigrated to Texas, and somehow became a horror movie junkie. She enjoys writing, painting, collecting cats, and making a scene.

Chris Benedict (*Dead of Night, Night of the Demon*) is a graphic designer and illustrator who has hosted a movie review web site at http://www.tranquility.net/~benedict since 1997. He lives in Columbia, Missouri. He actually has the heart of a small boy. He keeps it in a jar on his desk.

M. Binning (*Creature from the Black Lagoon*) is a 19-year-old female Law student from Wolverhampton in the U.K. She wrote her essay because it seemed much more interesting than writing the legal essay she was supposed to be working on at the time. She can be found posting on IMDb under the username shady402.

Andrew Black (*The Birds)* is an attorney from Canton, Michigan and the elder, wiser brother of Greg Black, whose piece on *Freaks* is also featured.

Gregory Black (*Freaks*) is a 21-year-old aspiring filmmaker and writer from Canton, Michigan. He is currently a student at Eastern Michigan University majoring in Creative Writing and Telecommunications (Film).

Matt Black (*The Haunting, The Mummy*) has an unhealthy obsession with "vintage culture," from the Victorian era to the 1960s. A film reviewer, jazz lover, and vegan troublemaker, Matt is also a frequent contributor to *Noctigram* magazine and *Film Fannaddict*.

James Blackford (*The Thing from Another World/The Thing*) 25, is a fan of most disreputable forms of cinema, particularly Italian exploitation and horror. He holds a B.A. (Hons) and a Masters in Film Studies. He is about to embark on his Ph.D thesis, "Cannibals, Critics and Consumers: The Production, Reception and Ideological Function of Italian Exploitation Cinema" at The University of London.

Wendy K. Bodine (*Alien/Aliens*) (EllenRipley112 on IMDb) is a mild-mannered assistant editor by day headquartered in central N.J. A single mom, she enjoys watching horror flicks when her daughter and mother aren't around. Her favorite films include the Alien Quadrilogy and pretty much anything with a zombie in it.

Nick Brown (*Suspiria*) is a horror fan hailing from Hull, England. He has been a fan of movies most of his life, in particular cult/Italian horror. Nick is currently in the final year of a Business Studies degree at Hull University, and hopes to use his qualifications to gain a highly paid job in the near future.

Darren Callahan (*Invasion of the Body Snatchers*) has written drama for the Sci-Fi Channel, NPR, and New York City's Radio Pacifica. He is a renowned playwright, novelist, and musician. Information on his works can be found at darrencallahan. com.

Andreas Charalambous (*Nosferatu*) lives in London where he lectures in Film and Media Studies. Maintaining his passion for horror through his academic work, he has published a thesis for his University's Department of Social Sciences entitled "The Critical Reception of Horror: An Analysis of Moral Panics." He is currently writing various other horror studies projects.

Aaron Christensen (*The Cabinet of Dr. Caligari, Cat People, The Phantom of the Opera*) is a Chicago-based actor and writer. He'd love to take a long, long nap, but the nefarious Dr. AC will not hear of it.

Peter Christensen (*The Body Snatcher, Island of Lost Souls*) has a B.A. from Hamilton College and a Ph.D from the University of Minnesota. An old—in many senses—fan of horror movies, he and his wife life in Chicago, where Peter teaches English at Columbia College.

Preston B. Collins (*The Phantom of the Opera*), mysterious, elusive, and all-powerful as he is, cannot be bothered with such trivial things as mini-biographies. When not busy watching films, he enjoys ignoring email messages, trivializing deadlines, and antagonizing editors from sea to shining sea.

Cory Colock (*The Blair Witch Project*) (screen name Golgo-13 on IMDb) has been an avid horror fan for nearly 20 years, as well as a fan of all genres of cinema. When not watching movies, he enjoys... nothing else. He currently resides in Pennsylvania.

Rob Dennehy (*The Shining*) (IMDb screen name BaseBallZombies) is a Mortgage Broker/Semi-Professional Poker Player from Illinois and an avid horror fan. Rob's favorite horror films include *The Texas Chain Saw Massacre* (1974), *Psycho* (1960), *Halloween* (1978) and George A. Romero's *Dead* films.

Mikey Diablo (*The Terminator*) was born and raised in south central Pennsylvania. His interest in horror began with the *Nightmare on Elm Street* series and Stephen King movies, such as *Children of the Corn*. His love of horror eventually led him to create and co-host the radio podcast *A Verbal Bloodletting*, heard bi-weekly at www.myspace.com/averbalbloodletting.

Jorge Didaco (*The Innocents*), a Brazil-based teacher of theater and film, has been under the spell of horror ever since the tender age of four. When the evil Maleficent (from Disney's *Sleeping Beauty*) cried out in fury, "Now shall you deal with me, and all the powers of hell!" It was love at first sight.

Mark Easteadt (*Scream*) hails from Lancaster County, Pennsylvania. When not watching, talking, or writing about horror films, he's tried such crazy things as having a job, trying to be an adult, and shamming at being a productive citizen. Given the choice, he'd choose writing about movies as his life's work. Ahh, maybe someday.

C.D. Ellefson (*I Walked With a Zombie*) works for a news media clipping bureau, and has enjoyed horror books and movies for 35 years. Favorite films include *Halloween* (1978), *Night of the Living Dead* (1968), and *The Blair Witch Project* (1999).

Danny Fuller (*Dr. Jekyll and Mr. Hyde, White Zombie*) graduated Magna Cum Laude from the University of Texas at Arlington. Married with one daughter, he works as a tax accountant for a major retailer headquartered in Plano, Texas. In his spare time, he plays sports, watches horror movies, and is the author of the children's book, *The Adventures of Polly Panda*.

Robert Gannon (*What Ever Happened to Baby Jane?*) is a full-time music business student at New York University. For information on his original writing, music, art, and film, visit his official website, http://www.associatedcontent.com/trentsketch.

Robie Gelpi (*The Stepford Wives*) resides in Washington State, U.S.A. with his wife and two furry babies named Prissy Love and Fat Boy. An incurable agnostic and lifelong hypochondriac, he is known among friends for his obsessions with Tennessee Williams, Agatha Christie, comic books, and anything related to theater and cinema.

A.D. Gillott (*A Nightmare on Elm Street, The Silence of the Lambs*) is 26, was born in Yorkshire, England, and currently resides in a cold, black, haunted tower atop a lonely mountain in Spain. He is an orthodox misanthrope and spends his days scowling down upon the ant-like villagers beneath him, screaming curses and obscenities. It ain't much, but it's a living.

Alexander Gold (*Eraserhead*) lives in New Jersey. In addition to watching film, he also listens to a wide variety of music, some of his favorite artists being Neil Young, The Beatles, Of Montreal, Joy Division, Elvis Costello, and A Tribe Called Quest. In the future, he aspires to become a film/pop music historian.

Mark Allan Gunnells (*Carrie, Village of the Damned*) holds degrees in English and Psychology. A lifelong horror fan, he has published close to 50 original horror stories. A small town boy at heart, he lives in his hometown of Gaffney, S.C., with his partner.

Brett Harrison (*The Return of the Living Dead*), mentally scarred at the age of 7 by *Jaws*, avoided horror until the lure of Romero's *Creepshow* in '82 proved too strong to resist. A resident of Hampshire, England, he is currently on a mission to see as much onscreen terror as possible.

Will Harvard (*Peeping Tom*) is from Alabama, and currently studies at Columbus State University in Georgia, where he is working on a Political Science major. A huge horror fan, he enjoys all types of horror films from 1930s Universal to Italian zombie films and can be found on IMDb as Count_Fistfuldollars.

Andrew Haubert (*Black Christmas, The Texas Chain Saw Massacre*) is a 26-year-old graduate of Ohio University, where he received a Bachelor of Communications. Currently at work expanding his screenwriting/production portfolio, he plans to pursue a graduate program in filmmaking. No surprise to his friends and family, most of his efforts to date revolve around the horror genre.

Eric Fraisher Hayes (*The 7th Voyage of Sinbad*) is an actor/director in the San Francisco Bay Area. At the age of eight, he was directing the neighborhood kids in re-enactments of the Universal classics. In the days before cable or video rentals, he watched five monster movies every weekend for two straight years. A trip to Scout camp ended the streak.

Jason Herr (*The Last House on the Left, Ringu*), a Maryland native, is an exploitation and "shock" film junkie who enjoys corrupting others with his extensive knowledge of "extreme" films on various online forums under the screen-names EVOL666 and SCUMDOG OF THE UNIVERSE. To commission reviews, interviews, or just talk twisted films, he can be contacted at (appropriately enough) scumfuck69@myactv. net.

Brian Huddleston (*Repulsion*) (aka Brian the Scarecrow and Scarecrow-88 online) is 29 years old and has been a horror fan since his teenage years. He and his wife Jennifer and their two beautiful children, Stephanie & Christopher, live in a state of bliss in the state of Mississippi in the good old United States of America.

Anish Jethmalani (*The Omen*) is a Chicago actor and has performed on the stages of several regional theaters including the Goodman and Steppenwolf. An ensemble member of Eclipse Theatre Company in Chicago, he has also been seen in the independent films *The Strip, Sugar Mountain*, and *Betaville*.

Jon Kitley (*The Beyond, Frankenstein/Bride of Frankenstein*) is the owner, head corpse, and webmaster of Kitley's Krypt (www.kitleyskrypt.com), a website devoted to the horror genre, both old and new. When he's not working on the site or watching horror movies, he's attending horror conventions to spread the gospel of the genre.

Laurent Kleinblatt (*Dawn of the Dead/Day of the Dead*) is a 28-year-old Belgian (raised in Antwerp, living in Brussels). A mathematician who works (way too much) as an actuary for a consulting company, Laurent's hobbies are cycling, jogging, cooking, learning Mandarin Chinese, and fooling around online as Rand_Corp. Despite appearances, he swears he is not a Goth.

Dave Kosanke (*Re-Animator, Videodrome*) lives in Franklin, Wisconsin, where he publishes, writes and edits *Liquid Cheese*, a fanzine devoted to horror and exploitation movies. His written work has appeared in *Scary Monsters, Batteries Not Included, Midnight Marquee*, and *Ultra Violent*.

Doug Lamoreux (*The Blob, Mystery of the Wax Museum/House of Wax*) is a former professional firefighter and a lifelong horror enthusiast. Now an actor and writer residing in Chicagoland, he is the co-author of the horror novel *Apparition Lake* and can be seen in *The Thirsting* (a shocker coming soon from Universal Home Video).

Charles S. Lore (*The Invisible Man*) cut his fangs on the simultaneous release of the Universal films to television and the Hammer and AIP films in the late 1950s. By age 15, he was a contributing editor of *Castle of Frankenstein* magazine. He is weighing a return to the printed page upon retirement.

Denise T. LoRusso (*Onibaba, The Wolf Man*) is a 50-something life-long horror fanatic residing in rural Pennsylvania, U.S.A. She is a retired registered nurse, post-secondary educator, and grandmother of four, and lives with her college professor husband, three cats, and a dog. She is a member of a local rescue group, often fostering abused and neglected dogs.

Kenneth Lund (*Jacob's Ladder*), 30 years old, resides in Odense, Denmark with his patient girlfriend. When not watching horror movies, reading horror novels, or nitpicking about minuscule details in horror movies with friends from the IMDb Horror Board, he earns a living as marketing manager in a large Danish speaker bureau.

Streebo Majic (*Shivers*) is a founding member of Mutantville Productions in Charlotte, North Carolina. As of this writing, Streebo is completing his work as writer-director-producer on his first full-length feature horror film, *C for Chaos*. Join the Mutantville Players at www.mutantville.com and by email at mutantville@hotmail.com

Lucas Matheson (*Child's Play*) (aka lost-in-limbo on IMDb.com) is a 22-year-old resident of Australia. Horror films didn't really matter until his mid-teens, when he started watching late-night telly of '80s horror flicks, including the one that kickstarted his appreciation of the genre: John Carpenter's *The Thing*.

Patrick Mathewes (*The Incredible Shrinking Man, Plan 9 from Outer Space*) can frequently be found as psychotronicbeatnik on the Horror Boards at IMDb. His favorite job was working as a projectionist and film presenter in a small repertory cinema. Currently, he hangs his beret and bongos in Oregon where he works in a library.

Kevin James Matthews (*The Evil Dead/Evil Dead II*) is a resident of Edinburgh, Scotland and has been for many years. He likes it there. Obviously. A life-long movie fan and part-time amateur writer, he welcomes this opportunity to combine his two passions and hopes to do much more in the future. Cheers to all.

Mark McCormac (*Witchfinder General*) (Prof Hieronymos Grost on IMDb) resides in Dublin, Ireland. Married 11 years now with two little boys, his first horror film was Hammer's *Captain Clegg*, and from there he was hooked. Favorites include *The Wicker Man*, Hammer, Amicus, Corman, Universal, and Italian Horror.

Justin McKinney (*The Masque of the Red Death*) lives in Pt. Pleasant, West Virginia (stomping grounds of the legendary Mothman). Having studied both film and environment science at Ohio University, he spends his free time writing screenplays and taking whatever acting roles come his way. Indie horror credits include *Brain Drain, Descend Into Darkness*, and *Chubby Killer*.

Cheryl Melville (*War of the Worlds*), a member of the IMDb message boards for over four years as AppleBlossom, has lived all her life in the "lucky country," Australia. Last year, A.B. created MovieBuffs United, an alternative movie message board to post on whatever you're interested in discussing concerning the film industry. Check it out sometime!

Brett Neveu (*Dracula*) is a playwright and screenwriter living in Chicago. He has worked with many theater companies around the world including The Goodman Theatre (Chicago), The New Group (New York), and The Royal Shakespeare Company (London and Stratford Upon Avon).

Seth Pearce (*The Sixth Sense*) is an avid hockey fan living in Colorado. For the last several years, Seth has endeavored to educate himself about cinema and the medium of performance art. His favorite directors include Akira Kurosawa, Roman Polanski, David Fincher, and Luc Besson. His favorite horror films are *Alien, The Thing*, and *Repulsion*.

Christopher Philippo (*Mad Love*) lives in Troy, New York and studies film at the University of Albany. He produced the low-budget horror movie *Daddy*, contributes to the 'zine *Ax Wound*, is writing a book about women horror directors, and was presumably killed by aliens in Spielberg's *War of the Worlds*. (www.chrisphilippo.com)

Crystal Porphir (*Hellraiser*), 34, a Multiple Sclerosis Advocate, lives in Tulsa, Oklahoma and was featured as a "Goth babe" on the Internet site, Gothic Babe of the Week in April 1998. An amateur horror writer and poet, she is currently writing two horror literary projects.

Lee Price (*The Golem, Jurassic Park*) is a grantwriter specializing in arts and cultural organizations. He lives in New Jersey with his wife, two children, and their dog, Riley. As lee-109 on the IMDb Classic Film board, he is the founder of two major exercises, Fixing the Oscars and Doubling the Canon.

Mark J. Price (*Jaws*) is a copy editor who writes for the *Akron Beacon Journal* in Akron, Ohio. On the IMDb message boards, he goes by the nickname Chillertheater.

Lawrence P. Raffel (*Cannibal Holocaust*) is the owner of *Monsters at Play* (www. monstersatplay.com), which has become one of the premier online destinations for educated and thoughtful genre criticism. Recently, Lawrence has taken to providing content for another popular online horror destination, FEARnet.com.

Anthony Revelas (*Black Sunday*) (aka Leroy Gomm on the IMDb boards) is an aspiring artist and illustrator. When he is not at the drawing table, he can often be found on message boards expostulating the virtues of classic horror films.

J. Luis Rivera (*The Fly '58/The Fly '86, House of Usher*) was born in Monterrey, México and has been watching movies most of his life. Currently working as Systems Engineer, in his spare time, J. writes movie reviews and is working on his own site aiming to become a respectable film critic.

Sean Robinson (*An American Werewolf in London/The Howling, The Exorcist*), 41 years old, hails from Maryport in Cumbria, England, where he lives with his bride Dawn and their two children, Curtis and Kenan. He is currently working on finishing two horror novels and a screenplay. You can find him on IMDb as UnholyOne.

Amanda Rose (*Poltergeist*) is a 33-year-old mother of two from London, naturally instructing her children in the ways of the dark heart of cinema. Recently, she worked alongside Alan Jones at Frightfest 2006, the U.K.'s premiere horror film festival, an experience she describes as "inspirational."

Jimmy Seiersen (*Night of the Living Dead*) is a 22-year-old wannabe filmmaker from Sweden. Being interested in movies, he studied media in high school and at the University of Skövde, and now hopes to get into the Swedish film industry.

Charley Sherman (*The Black Cat, Horror of Dracula*) grew up in Nottingham, England. He has been babbling about monsters in some form or other since he was 6 years old. His biggest contribution to the horror field was directing the stage adaptation of Clive Barker's short story "In the Flesh," which he and Steve Pickering adapted for The Organic Theater in Chicago in 1992.

Erika Shoemaker (*Blood Feast/2000 Maniacs!*), 29, suffers from the condition known as chronic procrastination. Trying to get her to meet deadlines was like trying to convince Ishtar that Chinese take-out would work just as well. For all you HGL fans out there, she coincidentally lives near a cemetery bearing the name...Pleasant Valley.

Sven Soetemans (*The Curse of Frankenstein*) (Coventry on IMDb) is a horror-obsessed amateur reviewer from Belgium, which is paradise for genre fanatics, since there hardly is any censorship and EVERYTHING is available. He works as a financial controller, which pretty much just means he checks if people are solvent enough to pay him.

Richard Sparks (*Rosemary's Baby*) is an illustrator and musician who currently lives in Chicago. Like Rosemary, he also has dreams. Unlike Rosemary, his are just kind of regular.

Dan Stearnes (*Halloween*) (aka Suspiria10) has been a horror lover since the womb thanks to his mother's fondness for the genre. Based smack dab in the Arizona desert, he one day hopes to do something fun within the genre.

Linda Townsend (*Them!*), 45, is from Arkansas, U.S.A. and has held such diverse occupations as KFC manager, caring for the mentally disabled, and factory worker for Whirlpool. Married 21 years to her husband/soul mate, she loves to watch all kinds of movies, but she prefers the classic sci-fi/horrors of the '50s and '60s.

Michelle Trudel (*Se7en*) is a licensed massage therapist and Reiki practitioner currently residing in Chicago. When not espousing the virtues of love, peace and meditation, she watches her favorite horror flicks wearing the sweetest pair of Godzilla slippers you'll ever see. And no, you can't have them.

Michael Vario (*The Beast from 20,000 Fathoms, Phantasm*) has been a fan of horror for over 40 years. He was raised on Long Island, New York and currently resides in New York City.

Gert Verbeeck (*Gojira*), lives in Brussels, Belgium. As a writer/director, his documentary short *House of an Architect* was accepted as an official selection of Cinéma des Indépendants (a Brussels short film festival) in May 2006. Also active as a musician/composer, Gert's current rock band, Carlos, recently finished recording the album, *An Evening with Maria Gomez.*

Jake W. (*King Kong*) is a writer (somewhat), an aspiring fantasy/horror artist, and has been a horror film fanatic ever since he can remember. He lives in the United States where he continues to waste each and every day rotting his brain with movies, both good and bad.

Joel R. Warren (*The Hunchback of Notre Dame, House on Haunted Hill*) is a mathematics teacher, film lover, and general-purpose curmudgeon. His love of movies can be traced back many years, to happy days of playing hooky from school to catch the afternoon feature.

Craig G. Watson (*The Uninvited*) was born in England and now lives in Milwaukee, Wisconsin with his wife and their two cats. He is a senior graphic designer by trade and enjoys writing horror fiction in his spare time. He is currently putting the finishing touches on his first horror novel, *The Safe House*.

David White (*Eyes Without a Face*) is the Associate Artistic Director of Passage Theatre in Trenton, New Jersey. He has contributed to *Video Watchdog* and the Turkish film magazine *Geceyarisi Cinemasi* (*Midnight Cinema*). David is the author of *Fantomas in America* (forthcoming from Black Coat Press), a novel based on the lost American movie serial directed by Edward Sedgewick.

William S. Wilson (*Martin*) is a certifiable horror/sci-fi genre addict, and has contributed to various genre publications and websites. He currently resides in Williamsburg, Virginia and graduated from the College of William & Mary. When not watching good movies, he is usually watching really bad ones.

Thierry Wybauw (*Profondo Rosso, Westworld*) resides in Antwerp, Belgium. As Dario the 2nd, he's proud to be one of the oldest (since 1999) regulars on the IMDb horror boards, continuing to spread the word so that generation after generation will be able to detect the roots of today's modern age of horror cinema. (www.fragments-of-fear.com)

Timothy Young (*Asylum*) is a) from Lancaster, U.K., b) a webmaster and chief reviewer at cult DVD site Mondo-Esoterica.net and c) a lifelong fan of obscure films from every decade and corner of the planet.

Zane Younger (*Psycho*) is a student living in Charleston, SC, U.S.A., and has been a horror fan for many years. Agatha Christie novels started his interest in the macabre when he was younger. Zane lives a happy normal life and plans to continue his happy existence for many, many years to come.

If you enjoyed this book
check out our other
film-related titles at
www.midmar.com
or call or write for a free catalog
Midnight Marquee Press, Inc.
9721 Britinay Lane
Baltimore, MD 21234
410-665-1198
(8 a.m. until 6 p.m. EST)
or MMarquee@aol.com